STUDIES
IN THE DEVELOPMENT
OF CAPITALISM

STUDIES IN THE DEVELOPMENT OF CAPITALISM

BY MAURICE DOBB, M.A.

LECTURER IN ECONOMICS IN THE UNIVERSITY OF CAMBRIDGE

INTERNATIONAL PUBLISHERS, NEW YORK

Copyright, 1947, by
INTERNATIONAL PUBLISHERS CO., INC.

Revised Edition
© COPYRIGHT 1963 BY MAURICE DOBB

Fifth Printing, 1975

ISBN 0-7178-0197-7
Library of Congress Catalog Card Number: 64-13744

Printed in the United States of America

CONTENTS

PREFACE

A work of this kind, which is concerned with generalizing about historical development on the basis of material already collected and arranged by other hands, runs a grave danger of falling between two stools, and of displeasing both the economist, who often has little time for history, and the historian, who may dismiss it as insufficiently grounded in the first-hand knowledge that comes from actual field-work. To the economist the author may appear as an irrelevant wanderer from his proper territory, and to the historian as an intruding amateur. Of this danger and of his own imperfect equipment for the task the author has, at least, not been unaware. He has, nevertheless, been encouraged to persevere by the obstinate belief that economic analysis only makes sense and can only bear fruit if it is joined to a study of historical development, and that the economist concerned with present-day problems has certain questions of his own to put to historical data. He has been fortified by the conviction that a study of Capitalism, in its origins and growth, so much neglected by economists (other than those of a Marxist persuasion), is an essential foundation for any realistic system of economics.

There are those who deny that history can do more for the economist than verify whether particular assumptions (e.g. the assumption of perfect competition) are in some simple sense true of particular periods, and that all else is facile and dangerous extrapolation of past trends into the future. Such persons seem to ignore, firstly the fact that any economic forecast must rest on certain assumptions about tendencies to change (or their absence) the probability of which cannot be estimated at all without reference to the past ; secondly, that the *relevance* of the questions which a particular theory tries to answer—whether a given structure of assumptions and definitions affords an abstract model which is sufficiently representative of actuality to be serviceable—can only be judged in the light of knowledge about the form of development and the sequence of events in the past. In other words, it is not a matter simply of verifying particular assumptions, but of examining the relationships within a complex set of assumptions and between this set as a whole and changing actuality. It is a matter of discovering from a study of its growth how a total situation is really constructed : which elements in that situation are more susceptible to change, and which are most influential in producing change in others. It is a matter of putting questions to economic development in order to discover what are the correct questions to ask both of the past and of the present and what are the crucial relationships on which to focus attention.

At any rate, this collection of historical studies has not been hastily undertaken, and the author has not lacked the guidance and instruction of friends who are themselves expert in various parts of the field. Having had its germ in some jejune chapters of twenty years ago about the origins of capitalist enterprise, the work has grown discontinuously over the intervening period. This disordered growth, with its periodic botching and reconstruction, may have caused the final form at many points to be shapeless and diffuse. But the child once born proved too intractable to be remoulded entirely, and had either to die in obscurity or to brave the public eye with all the ungainly traits of its upbringing.

For instruction in many aspects of the history of the late Middle Ages the author owes a considerable debt to Professor Postan, Dr. Beryl Smalley and Mr. Edward Miller, and for guidance concerning the Tudor and the Stuart age to Mr. Christopher Hill and Mr. Rodney Hilton, and concerning the industrial revolution to Mr. H. L. Beales. Mr. R. B. Braithwaite afforded guidance on a special point touching philosophy ; and Miss Dona Torr richly supplied suggestions and searching criticism from her store of historical knowledge, especially of the nineteenth century and of the literature of Marxism. But for the signs that remain in these pages of ignorance unconquered these guides can in no way be held responsible.

It should perhaps be added that no pretence is made that these studies do more than answer certain specific questions. Certain aspects only of economic development have been selected ; although the selection has been made in the belief that these aspects have paramount significance. Comparative data from other countries have been introduced in so far, but only in so far, as the comparison appeared to illuminate these particular enquiries. The author is under no illusion that he has written a history of Capitalism ; and a reader will perhaps be more tolerant of them if he remembers that these studies do not pretend to afford more than a first sketch for certain portions of a complete historical picture.

M. H. D.

CAMBRIDGE,
   November 1945.

NOTE TO THE SECOND EDITION

A brief postscript on the post-war scene has been added to bridge the decade and a half since the book was first published. Otherwise, no attempt has been made to revise or rewrite, and the text of the original has been left unchanged.

M. H. D.

CAMBRIDGE
   October 1962

CHAPTER ONE

CAPITALISM

I

It is perhaps not altogether surprising that the term Capitalism, which in recent years has enjoyed so wide a currency alike in popular talk and in historical writing, should have been used so variously, and that there should have been no common measure of agreement in its use. What is more remarkable is that in economic theory, as this has been expounded by the traditional schools, the term should have appeared so rarely, if at all.[1] There is even a school of thought, numbering its adherents both among economists and historians, which has refused to recognize that Capitalism as a title for a determinate economic system can be given an exact meaning. In the case of economists this is largely because the central concepts of their theory, as customarily stated, are modelled in a plane of abstraction that is innocent of those historically relative factors in terms of which Capitalism can alone be defined. In the case of historians who adopt this nihilistic standpoint, their attitude seems to spring from an emphasis upon the variety and complexity of historical events, so great as to reject any of those general categories which form the texture of most theories of historical interpretation and to deny any validity to frontier-lines between historical epochs. No period of history, it is said, is ever made of whole cloth ; and since all periods are complex admixtures of elements, it is a misleading simplification to label any section of the historical process with the title of a single element. A system like Capitalism may be spoken of abstractly as describing *an* aspect which in varying measure has characterized numerous periods of history. But as such it is an abstract economic notion, not an historical one ; and to trace back the

[1] Sombart, in his article on the subject in the *Encyclopedia of the Social Sciences*, says : " This term is not found in Gide, Cauwes, Marshall, Seligman or Cassel, to mention only the best-known texts. In other treatises such as those of Schendler, Adolf Wagner, Richard Ehrenburg and Philipovich, there is some discussion of capitalism, but the concept is subsequently rejected." Neither *Palgrave's Dictionary of Political Economy* nor the *Dictionnaire de l'Économie Politique* includes the term Capitalism.

origins of any such " system " is generally a vain pursuit that can have no end. One may suspect that this attitude is reinforced by a more topical consideration. If Capitalism does not exist as an historical entity, critics of the present economic order who call for a change of system are tilting at windmills ; and Marx in particular, who was originally responsible for the talk about a capitalist system, was following a will o' the wisp. Some have been quite outspoken about this, and, like a reviewer of Professor Tawney's *Religion and the Rise of Capitalism,* have denounced the term as being no more than a political catchword.

To-day, after half a century of intensive research in economic history, this attitude is rarely regarded by economic historians as tenable, even if they may still hold the origin of the term to be suspect. True, we find the leading historian of Mercantilism dismissing the notion of " modern capitalism " as " that unwholesome Irish stew ".[1] But the prevailing view of those who have studied the economic development of modern times is summed up by Professor Tawney in a well-known passage. " After more than half a century of work on the subject by scholars of half a dozen different nationalities and of every variety of political opinion, to deny that the phenomenon exists, or to suggest that if it does exist, it is unique among human institutions in having, like Melchizedek, existed from eternity, or to imply that, if it has a history, propriety forbids that history to be disinterred, is to run wilfully in blinkers. . . . An author . . . is unlikely to make much of the history of Europe during the last three centuries if, in addition to eschewing the word, he ignores the fact." [2] But if to-day Capitalism has received authoritative recognition as an historical category, this affords no assurance that those who claim to study this system are talking about the same thing. Some might think that a variety of usage gave little ground for comment and could do no great harm. But the difference of verbal usage is not only associated with a different emphasis in the search for what is relevant among the multitude of historical incidents and with a different principle of selection in composing the chronicle of events, but is apt to lead to a different mode of interpretation and a different causal-genetic

---

[1] Professor E. Heckscher in *Economic History Review,* vol. VII, p. 45. He adds that it can only have " a distinct meaning " if it is " connected with what is called in economic science capital "—in which sense, i.e. of the existence of capital, different stages of history have differed only in degree.

[2] Preface to 1937 Edition of *Religion and the Rise of Capitalism.*

story. If it is the pattern which historical events force upon us, and not our own predilections, that is decisive in our use of the term Capitalism, there must then be one definition that accords with the actual shape which historical development possesses, and others which, by contrast with it, are wrong. Even a believer in historical relativism must, surely, believe that there is one picture that is right from the standpoint of any given homogeneous set of historical observations. Moreover, it not infrequently happens that those who write about Capitalism are unaware, apparently, of any problem of meaning ; failing to make clear the sense in which they intend the word to be taken, and even themselves showing no great consistency in its employment.

One should, perhaps, at once make it clear that the word " capitalist*ic* " which has become fashionable among some economists, especially those who lean towards the Austrian School, has little in common with Capitalism as a category of historical interpretation. " Capitalistic " has been used by economists in a purely technical sense to refer to the use of so-called " roundabout " or time-using methods of production, and has been largely associated with a particular view of the nature of capital. It has no reference to the way in which the instruments of production are *owned*, and refers only to their economic origin and the extent of their use. Since production beyond the most primitive has always been in some degree " capitalistic " in this technical sense, the term has little value for purposes of historical differentiation, and its inventors have not attempted to employ it in this way. Their use of it, indeed, is by implication a denial of any specific meaning to Capitalism as a special historical system.

Scarcely more helpful is another conception which we find implicit in the context in which the term is frequently used, and which has the weakness of confining Capitalism to such a narrow span of years as to draw a boundary between social phenomena that bear the strongest marks of family resemblance. According to this, Capitalism is identified with a system of unfettered individual enterprise : a system where economic and social relations are ruled by contract, where men are free agents in seeking their livelihood, and legal compulsions and restrictions are absent.[1] Thereby Capitalism is made virtually synonymous

[1] One may quote as a not very serious example, perhaps, of this the following : " True capitalism means an economy of free and fair competition for profit and continuous work opportunity for all " (J. H. R. Cromwell and H. E. Czerwonky,

with a régime of *laissez-faire* and in some usages of the term with
a régime of free competition. Dicey did not employ the term
Capitalism ; but he treated as crucial the contrast between
what he called the period of Individualism, in a sense corresponding to the notion that we are discussing, and the period of
Collectivism, dating the opening of the latter from the 1870's.[1]
Although a preoccupation with this kind of distinction between
Individualism and *Étatisme* may, perhaps, be said to belong to
the past rather than to the present, and among economic historians
has seldom, if ever, been made a basis for defining Capitalism, its
imprint on thought still lingers ; and much of the talk that one
meets to-day seems by implication to identify Capitalism with
a system of " free enterprise " and to contrast it with any
encroachment of State control at the expense of *laissez-faire*.
The deficiency of so confined a meaning is evident enough.
Few countries other than Britain and U.S.A. in the nineteenth
century conformed at all closely to a régime of " pure individualism " of the classic Manchester type ; and even Britain
and U.S.A. were soon to pass out of it into an age of corporate
enterprise and monopoly or quasi-monopoly, when *laissez-faire*
as a policy has been in decline. If Capitalism is to be so
straitly limited in time as this, how are we to characterize
the system which preceded it and the system which followed
after, both of which resembled it closely in a number of leading
respects ?

As having exercised a major influence on historical research
and historical interpretation three separate meanings assigned
to the notion of Capitalism stand out prominently in relief.
While in some respects they overlap, each of them is associated
with a distinctive view of the nature of historical development ;
each involves the drawing of rather different time-frontiers
to the system ; and each results in a different causal story
of the origin of Capitalism and the growth of the modern
world.

Firstly, and most widely familiar perhaps, is the meaning
that has been popularized by the writings of Werner Sombart.

In Defence of Capitalism, 5). This definition is so exacting in the virtues it records
as to make one doubt whether " true Capitalism " can have ever existed. More
weighty examples are found among writers who sometimes refuse the term Capitalism
to a Fascist economy and contrast Capitalism with " Totalitarianism ". C.f. also
the *Handwörterbuch der Staatswissenschaften* (1923): " Der Kapitalismus hat die privat-
wirtschaftliche oder individualistische Wirtschaftsordnung zur Voraussetzung und
ist ohne diese gar nicht denkbar."
[1] *Law and Opinion in England, passim.*

Sombart has sought the essence of Capitalism, not in any one aspect of its economic anatomy or its physiology, but in the totality of those aspects as represented in the *geist* or *spirit* that has inspired the life of a whole epoch. This spirit is a synthesis of the spirit of enterprise or adventure with " the bourgeois spirit " of calculation and rationality. Believing that " at different times different economic attitudes have always reigned, and that it is this spirit which has created the suitable form for itself and thereby an economic organisation ",[1] he sought the origin of Capitalism in the development of states of mind and human behaviour conducive to the existence of those economic forms and relationships which are characteristic of the modern world. " At some time in the distant past the capitalist spirit must have been in existence—in embryo if you like—before any capitalist undertaking could become a reality."[2] The pre-capitalist man was " a natural man " who conceived of economic activity as simply catering for his natural wants ; and in pre-capitalist times " at the centre of all effort and all care stood living man : he is the measure of all things—*mensura omnium rerum homo* ".[3] By contrast, the capitalist, " root(ing) up the natural man " with his " primitive and original outlook " and " turn(ing) topsy-turvy all the values of life ", sees the amassing of capital as the dominant motive of economic activity, and in an attitude of sober rationality and by the methods of precise quantitative calculation subordinates everything in life to this end.[4] More simply Max Weber defined Capitalism as " present wherever the industrial provision for the needs of a human group is carried out by the method of enterprise ", and " a rational capitalistic establishment " as " one with capital accounting " ; and he used the spirit of Capitalism " to describe that attitude which seeks profit rationally and systematically ".[5]

Secondly, there is a meaning, more often found implicit in the treatment of historical material than explicitly formulated,

[1] *Der Moderne Kapitalismus* (1928 Ed.), I, 25. This he described as " the fundamental idea (*Grundgedanke*) " of his work.
[2] *Quintessence of Capitalism*, 343-4.
[3] *Der Moderne Kapitalismus*, vol. I, 31.
[4] *Quintessence*, 13-21, 239.
[5] *General Economic History*, 275 ; *The Protestant Ethic and the Spirit of Capitalism*, 64. Weber's view is closely associated with Sombart's ; but at the same time it has certain differences. Mr. Talcott Parsons has emphasized that there is a distinction between Weber's " capitalism in general ", which " is a purely economic category " (unlike Sombart's) and refers to any rationally conducted exchange for profit (which comes close to the second meaning we are about to mention), and his historical notion of " modern Capitalism " which is the same as Sombart's. (*Journal of Political Economy*, vol. 37, p. 34.)

which virtually identifies Capitalism with the organization of production for a distant market.[1] Whereas the régime of the early craft gild, where the craftsman sold his products retail in the town market, would presumably be excluded by this definition, Capitalism could be regarded as being present as soon as the acts of production and of retail sale came to be separated in space and time by the intervention of a wholesale merchant who advanced money for the purchase of wares with the object of subsequent sale at a profit. To a large extent this notion is a lineal descendant of the scheme of development employed by the German Historical School, with its primary distinction between the " natural economy " of the mediæval world and the " money economy " that succeeded it, and its emphasis on the area of the market as defining the stages in the growth of the modern economic world. In the words of Bücher, the essential criterion is " the relation which exists between the production and consumption of goods ; or to be more exact, the length of the route which the goods traverse in passing from producer to consumer ".[2] This is not uncommonly found in close conjunction with a definition of Capitalism as a system of economic activity that is dominated by a certain type of motive, the profit-motive ; the existence in any period of a substantial number of persons who rely on the investment of money with the object of deriving an income, whether this investment be in trade or in usury or in production, being taken as evidence of the existence of an element of Capitalism. Thus we find Capitalism described by Professor Earl Hamilton, the historian of the sixteenth century price-revolution, as " the system in which wealth other than land is used for the definite purpose of securing an income " ;[3] while Pirenne seems to apply the term to any " acquisitive " use of money, and declares that " mediæval sources place the existence of capitalism in the twelfth century beyond a doubt ".[4] When this notion is married to that of Capitalism as a commercial system—as production for the market—we have the kind of definition that we find used by Professor Nussbaum : " a system of exchange economy " in which the " orienting principle of economic activity is unrestricted profit " (to which, however, he

---

[1] Cf. Marx's reference to Mommsen, the historian of ancient Rome, as one who " discover(s) a capitalist mode of production in every monetary economy " (*Capital*, vol. III, 914).

[2] *Industrial Evolution*, 89. Cf. also Schmoller, *Principes d'Économie Politique, passim.*

[3] In *Economica*, Nov. 1929, 339.

[4] *Economic and Social History of Mediæval Europe*, 163 ; cf. also Pirenne in *American Historical Review*, 1914, 494 seq.

adds as an additional characteristic that such a system is marked by a differentiation of the population into " owners and property-less workers ".[1]) The tendency of those who give this emphasis to the term is to seek the origins of Capitalism in the first encroachments of specifically commercial dealings upon the narrow economic horizons and the supposedly " natural economy " of the mediæval world, and to mark the main stages in the growth of Capitalism according to stages in the widening of the market or to the changing forms of investment and business enterprise with which this widening was associated. In many respects this notion has affinity with Sombart's, and overlaps with the latter ; but the focus of its attention remains substantially different.

Thirdly, we have the meaning originally given by Marx, who sought the essence of Capitalism neither in a spirit of enterprise nor in the use of money to finance a series of exchange transactions with the object of gain, but in a particular mode of production. By mode of production he did not refer merely to the state of technique—to what he termed the state of the productive forces—but to the way in which the means of production were owned and to the social relations between men which resulted from their connections with the process of production. Thus Capitalism was not simply a system of production for the market—a system of commodity-production as Marx termed it—but a system under which labour-power had " itself become a commodity " and was bought and sold on the market like any other object of exchange. Its historical prerequisite was the concentration of ownership of the means of production in the hands of a class, consisting of only a minor section of society, and the consequential emergence of a propertyless class for whom the sale of their labour-power was their only source of livelihood. Productive activity was furnished, accordingly, by the latter, not by virtue of legal compulsion, but on the basis of a wage-contract. It is clear that such a definition excludes the system of independent handicraft production where the craftsman owned his own petty implements of production and undertook the sale of his own wares. Here there was no divorce between ownership and work ; and except where he relied to any extent on the employment of journeymen, it was the purchase and sale of inanimate wares and not of human labour-power that was his

[1] *History of Economic Institutions of Europe*, 61. Elsewhere in this work, however, the author appears as a fairly close adherent of Sombart's view.

primary concern. What differentiates the use of this definition from others is that the existence of trade and of money-lending and the presence of a specialized class of merchants or financiers, even though they be men of substance, does not suffice to constitute a capitalist society. Men of capital, however acquisitive, are not enough : their capital must be used to yoke labour to the creation of surplus-value in production.

It is not our purpose here to debate the merits of rival definitions : merely to make clear that in the studies which follow the last of these three senses is the one in which Capitalism will be used, and to underline some of the implications of using the term in this way. The justification of any definition must ultimately rest on its successful employment in illuminating the actual process of historical development : on the extent to which it gives a shape to our picture of the process corresponding to the contours which the historical landscape proves to have. As our ground for rejecting the other two of this trio of familiar meanings the following all-too-cursory observations must suffice.

Both Sombart's conception of the capitalist spirit and a conception of Capitalism as primarily a *commercial* system share the defect, in common with conceptions which focus attention on the fact of acquisitive investment of money, that they are insufficiently restrictive to confine the term to any one epoch of history, and that they seem to lead inexorably to the conclusion that nearly all periods of history have been capitalist, at least in some degree. As our knowledge of earlier economic societies has increased, the tendency on the part of those who give such meanings to the term has been to extend the boundaries of Capitalism further back in time. It is now realized that money dealings and production for a market were much more common in mediæval times than used to be supposed. As Brentano remarked, the Fourth Crusade already disclosed " a very orgy of Capitalism " in this sense of the word.[1] And as our knowledge of the economic conditions of the ancient world extends, evidence accumulates to show that, on such definitions, the presence of Capitalism cannot be denied even in classical Greece and Rome. The acquisitive use of money is not exclusively modern. The purchase of slaves in antiquity was presumably an " acquisitive "

[1] Sombart frankly admitted that this was so. He rather unconvincingly tried to meet the objection by asserting that commerce in mediæval times was not commerce in any mature sense, but was inspired by the spirit of handicraft and not by a capitalist spirit.

employment of money as much as is the hire of wage-earners to-day. The classical world had its usurers, and *lucri rabies* was not a sin unknown to the mediæval world. If both are to be regarded as capitalist societies, one has to conclude that any search for the origins of the system within the confines of the last eight centuries is useless, and that Capitalism must have been present intermittently throughout most of recorded history. What we clearly need, however, is a definition to describe the distinctive economic institutions of the modern world of recent centuries ; and what cannot do this is useless for the purpose that most people intend.

The further difficulty attaches to the idealist conception of Sombart and Weber and their school, that if Capitalism as an economic form is the creation of the capitalist spirit, the genesis of the latter must first of all be accounted for before the origin of Capitalism can be explained. If this capitalist spirit is itself an historical product, what caused its appearance on the historical stage ? To this riddle no very satisfactory answer has been propounded to-date, other than the accidental coincidence in time of various states of mind, which conveniently fused in a marriage of enterprise and rationality to form the *élan vital* of a capitalist age. The search for a cause has led to the unsatisfactory and inconclusive debate as to whether it be true that Protestantism begat the capitalist spirit (as Weber and Troeltsch have claimed) ; and there seems to be scarcely more reason to regard Capitalism as the child of the Reformation than to hold, with Sombart, that it was largely the creation of the Jews.[1] Nor is this difficulty of tracing back the *causæ causantes* one which also attaches, *mutatis mutandis*, as is sometimes supposed, to an explanation of capitalist origins that runs in purely economic terms. While it is true that behind any economic change one has to look for some human action, the action which initiates the crucial change may be inspired by an intention which is quite alien to the final outcome, and hence be a simple product of the preceding situation ; whereas, if the emergence of a new economic system

[1] To the claim of Weber and Troeltsch that the Protestant ethic encouraged the spirit of calculation Mr. H. M. Robertson (in *Aspects of the Rise of Economic Individualism*) has replied, with some effect, that there was little to choose between Protestant and Catholic writers in their attitudes to such matters as commercial calculation and free trade ; and Brentano and others since his day (e.g. Pirenne) have shown that it is possible to find plenty of calculating acquisitiveness before the Reformation. Cf. P. C. Gordon Walker on " Capitalism and the Reformation " in *Econ. Hist. Review*, Nov. 1937 ; also A. E. Sayous in *Revue d'Histoire Économique et Sociale*, 1930, 427-44.

is to be explained in terms of an *idea*, this idea must embody " in embryo " the essence of the future system in advance ; and the emergence full-grown of the idea of that system, before and in the absence of the system itself, has to be explained.

On the other hand, it is clear that, as our knowledge has been enriched by the extension of research into modern economic history in the last few decades, the definition of Capitalism in actual use in historiography has moved increasingly towards that which was first adopted and developed by Marx. Emphasis has increasingly come to be placed on the emergence of a new type of class differentiation between capitalist and proletarian rather than on profit as a motive of economic activity ; and attention has increasingly been focused upon the appearance of a relationship between producer and capitalist, analogous to the employment relation between master and wage-earner in the fully matured industrial system of the nineteenth century. On the whole it seems more likely that this is because the material which research has disclosed has forced this emphasis upon the attention of historians in their search for the essential differentia of the modern age, than because they have been predisposed towards it by the writings of Marx. Thus, Mr. Lipson, in claiming that the essentials of Capitalism were present some centuries before the industrial revolution, states that " the fundamental feature of capitalism is the wage-system under which the worker has no right of ownership in the wares which he manufactures : he sells not the fruits of his labour but the labour itself—a distinction of vital economic significance " [1] Even Cunningham came close to this standpoint when he said that " the distinguishing feature of capitalist organisation of industry is the possession of the materials by the employer, who engages the workman and pays his wages ; he subsequently makes a profit by the sale of the goods " ; adding that " the intrusion of capital may not make much apparent change in the conditions under which the work is done, but it makes a tremendous change in the personal relations of the workman to his fellowmen when he is reduced to a position of dependence ".

---

[1] *Economic History*, 3rd Ed., vol. II, xxvi. Mr. Lipson adds to this, however, that " if the goods do not belong to him because the material is provided by another person, then he is a wage-earner whether the instruments of production belong to him or not ". If, however, " the true test is whether the worker has any property in the goods which he makes ", and ownership of the means of production is disregarded, will not the definition be extensible also to what is customarily called a socialist system ? In another place, curiously enough, Mr. Lipson speaks of " the mediæval village " as " organized on a capitalist basis " (*Ibid.*, 372).

He did not, however, confine the term Capitalism to a particular organization of industry, but gave it a wider, and commercial, definition as "a phase when the possession of capital and the habit of pushing trade have become dominant in all the institutions of society".[1]

II

In our preoccupation with the definition of an economic system, we must not let it be implied that the frontiers between systems are to be drawn across a page of history as a sharp dividing line. As those who distrust all such talk of epochs have correctly insisted, systems are never in reality to be found in their pure form, and in any period of history elements characteristic both of preceding and of succeeding periods are to be found, sometimes mingled in extraordinary complexity. Important elements of each new society, although not necessarily the complete embryo of it, are contained within the womb of the old ; and relics of an old society survive for long into the new. What is implied in a conception of Capitalism such as we have adopted is that, save for comparatively brief intervals of transition, each historical period is moulded under the preponderating influence of a single, more or less homogeneous, economic form, and is to be characterized according to the nature of this predominant type of socio-economic relationship. Hence in any given period to speak in terms of a homogeneous system and to ignore the complexities of the situation is more illuminating, at least as a first approximation, than the contrary would be. Our chief interest will not lie in the first appearance of some new economic form. Nor will the mere appearance of it justify a description of the succeeding period by a new name. Of much greater significance will be the stage when the new form has grown to proportions which enable it to place its imprint upon the whole of society and to exert a major influence in moulding the trend of development. Again, it is true that the process of historical change is for the most part gradual and continuous. In the sense that there is no event which cannot be connected with some immediately antecedent event in a rational chain it can be described as continuous throughout. But what seems necessarily to be implied in any conception of development as divided into periods or epochs, each characterized

[1] *The Progress of Capitalism in England*, 24, 73.

by its distinctive economic system, is that there are crucial points in economic development at which the *tempo* is abnormally accelerated, and at which continuity is broken, in the sense of a sharp change of direction in the current of events.

These points of abrupt change in the direction of the historical flow correspond to the social revolutions which mark the transition from an old system to a new one. The view that development is characterized by periodic revolutions stands, therefore, in contrast to those views of economic development, moulded exclusively in terms of continuous quantitative variation, which see change as a simple function of some increasing factor, whether it be population or productivity or markets or division of labour or the stock of capital. A leading defect of the latter is their tendency to ignore, or at any rate to belittle, those crucial new properties which at certain stages may emerge and radically transform the outcome—whether it be the adventurous ambition of the capitalist entrepreneur in a period of expanding profit-making opportunities, or the new attitude to work in a collectivist and egalitarian society—and the bias they are apt to give the mind towards interpreting new situations in categories of thought which were product of past situations and towards super-historical " universal truths ", fashioned out of what are deemed to be immutable traits of human nature or certain invariable sorts of economic or social " necessity ". This tendency theories of development that are cast in terms of the unique " spirit of an epoch " have, at least, the merit of avoiding. When we cease to speak in metaphor, however, it is not easy immediately to define the type of events to which the phrase social revolution is usually intended to refer. While a social revolution seems to contain the notion of discontinuity, in the sense in which we have referred to an abrupt change of direction, this loses its simple meaning when we cease to express it in terms of spatial analogies. While, again, such a revolution evidently includes the notion of a quickened *tempo* of change, its meaning is not confined thereto. Those who conceive of change in terms of simple quantitative growth may admit that the rate of growth is not constant but subject to fluctuations, passing at times through phases of accelerated increase, as with population increase in the later eighteenth century, without introducing into their picture any notion of revolutionary transitions in which a qualitative change of system occurs.

If it be right to maintain that the conception of socio-economic systems, marking distinct stages in historical development, is not merely a matter of convenience but an obligation—not a matter of suitable chapter-headings but something that concerns the essential construction of the story if the story is to be true—then this must be because there is a quality in historical situations which both makes for homogeneity of pattern at any given time and renders periods of transition, when there is an even balance of discrete elements, inherently unstable. It must be because society is so constituted that conflict and interaction of its leading elements, rather than the simple growth of some single element, form the principal agency of movement and change, at least so far as major transformations are concerned. If such be the case, once development has reached a certain level and the various elements which constitute that society are poised in a certain way, events are likely to move with unusual rapidity, not merely in the sense of quantitative growth, but in the sense of a change of balance of the constituent elements, resulting in the appearance of novel compositions and more or less abrupt changes in the texture of society. To use a topical analogy : it is as though at certain levels of development something like a chain-reaction is set in motion.

Clearly the feature of economic society which produces this result, and is accordingly fundamental to our conception of Capitalism as a distinctive economic order, characteristic of a distinctive period of history, is that history has been to-date the history of *class societies* : namely, of societies divided into classes, in which either one class, or else a coalition of classes with some common interest, constitutes the dominant class, and stands in partial or complete antagonism to another class or classes.[1] The fact that this is so tends to impose on any given historical period a certain qualitative uniformity ; since the class that is socially and politically dominant at the time will naturally use its power to preserve and to extend that particular mode of production—that particular form of relationship between classes, —on which its income depends. If change within that society should reach a point where the continued hegemony of this

[1] Cf. the remarks of Pirenne which show an approach to this conception of discontinuous development due to the successive rise of different classes : " I believe that for each period into which our economic history [of Capitalism] may be divided there is a distinct and separate class of capitalists." Since the capitalist group of one epoch " does not spring from the capitalist group of the preceding epoch ", it follows that " at every change in economic organization we find a breach of continuity ", and history is not an inclined plane but a staircase (" Stages in the Social History of Capitalism " in *American Historical Review*, 1914, 494-5).

dominant class is seriously called in question, and the old stable balance of forces shows signs of being disturbed, development will have reached a critical stage, where either the change that has been proceeding hitherto must somehow be halted, or if it should continue the dominant class can be dominant no longer and the new and growing one must take its place. Once this shift in the balance of power has occurred, the interest of the class which now occupies the strategic positions will clearly lie in accelerating the transition, in breaking up the strongholds of its rival and predecessor and in extending its own. The old mode of production will not necessarily be eliminated entirely ; but it will quickly be reduced in scale until it is no longer a serious competitor to the new.[1] For a period the new mode of production, associated with new productive forces and novel economic potentialities, is likely to expand far beyond the limits within which the old system was destined to move ; until in turn the particular class relations and the political forms in which the new ruling class asserts its power come into conflict with some further development of the productive forces, and the struggle between the two is fought to a climax once again. In the nineteenth century, largely under the influence of Hegel, the history of civilization was generally believed to consist of a succession of epochs marked by the dominance of successive national cultures. According to our present emphasis, it has rather consisted of a succession of class systems, each having its own peculiar mode of extracting an income for its ruling class. In the economic history of Europe, at least, one thing stands out and is worthy of particular remark. This is the surprising degree of similarity of the main stages through which economic development has passed. The timing of these stages has, of course, been very diverse, and the detail of the story, and the particular forms and phases within each main stage, have been notably dissimilar. But such unity as Europe can be said to possess seems most likely to have been due to the fundamental similarity of shape which the economic development of its various parts has exhibited over the past ten centuries.

The common interest which constitutes a certain social grouping a class, in the sense of which we have been speaking,

---

[1] It is not necessary to assume that this is done as part of a conscious long-term plan ; although, in so far as the dominant class pursues a definite political policy, this will be so. But it assumes at least that members of a class take common action over particular questions (e.g. access to land or markets or labour), and that greater strength enables them to oust their rivals.

does not derive from a quantitative similarity of income, as is sometimes supposed : a class does not necessarily consist of people on the same income level, nor are people at, or near, a given income level necessarily united by identity of aims. Nor is it sufficient to say simply that a class consists of those who derive their income from a common source ; although it is source rather than size of income that is here important. In this context one must be referring to something quite funda- mental concerning the roots which a social group has in a particu- lar society : namely to the relationship in which the group as a whole stands to the process of production and hence to other sections of society. In other words, the relationship from which in one case a common interest in preserving and extending a particular economic system and in the other case an antagonism of interest on this issue can alone derive must be a relationship with a particular mode of extracting and distributing the fruits of surplus labour, over and above the labour which goes to supply the consumption of the actual producer. Since this surplus labour constitutes its life-blood, any ruling class will of necessity treat its particular relationship to the labour-process as crucial to its own survival ; and any rising class that aspires to live without labour is bound to regard its own future career, prosperity and influence as dependent on the acquisition of some claim upon the surplus labour of others. " A surplus of the product of labour over and above the costs of maintenance of the labour," said Friedrich Engels, " and the formation and enlargement, by means of this surplus, of a social production and reserve fund, was and is the basis of all social, political and intellectual progress. In history up to the present, this fund has been the possession of a privileged class, on which also devolved, along with this possession, political supremacy and intellectual leadership." [1]

The form in which surplus labour has been appropriated has differed at different stages of society ; and these varieties of form have been associated with the use of various methods and instruments of production and with different levels of productivity. Marx spoke of Capitalism itself as being, " like any other definite mode of production, conditioned upon a certain stage of social productivity and upon the historically developed form of the productive forces. This historical prerequisite is itself the historical result and product of a preceding process, from which

[1] *Anti-Dühring*, 221.

the new mode of production takes its departure as from its given foundation. The conditions of production corresponding to this specific, historically determined, mode of production have a specific, historical passing character."[1] At a stage of social development when the productivity of labour is very low, any substantial and regular income for a leisured class, living on production but not contributing thereto, will be inconceivable unless it is grounded in the rigorous compulsion of producers ; and in this sense, as Engels remarked, the division into classes at a primitive stage of economic development " has a certain historical justification ".[2] In a predominantly agricultural society the crucial relationships will be connected with the holding of land ; and since the division of labour and exchange are likely to be little developed, surplus labour will tend to be performed directly as a personal obligation or to take the form of the delivery of a certain quota of his produce by the cultivator as tribute in natural form to an overlord. The growth of industry, which implies the invention of new and varied instruments of production, will beget new classes and by creating new economic problems will require new forms of appropriating surplus labour for the benefit of the owners of the new instruments of production. Mediæval society was characterized by the compulsory performance of surplus labour by producers : producers who were in possession of their own primitive instruments of cultivation and were attached to the land. Modern society, by contrast, is characterized, as we have seen, by a relationship between worker and capitalist which takes a purely contractual form, and which is indistinguishable in appearance from any of the other manifold free-market transactions of an exchange society. The transformation from the mediæval form of exploitation of surplus labour to the modern was no simple process that can be depicted as some genealogical table of direct descent. Yet among the eddies of this movement it is possible for the eye to discern certain lines of direction of the flow. These include, not only changes in technique and the appearance of new instruments of production, which greatly enhanced the productivity of labour, but a growing division of labour and consequently the development of exchange, and also a growing separation of the producer from the land and from the means of production and his appear-

---

[1] *Capital*, vol. III, 1023-4. Marx adds that " the conditions of distribution are essentially identical with these conditions of production, being their reverse side ".
[2] *Op. cit.*, 316.

ance as a proletarian.   Of these guiding tendencies in the history of the past five centuries a special significance attaches to the latter ; not only because it has been traditionally glossed over and decently veiled behind formulas about the passage from status to contract, but because into the centre of the historical stage it has brought a form of compulsion to labour for another that is purely economic and " objective " ; thus laying a basis for that peculiar and mystifying form whereby a leisured class can exploit the surplus labour of others which is the essence of the modern system that we call Capitalism.

III

The development of Capitalism falls into a number of stages, characterized by different levels of maturity and each of them recognizable by fairly distinctive traits.   But when we seek to trace these stages and to select one of them as marking the opening stage of Capitalism, there is an immediate consideration about which it is of some importance that there should be no confusion. If we are speaking of Capitalism as a specific mode of production, then it follows that we cannot date the dawn of this system from the first signs of the appearance of large-scale trading and of a merchant class, and we cannot speak of a special period of " Merchant Capitalism ", as many have done.   We must look for the opening of the capitalist period only when changes in the mode of production occur, in the sense of a direct subordination of the producer to a capitalist.[1] This is not just a point of terminology, but of substance ; since it means that, if we are right, the appearance of a purely trading class will have of itself no revolutionary significance ; that its rise will exert a much less fundamental influence on the economic pattern of society than will the appearance of a class of capitalists whose fortunes are intimately linked with industry ; and that, while a ruling class, whether of slave-owners or feudal lords, may take to trading or enter into a close alliance with traders, a merchant class, whose activities are essentially those of an intermediary between producer and consumer, is unlikely to strive to become a dominant class in quite that radical and exclusive sense of which we were speaking a moment ago.   Since its fortunes will tend

---

[1] Some seem, however, to have used the term " Merchant Capitalism " to apply, not to the mere existence of large capitals and specialized merchants in the sphere of trade, but to the early period of Capitalism when production was subordinated to the " merchant manufacturer " under the putting-out system.   The strictures in the text do not, of course, refer to this usage of the term.

to be bound up with the existing mode of production, it is more likely to be under an inducement to preserve that mode of production than to transform it. It is likely to struggle to " muscle in " upon an existing form of appropriating surplus labour ; but it is unlikely to try to change this form.

When we look at the history of Capitalism, conceived in this way, it becomes clear that we must date its opening phase in England, not in the twelfth century as does Pirenne (who is thinking primarily of the Netherlands) nor even in the fourteenth century with its urban trade and gild handicrafts as others have done, but in the latter half of the sixteenth and the early seventeenth century when capital began to penetrate production on a considerable scale, either in the form of a fairly matured relationship between capitalist and hired wage-earners or in the less developed form of the subordination of domestic handicraftsmen, working in their own homes, to a capitalist on the so-called " putting-out system ". It is true that already prior to this fairly numerous examples are to be found of a transitional situation where the craftsman had lost much of his independence, through debt or in face of the monopoly of wholesale traders, and already stood in relations of some dependence on a merchant, who was a man of capital. It is also true that in the fourteenth century or even earlier there was a good deal of what one may call (to use modern terminology) *kulak* types of enterprise—the well-to-do peasant in the village or the local trader or worker-owner in town handicrafts, employing hired labour. But these seem to have been too small in scale and insufficiently matured to be regarded as much more than adolescent Capitalism, and scarcely justify one in dating Capitalism as a new mode of production, sufficiently clear-cut and extensive to constitute any serious challenge to an older one, as early as this. At any rate, one can say with considerable assurance that a capitalist mode of production, and a special class of capitalists specifically associated with it, did not attain to any decisive significance as an influence on social and economic development until the closing decades of the Tudor era.

In the career of Capitalism since this date it is evident that there are two decisive moments. One of them resides in the seventeenth century : in the political and social transformations of that decisive period, including the struggle within the chartered corporations, which the researches of Unwin have brought to light, and the Parliamentary struggle against monopoly, reaching its apex in the Cromwellian revolution, the results of which were very far from being submerged, despite a certain measure of compromise and reaction at the Restoration. The second consists of the industrial revolution of the late eighteenth and earlier half of the nineteenth century, which was primarily of economic significance ; it had a less dramatic, but far from unimportant, reflection in the political sphere. So decisive was it for the whole future of capitalist economy, so radical a transformation of the structure and organization of industry did it represent, as to have caused some to regard it as the birth pangs of modern Capitalism, and hence as the most decisive moment in economic and social development since the Middle Ages. Maturer knowledge and judgement to-day clearly indicate, however, that what the industrial revolution represented was a transition from an early and still immature stage of Capitalism, where the pre-capitalist petty mode of production had been penetrated by the influence of capital, subordinated to capital, robbed of its independence as an economic form but not yet completely transformed, to a stage where Capitalism, on the basis of technical change, had achieved its own specific production process resting on the collective large-scale production unit of the factory, thereby effecting a final divorce of the producer from his remaining hold on the means of production and establishing a simple and direct relationship between capitalist and wage-earners.

But if we date the origin of the capitalist mode of production in this way, a crucial difficulty seems immediately to confront us. To be consistent, must we not recognize not merely two but three decisive moments in the transition from the mediæval mode of production to the capitalist : the third and earliest of these marking the disintegration of Feudalism ? And if we admit that there was such an earlier decisive period of transition, how are we to speak of the economic system in the intervening period between then and the later sixteenth century : a period which, according to our dating, seems to have been neither feudal nor yet capitalist so far as its mode of production was concerned ? It is certainly true that the fourteenth century witnessed a crisis of the old feudal order, following closely on the heels of the rise of corporate towns to a large measure of local autonomy, political and economic, as well as to a greatly enhanced influence in national affairs. In this crisis the feudal mode of production, based on serfdom, was seriously shaken and reached an advanced stage of disintegration, the effects of which were seen in the *malaise* of landlord economy in the following century. But unless one is to identify the end of Feudalism with the process of commutation—a subject about which more will be said later—one cannot yet speak of the end of the mediæval system, still less of the dethronement of the mediæval ruling class. It is also true, and of outstanding importance for any proper understanding of this transition, that the disintegration of the feudal mode of production had already reached an advanced stage *before* the capitalist mode of production developed, and that this disintegration did not proceed in any close association with the growth of the new mode of production within the womb of the old. The two hundred-odd years which separated Edward III and Elizabeth were certainly transitional in character. A merchant bourgeoisie had grown to wealth and to influence. Having won a measure of privilege, it stood in a position of co-partner rather than antagonist to the nobility, and in Tudor times partly merged with it. Its appearance exercised little direct effect upon the mode of production, and its profits were derived from taking advantage of price-differences in space and time, due to the prevailing immobility of producers and their meagre resources—price-differences which it sought to maintain and even widen by its privileges of monopoly.[1] In the urban handicrafts and in the rise of well-to-do and middling-well-to-do freehold farmers one sees a mode of production which had won its independence from Feudalism : petty production of the worker-owner, artisan or peasant type, which was not yet capitalist, although containing within itself the embryo of capitalist relations and even showing signs of coming into subjection to capital from outside. But this type of economy remained a subordinate element in society ; and one has to remember that the majority of small tenants, although they paid a money rent (which was, however, more often a customary payment than an " economic rent "), were still largely tied in various ways and subordinated to manorial authority ; and while the estates were

---

[1] Cf. Marx's penetrating comment that " Merchant Capital is the historical form of capital long before capital has subjected production to its control. . . . Capital develops on the basis of a mode of production independent and outside it, (and) the independent development of merchant capital stands therefore in inverse ratio to the general development of society " (*Capital*, vol. III, 384). Also Pirenne : " In an age when local famines were continual one had only to buy a small quantity of grain cheaply in regions where it was abundant to realize fabulous profit, which could then be increased by the same methods. Thus speculation . . . largely contributed to the foundation of the first commercial fortunes " (*Economic and Social History of Medieval Europe*, 48).

for the most part farmed by hired labour, this labour was still subject to a good deal of *de facto* compulsion and to a large extent came from persons who still treated wages as a supplementary, rather than the sole, form of livelihood. The labourer could be forced to accept work at legal rates, and he was restricted in moving from his village without the sanction of the local lord. Indeed, the legislation of the fourteenth century robbed the poorer freemen of what had previously distinguished them from the *villani adscripti glebæ* : freedom to move at will. Social relations in the countryside between producers and their lords and masters retained much of their mediæval character, and much of the tegument at least of the feudal order remained.

Discussion as to whether certain changes, such as those of the late eighteenth century, deserve to be given the title of a revolution has frequently concentrated, not only upon the *tempo* of change, but upon its simultaneity in different branches of industry, as though this were a crucial issue. To avoid misapprehension, it should perhaps be stated forthwith that the history of Capitalism, and the stages in its development, do not necessarily have the same dating for different parts of the country or for different industries ; and in a certain sense one would be right in talking, not of a single history of Capitalism, and of the general shape which this has, but of a collection of histories of Capitalism, all of them having a general similarity of shape, but each of them separately dated as regards its main stages. In other words, different regions of England (and to some extent even different towns) had in, say, the fourteenth and fifteenth centuries their different economic histories, in the same way as the economic development of different nations of Europe in the nineteenth century is rightly treated as largely separate stories. This seems more likely to be true the further one's gaze travels back across the centuries, and least true of the present age. In this respect the appearance of Capitalism itself is a powerful co-ordinating influence. When we view the country as a whole, some crucial transition may give the appearance of being so long-drawn-out a process as to make the title of an economic revolution a misnomer. Yet in any one semi-autonomous sector the rhythm of movement may be much more sharply outlined. What is significant is the speed with which in any given sector a chain of consequential changes follows the occurrence of some crucial event—speed compared with the rate of change in these factors in more normal times—and not necessarily the simultaneity of this crucial event and its chain of consequences in different sectors. In this connection, indeed, we meet an important distinction between major transitions from one form of class hegemony to another, of which we have spoken, and those minor transitions which mark stages within the life-span of a given economic system (to which Professor Pirenne was apparently referring when he spoke of the development of Capitalism as having the shape of " a staircase "). Where a new class, linked with a new mode of production, makes itself the dominant class, and ousts the representatives of the old economic and social order who previously held sway, the influence of this political revolution must necessarily be felt over the whole area of whatever is the political unit within which power has been transferred, and the immediate consequences must in this case be approximately simultaneous throughout this area. It is this change of policy, and hence of the direction in which its influence is exerted, at a *national* level that gives to such moments as the English revolution of the seventeenth century or 1789 in France or 1917 in Russia their special significance.

The development of Capitalism through the main phases into which its history falls has been associated essentially with technical change affecting the character of production ; and for this reason the capitalists associated with each new phase have tended to be, initially at least, a different stratum of capitalists from those who had sunk their capital in the older type of production. This was markedly the case in the industrial revolution. The pioneers of the new technical forms were for the most part new men, devoid of privilege or social standing, who carried on a struggle against the privileges of older established interests in the name of economic liberalism. In order to expand, these new men had often to rely for capital on partnership with capitalists of longer standing ; sometimes merchant manufacturers who had previously financed domestic industry set up factories ; and gradually capital was transferred from the old into the new, so that antagonism between the older capitalist strata and the *nouveaux riches* of the new industry never went very deep. In turn, the change in the structure of industry affected the social relations within the capitalist mode of production : it radically influenced the division of labour, thinned the ranks of the small sub-contracting worker-owner type of artisan intermediate between capitalist and wage-earner, and transformed the relation of the worker to the productive process itself.

But it would be a mistake to suppose that these social relations were the passive reflection of technical processes and to ignore the extent to which changes in them exercised a reciprocal influence, at times a decisive influence, upon the shape of development. They are, indeed, the shell within which technical growth itself proceeds. If the conception of Capitalism and its development that we have here adopted be a valid one, it would seem to follow that any change in the circumstances affecting the sale of that crucial commodity labour-power, whether this concerns the relative abundance and scarcity of labour or the degree to which workers are organized and act in concert or can exert political influence, must vitally affect the prosperity of the system, and hence the impetus of its movement, the social and economic policies of the rulers of industry and even the nature of industrial organization and the march of technique. In the extreme case it will be decisive in affecting the stability of the system. In the chapters which follow, the influence exerted by changing states of the labour market will, rightly or wrongly, be a recurring theme. It may well be that this influence extends to spheres which fall outside the scope of this present study, with effects that are less evident than those of which we shall presently speak. For example, two writers have recently suggested a connection between the changing state of the labour market and the attitude of the State towards the punishment of crime ; this attitude being apparently less harsh and more prone to humane considerations at times of labour-scarcity when convict labour was in demand than at times when the labour reserve was large and proletarian life was consequently cheap.[1] Concerning the influence of this factor upon economic policy we will venture to make one general statement, if only as an hypothesis for more expert enquiry. There seems to be at least *prima facie* evidence for connecting periods when the policy of the State in a class society moves in the direction of economic regulation with periods of actual or apprehended labour-scarcity, and periods when State policy is inspired by a spirit of economic liberalism with an opposite situation. The reasons which prompt the State at any time towards intervention in production may be various and complex ; as are also the possible forms and objects of intervention. A situation conducive to one type of intervention may not be conducive to another. But when State intervention has occurred in the past as a considered and settled

[1] G. Rüsche and Kirchheimer, *Punishment and Social Structure.*

policy adapted to the normal circumstances of peace-time, the two objects which mainly seem to have actuated it are the enforcement of a monopoly in favour of some group of capitalists or the tightening of the bonds of labour discipline [1] ; and one might expect that the efforts of the State in a capitalist society to control wages and to restrict the freedom of movement of the labourer would be greater when the labour reserve was depleted than when it was swollen. Support is lent to the supposition that a ruling *motif* of *Étatisme* in a class society lies in control of the labour market by the fact that State intervention tended to grow in countries of Western Europe in the fourteenth and early fifteenth century, which was a period of almost universal labour scarcity (for example, in France the proclamation of John the Good designed to control the craft organizations in Paris and in England statutory control of wages) and again in the seventeenth century, which was in France, for example, the age of Sully, Laffemas and Colbert ; whereas the nineteenth century, a period of an abundant labour reserve and rapid increase of population, witnessed the greatest triumphs of *laissez-faire*.[2] The hypothesis has, at least, a good deal to recommend it, that freedom flourishes

[1] One is speaking here primarily of regulations and controls governing price or output or entry to a trade or change of employment, of the type common under the Mercantilist system and again in recent times, and not of legislation such as Factory Acts or social insurance which do not so directly affect the relations of exchange or of production and generally have a different motivation and significance.

[2] Cf. E. Heckscher (*Mercantilism*, vol. I), who suggests that the rise of wages after the Black Death " provided a powerful motive for the first interference on the part of the State " (p. 138), which " was nearly always exerted on the side of the masters " (p. 148).   Towards the end of the fifteenth century, however, there was a modification of official policy in France, and a partial reversion to a régime of gild self-government.   For the seventeenth century cf. P. Boissonnade, *Le Socialisme d'État : l'Industrie et les Classes Industrielles en France, 1455–1661*, who refers to the rigid discipline to which apprentices and workers were submitted in the seventeenth century, " similar to that of the barracks or the convent ", and to the State policy towards the gilds which favoured the *patronat* against the worker, and in face of general complaints of labour shortage prohibited workers' associations and assemblies and punished those who changed their employment (pp. 295–305).   Despite illegal *syndicats* and workers' revolts and insurrections in several towns in various years between 1622 and 1660, this seems to have been a period of worsening conditions among the workers, who " live in a state bordering on nakedness " in conditions of " frightful misery " (pp. 307–8) : a state of affairs which continued under Colbert (Boissonnade, *Colbert, 1661–83* ; H. Hauser, *Les Débuts du Capitalisme*, 36–9, 102–6, 161 seq.).   Cf. also Weber's reference to the undeveloped character of a proletariat on the continent of Europe as the reason for the " deliberate cultivation by the state " of industry in France and Germany (*General Econ. History*, 164).   It is true that in the present century we have again an age of compulsory arbitration, of both minimum and maximum wages, and of the Corporate State, combined with a swollen unemployment total between the two wars.   But this modern situation is a peculiar one in this respect, that it is dominated by the rise of powerful organizations of the wage-earning class.   There is an evident connection, however, between the growth of armament expenditure in the 1930's, depleting the labour reserve, and the growth of coercion by the State over labour.

most under Capitalism when, by reason of a superabundant proletariat, the mode of production is secure, whereas legal compulsion stands at a premium as soon as jobs compete for men and the mode of production grows less profitable as a source of income on capital and less stable.

By contrast with the picture of a fluctuating policy of the State towards industry, as we actually find it, Capitalism has sometimes been represented as constantly striving towards economic freedom, since only in the absence of regulation and control can it find favourable conditions for expansion. Capitalism, to this view, is the historical enemy of legal restraint and monopoly, and monopoly is the product of illegitimate intrusion of the State into the economic domain, in pursuit of power instead of plenty or of social stability at the cost of commercial prosperity. But this bears little resemblance to the true picture ; and in what follows the rôle of monopoly at various stages of Capitalism, at one time aiding the emergence of the bourgeoisie and the progress of capital accumulation, at another time arresting technical development, will be frequently emphasized. While in its coming-of-age Capitalism made war upon the monopolistic privileges of craft gilds and trading corporations which barred its way, subsequently it showed itself to be not at all averse to the acceptance of economic privileges and State regulation of trade in its own interests, as the later history of Mercantilism bears witness. In the nineteenth century, again, especially in England, the new factory industry raised the banner of unfettered access to markets and to labour supplies, and claimed the right to compete on equal terms with older established rivals, in order to give headroom to its remarkably enhanced productive powers. But, except in the specially favourable circumstances of England as pioneer of the new technique, this enthusiasm for freedom of trade was seldom unqualified ; and by the end of the century competition was once again to yield place to monopoly, and free trade to retire before the dawn of what has been termed an era of neo-Mercantilism. One might even say that it is only in exceptional periods, when markets and profit-opportunities are expanding in an unusual degree, that the chronic fear of increase of products and of productive capacity which this system seems to nurture is held in check, and its native tendency towards restrictive policies, born of this fear, is in abeyance.

Two final comments of a general nature seem to be relevant as introduction to the more detailed studies which follow. The emphasis of our approach to the interpretation of Capitalism is that changes in the character of production, and in the social relations that hinge upon it, have generally exerted a more profound and potent influence upon society than have changes in trade relations *per se*. But this must not be held to imply that trade and markets have not in their turn had an important reciprocal influence on production and are not to be assigned a leading rôle at various points in the story. Not only was trade the soil from which a bourgeoisie first grew ; not only did its impact on the mediæval village have a potent influence, if only an indirect one by promoting a differentiation among the peasantry into well-to-do peasants and poor, thereby fostering the growth of a rural semi-proletariat from among the latter ; not only have markets shaped the moulds into which industry settled, as well as themselves being contingent on the growth of production ; but one can say that it is periods of rapidly expanding markets as well as of expanding labour supply which are the periods *par excellence* of industrial expansion, of progress both in productive technique and in forms of organization ; whereas it is apparently when markets are straitened that concern for a safe routine and the consolidation of an established position tends to oust the spirit of adventure and a stiffening of the joints of capitalist industry sets in. Compared with previous systems, there can be no doubt that modern Capitalism has been progressive in a high degree : according to the well-known tribute paid to it by Marx and Engels in the *Communist Manifesto*, " the bourgeoisie has played an extremely revolutionary rôle upon the stage of history . . . (it) was the first to show us what human activity is capable of achieving . . . (it) cannot exist without incessantly revolutionizing the instruments of production, and, consequently, the relations of production ". But this progressive influence of Capitalism was less because, by some enduring quality of its nature, the system thrives on continuous innovation, than because its period of maturity was associated with an unusual buoyancy of markets as well as with an abnormal rate of increase of its labour supply. That this should have been the case in the nineteenth century, and in America for the first three decades of the twentieth, does not justify us in supposing that this favourable constellation will indefinitely continue ; and we shall see that evidence is not lacking to suggest that this may be already a thing of the past. Such long-term influence, however, as the changing configuration of markets has exerted upon economic development seems to have been primarily *via* its effect on production, as one of the latter's conditioning factors ; and, apart from this, the sphere of trade does not seem to have been the seat of any powerful waves of influence which have directly spread thence in wide circles over the surface of society.[1]

If the shape of economic development is as we have described it, a specific corollary seems to follow for economic analysis : a corollary, moreover, of crucial importance. This is that, for understanding the larger movements of the economic system at any given period, the qualities peculiar to the system are more important than the qualities it may have in common with other systems ; and that one is unlikely to make much of its long-term tendencies of development if one derives one's concepts simply from relations of exchange, drawing a line between these and that special type of institutional factor which composes what Marx termed the mode of production of the epoch. Economic theory, at least since Jevons and the Austrians, has increasingly been cast in terms of properties that are common to any type of exchange society ; and the central economic laws have been formulated at this level of abstraction.[2] Institutional, or his-

---

[1] This is not intended to be a statement about the order of " importance " of different factors in promoting change. It is a statement simply about the *modus operandi* of causal sequences and about the different operational rôle of different factors in a process of development. The distinction referred to seems to be akin to that made by J. S. Mill between an event which is the immediate *cause* of some change and an event (or events), which exerts an influence, not by directly producing the change, but by *predisposing* certain elements in a situation in the relevant direction, " a case of causation in which the effect is to invest an object with a certain property " or " the preparation of an object for producing an effect " (*System of Logic*, 9th Ed., vol. I, 388–90).

[2] Some seem to have claimed for the propositions of economic theory a universal and necessary character akin to that of so-called " synthetic *a priori* propositions ". Professor Hayek, following a line of thought opened up by Weber, has declared that the objects which form the subject-matter of the social sciences are " not physical facts ", but are wholes " constituted " out of " familiar categories of our own minds ". " Theories of the social sciences do not consist of ' laws ' in the sense of empirical rules about the behaviour of objects definable in physical terms " : all they provide is " a technique of reasoning which assists us in connecting individual facts, but which, like logic or mathematics, is not about the facts ", and " can never be verified or falsified by reference to facts ". " All that we can and must verify is the presence of our assumptions in the particular case. . . . The theory itself . . . can only be tested for consistency " (" The Facts of the Social Sciences " in *Ethics*, Oct. 1943, pp. 11, 13).

This rather startling claim derives from the view that the " wholes " with which social theories deal are concerned with relations which are not definable in terms of common physical properties but only in *teleological* terms of attitudes which we recognize as similar by analogy with the character of our own minds. Hence from knowledge of our own minds we can derive *a priori* all the general notions which form the subject-matter of social theory. So far as economics is concerned, this view seems to depend on the selection of *the market* as the sole province of economics, and of the problem of " adapting scarce means to given ends " as the aspect of the

torico-relative, material, while it has not been excluded entirely, has only been introduced into the second storey of the building, being treated in the main as changes in " data " which may influence the value of the relevant variables, but do not alter the main equations themselves by which the governing relationships are defined. Hence a line of demarcation is drawn between an autonomous sphere of exchange-relations, possessed of properties and ruled by necessities that are, in the main, independent of any change of " system "—a sphere which is the province of economists—and the sphere of property institutions and class relations which is the territory where sociologists and historians of institutions, with their talk of " systems ", can riot to their hearts' content. But if the major factor in the economic and social, if not the political, development of the past four to five centuries has been something called Capitalism, and Capitalism is as we have described it, such a dichotomy is untenable.[1] An autonomous sphere of exchange-relationships, whose concepts ignore the qualitative difference in the connection of various classes with production and hence with one another, in order to

market upon which economic study is focused (" ends " being defined subjectively in terms of human desires).

This view is admittedly not applicable to phenomena capable of statistical measurement (e.g. vital statistics) ; nor presumably to institutions such as forced labour, individual ownership of property, the distinction between men with property and men without : all these seem quite capable of classification in terms of their physical properties, without reference to mental attitudes. Moreover, it is not at all clear why the assumption is made that such things as money or capital are not definable in terms of the actual uses to which we find that they are put, instead of " in terms of the opinions people hold about them ". [If money is defined as something which does not give direct enjoyment but is *regarded* only as a means by which things yielding enjoyment can be acquired, then this definition must be in terms of people's mental judgements ; but not if money is defined substantially as something that is customarily *used* as a means of acquiring things which people eat or wear or use as fuel or adorn their houses with, without itself being used in any of these ways. The fact that we may not always be able to decide whether to classify as ornaments or as money certain objects worn round the necks of South Sea islanders without intuition as to their mental processes does not seem sufficient to invalidate the latter type of definition for most purposes.] It is not a question as to whether in certain circumstances we may not be able to learn *more* by deducing other people's motives from our own than by simply generalizing about their behaviour : it is a question as to whether the subject-matter of economic theory and historical interpretation is confined to what we can learn from the former.

[1] J. S. Mill made the considerable concession of maintaining that the laws of distribution were relative to particular institutions ; but maintained that the laws of production were not. But this view (called by Marx " an idea begotten by the incipient, but still handicapped, critique of bourgeois economy " : *Capital*, vol. III, 1030), draws a dichotomy within the corpus of economics itself which seems to be even more difficult to maintain. For example, in Mill's doctrine the rate of profit, which figured in the determination of value, depended on those conditions which determined distribution ; and in this sense the theory of value rested on a theory of distribution. Modern economics, however, has left no room for this kind of dichotomy, since it has formally integrated distribution (i.e. the pricing of factors of production) into the structure of general price-equilibrium.

concentrate on their similarity as quantitative factors in an abstract pricing-problem, clearly cannot tell us much about the economic development of modern society. Moreover, the alleged autonomy of this sphere is itself brought into question.

To regard exchange-relationships as an autonomous territory for a special science of economics seems to mean that a fairly complete causal story of essential processes can be constructed without going outside its boundaries. There are those who hold that, while a study of exchange relations by themselves must admittedly be incomplete, unless it proceeds to take account of the influence upon them of particular institutions such as the class structure of society, the laws revealed by the former are nevertheless fundamental and express necessities which rule any type of economic system. In what sense the modern theory of price-equilibrium can be held to express " necessities " for any type of society, and how much remains of such " necessities " when they have had to be supplemented to any large extent by historically-relative institutional data, is not altogether clear.[1] But, expressed in formal terms, a possible meaning to be given to this claim is that the influence of the institutional factors upon exchange-relationships is not such as to change any of the governing equations or to rob any of the independent variables which have figured in these equations of their assumed independence. If this condition holds, changes in institutional factors can reasonably be treated simply as changes in " data ", which affect the values to be assigned to these variables without affecting anything else. If, however, this convenient assumption does not hold—if the influence of the particular institutional data is more radical than this—then the necessities which these laws express will change their character with any fundamental change of system ; and the very statement of them in a form that is simultaneously realistic and determinate will be impossible unless the institutional situation is taken into account.

The claim that economic principles can be formulated without regard to particular institutional conditions may seem to many to be open to such an obvious objection as to make it surprising that such a claim could have been seriously advanced. Is it not obvious that the manner in which prices are determined,

[1] A particular meaning that those who subscribe to this view have themselves given to it is the alleged necessity for the adoption of certain price- and market-mechanisms by a socialist economy, which has figured in the discussion about the problem of economic calculation in a socialist economy, around which there has grown quite a considerable literature.

and exchange is regulated, under conditions of competition *must* be different from the manner in which they are determined under conditions of monopoly ; or, again, that the pattern of prices at any particular time (and hence movements of prices over time) must be different when each seller is ignorant of the intended actions of other sellers from what it would be where this ignorance was partly or wholly absent (as would be the case under conditions of economic planning) ? If this be so, the statement that a change of circumstance does not affect the equations themselves by which economic " necessities " are defined cannot be true so far as the determination of prices is concerned. Presumably the statement can only be seriously intended to apply to postulates at some higher level of generality : to principles of which the particular theories of particular situations can be treated as special cases.[1] The only postulates that can possibly be of this kind are ones concerning the relationship of prices to demand : postulates which state that a given structure of prices will have a determinate effect on demand, and which have been held to yield the corollary that, in any given state of supply of productive resources, only one set of prices (and an allocation of productive resources corresponding to it) will result in an " optimum satisfaction " of demand—a corollary which requires also for its validity certain assumptions about the nature of consumers' preference or about utility. But these statements do not suffice to afford a determinate account of how relationships of exchange are in fact determined.

An analogy which, because it is familiar, may perhaps commend itself to economists, can be cited from recent discussions about the Quantity Theory of Money. This theory, expressing an invariant relationship between changes in the quantity of money and changes in prices, used to be stated in a form in which it was regarded as having general validity for any type of situation. This was largely by virtue of an implicit assumption that certain other crucial variables were independent of the quantity of money, or that, if they were connected with

[1] The difference between the determination of price under competition and under imperfect competition has been formally stated in this way : namely, that output will be determined by the condition of equality of marginal cost and marginal revenue ; perfect competition being treated as a special case where marginal and average revenue are equal (since the demand is infinitely elastic), and hence marginal cost is equal to price, instead of less than price. But when one is dealing with the industry as a whole, this crucial condition (the elasticity of demand for the individual firm) has to be introduced when competition is imperfect as a separate condition (separate, that is, from the demand for the whole industry) ; as has also such a condition as the presence of restrictions on entry of firms into the industry.

the latter, this connection was limited to a certain form.[1] It is now realized that this assumption does not hold true of all types of situation : in particular, of a situation characterized by excess-capacity of man-power and machinery. In so far, therefore, as the theory claims to tell a causal story, its alleged generality breaks down, since there are situations in which the relationship it asserts between money and prices is not true ; whereas, if it modifies its status to that of a mere " equation of identity ", the causal story [2] of the actual relationship between money and prices remains to be told, and told in terms of particular situations. When this fuller causal story has been completely told, it may be that some new general principle emerges, in terms of which in a purely formal sense particular situations can again be expressed as special cases (e.g. a state of full employment as one where supply of output has a zero, instead of some positive, elasticity). The point is that such general principles can only properly emerge as a result of prior classification and analysis of the concrete peculiarities of particular situations, and not as a result of isolating a few common features of those situations by a method of superficial analogy. The comparative study of social institutions affords a strong presumption, to say the least, that the modern theory of price-equilibrium may have considerable analogy with the Quantity Theory of Money in this respect. In Friedrich Engels' words, Political Economy as an " historical science " " must first investigate the special laws of each separate stage in the evolution of production and exchange, and only when it has completed this investigation will it be able to establish the few quite general laws which hold good for production and exchange considered as a whole ".[3]

This is not a theme that can here be fittingly pursued. But it is also not one that in the present context could be entirely ignored. While no one could seriously deny that there are features which different types of economic society have in common, and that such analogies are deserving of study and have their share of importance when placed in proper setting,

---

[1] For example, that in so far as velocity of circulation changed as a consequence of price-changes (or of the expectation of such changes) this was likely to be in a direction that would *reinforce*, and not counteract, the influence of changes in quantity of money on prices. Output was held to be unaffected by changes in demand by virtue of an implicit assumption of full employment, i.e. inelastic supply of output as a whole.

[2] Causal story is used here in the sense of a theory adequate to enable one to make some prediction about actual events : in this case about the probable effect of a given change in the quantity of money.

[3] *Anti-Dühring*, 167–8.

it seems abundantly clear that the leading questions concerning economic *development*, such as those with which the following studies are concerned, cannot be answered at all unless one goes outside the bounds of that limited traditional type of economic analysis in which realism is so ruthlessly sacrificed to generality, and unless the existing frontier between what it is fashionable to label as " economic factors " and as " social factors " is abolished.   Moreover, it is not only that this limited type of economic enquiry is powerless to provide answers to certain questions.   By confining its examination of society to the level of the market, this type of enquiry also contributes to that mystification about the essential nature of capitalist society of which the history of economics, with its abstinence-theories and its word-play about " productivity ", is so prolific of examples.   At the level of the market all things available to be exchanged, including the labour-power of proletarians, appear as similar entities, since abstraction has been made of almost every other quality except that of being an object of exchange.   Hence at this level of analysis everything is seen as an exchange of equivalents ;   to the exchange-process the owner of titles to property contributes as much as the labourer ;   and the essence of Capitalism as a particular form of the appropriation of surplus labour by a class possessing economic power and privilege is thus by sleight of hand concealed.   To shift the focus of economic enquiry from a study of exchange societies in general to a study of the physiology and growth of a specifically capitalist economy—a study which must necessarily be associated with a comparative study of different forms of economy—is a change of emphasis which seems, in this country at least, to be long overdue.

CHAPTER TWO

THE DECLINE OF FEUDALISM AND THE GROWTH OF TOWNS

I

This country has not been immune to discussion about the meaning of Feudalism, and usages of the term have been various and conflicting. As Dr. Helen Cam has remarked, the constitutional historian has tended to find the essence of Feudalism in the fact that " landholding is the source of political power " ; to the lawyer its essence has been that " status is determined by tenure " and to the economic historian " the cultivation of land by the exercise of rights over persons ".[1] But in general the matter has here excited little controversy. Definition has not been linked with rival social philosophies as has elsewhere been the case, most notably in nineteenth-century Russia. The very existence of such a system has not been called in question ; and design for the future has not been made to depend on any imprint which this system may have left upon the present. In Russia, by contrast, the discussion has exercised opinion more powerfully than elsewhere, and the question whether Feudalism in the Western sense had ever existed formed a principal issue in the famous debate between Westerners and Slavophils in the first half and middle of the nineteenth century. At first emphasis was laid on the relationship in which the vassal stood to his prince or sovereign and on the form of landholding, yielding what was in the main a juridical definition : a definition certainly according with the etymology of the word, since as Maine observed the term Feudalism " has the defect of calling attention to one set only of its characteristic incidents ". A matured example of this is the definition which the late Professor P. Struve recently contributed to the *Cambridge Economic History of Europe* : " a contractual but indissoluble bond between service and land grant, between personal obligation and real right ". From this definition it followed that, although Feudalism had existed in Russia, its beginning was only to be dated from around 1350 with the

[1] *History*, vol. XXV (1940–1), p. 216.

termination of allodial landholding and the rise of service-tenures, and that it presumably terminated in the seventeenth century, when the *pomiestie* became assimilated to the *votchina* (i.e. became hereditary) and there was a reversion to the allodial principle.[1] With the growing influence of Marxism on Russian studies of agrarian history, a second type of definition came into prominence, giving pride of place to economic rather than to juridical relations. Professor M. N. Pokrovsky, for instance, who for many years was the *doyen* of Marxist historians, seems to have regarded Feudalism *inter alia* as a system of self-sufficient " natural economy ", by contrast with a moneyed " exchange economy "—as " an economy that has consumption as its object ".[2] This notion that Feudalism rested on natural economy as its economic base is one which, implicitly at least, seems to be shared by a number of economic historians in the West, and might be said to have more affinity with the conceptions of writers of the German Historical School, like Schmoller, than with those of Marx. There is a good deal of evidence to suggest that markets and money played a more prominent part in the Middle Ages than used to be supposed. But this notion, at any rate, shares with the purely juridical one the great inconvenience (to say the least) of making the term not even approximately coterminous with the institution of serfdom. In Pokrovsky's case, for example, this definition leads him to speak of the sixteenth century in Russia as a period of decline of Feudalism (entitling the relevant chapter in his *Brief History* " The Dissolution of Feudalism in Muscovy "), for the reason that commerce was reviving at this time and production for a market on the increase. Yet the sixteenth century was the very period when enserfment of previously free or semi-free peasants was taking place extensively and feudal burdens (in the common economic usage of the word) on the peasantry were being greatly augmented. Some English economic historians have apparently tried to evade this dilemma, firstly, by a virtual identification of serfdom with the performance of labour-services, or obligatory work directly performed upon the lord's estate, and, secondly, by attempting

---

[1] *Cambridge Economic History of Europe*, vol. I, 427, 432.
[2] *Brief History of Russia*, vol. I, 289. This definition *inter alia* earned him strong criticism from other Soviet historians in the early '30's. Pokrovsky's critics alleged that he tried simultaneously to ride both this conception and a purely political and juridical one ; and that influenced in particular by a much-discussed work of Pavlov-Silvanski in 1907 (which championed the idea that Feudalism in the Western sense had existed in Russia), he never completely broke away from the latter conception (cf. S. Bakhrushin in *Protiv Historicheski Conseptsii M. N. Pokrovskovo*, 117-18).

to show that such labour-services usually disappeared and were commuted into a contractual relationship in terms of money in the degree that trade and production for exchange in a wide market developed at the close of the Middle Ages. But this does not seem to provide at all a satisfactory way of escape, as what follows in this chapter will attempt to show.

The English mind is wont to dismiss arguments about definition as mere disputation about words : an instinct which is probably a healthy one seeing that so much argument of this kind has been little more than an exercise for pedants. But questions of definition cannot be entirely dismissed from our reckoning, however keen we may be on letting facts speak for themselves. We have already said that in attaching a definite meaning, whether explicitly or implicitly, to a term like Feudalism or Capitalism, one is *ipso facto* adopting a principle of classification to be applied in one's selection and assembly of historical events. One is deciding how one will break up the *continuum* of the historical process, the raw material that history presents to historiography—what events and what sequences are to be thrown into relief.   Since classification must necessarily precede and form the groundwork for analysis, it follows that, as soon as one passes from description to analysis, the definitions one has adopted must have a crucial influence on the result.

To avoid undue proxility, it must suffice, without further parade of argument, to postulate the definition of Feudalism which in the sequel it is proposed to adopt. The emphasis of this definition will lie, not in the juridical relation between vassal and sovereign, nor in the relation between production and the destination of the product, but in the relation between the direct producer (whether he be artisan in some workshop or peasant cultivator on the land) and his immediate superior or overlord and in the social-economic content of the obligation which connects them.   Conformably with the notion of Capitalism discussed in the previous chapter, this definition will characterize Feudalism primarily as a " mode of production " ; and this will form the essence of our definition. As such it will be virtually identical with what we generally mean by serfdom : an obligation laid on the producer by force and independently of his own volition to fulfil certain economic demands of an overlord, whether these demands take the form of services to be performed or of dues to be paid in money or in kind—of work or of what Dr. Neilson has termed " gifts to the lord's

larder ".[1]   This coercive force may be that of military strength,
possessed by the feudal superior, or of custom backed by some
kind of juridical procedure, or the force of law.   This system of
production contrasts, on the one hand, with slavery in that (as
Marx has expressed it) " the direct producer is here in possession
of his means of production, of the material labour conditions
required for the realization of his labour and the production of
his means of subsistence.   He carries on his agriculture and the
rural house industries connected with it as an independent
producer ", whereas " the slave works with conditions of labour
belonging to another ".   At the same time, serfdom implies that
" the property relation must assert itself as a direct relation
between rulers and servants, so that the direct producer is not
free " :   " a lack of freedom which may be modified from serfdom with forced labour to the point of a mere tributary
relation ".[2]   It contrasts with Capitalism in that under the latter
the labourer, in the first place (as under slavery), is no longer
an independent producer but is divorced from his means of
production and from the possibility of providing his own subsistence, but in the second place (unlike slavery), his relationship to the owner of the means of production who employs him
is a purely contractual one (an act of sale or hire terminable
at short notice) : in the face of the law he is free both to choose
his master and to change masters ; and he is not under any
obligation, other than that imposed by a contract of service, to
contribute work or payment to a master.   This system of social
relations to which we refer as Feudal Serfdom has been associated
in history, for a number of reasons, with a low level of technique,
in which the instruments of production are simple and generally
inexpensive, and the act of production is largely individual in

---

[1] N. Neilson, *Customary Rents* (in *Oxford Studies in Social and Legal History*), 15.
Cf. Vinogradoff, *Villeinage in England*, 405 : " The labour-service relation, although
very marked and prevalent in most cases [in the feudal period], is by no means the
only one that should be taken into account."

[2] *Capital*, vol. III, 918.   Marx goes on to say that " under such conditions the
surplus labour for the nominal owner of the land cannot be filched from them [the
serfs] by any economic measures but must be forced from them by other measures,
whatever may be the form assumed by them " ; to which he adds the following
remarks : " The specific economic form in which unpaid surplus labour is pumped
out of the direct producers determines the relations of rulers and ruled. . . . It is
always the direct relation of the owners of the conditions of production to the direct
producers which reveals the innermost secret, the hidden foundation of the entire
social construction, and . . . of the corresponding form of the state." Yet " this
does not prevent the same economic basis from showing infinite variations and
gradations in its appearance ", due to " numerous outside circumstances, natural
environment, race peculiarities, outside historical influences, and so forth, all of
which must be ascertained by careful analysis ".

character ; the division of labour (and hence the co-ordination of individuals in production as a socially-integrated process) being at a very primitive level of development. Historically it has also been associated (and for a similar reason in the main) with conditions of production for the immediate needs of the household or village-community and not for a wider market ; although " natural economy " and serfdom are far from being coterminous, as we shall see. The summit of its development was characterized by demesne-farming : farming of the lord's estate, often on a considerable scale, by compulsory labour-services. But the feudal mode of production was not confined to this classic form. Finally, this economic system has been associated, for part of its life-history at least and often in its origins, with forms of political decentralization, with the conditional holding of land by lords on some kind of service-tenure, and (more generally) with the possession by a lord of judicial or quasi-judicial functions in relation to the dependent population. But, again, this association is not invariable, and serfdom can be found in company both with fairly centralized State-forms and with hereditary landholding instead of service-tenures. To invert a description of Vinogradoff (who speaks of serfdom as " a characteristic corollary of Feudalism " [1]), we may say that the holding of land in fief is a common characteristic, but not an invariable characteristic, of Feudal Serfdom as an economic system in the sense in which we are using it.

II

The revival of commerce in Western Europe after A.D. 1100 and its disruptive effect on feudal society is a sufficiently familiar story. How the growth of trade carried in its wake the trader and the trading community, which nourished itself like an alien body within the pores of feudal society ; how with exchange came an increasing percolation of money into the self-sufficiency of manorial economy ; how the presence of the merchant encouraged a growing inclination to barter surplus products and produce for the market—all this, with much richness of detail, has been told many times. The consequences for the texture of the old order were radical enough. Money revenue as well as services of bondmen grew to be a lordly ambition ; a market in loans developed and also a market in land. As one writer,

[1] Article on Serfdom in *Encyclopedia Britannica*.

speaking of England, has said : " the great roads which join London to the seaboard are the arteries along which flows money, the most destructive solvent of seigniorial power ".[1]

That this process was of outstanding importance in these centuries can scarcely be doubted. That it was connected with the changes that were so marked at the end of the Middle Ages is evident enough. The tendency that developed to commute labour-services for a money-payment and either to lease out the seigniorial demesne for a money-rent or to continue its cultivation with hired labour obviously had the growth of the market and of money-dealings as their necessary condition. What is questionable, however, is whether the connection was as simple and direct as has often been depicted, and whether the widening of the market can be held to have been a *sufficient* condition for the decline of Feudalism—whether an explanation is possible in terms of this as the sole or even the decisive factor. It has been not uncommon for the solvent effect of exchange and of money to be assigned, not only an outstanding, but a unique influence in the transformation of society from feudal to capitalist. We are often presented with the picture of a more or less stable economy that was disintegrated by the impact of commerce acting as an external force and developing outside the system that it finally overwhelmed. We are given an interpretation of the transition from the old order to the new that finds the dominant causal sequences within the sphere of exchange between manorial economy and the outside world. " Natural economy " and " exchange economy " are two economic orders that cannot mix, and the presence of the latter, we are told, is sufficient to cause the former to go into dissolution.

Serious doubt about the adequacy of such an interpretation arises as soon as the influence of trade on the structure of Feudalism in different parts of Europe, or even in different parts of England, is subjected to comparative study. For example, if the destructive effects of money-dealings on the old order, based on servile labour, were truly the decisive factor at work, one could naturally expect to find most evidence of commutation of services for a money-payment in England by (say) the fourteenth century in counties nearest to the London market—in closest

[1] W. H. R. Curtler, *The Enclosure and Redistribution of our Land*, 41. Pirenne says that " the decay of the seigneurial system advanced in proportion to the development of commerce " (*op. cit.*, 84). Professor Nabholz attributes the transition from feudal dues to money rents to the fact that " the lord must adjust himself to a money economy " (*Cambridge Economic History*, vol. I, 503 ; also 554–5).

touch with those " arteries along which flows money, the most destructive solvent of seigniorial power ". Actually, it was the south-east of England that showed the largest proportion of labour services at this date and the north and west of England the smallest.[1] This of itself might be held to be insufficient as rebutting evidence, since the relative importance of labour services among feudal dues varied in different parts of the country with the type of cultivation and the size of the arable demesne ; and many money-payments were survivals of long standing and not products of recent commutation. But it is also true, when we study the trend over several centuries, that " in the more backward parts of the country, farthest from great markets, above all in the north-west, labour services were shed first, while the more progressive south-east retained them longest ".[2] Secondly, an explanation of the change in terms of market influences would lead one to expect to find a close correlation between the development of trade and the decline of serfdom in different areas of Europe. To some extent it is true that there is this correlation. But the exceptions are sufficiently remarkable. The outstanding case where the connection does not hold is the recrudescence of Feudalism in Eastern Europe at the end of the fifteenth century—that " second serfdom " of which Friedrich Engels wrote [3] : a revival of the old system which was associated with the growth of production for the market. Alike in the Baltic States, in Poland and Bohemia expanding opportunities for grain export led, not to the abolition, but to the augmentation or revival of servile obligations on the peasantry, and to arable cultivation for the market on the large estates on a basis of serf labour.[4] Similarly in Hungary the growth of trade, the growth of large estate-farming and increased impositions on the peasants went hand in hand.[5] Thirdly, there is no evidence that the start of commutation in England was connected with the growth of production for the market, even if the two were associated in the later stages of the decline

---

[1] Cf. H. L. Gray in *English Historical Review*, Oct. 1934, 635–6. It is true that London had not yet the pre-eminence over other cities that it later had. But the two next cities in importance, Norwich and Bristol, were also in the southern half of England.

[2] M. Postan in *Trans. Ryl. Hist. Society* (NS.), vol. XX, 171.

[3] *Marx–Engels Correspondence*, 407–8.

[4] Cf. H. Sée, *Modern Capitalism*, 161 ; also cf. W. Stark, *Ursprung und Aufstieg des landwirtschaftlichen Grossbetriebs in den Böhmischen Ländern ; Camb. Econ. History*, vol I, 405.

[5] *Camb. Econ. History*, vol. I, 410.

of serfdom.[1]   It is now recognized that there was a fairly considerable movement towards commutation as early as the twelfth
century, which was succeeded in the thirteenth century by a
reaction towards an increase of labour services and an intensification of pressure on the peasantry.[2]   Yet the growth of trade
and of urban markets was a feature of the thirteenth century,
when feudal reaction was occurring, and not of the twelfth
century when the drift towards commutation is found.

There seems, in fact, to be as much evidence that the growth
of a money economy *per se* led to an intensification of serfdom
as there is evidence that it was the cause of the feudal decline.
If we wish to multiply examples we shall find the history of
eastern Europe particularly rich in testimony of the former
kind.   The fact that the Greek colonies on the shores of the
Black Sea in the second and third centuries A.D. were so largely
trading colonies did not prevent them from being (in Rostovstev's
description of them) " military communit(ies) of landowners
and traders who ruled over a native population of serfs ".[3]   The
fact that the early Russian cities like Kiev and Novgorod so
largely thrived as centres of trade along the great Baltic-Lake
Ladoga-Dnieper-Black Sea trade route did not prevent their
ruling class from having slaves as objects of production as well
as of trade and from developing a form of serfdom on their
lands.[4]   Four centuries later, it was precisely wealthy monasteries like the Troitsa Sergeievsky near Moscow or that of St.
Cyril on the White Sea, among the most enterprising and successful traders of the period, that were the earliest to impose
labour services (instead of dues in money or kind) upon peasantry
on their estates.   Something similar was true of German monasteries and of Church colonizing enterprises east of the Elbe,
which reduced the indigenous Wendish peasantry to serfdom or
even slavery upon their own once-free lands, and generally maintained a more severe régime of bondage on Church lands than
prevailed on lay estates.   In Poland in the fifteenth century a
transition from a system of tribute-payments in money and in

---

[1] This association is scarcely true of the fifteenth century, however.   This century
witnessed a very rapid growth of hired labour in agriculture ; yet it was a century,
for the most part, of declining rather than of expanding trade.

[2] Cf. Kosminsky in *Econ. Hist. Review*, vol. V, No. 2, pp. 43–4, who speaks of an
actual " asservation of the free " ; also his *Angliskaia Derevnia v. 13° veke*, 211–16,
219, of which the article is a summary ; and Postan, *loc. cit.*, 174–8, 185–7 ; N.
Neilson, *Economic Conditions on the Manors of Ramsey Abbey*, 50 and *passim*.

[3] M. Rostovstev in *American Historical Review*, vol. XXVI, 222.

[4] See below, p. 67.

kind (which had characterized the earlier period of colonization of new land) to an extensive system of labour-services coincided with the growth of corn export, following the Peace of Torun in 1466, which had given Poland an outlet to the sea [1] ; and in the Polish-occupied Ukraine of the sixteenth century we find that " serfdom made its initial appearance in western Ukraine where the demand for grain (for export) first appeared in the latter half of the sixteenth century ".[2]   The eighteenth century in Russia—the century of Peter the Great and of the enlightened Catherine, that " golden age of the Russian nobility "—was one in which Russian serfdom approximated more closely than it had ever done to slavery ; the serf being virtually the chattel of his lord who could sell his peasant apart from the land and could torture (even kill) him almost with impunity.   Yet it was also the century that witnessed a higher development of commerce than in any previous century since the glories of Kiev and a not inconsiderable growth of manufacture.

To the question whether there is any reason to suppose that the growth of money economy of itself should encourage a feudal lord to cancel or relax the traditional obligations of his serfs and substitute a contractual relationship in their stead, the answer is, I think, bound to be that there is none.   That the lord would have no inducement at all to commute labour-services for a money-payment unless the use of money were developed to some extent is obvious enough ; and it is in this sense that a certain growth of the market was an essential condition of the change. But it does not follow from this that the spread of trade and of the use of money necessarily leads to the commutation of labour services (still less to the emancipation of the producer from all feudal obligations) and to the leasing of the lord's estate or the farming of it on the basis of hired labour.   Is there not equally good ground for expecting the growth of trade to occasion an intensification of serfdom in order to provide forced labour to cultivate the estate for purposes of the market ?   Is there not as good reason to regard what occurred in eastern Europe or in thirteenth-century England as the natural consequence of expanding commerce as what occurred in fourteenth- and fifteenth-century England or fourteenth- and fifteenth-century France

---

[1] J. Rutkowski, *Histoire Economique de la Pologne avant les Partages,* 31–6. The change seems to have come earlier, and to have been most complete, in the neighbourhood of navigable rivers such as the Vistula, and to have been tardier and least developed in remote regions where transport was difficult.

[2] M. Hrushevsky, *A History of the Ukraine,* 172–4.

and the Rhineland ? If either of the two were to be regarded
as the more probable outcome, it would seem to be the former,
since at earlier periods of history the effect of commerce had been
apparently to encourage a substitution of slavery, which permits
a higher degree of organization and discipline, for the looser
bonds of serfdom.[1]   In past discussion of the decline of Feudalism
the assumption that production of commodities for a market
necessarily implies production on the basis of wage-labour seems
too often to have slipped into the argument unawares.

What is clearly missing in the traditional interpretation is
an analysis of the internal relationships of Feudalism as a mode
of production and the part which these played in determining
the system's disintegration or survival. And while the actual
outcome has to be treated as a result of a complex interaction
between the external impact of the market and these internal
relationships of the system, there is a sense in which it is the
latter that can be said to have exercised the decisive influence.
As Marx observed, the " dissolving influence " that commerce
will have upon the old order depends upon the character of this
system, " its solidity and internal articulation " ; and, in particular, " what new mode of production will take the place of
the old does not depend on commerce but on the character of
the old mode of production itself ".[2]

As soon as we enquire how far forces internal to feudal
economy were responsible for its decline, we turn in a direction
to which less study has been devoted and where the evidence is
neither very plentiful nor conclusive. But such evidence as we
possess strongly indicates that it was the inefficiency of Feudalism
as a system of production, coupled with the growing needs of
the ruling class for revenue, that was primarily responsible for
its decline ; since this need for additional revenue promoted an
increase in the pressure on the producer to a point where this
pressure became literally unendurable. The source from which
the feudal ruling class derived its income, and the only source
from which this income could be augmented, was the surplus
labour-time of the servile class over and above what was
necessary to provide for the latter's own subsistence. With the
low and stationary state of labour-productivity of the time,
there was little margin to spare from which this surplus product

[1] Marx comments on the fact that " in the antique world the effect of commerce
and the development of merchant capital always results in slave economy " (*Capital*,
vol. III, 390).
   [2] *Ibid.*

could be increased ; and any attempt to increase it was bound to be at the expense of the time devoted by the producer to the cultivation of his own meagre holding and bound very soon either to tax the producer's strength beyond human endurance or else to reduce his subsistence below the level of mere animal existence. That this was so did not, of course, prevent the pressure to obtain a larger surplus from being exerted ; but the eventual result for the system at large remained disastrous, since in the end it led to an exhaustion, or actual disappearance, of the labour-force by which the system was nourished. In the words of a French writer : " To the knight or baron the peasant, serf or free, was only a source of revenue ; in time of peace they oppressed him at home as much as they could with imposts and *corvées* ; in time of war in foreign territories they pillaged, murdered, burnt, trampled upon him. . . . The peasant was a creature to exploit at home, and to destroy abroad, and nothing more." Even in the literature of the time, such as the *chansons de geste,* full of gentle chivalry, " there is not a word of pity for the peasants whose houses and crops are burned and who are massacred by hundreds or carried away with feet and wrists in bonds ".[1] The villein we find everywhere despised as an inferior creature : regarded not at all as an end of policy but simply as an instrument—as a means to the enrichment of their lords. For the system that rested on these foundations history was to have its own peculiar reckoning.

Not only did the productivity of labour remain very low in the manorial economy, owing both to the methods in use and the lack of incentive to labour, but the yield of land remained so meagre as to lead some authorities to suggest an actual tendency for the system of cultivation to result in exhaustion of the soil. The primitive rotation, the lack of sufficient root crops and sown-grasses like lucerne, gave little chance to the soil to recover after it was cropped ; and while manuring was known and sometimes practised, the average peasant's poverty prevented him from the adequate manuring of his own land which " soil cultivated under the mediæval cropping system required if it was not to lose its productive power ".[2] Even the folding of his own sheep on his holding was not always possible owing to the *jus faldae* of the lord—his right of requiring the manorial sheep to be folded on his demesne. At any rate there was little

[1] A. Luchaire, *Social France at the time of Philip Augustus,* p. 384.
[2] H. S. Bennett, *Life on the English Manor, 1150–1400,* p. 78.

or no incentive to improvement. As an authority on mediæval Europe has written, " any improvement in the soil was but the pretext for some new exaction ", and the lord, being " a mere parasite . . . discouraged initiative and dried up all energy at its source by taking from the villein an exorbitant part of the fruits of his work, so that labour was half sterile ".[1] It is hardly surprising that masters should complain of villeins who " will labour fervently before a man's face but feebly and remissly behind his back ", or that it should have been said of bond-servants (the most exploited section of feudal society) that, " being bought and sold like beasts, and beat with rods, and scarcely suffered to rest or to take breath ", they should, " when they be not held low with dread, wax stout and proud against the commandments of their sovereigns ".[2] How wretched was the plight of the mass of the producers and how close to the irreducible minimum they were is graphically shown by con-temporary accounts, like that of the man who " drove four heifers before him that had become feeble, so that men might count their every rib, so sorry looking they were " ; and " as he trod the soil his toes peered out of his worn shoes, his hose hung about his hocks on all sides ", while his wife beside him " went barefoot on the ice so that the blood flowed ". The common bailiffs' doctrine was that " the churl, like the willow, sprouts the better for being cropped "—a doctrine that, even if true, must have operated within very narrow limits ; and a not unenvied title that bailiffs frequently earned was *excoriator rusticorum*. The Abbot of Burton hardly needed to remind his serfs that they possessed *nihil praeter ventrem*.[3]

At the same time the needs of the feudal ruling class for an

---

[1] P. Boissonnade, *Life and Work in Mediæval Europe*, pp. 140–1, also p. 145. Cf. the remarks of Adam Smith, *Wealth of Nations*, 1826 Ed., pp. 360–3. Denton refers to the fertility of English arable land at the end of the fifteenth century as exhausted (*England in the Fifteenth Century*, p. 153), and Lord Ernle has even suggested a decline of 30 or 40 per cent. in yield per acre between the thirteenth and fifteenth centuries. Cf. also Harriet Bradley, *Enclosures in England*, p. 47 seq., where reference is made to " the overwhelming evidence of the poverty of the fourteenth-century peasant—poverty which can only be explained by the barrenness of their land " (56). For an opposite opinion cf. R. Leonard in *Econ. Journal*, March 1922 ; also on the wider question of soil exhaustion and history A. P. Usher in *Quarterly Journal of Economics*, May 1923, p. 385. Fuller statistical data (e.g. of Sir Wm. Beveridge) does not support the view that there was an actual decline in yield over this period, but rather, as a recent writer has summarized it, " gives the impression that the period was one characterized by agricultural stagnation, but not by retrogression, because the level of agricultural technique may at the beginning have been about as low as it could be " (M. K. Bennett in *Econ. History*, Feb. 1935, 22).

[2] Cit. G. G. Coulton, *Social Life in Britain from the Conquest to the Reformation*, pp. 340, 341–2.

[3] H. S. Bennett, *op. cit.*, pp. 164, 185–6, 305.

increasing revenue demanded an intensified pressure and novel exactions on the producers. In the first place there was a tendency (which seems to have operated more forcibly on the Continent than in England) for the number of vassals to be multiplied, by a process known as sub-infeudation, in order to strengthen the military resources of the greater lords. This, combined with the natural growth of noble families and an increase in the number of retainers, swelled the size of the parasitic class that had to be supported from the surplus labour of the serf population.[1] Added to this were the effects of war and of brigandage, which could almost be said to be integral parts of the feudal order, and which swelled the expenses of feudal households and of the Crown at the same time as it spread waste and devastation over the land.[2] While exaction and pillage diminished productive powers, the demands that the producer was required to meet were augmented. The series of Crusades involved a special drain on feudal revenues at this period ; and as the age of chivalry advanced, the extravagances of noble households advanced also, with their lavish feasts and costly displays, vying in emulation in their cult of *magnificentia*. At first the growth of trade, with the attraction of exotic wares that it made available and the possibilities it opened of producing a surplus for the market, reinforced the tendency to intensify feudal pressure on the peasantry ; and, as we have already noticed, the thirteenth century in England was marked by an increase of labour dues on the larger estates in England, and especially on monastic lands. A contemporary account complains that the lords are " destroying the peasants by exactions and tallage " and " exacting tallage from them by force and oppression ".[3] Probably this was the root of that change of which Vinogradoff remarked, when he said that " the will and influence of the lord is much more distinct and overbearing in the documents of the later thirteenth and of the fourteenth century than in the earlier records ".[4] At the same time it is possible that the smaller estates, which were apt to be badly supplied with unfree labour, may have had a tendency to encourage money-rents from tenants and to rely for cultivating the demesne, where

---

[1] As regards the size of Church establishments in the later Middle Ages, cf. some remarks of Sombart, *Der Moderne Kapitalismus*, vol. I, 160–2.
[2] Cf. the remarks of M. Bloch, *La Société Féodale : les classes et le gouvernement des hommes*, 16–24. Also see footnote to p. 49.
[3] Cit. H. S. Bennett, *op. cit.*, pp. 138–9 ; also 105.
[4] *Villeinage in England*, p. 408.

this was practicable, on the hired labour of freemen.[1] In twelfth-century France we hear occasional voices like that of the Abbé de Cluny denouncing the oppressors of the peasantry, who, not content with the customary obligations, make novel and additional demands.[2]

The result of this increased pressure was not only to exhaust the goose that laid golden eggs for the castle, but to provoke, from sheer desperation, a movement of illegal emigration from the manors : a desertion *en masse* on the part of the producers, which was destined to drain the system of its essential life-blood and to provoke the series of crises in which feudal economy was to find itself engulfed in the fourteenth and fifteenth centuries. This flight of villeins from the land often assumed catastrophic proportions both in England and elsewhere, and not only served to swell the population of the rising towns but especially on the Continent contributed to a prevalence of outlaw-bands and vagabondage and periodic *jacqueries*.[3] In France " when the lord remained inflexible, his land was deserted : it meant the exodus of the whole village, or even the whole canton ", and " desertions were numerous, continuous ".[4] For example, in the twelfth century the inhabitants of the Île de Ré deserted *en masse* owing to their lord's severity, and the lord was forced to introduce concessions in order to retain any labour at all.[5] The lords in their turn resorted to agreements between themselves in the twelfth and thirteenth centuries for mutual assistance in the capture of fugitive serfs : agreements which provided for an exchange of captives or gave the right of pursuit in another's territory. But so considerable did the problem of fugitives become, and so great the hunger for labour, that, despite treaties and mutual promises, an actual competition developed to entice and steal the serfs of a neighbouring domain—a competition which necessarily involved the making of certain concessions, and the existence of which imposed its own limits on the further

[1] Kosminsky, *loc. cit.*
[2] Cit. Levasseur, *La Population Française*, vol. I, p. 147. Pirenne refers to a state of financial embarrassment among knights and monasteries in the mid-thirteenth century on the Continent. (*Op. cit.*, p. 82.)
[3] English legislation enacted severe penalties for such flight from feudal service : penalties which included imprisonment or branding on the forehead. There were even penalties against learning a handicraft on the part of those attached to a manor ; and it was prohibited for any man owning land of less than £20 annual value to apprentice his son to a trade (Denton, *op. cit.*, p. 222). Cf. also Lipson : " The manorial system was undermined not by commutation, but by the dispersion of the peasantry. . . . Desertion *en masse* from the manor accelerated the end of villeinage in England." *Econ. History of England*, vol. I (Middle Ages), 1937 Ed., 92–4.
[4] A. Luchaire, *op. cit.*, pp. 407–8.   [5] *Ibid.*, 407.

increase of feudal exploitation.   In some cases a lord, to repeople his land which had grown deserted by reason of his own oppression, was forced into the sale of franchises, setting bounds to seigniorial exactions, in return for a rent or a cash payment ; and in certain provinces of France there developed in this way a number of rural communes, formed from an association of villages, which, like towns, possessed a mayor and a jurisdiction of their own.[1]

To some extent the feudal lust for expanded revenue was met by an increase of population ; and the fact that there was some growth of population up to A.D. 1300 suggests that until this date there were certain areas where fresh supplies of cultivable land were available or else the pressure of feudal exactions had not yet reached its limit.   Data concerning population in this age are scanty ;   but there was apparently a considerable growth of population both in England and on the Continent in the twelfth and thirteenth centuries.[2]   This, it is true, would have served to provide more labour to support the system and to furnish additional feudal revenue.   But except in areas where the increase in numbers was accompanied by an increase in cultivable land available to the peasants (which would in turn have required a sufficient increase in draught animals and instruments in the hands of the cultivators), the eventual result was bound to be an increase in the peasants' burden owing to the increased pressure on the available land.   True, considerable attempts were made to extend the area of cultivation in the course of the Middle Ages. There were some brave efforts at colonization and land-reclamation, to which certain religious orders such as the Cluniac and the Cistercian made an important contribution, as they did also towards the upkeep of roads and the encouragement of crafts ; in England there were encroachments on the waste, and clearings in the primeval forest were made ;   in Flanders there was reclamation of land from the sea in the twelfth century ;   in Germany the marshes of the Elbe, Oder and Vistula were drained. But generally there was little incentive or means to improve the land ;   and there is sufficient evidence of land-hunger by the end

[1] *Ibid.*, 404–6, 411–14 ;   M. Bloch, *La Société Féodale : La Formation des Liens de Dépendance*, 422–3.

[2] In England the population seems to have grown from about 2 million to $3\frac{1}{2}$ million between the Norman Conquest and the beginning of the fourteenth century. In France the increase was probably even greater.   Levasseur suggests a rise from 7 million in the eleventh century to between 20 and 22 million in the fourteenth : a figure which was not exceeded in the sixteenth century or even until after the early eighteenth century (*La Population Française*, vol. I, p. 169).

of the thirteenth century to suggest that the extension of the area of cultivable land lagged behind population-increase, and save in a few places was probably of too small a magnitude to offset the tendency to declining labour-productivity. Pressure on the soil was already showing itself in the Netherlands, in Saxony, the Rhineland, Bavaria and the Tyrol by 1200 and was a factor in the start of eastward migration ; [1] and it has been stated that after the later part of the fourteenth century " the limits of land acquisition on forest soil in North-East Germany and the interior of Bohemia were already reached ".[2]

After 1300, however, the population over most of Western Europe, instead of increasing as it had done since A.D. 1000, seems to have begun a sharp decline.[3] Whether this was connected with a declining productivity of labour on the peasants' lands by reason of the population growth of previous centuries or was a direct result of increased feudal burdens on the peasantry is impossible to say with any approach to certainty. That there was some connection seems on the face of it very likely. At any rate, its immediate effect was to threaten feudal society with a shrinkage of revenue and to precipitate what may be called a crisis of feudal economy in the fourteenth century. Usually this decline, both in numbers and in feudal revenue, has been attributed exclusively to the devastation of wars and the plague. War and plague were clearly responsible for a great deal. But since the decline started some decades before the onset of the Black Death,[4] it evidently had economic roots. The destructive effect of the plague itself must have been fanned by the malnutrition of the population (mortality from the pestilence apparently being proportionately greater among the masses), and local famines have taken the toll

[1] J. Westfall Thompson, *Feudal Germany*, 496 and 52ľ : " In the twelfth century in some prosperous districts land seems to have attained twelve times the value it had in the ninth, and afterwards even down to the second half of the thirteenth century an increase of about 50 per cent. is to be observed."

[2] Nabholz in *Camb. Econ. History*, vol. I, 396.

[3] Denton suggests that in England the population stopped increasing about the end of the reign of Edward II, and then fell sharply in the mid-fourteenth century, after which it tended to remain stationary at a level scarcely higher than the Domesday figure until the accession of Henry VII (*England in the Fifteenth Century*, pp. 129-30). Of Europe generally in the fourteenth century Pirenne speaks as entering on a period of " not perhaps a decline but a cessation of all advance " (*loc. cit.*, p. 193).

[4] Lipson, for instance, speaks of wages as having been " rising for a generation before the plague swept over England ", and adds : " hence the great pestilence only intensified but did not originate the economic crisis, for the altered equilibrium of the labour market had already begun to produce its effects". (*Econ. History of England*, vol. I, 1937 Ed., pp. 113-14.)

they did because of the absence of reserves. There is some evidence to suggest that agricultural decline in England set in soon after 1300,[1] and probably at about the same date in France. In fourteenth-century England depopulation of the countryside, and with it scarcity of labour, had gone so far even before the Black Death as to cause a serious fall of feudal income and a tendency, on the contrary to improving the demesne, to reduce its size by leases to peasant holders. It now seems clear that this leasing of the demesnes was an expression of economic crises rather than fruit of growing ambition to trade and to improve, to which it has been commonly attributed in the past. In the fifteenth century the evidence indicates that there was a reduction in the total cultivated area, more land being withdrawn from the demesnes than was leased to tenants.[2]

In France labour scarcity seems even earlier to have been a factor hindering the extension of demesne cultivation. Not only had large land-grants been made by seigneurs to vassals and men-at-arms, but also land leased to small tenants in return for a share of the harvest (*tenures à champart*). We have mentioned the attempt to retain labour on the land as a source of revenue by partial emancipations of serfs from the thirteenth century onwards : a tendency that we find not only in France but also in the Rhineland and in Flanders, sometimes by individual manumission and sometimes by the sale of freedom to whole villages (in Burgundy, where the peasantry was especially poor, in return for the surrender of part of their land to the lord). In

---

[1] Mr. R. A. L. Smith has given the years just before 1320 as the start of " acute agricultural depression " in Kent ; and from that time dates a policy of demanding once more the performance of labour-services previously commuted on the estates of Christ Church, Canterbury—" the monks strove to exploit to the full their resources of compulsory labour " (*Canterbury Cathedral Priory*, 125-7).

[2] M. Postan, in *Econ. Hist. Review*, May 1939. Professor Postan asks the question : how far was this decline in seigniorial revenues responsible for " the political gangsterdom of the times ", which had the effect of further sapping the strength of the feudal nobility ? This gangsterdom, though it probably increased in the fifteenth century, seems also to have characterized Feudalism in earlier centuries (as it did even more notoriously on the Continent, e.g. the " robber barons " of the Rhineland and elsewhere). Jusserand gives examples of highway robbery and racketeering by armed gangs in the fourteenth century : gangs which, under the system known as " maintenance ", received support from the highest of the land, including persons at Court and members of the Royal Family, not excluding the Prince of Wales and the prelates of the Church and Edward III's " dearest consort, the queen ". " The great of the land and some lesser people too had their own men, sworn to their service and ready to do anything they were commanded, which consisted in the most monstrous deeds, such as securing property or other goods to which neither their masters nor any claimants, paying their master in order to be ' protected ', had any title. They terrorized the rightful owners, the judges and the juries, ransoming, beating and maiming any opponent." (J. J. Jusserand, *Eng. Wayfaring Life in the Middle Ages*, 150-7.)

company with this marched a tendency to exchange *corvées* services on the seigniorial estate for payments in money or in kind. But these measures, forced as they were by revolt and flight more often than at the initiative of the lord, did not suffice to check the tendency to depopulation. " In all parts (of France) entire villages, sometimes for generations, were abandoned ", the forest in some areas invading former fields and vineyards ; and " the two last centuries of the Middle Ages were in all Western and Central Europe a period of rural ' malaise ' and of depopulation ".[1] In Western and Central Germany an important influence was the eastern migration which had started in the twelfth century under the attraction of the colonizing movement, sponsored by warrior-lords and by the Church in the new lands beyond the Elbe : a colonization which gathered momentum after the " crusade against the Wends " (that " sinister mixture of bigotry and lust for land ", as Westfall Thompson calls it), resulting in the partial extermination of the subjugated tribes and a pressing need on the part of monasteries and Church for a labour supply to replace tribute-paying Slavs in the new territories. In order to people these lands special concessions were made at first to attract colonists. The result was to spread the scarcity of labour not only to Saxony and Westphalia, but even as far as Holland and Flanders whence the migrants came.[2] The constant threat of losing the population from their lands, especially in the regions where growing towns and privileged *bourgs* acted as a powerful magnet, combined with the steady resistance of the peasantry to the performance of labour services, was a leading factor in Western Germany in the decline of demesne farming, and in the tendency of lords " to reduce their demands for labour services in order to dissuade tenants from deserting their estates ", which operated fairly steadily after the twelfth century.[3]

III

The reaction of the nobility to this situation was not at all a uniform one ; and it is on the difference in this reaction in

---

[1] M. Bloch, *Les Caractères Originaux de l'histoire rurale française*, 117–18 ; also 99–100, 104, 111–14 ; also cf. *Camb. Econ. Hist.*, vol. I, 295–321, and Bloch, *La Société Féodale : la formation des liens de dépendance*, 422–5. By the sixteenth century the seigniorial attitude towards manumission of serfs had hardened, and willingness gave way to opposition to further concessions.
[2] J. Westfall Thompson, *Feudal Germany*, 400–39, 485, 501–2, 610.
[3] F. L. Ganshof in *Camb. Econ. History*, vol. I, 295.

different areas of Europe that a large part of the difference in the economic history of the ensuing centuries depends.   In some cases, in order to attract or retain labour (as in parts of France, especially the south, after the Hundred Years' War), the lords were forced into concessions which represented a mitigation of servile burdens and even on occasions a substitution of a contractual relationship, embodied in a money-payment, for an obligatory one.   In yet other cases they responded with a tightening of feudal burdens, with firmer measures for the attachment of bondmen to an estate and for the recapture of fugitives, and a reimposition of servile obligations where these had previously been relaxed—the " feudal reaction " about which there has been much debate.   In Eastern Europe the latter was most marked and most successful.   Even in England there is evidence of an attempt to tighten the bonds of serfdom in the fourteenth century.   To-day it is generally held that this response to the scarcity of labour which followed the Black Death was less widespread than used to be supposed and that it seldom had any large measure of success.   That the attempt was made, however, especially on certain monastic estates, is fairly clear.[1]   Of the virtual renaissance of serfdom which occurred in some parts of the Continent we have already quoted examples : we find it in Denmark and in the Balkans, as well as later in the Baltic States and Russia, in Poland, Hungary and Bohemia.   In Spain Moslems and Jews on the estates were reduced to serfdom and the peasant lot was so degraded as to be subsequently described as " worse than that of a galley slave ".   There was even some revival of the slave trade in the Mediterranean to supply landowners with cultivators.[2]

Evidently political and social factors played a large part here in determining the course of events.   The strength of peasant resistance, the political and military power of local lords, render-

---

[1] Namely at Canterbury (where it started before 1330), Ely, Crowland, and on some estates of the Bishopric of Durham.   It has to be remembered, moreover, that the Statute of Labourers of 1351 not only provided for the control of wages but also made service to a master compulsory for all poor persons *whether bond or free* and placed restrictions on their freedom of movement ; while decisions of the higher courts on its enforcement provided that a lord might re-capture a villein, despite a statutory contract between the latter and another employer.   This suggests that " the machinery of the manorial courts had become inadequate for the task of recovering fugitive villeins, and that the lords needed some other means of securing labourers, and that therefore a remedy was provided for them by the agency of the central government " (B. H. Putnam, *Enforcement of the Statutes of Labourers*, 222, also 200–6).

[2] Cf. Boissonnade, *op. cit.*, 325–6.   Also J. S. Schapiro, *Social Reform and the Reformation*, 54 seq. ; J. K Ingram, *History of Slavery and Serfdom*, 113 seq.

ing it easy or difficult as the case might be to overcome peasant resistance and forcibly to prevent desertion of the manors, and the extent to which the royal power exerted its influence to strengthen seigniorial authority or on the contrary welcomed an opportunity of weakening the position of rival sections of the nobility—all this was of great importance in deciding whether concession or renewed coercion was to be the seigniorial answer to desertion and depopulation, and whether, if coercion was attempted, it was to prove successful. Some writers have advanced the view that in England the influence of the king's courts and justices acted as a protection (doubtless no more than partial) for villein rights against arbitrary acts of oppression by their lords, at any rate if these acts were unhallowed by tradition,[1] and that in France the triumph of the absolute monarchy when it occurred served to limit the extent of the " feudal reaction ".[2] By contrast the territories east of the Rhine (until one came to Poland and Muscovy) witnessed no comparable central power, jealous of the autonomy of lords and princes and competent to curb the unbridled exercise of their authority. In Eastern Europe and in Spain it would seem that both the military strength and the political authority of the local seigneurs remained relatively high. In France and in Flanders Feudalism had been seriously weakened by the Hundred Years' War ; yet in certain parts of France the political authority of the seigneurs apparently remained for some time little impaired, and above all the Church, as a closely-knit international organization, retained its strength. In England the baronage which had never been strong by contrast with the Crown (which by virtue of the Norman Conquest had secured to itself an independent source of revenue in the extensive Crown estates) were further weakened by the Wars of the Roses : so much so that the noblemen summoned to attend the first Parliament of Henry VII numbered scarcely more than a half those who had been summoned at the beginning of the century.[3]

But while they may have been contributory, political factors of this kind can hardly be regarded as sufficient to account for the differences in the course of events in various parts of Europe.

---

[1] This fact is denied, however, by Kosminsky (and before him by such authorities as Pollock and Maitland), who asserts that the English common law defended the right of lords to increase villein services without restriction and refused to hear villeins' suits against their lords (*Angliskaia Derevnia v. 13° veke*, 206-9). Protection, when it was given in later times, probably came from the prerogative courts rather than from the courts of common law.

[2] M. Bloch, *op. cit.*, 132, 139.   [3] Denton, *op. cit.*, 257.

Political centralization in Muscovy and the curbing of the power of the *boyars* went hand-in-hand with an intensification of serfdom ; and while the rise of absolute monarchy in France may have put bounds to feudal reaction, it did not (at least as an early consequence) reverse it. All the indications suggest that in deciding the outcome economic factors must have exercised the outstanding influence. Yet regarding the precise character and importance of such factors we are not very plentifully supplied with reliable data. An influence to which one's attention is immediately directed is the prevailing type of cultivation. For example, a predominance of pasture over arable would clearly affect the seigniorial desire for labour services, as well as itself being influenced by the scarcity or plentifulness of labour. The suitability of large areas in the west and north of England for sheep rearing, as well as the development of the wool trade, must evidently have predisposed lords in these areas towards money-payments rather than the labour-services which would be needed in much larger quantities as the basis for the cultivation of arable demesnes. In the case of Bohemia a factor to which Dr. Stark [1] has drawn attention was the need which the export trade in corn and the narrowness of the home market imposed for extensive cultivation on the cheapest possible basis. Had more intensive cultivation prevailed, quality of labour would have proved a more important consideration compared with its cheapness, and the preference of lords for compulsory serf labour on large *latifundia* might not have prevailed. That this can hardly of itself be accepted as a satisfactory explanation is suggested, however, when we consider that the choice of extensive methods of cultivation in such a case must itself have been determined by the scarcity and dearness of labour for hire (or, alternatively, the availability or non-availability of potential tenant-farmers to cultivate land for a money-rent) compared to the plentifulness of land ; and that there were other cases, for example England and the Netherlands, where expanding corn export coexisted with an ultimate tendency that was away from labour-services. [2]

In some cases where labour-services fixed by custom were light there might be difficulty in raising them ; and in such

---

[1] Stark, *op. cit.*
[2] In the thirteenth century it may have been true of England that the growth of corn export strengthened serfdom. Kosminsky points out that in that century production for export strengthened serfdom, most notably in the corn-exporting regions, the Midlands and Thames Valley (*ibid.*, 227–8).

cases a change to money dues might be a way of increasing the
serf's obligations which was the more acceptable to him because
it offered more personal freedom, and so presented to a lord the
line of least resistance. It is, again, a well-known fact that
compulsory labour was apt to be much less efficient than labour
expended by the cultivators on their own holdings in their own
time ; and even if the lord took much trouble to provide adequate
supervision of the work the yield of these obligatory services often
remained both uncertain and low. At times seemingly trifling
matters, such as the price of provisions, may have influenced the
decision (where some provisions were supplied to workers on the
demesnes, even though no more than a loaf or a fish and some
ale) ; and one meets the remark, " the work is not worth the
breakfast ", several times in the Winchester Pipe Rolls in the
course of the fourteenth century.[1]   In such cases the substitution of dues in kind or in money (paid from the more efficient
labour of the serf on his own holding) for work on the estate
might have proved a profitable bargain for the lord.

But while, no doubt, many factors such as these exercised
again a contributory influence, it seems evident that the fundamental consideration must have been the abundance or scarcity,
the cheapness or dearness, of hired labour in determining whether
or not the lord was willing or unwilling to commute labour-
services for a money-payment, and whether this was a profitable
or a profitless thing for him to do if he was forced into it.[2]   At
any rate, this consideration must have ruled where the concern
of feudal economy was to produce for a market and not simply
to provision directly the seigniorial household.   If the feudal lord
dispensed with direct labour-services, the alternatives open to
him were to lease out the *demesne* or to hire labour for its cultivation
at a money-wage.   Let us take the case where he chose the latter.
What he was then doing was to convert an existing type of
surplus (that of his serfs) from one form into another (from direct
services to a payment in money or in kind) and to invest in the
acquisition of a new type of surplus—that yielded by hired
labour.   For the employment of this additional labour, the
retention of part of the land as demesne land was necessary, and
the substitution of the new labour for the old serf labour in its
cultivation.   The latter now laboured for all their working time,

---

[1] A. E. Levett, *Results of the Black Death* in *Oxford Studies in Social and Legal Hist.*,
vol. V., 157.
[2] Cf. the remarks of Kosminsky, *Angliskaia Derevnia v. 13° veke*, 52, 163 ; and of
M. Postan in *Trans. Ryl. Hist. Society*, 1937, 192–3.

instead of only for part of it, on their " own " land—the land to which they had been traditionally attached ; paying over to the lord the produce of this additional labour-time (or else the proceeds of its sale in the local market). But the new type of demesne cultivation had this difference from the old. Any labour-time devoted to the demesne under the régime of labour-services was pure surplus for the lord (apart from a few incidental expenses such as the bread and ale supplied to the harvesters in the fields that we have mentioned). The producers' subsistence was provided, not from the produce of this labour, but from the labour-time spent on their own holdings. It was the latter which provided, as it were, the lord's " outlay "—the land allotted to his serfs for their own cultivation and such labour-time as he laid no claim upon for himself but left available for the provision of their own subsistence. Demesne cultivation, therefore, by this method could be profitable even at a low level of labour-productivity. Low productivity reduced the amount of produce available to feed the producer and his family as well as the size of the lord's produce (given the division of the serf's working time between working for himself and obligatory labour for his master). As under the *métayage* system of produce-sharing, bad harvests made the share of peasant and landlord alike smaller, but could not make the latter share disappear altogether as long as there was a net product at all to be divided. Under the new type of demesne cultivation, however, the labour-power had first of all to be purchased with wages ; and from the produce of this labour the equivalent of these wages had to be subtracted before what was surplus for the lord began. For this new type of cultivation to be of advantage—to add to the surplus available as feudal revenue under the traditional methods —it was not sufficient that hired labour should be more efficient than compulsory serf-labour. Productivity must have reached a certain *minimum level*. In short, one can say that the preconditions for a commutation of labour-services and the transition to demesne cultivation by hired labour were two-fold : the existence of a reserve of labour (either labour without land, or labour with insufficient land to maintain a livelihood, like the bulk of the English " cotters ", and with labour-time to spare) and a level of productivity of this hired labour that was greater than its wages by a significant amount. This " significant amount " which the surplus available from the new mode of production had to reach was a sort of *minimum sensibile* necessary to attract estate-owners to its use. Sometimes, it is clear, this margin would have to be fairly large to overcome natural conservatism and to persuade estate-owners that cultivation by hired labour had substantial and enduring advantages. But in the case of estates which had always been deficiently supplied with serf-labour, the fact that hired labour could produce even a narrow margin of surplus above the equivalent of its own wages might suffice for its adoption, provided that the reserve of labour was readily available. One has, indeed, the paradox that, provided only that this crucial level of productivity (relative to the price of hired labour) had been reached, hired labour might even have been *less* efficient than bond-labour and its use still have proved an advantage.[1]

This condition that we have postulated for the operation of a tendency to commutation at the lord's initiative could be fulfilled either by labour being exceptionally cheap or by labour being exceptionally productive relative to the primitive standards of the times. But in addition to being cheap or productive it had to be available at the given time and place in fair abundance. It follows that the transition to hired labour was more likely to occur in types of cultivation where the net product of labour was high, and that serf-labour was more likely to be retained where types of cultivation prevailed in which the productivity of labour was low, or over periods of economic history when productive methods had not advanced beyond a very low level (unless this was offset by the price of hired labour being equivalently low owing to the misery of the population). We are also confronted with this further paradox : the very misery of the peasantry, such as we have described, creating the danger of depopulation of manors, might incline the lords to be more amenable to concessions which lessened feudal burdens or to commute labour-services for a rent, both in an effort to avoid depopulation and because the misery which provoked mass migration tended to make labour for hire very cheap (as may have been a significant factor in France, for example, during and after the Hundred

---

[1] The surplus available from hired labour did not need to be *larger* than that yielded by serf-labour (= the product of serf-labour when working for the lord), since, although we are assuming that hired labour is being substituted for serf-labour on the demesne, it is not being substituted for, but *added to*, serf-labour as a *source of surplus*. If we assume that the lord has commuted labour-services at the equivalent of what the surplus labour-time of serfs could produce when devoted to demesne cultivation, then the lord will gain from the change if the new hired labour produces any surplus at all above their wages, since he will now have this surplus as an addition to what he receives as commuted dues from his serfs.

Years' War and in Flanders in the thirteenth century).[1] Conversely, where the plight of the cultivator was less desperate and land available to him was more plentiful, or alternatively where labour was exceptionally scarce because depopulation had already reached an advanced stage (as appears to have been a decisive factor in Eastern Europe after the Thirty Years' War) seigniorial authority would have tended to insist on the retention of labour-services and to augment them by new exactions rather than to commute them.   It is, surely, a very significant witness to the leading importance of this principle which we have cited that the century of scarce labour and of dear labour in England should have seen attempts to reimpose the old obligations, whereas this reaction should have weakened and given place to a renewed tendency to commutation in the middle of the fifteenth century, when the gaps in the population had been sufficiently filled for some fall in wages from their late-fourteenth century peak to have occurred.[2]   It is, surely, also significant that it was east of the Elbe, where labour was most thinly spread compared to available land, that the " second serfdom " should have found its most secure foothold ; and that in Russia, for example, it was in the centuries when the expanding frontier of Cossack settlement to the south and south-east came into prominence, draining away fugitive peasant labour from central Muscovy with the lure of free land, that the movement towards the definitive bonding of the cultivator and his legal attachment to the soil should have developed.[3]

If we consider the other alternative available to the feudal lord—that of exchanging labour-services, not for cultivation of his estate by hired labour, but for leasing of the demesne to

---

[1] There seems to be some evidence that the tendency to commutation and manumission which occurred in Flanders from the second half of the twelfth century was accompanied by the appearance of a substantial class of peasants with holdings too small for a livelihood and even of a landless class (cf. L. Dechesne, *Histoire Economique et Sociale de la Belgique*, 62–5).

[2] Cf. H. Nabholz in *Camb. Econ. History*, vol. I, 520.   Wages, however, continued to remain substantially higher than at the *beginning* of the fourteenth century, and in 1500 may have been about double what they had been in 1300.

[3] For labour scarcity at the time cf. P. Liashchenko, *Istoria Narodnovo Khoziaistva, S.S.S.R.*, vol. I, 157 ; A. Eck, *Le Moyen Age Russe*, 225, 257.   There is no real contradiction between what is said here and the reference made above to the flight of peasants in thirteenth-century France and elsewhere prompting seigniorial concessions in the form of manumissions and commutation.   Such a tendency in its early stages may result in concessions to *restrain* the exodus ; but when it has gone to the length of actual depopulation it is clearly more likely to result in compulsory measures to bring back the fugitives and to attach them to the soil.   There is also a distinction between commutation *forced* on a lord against his will by threat of peasant revolt and commutation to which he accedes *willingly*, or even initiates.

tenants—analogous considerations seem to apply. It is true that
to the landlord's choice of leasing the demesne, certain special
considerations are relevant which have no parallel among the
influences which decide his choice between cultivating the
demesne with serf or with hired labour. For example, by
leasing he might save a certain (perhaps a considerable) amount
on overhead expenses of estate management—rent-collecting, in
other words, might prove much cheaper than the maintenance
of a staff of stewards and bailiffs. Perhaps more important
might be the favourable or unfavourable state of the local market
for the products of the estate : in particular the ratio of agricultural prices to prices of handicraft products and imported goods ;
an unfavourable movement of which in the fourteenth century
(due partly to the growing strength of the urban gilds) may
have been a factor in predisposing estate-owners to leases of the
demesne in that century.[1]   A contributory factor may sometimes
have been the rise of a stratum of more well-to-do peasants,
eager to add field to field as a means of improved farming and of
social advancement, about which something will be said below.
Such factors as these were, no doubt, decisive in determining
which alternative to labour-services he adopted : leasing or hired
labour.   But, broadly speaking, to his choice between labour-
services and leases and his choice between labour-services and
hired labour, the same fundamental factors in the situation in
both cases were evidently relevant. The scarcer was land
relative to labour at any given time and place, the higher was
likely to be the rentability of land, and hence the greater the
inducement to adopt a policy of leases instead of estate-farming
with labour-services ; while the converse was likely to be true
where land was plentiful and human beings were scarce.

When, however, we allude here to what we may perhaps term
the land-labour ratio at a particular time and place, we must be
careful not to conceive of this in too abstract a sense.   What was

---

[1] For this point I am indebted to Mr. E. Miller, of St. John's College, Cambridge, who ascribes to changes in this "price scissors" a leading rôle in the
events of the later Middle Ages.   The precise effect of such price-changes might not
always be uniform, however, since it would depend on how inelastic was the estate-
owners demand for income, on the one hand, and on the possibilities of leasing the
demesne on favourable terms, on the other hand. We have noted above that on
the estates of Christ Church Priory, Canterbury, the decline of revenues from corn-
sales from the third decade of the fourteenth century onward, which may have been
connected with an unfavourable movement of market-prices, was accompanied by
an *intensification* of labour-services and not the reverse.   " The account-rolls of all
the manors show that in the years between 1340 and 1390 full labour-services were
performed " (Smith, *op. cit.*, 127).

relevant to the lord's demand for labour (or alternatively for tenants) was, of course, the land in his possession (and in the case of his demand for labour, the amount of it he chose to cultivate) over and above the land which, by long tradition, was peasants' land ; whereas it was not only the absence or plentifulness of man-power available to meet that seigniorial demand which was decisive, but also its exploitableness—its willingness to have burdens heaped upon it for a meagre return, or to be charged a heavy rent as the price of a meagre grant of land ; and this tended to be in inverse ratio to the amount of *peasant-land* that was available, compared to the peasant population, and also to the amount of cattle, draught animals and instruments of tillage that the peasant possessed and to the quality of the soil and of village agricultural technique. Moreover, the extent of social differentiation among the peasantry themselves, creating a *stratum* of impoverished peasants with meagre holdings, might in this connection be even more important than the total area of peasant land available to the whole village ; and it may well be that any connection that there was between growth of the market and the transition to leases or to hired labour operated *via* the effect of trade on this process of differentiation among the peasantry themselves rather than *via* its direct influence on the economic policy of the lord, as has been customarily assumed.

Again, to avoid undue simplification, we have to bear in mind that the position with regard to the supply of serf-labour was often different on differently-sized estates : a consideration that explains much which at first appears contradictory as well as much in the conflicting policies among the different ranks of feudal nobility. It frequently happened that the smaller estates —the *barones minori* in England, the knights in Germany and the sixteenth-century small *pomiestchiki* in Russia—were much less well supplied with serf-labour compared to their needs than was the case with the larger estates, especially those of the Church. Moreover, when " enticements " or forcible kidnappings of serfs by one estate-owner from another occurred, it was the smaller estates that were most liable to suffer from the competition and the depredations of their richer and more powerful neighbours, and hence were most anxious to acquire protection from the law in order to fetter labour to the land and to restore fugitives to their original owners. For illustration one has only to look at the legislation of Boris Godunov in Russia, and in particular his decrees of 1597 and 1601 : of the Tsar who excited the enmity of the large *boyars* through his regard for the interests of the small landowner. But sometimes, as we have noted, this had an opposite effect. If the amount of serf-labour that an estate could command fell below a certain crucial figure, its lord, if he found it worth while to cultivate the demesne at all, was of necessity forced to place reliance in the main on hired labour ; and the question of the amount of compulsory services he could command from each of his serfs was of relatively little concern to him, at any rate of much less concern to him than to his richer neighbour. If hired labour was not available, the alternative open to him was not to increase or extend labour-services (since these would have been inadequate in any case), but to abandon demesne cultivation and instead to find such tenants for the land as he could to pay him a rent for its use.[1]

Whether the economic plight particularly of these small estates in the difficult years of the fourteenth and fifteenth centuries in England or the enterprise of ambitious villagers was the more responsible, a further series of events seems to have contributed in no small degree to the extension of leases and the growing use of hired labour. This was the growing economic differentiation among the peasantry themselves, which we have already mentioned, and the rise of a section of relatively well-to-do peasant-farmers in the village about this time. Ambitious and able to accumulate a small amount of capital, and encouraged by the growth of local trade and local markets, these farmers were probably capable of more efficient cultivation and anxious both to enlarge their holdings by leases of additional land and to make use of the hired services of their poorer neighbours. As solvent tenants for such leases from the lord of the manor, what they lacked in exploitableness which derives from poverty (on that score they could no doubt afford to be pretty shrewd bargainers), they may well have more than made up in eagerness to acquire additional land as a speculation on the enhanced profits of improved farming. The detailed record of their husbandry was not retained in " bailiffs " accounts, as was that of demesne farming, and they remain accordingly a more obscure page of history. But it seems likely that they made up a sort of *kulak* class in the fourteenth- and fifteenth-century English village, whose story, when it is fully told, may have much

[1] Cf. Eileen Power on " Effects of the Black Death on Rural Organization in England " in *History*, iii (NS.), 113.

in common with their counterpart in the history of the Russian village in the nineteenth century. Such a development at such a time may well seem at first to stand in contradiction to the picture of village poverty and agrarian crises which was drawn above. A qualification of this picture it certainly is. But a contradiction it ceases to be if we examine the situation more closely. In fact, the inclusion of this element into our picture may succeed in explaining much that appears baffling in the contrary evidence about village economy at the time. It is clear that inequalities in type of soil and situation and in fortune would naturally give rise to differentiation among the peasantry themselves, even among the population of a particular manor : differentiation which in the course of a century would tend to increase and become considerable in ways that are nowadays sufficiently familiar. It may be that an appreciable number of those who rented (or even sometimes purchased) land at this period were persons in a special position like reeves or manorial officials.[1] Marx made the comment that " some historians have expressed astonishment that it should be possible for forced labourers, or serfs, to acquire any independent property . . . under such circumstances, since the direct producer is not an owner, but only a possessor, and since all his surplus labour belongs legally to the landlord " ; and pointed out that in feudal society tradition and custom play a very powerful rôle and fix the sharing of the produce between serf and lord over long periods of time. The result may therefore be that the lord is precluded from claiming the fruits of any abnormal productivity of a serf's own labour-time devoted to his own holding.[2] In thirteenth-century England Kosminsky claims to find " a distinct stratum of upper peasantry ", together with " a very significant section of poor peasantry ", this differentiation being observable both among villein holdings and " free " holdings, although more pronounced among the latter than among the former.[3] Between then and the opening of the fifteenth century these differences

---

[1] Cf. M. Postan in *Econ. Hist. Review*, vol. XII, 11–12. On the Kent manors of Christ Church Priory at the end of the fourteenth century leases of the demesne were sometimes taken by the serjeants of a manor—officials who were " chiefly recruited from the growing class of prosperous peasants ". In general, " there is much evidence to show that the *firmarii* were usually prosperous peasants and small land-owners " (Smith, *op. cit.*, 193).

[2] *Capital*, vol. III, 923–4.

[3] Article on " The English Peasantry in the Thirteenth Century " in *Srednia Veka*, pub. by Institute of History, Academy of Sciences, U.S.S.R., p. 46 ; and *op. cit.*, 219–23. Kosminsky admits, however, that his evidence about this upper stratum is less adequate than he would like.

must have increased quite considerably. In 1435 a serf on a manor of Castle Combe is said to have left £2,000 at death, and bond tenants are found farming several hundred acres.[1] The fact that the mass of the village population on which the system relied for its labour was wretchedly poor was not to prevent an upper *kulak* layer, which had accumulated enough capital to afford improved methods and more land and some hired labour (perhaps only at certain seasons), from being moderately prosperous. On the contrary, village poverty has always been the soil on which village usurer and petty employer can best feed. There is evidence that cotters sometimes served as labourers under the larger tenants and that some villagers even hired labour to assist them in performing harvest work for the lord [2] ; and the growing number of those whose holdings or equipment were inadequate to support them, which was one aspect of economic differentiation, was evidently itself an important factor in the economic changes of the fifteenth and sixteenth centuries, affecting as it did so directly the immediate reserve of cheap labour for hire. Nor was the prosperity of these plebeian improving farmers inconsistent with a crisis of demesne farming. It may well be that the emergence of this layer of more prosperous peasants was connected with the tendency to consolidation of strips and to improved rotation that is to be observed towards the end of the fifteenth century, and that this favoured group of the rural population were considerable gainers from the fall in the value of money in Tudor times, which (in face of fixed or " sticky " money-rents) served to transfer income to them from the landowning class, and thereby to assimilate lower gentry and upper peasantry in the manner that was so characteristic of Tudor England.[3]

---

[1] Curtler, *op. cit.*, 62.

[2] Cf. *Custumals of Battle Abbey* (Camden Socy. Pubns.) xviii, xxxix, 22–3. For an example in the fourteenth century of villeins who employ ploughmen and who bring an unsuccessful suit against their lord the abbot on the ground that he has taken away their servants, see B. H. Putnam, *op. cit.*, 95.

[3] For detailed evidence of this rise of a well-to-do section of the peasantry, cf. Tawney, *Agrarian Problem in the Sixteenth Century*, esp. 72–97. The writer is also indebted to Mr. Rodney Hilton, of Balliol, Oxford, for enlightenment on this point from unpublished work of his own. In Leicestershire in the sixteenth century a study of inventories shows that " even if we omit the Squirearchy (who were less wealthy than many a yeoman, in personal estate at least), we find that 4 per cent. of the rural population owned a quarter of the personal estate and 15½ per cent. owned half of it ", there probably being " a greater measure of inequality in ownership of land " (W. G. Hoskins, *The Leicestershire Farmer in the Sixteenth Century*, 7–8). In the second half of the century there were extensive purchases of land by yeomen, including whole manors, yeomen thereby rising to be squires (*ibid.*, 29).

It must not, however, be assumed that the mere fact of a change from labour-services to money-payments or a transition to leases of the demesne represented a release of the cultivator from servile obligations and the substitution of a free contractual relationship between him and the owner of the soil. And the not uncommon view which virtually identifies a decline of labour-services with a dissolution of Feudal Serfdom is clearly false. The movement that had occurred at an early stage of Feudalism from a system of compulsory tribute, in kind or in money, to a system of demesne farming with labour-services, in an age when feudal need of revenue had grown relatively great and labour relatively scarce, was now reversed. But although tribute once more replaced services, it did not necessarily lose its compulsory character, so long as the producer was not free to move and his livelihood was virtually at the lord's will. Nor can it always be assumed that commutation involved an actual lightening of feudal burdens. How far commutation constituted a substantial modification of feudal relationships varied widely with the circumstances of the case. In many cases it is true that the change from obligatory services to a money-payment represented some modification of the older burdens and a change of form which paved the way for more substantial alterations at a later date. Where the change occurred as a concession wrung by pressure of the cultivators themselves, this was most noticeably the case ; and the same was true of leasing of the demesne that was primarily due to the economic embarrassments of the estate-owner. But there were also plenty of instances where commutation involved not a mitigation but an augmenting of feudal burdens. Here it was merely an alternative to a direct imposition of additional services. Commutation was most likely to have this character where resort to it was primarily at the lord's initiative ; the attempt to increase feudal revenue presumably taking this form because of a relative abundance of labour. It may well be that the tendency towards commutation which we find in England as early as the twelfth century was of this kind. Much of the commutation occurring at this period was apparently at a price considerably in excess of the market-value of the services (so far as this can be computed). By no means all changes to money-payments were commutation in the proper sense of the term. Many of them took the form of *opera vendita*, not permanently, but from year to year at the lord's discretion ; the latter retaining the right to revert to his claim for labour-services when it pleased him to do so.[1] Probably it was the pressure of population upon the available land of the village, rendering it harder for the villager to obtain his subsistence and hence making hired labour cheap and relatively plentiful—the spare-time labour of the poorer cottagers and of families for whom there was no land in the open fields—that furnished the inducement to this commutation.[2] Professor Kosminsky, who speaks of "cotters economy" at this time as representing "a reserve reservoir of labouring hands for the estates", also observes that "'freeholding' as a rule is feudal-dependent holding, paying feudal rent, often close in appearance to a villein holding, out of which it has recently come. Leaseholds, in whatever form they appear, very often are linked with the carrying out of obligations of villein type".[3] By contrast, the reverse tendency towards the restoration of labour-services a century later may have been due to a drain of labour into the rising towns as much as to the stimulus given by an expanding market to demesne farming ; just as it was the labour scarcity and the rising wages of the middle decades of the fourteenth century that once more hardened the reluctance of landlords to accept money-payments *in lieu* of labour-services, and caused them to charge an augmented money-price for the commutation where it occurred [4] (even though the threat of desertion of the manor, which after the Black Death assumed serious proportions, very soon and in most cases forced lords to make substantial concessions to their dependents).

[1] Lipson, *op. cit.*, 91–2 ; Levett, *op. cit.*, 150. On the temporary nature of many money-payments and the right of the lord to revert to labour-services cf. *Camb. Econ. History*, vol. I, 511 ; also N. Neilson, *Customary Rents* (in *Oxford Studies in Social and Legal History*), 49. On the estates of Canterbury Priory, services which had previously been placed *ad denarios* were claimed again after about 1315. (Cf. R. A. L. Smith, *op. cit.*, 125–6). This may well have been connected with the slight rise of wages which seems to have followed the harvest failures (and labour shortage as a result of deaths) in 1315, 1316 and 1321. (Thorold Rogers in *Economic Interpretation*, 16–17.)

As a matter of fact, as Richard Jones pointed out, money rents, on the contrary to being a hallmark of independence for the cultivator, generally act in primitive communities to the latter's disadvantage and the lord's advantage, since they lay the difficulties and risks of marketing upon the peasant's shoulders (*Lectures and Tracts on Pol. Economy*, Ed. Whewell, 434).

[2] Kosminsky, *op. cit.*, 114.

[3] Kosminsky, "Angliskoe Krestianstvo v. 13° veke" in *Collected Papers, History*, Moscow State Univ., 41, 1940, pp. 113–14. Kosminsky elsewhere points out that " the villein paying money-rent remained a villein, and his holding was held at the will of the lord and according to manorial custom ", (in *Srednia Veka*, Inst. of History, Academy of Sciences, U.S.S.R., 63) while stressing at the same time that " the boundaries (between villein and ' free ' holding), so clear in juridical theory, in practice were very far from clear, the latter sometimes being subject to such obligations as merchet and heriot." (*Ibid.*, 44.)

[4] Lipson, *op. cit.*, 106.

It may perhaps be the case that the amount of commutation taking place at the earlier period has been exaggerated, and that those who have stressed it have been led to do so, partly by a too-ready assumption that where money-rents were found these were products of commutation at some recent date, instead of being survivals throughout the feudal period (as Professor Kosminsky and Dr. Neilson both suggest),[1] and partly because, they have supposed that obligations to a lord that were *valued* in money in the records were necessarily *paid* to him always in a money form.[2] But whether it was large in extent or relatively small, this earlier transition from services to money-payments was no more than the beginnings of a tendency which was to operate with much greater force in the fifteenth century. By the end of the fifteenth century the feudal order had disintegrated and grown weaker in a number of ways. The peasant revolt of the previous century, it is true, had been suppressed, (though by trickery as much as by force of arms). But it had left its ghost to haunt the old order in the form of a standing threat of peasant flight from the manor into the woods or hills or to swell the growing number of day labourers and artisans of the towns. The ranks of the old nobility were thinned and divided ; and the smaller estates, lacking sufficient labour-services, had taken to leasing or to wage-labour as soon as the increase of population and in particular of the ranks of the poorer peasantry had made labour cheap again. Merchants were buying land ; estates were being mortgaged ; and a *kulak* class of improving peasant farmers were becoming serious competitors in local markets and as rural employers of labour. But the end was not yet ; and neither the Battle of Bosworth nor the en-closures of the sixteenth century marked the final disintegration of the feudal mode of production. This was not to occur until the century of the English civil war. " Personal serfdom " (as Lipson puts it) " survived the decay of economic serfdom " ; many bondmen continued under the Tudors ; in 1537 the House of Lords rejected a Bill for the manumission of villeins ; obligation to grind at the lord's mill, payment of heriot, custom works and even " harvest journeys " survived in some parts of the country

---

[1] Neilson, *op. cit.*, 48 ; Kosminsky *Angliskaia Derevnia v. 13 veka*, 75–6, 176–80.
[2] *Ibid.*, 96. For evidence relating to East Anglia of widespread money-payments both by free and non-free tenants in the twelfth century, cf. D. C. Douglas in vol. IX of *Oxford Studies in Social and Legal History*. For money-rents still earlier, in Saxon England, which may well have survived into Norman England, cf. J. E. A. Jolliffe, *Constitutional Hist. of Mediæval England*, 20–1, and *Pre-Feudal England*, *passim*.

at the end of the sixteenth century ; copyholders continued into the seventeenth century to hold their land " by the custom of the manor " (i.e. subject to the jurisdiction of the manorial court) ; and it was not until 1646, under the Commonwealth, that feudal tenures were finally abolished.[1]   Moreover, throughout the seventeenth century, and even the eighteenth, the freedom of movement of the labourer in the countryside was in practice severely restricted by the fact that to leave the parish and go elsewhere virtually required the permission of his former master (under the system whereby he had to obtain a testimonial under the seal of the Constable, to make his departure lawful).[2]

Concerning feudal obligations there are, therefore, two analytically distinct questions which are less often distinguished than clarity of thought demands.   There is first the question of the *nature* of the obligation imposed on the serf, e.g. whether the surplus is exacted from him in the form of direct labour on the seigniorial *demesnes* or in the form of produce which he has grown on his own land (e.g., the old Saxon *gafol*), either directly as produce or in money as a part of the proceeds of that produce after it has been sold.   Secondly there is the question of the *degree* of subordination in which the serf is placed relative to his lord and the consequential degree of exploitation to which he is subject.   A change in the former is by no means always yoked with a change in the latter ; and the reasons for an alteration in the amount of feudal obligations and in their nature do not necessarily bear close affinity to one another.   It happened that in the " feudal reaction " the desire to fetter the peasant more firmly to the land, depriving him of freedom of movement, and to increase the obligations laid upon him coincided in most cases with a tendency to revert to the use of labour-services in the cultivation of the demesne ; while in England in the latter days of serfdom the tendency to commutation seems to have run parallel with a relaxation of feudal burdens.   But this coincidence was not always found.   In their historical roots the two types of change do, however, seem to have this much in common :

---

[1] Lipson, *op. cit.*, 111–12. Also A. L. Rowse, *Tudor Cornwall*, 48–9.
[2] This passport or license system for labourers dated from a Statute of 1388, which enacted that " no servant or labourer, be it man or woman, depart . . . to serve or dwell elsewhere unless he carry a letter patent containing the cause of his going and the time of his return, if he ought to return, under the King's seal ". Cf. *English Economic History : Select Documents*, Ed. Bland, Brown and Tawney, 171–6, also 334–5, 352–3 ; also E. Trotter, *Seventeenth-Century Life in the Country Parish*, 138–9, where an example is also given of rent-paying tenants still being " tyed " to do certain services in the seventeenth century (in Yorkshire), *ibid.* 162.

we have seen that scarcity of labour (compared to the land that the lord has available for cultivation and to the needs of the prevailing modes of cultivation) will generally place a premium on measures of compulsion to tie labour to the land and to enhance the obligations to which it is subject, while, if demesne farming is practised by the lord, this scarcity of labour will at the same time place a premium on farming that land by direct labour-services rather than with hired labour. Plentifulness and cheapness of labour will in each case tend to have a contrary effect. There is, therefore, this much reason, if other things are equal, to expect to find feudal reaction and a growth of labour-services associated together and a decline in labour-services associated with a loosening of feudal bonds.[1]

Although it is a far cry from Feudalism in England to Feudalism in Russia, with its different chronology and environmental conditions, the history of the latter affords so clear an illustration of the fact that transition from labour-dues to dues in money is not inconsistent with the preservation of the essential features of serfdom as to deserve our attention. In Russia, not only has the predominance at one time of dues in money or in kind (obrok) and at another of labour-services (barshchina) characterized different stages of serfdom, but their changing relative importance has shown no close correlation with the degree of freedom or servitude of the cultivator.

In the Kievan Rus of the eleventh and twelfth centuries there were persons in a serf position cultivating estates of princes and boyars ; some of these being slaves settled on the land (kholopi), others called zakupi who worked with a plough and harrow and sometimes even a horse provided by their masters—" a recent peasant who had lost the possibility of carrying on his independent economy and was under the necessity of entering through bonds of indebtedness into dependence on a creditor-master, for whom he was obliged to work part of his time, leaving the rest for himself ".[2]

---

[1] Discussion is sometimes conducted as though the crucial question were whether conditions (e.g. the existence of a market or the type of soil) favoured large demesnes cultivation in the first place. But clearly the needs either of a market or of the lord's own household can equally well be met *either* by demesnes cultivation, (a) with compulsory labour, (b) with hired labour, *or* by dues in kind (or in money) from tenants. The decisive factor will be the relative profitability of one method of serving a given end as compared with others. Where the type of soil and hence of predominant type of cultivation may come in, is the extent to which it makes scarcity or plentifulness of labour of little or no account (e.g. the comparison between sheep-farming and arable).

[2] B. Grekov in Introduction to *Khoziaistvo Krupnovo Feodala 17⁰ veka*, vol. I ; also Grekov, *Kievskaia Rus* (4th Ed., 1944), 113 seq.

In addition there were half-free peasants (*smerdi*), who possessed their own land and implements of tillage but came to stand in some kind of tributary relationship to an overlord, to whom they paid dues in kind.[1]   In the period which succeeded the glory of Kiev and saw the settlement of the area between the Oka and the Volga which was later to become Muscovy, the prevailing relationship in these newly-settled territories seems to have been a tributary one. Squatters on the so-called " black lands " were gradually subjected to the overlordship of some prince and his vassals, and laid under the obligation of paying dues in kind to the latter (either fixed dues or some kind of produce-sharing). Princes and *boyars*, and especially monasteries, also had their estates which were worked by bonded *kholopi*.   But the supply of these was scarce and soon became insufficient for the needs of the feudal household ; and one historian of mediæval Russia has written that " the question of agricultural man-power dominates the history of the seigniorial domain in mediæval Russia . . . and the struggle for man-power is one of the principal phenomena of social evolution in this epoch ".[2] Between the fourteenth and the sixteenth centuries a tendency grows to exact labour-services from peasantry on the land of the large proprietors. On monastic estates we find such services as early as the fourteenth century ;[3] and in the reign of Ivan III we meet the statement of a German writer that as much as six days' work a week was being demanded of their peasants by monastic estates. This can hardly have been at all general at this period ; and in the sixteenth century we still seem to find a considerable admixture of dues in kind, dues in money, and labour-services or *barshchina*. In the central districts not more than 10 per cent. of the peasant households performed work on the seigniorial estate ; although in the steppe region the proportion was considerably higher and in the Orel region more than 50 per cent.[4] The remainder of the peasantry were subject to money-dues or to some kind of *métayage* system. But at the end of the sixteenth century there takes place a rapid growth of labour-services over money dues : an increase which was only halted by the crisis of seigniorial economy consequent on that

---

[1] The process of bonding (*zakabalenie*) of the *smerd* seems to have begun in the tenth century, and by the eleventh century a substantial section of them approached in the servility of their status to the *kholops* settled on the land, although some *smerds* may have themselves owned *kholops*. (Liashchenko, *op. cit.*, 90–2.)
[2] A. Eck, *Le Moyen Âge Russe*, 225.   [3] *Ibid.*, 145.
[4] *Ibid.*, 225 ; Liashchenko, *op. cit.*, 157–8.

extensive depopulation of the years before and after the Times of Troubles, which was the joint result of war and famine and of the flight of peasants to the free frontier-lands of the south—depopulation of a magnitude to cause anything from a half to nine-tenths of the cultivated land in many areas to be abandoned, and a reversion from the three-field system to more primitive and extensive methods of cultivation.[1] This labour shortage in central Muscovy in the first half of the seventeenth century led to a decline in demesne cultivation and in labour-services at the same time as it prompted stringent legal measures to bring back fugitive peasants and to bind the *krestianin* to his lord's estate : what Kluchevsky called " the crowning work in the juridical construction of peasant serfdom " on the part of the Muscovite State.[2] In the eighteenth century, the century of Peter the Great and Catharine, of the architecture of the Rastrellis and of the opening of Russia's " window on the West ", we find both *barshchina* and *obrok* in force, with a tendency apparently (apart from peasants assigned to work in the new manufactories and mines) for the latter to make headway over the former, and for the burden of *obrok* to grow, especially between the '60's and '90's (possibly as much as doubling on the average over the whole century). Even at this epoch dues in kind—in such varied things as eggs, poultry, meat and homespun—continued to be found alongside money-payments and direct service-obligations : a reflection, perhaps, of the undeveloped character of the local market in which the peasant could sell his produce and find the wherewithal to make a money-payment.

A striking fact of the ensuing century, the century of the Emancipation, was the growth in importance once again of labour-services over other dues. This chiefly applied to the steppe region and was evidently stimulated by the expansion of the market in corn and of corn export. By the time of the Emancipation about two-thirds of the serfs on private estates in the steppe regions were on *barshchina* and not *obrok*. Yet curiously enough it was not these southern landlords who were most opposed to the Emperor's project of Emancipation,

---

[1] Cf. the often-quoted passage from the report of an Ambassador from Queen Elizabeth of England in the year 1588 : " Many villages and townes of half a mile and a mile long stande all unhabited : the people being fled all into other places, by reason of the extream usage and exactions done upon them. So that in the way towards Mosko, betwixt Vologda and Yaruslaveley there are in sight fiftie villages at the least, some halfe a mile long, that stand vacant and desolate without any inhabitant." (Giles Fletcher, *Of the Russe Common Wealth*, 61.)

[2] V. O. Kluchevsky, *History of Russia*, vol. 3, 191.

but rather the reverse. The reason is not far to seek, and accords well with the type of explanation that we have advanced above. Peasant holdings in this part of the country were generally very small, too small in many cases to yield enough to keep a family alive. There was accordingly every prospect of a plentiful and cheap supply of wage-labour to cultivate the large estates if the traditional labour-service obligations were removed.[1]

IV

So far as the growth of the market exercised a disintegrating influence on the structure of Feudalism, and prepared the soil for the growth of forces which were to weaken and supplant it, the story of this influence can largely be identified with the rise of towns as corporate bodies, as these came to possess economic and political independence in varying degrees. The influence of their presence as trading centres, especially on the smaller estates of the knights, was a profound one. Their existence provided a basis for money dealings, and hence for money-payments from peasant to lord (which, however, were never entirely absent during the feudal period) ; and, if the pressure of feudal exploitation and the decline of agriculture helped to feed the towns with immigrants, the existence of the towns, as more or less free oases in an unfree society, itself acted as a magnet to the rural population, encouraging that exodus from the manors to escape the pressure of feudal exactions which played the powerful rôle in the declining phase of the feudal system that we have tried to describe. In England the owners of the smaller estates, who were most susceptible to the urban influence, increasingly adopted the habit of borrowing from merchants, especially when times were dark and war or famine confronted them with ruin. Often they would apprentice sons to an urban craft or even marry a son to a merchant's daughter—that " market for heiresses among the English aristocracy ", of which Professor Tawney speaks.[2] When times were favourable and they accumulated a surplus, they would sometimes pur-

---

[1] G. T. Robinson, *Rural Russia under the Old Régime*, 12–60 ; P. Liashchenko, *op. cit.*, esp. 90 seq., 119–25, 157–162 ; B. Grekov on " Kiev Russia " and S. Bakhrushin on " Feudal Order " in *Protiv Historicheski Konseptsii M. N. Pokrovskovo*, 70–116, 117–39 ; A. Eck, *op. cit.*, esp. 84–93, 225, 257–8, 273–95 ; V. O. Kluchevsky, *op. cit.*, esp. vol. 1, 185 seq., 343 seq., vol. 2, 217–241, vol. 3, 175–193, vol. 5, 60–75.
[2] *The Agrarian Problem in the Sixteenth Century*, 187.

chase membership of an urban gild and engage in trade. Many of them, under the incentive of the wool trade, in the sixteenth century enclosed land for pasture and at times became middlemen themselves. As an Italian writer remarked with surprise, " even men of gentle blood attend to country business and sell their wool and cattle, not thinking it any disparagement to engage in rural industry ".[1]

But while these urban communities, to the extent that they were independent centres of trade and of contractual dealings, were in a sense alien bodies whose growth aided in the disintegration of the feudal order, it would be wrong to regard them as being, at this stage, microcosms of Capitalism. To do so would be to anticipate developments that belong to a later stage. Nor can one regard their existence as necessarily in all circumstances a solvent of feudal relations. True, the trading element that these communities nourished were gathering between their hands the first germs of merchant and money-lending capital that was later to be employed on a larger scale. But other instruments of accumulation than a mere snowball-tendency had to intervene before this capital became as dominant and ubiquitous as it was to be in later centuries. In their early stage many, if not most, towns were themselves subordinated to feudal authority ; in this respect only differing in degree from free tenants of a manor, who, while spared the onerous services of a villein, still owed certain obligations to a lord. At least, in their early stage these communities were half servants of and half parasites upon the body of feudal economy. The mode of production which they enshrined in the urban handicrafts represented a form of simple commodity production, of a non-class, peasant type, where such tools as were used were in the ownership of the craftsmen : a form which differed from the crafts undertaken on a feudal estate only to the extent that the craftsman was making his wares for sale on a market and not making them as an obligation of service for a lord (and the latter might sometimes apply to village craftsmen as well). There was nothing in these early days (i.e. prior to the end of the fifteenth century) in England [2] about this mode

---

[1] *Cit.* J. R. Green, *History of the English People*, 18.

[2] This statement is not true of certain parts of the Continent, such as the Netherlands and some Italian towns, where merchant capital was much more developed and there were some signs of actual capitalist penetration into production as early as 1200.

One must remember that many towns of this period were scarcely larger than

of production that made it capitalistic : even though the crafts-man took apprentices and employed a journeyman or two to help him, this reliance on the labour of others was still on too small a scale to constitute in any sense the mainstay of the crafts-man's income or to qualify his status as a self-employing worker. It needed some important historical developments, which will be the subject of later consideration, for a transition to be made from this free and small-scale handicraft to a specifically capitalist mode of production. It is true, however, that these communities in the course of time won their freedom, generally not without struggle, from seigniorial authority, and that in doing so they sapped the strength of feudal economy, since the economic control which they now exercised enabled them so to regulate their trading relations with the countryside as to transfer to themselves the profit on this trade, which would otherwise have accrued to the prince or lord or *abbé* of the place. And it is also true that contemporaneously with this growing freedom and prosperity of the towns there appeared the first signs of class differentiation within the urban community itself, and the appearance of an ex-clusively trading oligarchy within the major gilds and the town government.

The origin of these urban communities is far from clear, and has been the matter of some controversy. Evidence is scanty and conditions vary greatly from town to town and from one country to another. The suggestion has sometimes been made that mediæval towns were survivals of older Roman cities, which having declined in the days of anarchy rose again to prominence when some measure of order brought a respite and a return of prosperity. One or two of the larger towns,[1] it is true, probably maintained some continuity of institutions throughout the period of barbarian devastations. It may have been the case that feudal garrisons and episcopal establishments continued in these old centres, and that later separate town life grew up around them ; or that the mediæval urban congregations were drawn

---

what we should call large villages to-day. It was rare for a town to exceed 20,000 inhabitants ; and in the fourteenth century cities as large as 40,000-50,000 inhabit-ants were only found in Italy and Flanders. York only had some 11,000 and Bristol 9,500. Even in the fifteenth century Hamburg only had some 22,000, Nürnberg 20,000-25,000, Ulm 20,000 and Augsburg 18,000. (Sombart, *Der Moderne Kapitalis-mus*, I, 215-16.)

[1] E.g. Cologne, Mayence, Strasbourg, Rheims, Paris. Cf. Cunningham, *Western Civilization*, 58 ; also F. L. Ganshof in *Bulletin of the International Committee of Historical Sciences*, 1938, 243.

to what were almost deserted sites of earlier towns. But as a general explanation this theory of continuity seems manifestly inadequate. Most authorities nowadays appear to hold that the Dark Ages were sufficiently devastating in their effects on urban life to make any considerable continuity from the old towns to the new improbable.[1] We should remember that it is continuity, not of sites or buildings, or even of some elements of population, but of institutions and of modes of life that is important in the present context. It may be that there was continuity in this relevant sense in one or two of the more important Roman centres ; but one finds it hard to believe that this happened at all generally. Of England, Lipson tells us that " to all appearances there was no continuity of development between the towns of Roman Britain and those of Saxon England. . . . In general the towns were abandoned, and when not actually destroyed by fire they were left bare of inhabitants—a fate which for many years apparently befell even London and Canterbury." [2] In most cases we are dealing with new groupings of the population and new kinds of association, which sprang to life after the ninth century ; and even though these may have gathered round the site of a former Roman town, the fact that this congregation took place at the time it did requires an explanation.

Some, again, have argued that the towns of this period had a purely rural origin, having grown from the thickening of population in certain rural hundreds. There was continuity between village community and town community, and in particular between the earlier hundred court and the later town tribunal : a view which was sponsored by no less an authority than Stubbs. On the Continent the genesis of the town has been traced by an influential school of writers to the *landgemeinde* or rural township (for example, in the writings of Maurer and Below). Since the town grew up within the structure of feudal society, its inhabitants retained certain relationships of dependence to an overlord ; and qualification for citizenship remained essentially agricultural—the ownership of land within the boundaries ; trade only subsequently becoming a main occupation of the inhabitants. The only dividing line which can be drawn, it is said, between earlier village and later town lies in the fortification of the place at a certain date with a wall, for the protection of its inhabitants, thereby converting it into an

---

[1] Cf. Ashley, *Surveys*, 179 and 195.
[2] *Econ. History*, vol. I (Revised Ed.), 188.

oppidum.[1]   But even in cases where this explanation may be true, one is still left with the crucial question as to why a community that was agricultural in its origin should at some stage have adopted trade and handicraft as its economic basis. Least of all can a theory of continuity with the village explain this transition.

Thirdly, we have an explanation, which we owe chiefly to Pirenne, that towns originated in settlements of merchants' caravans. Traders who at first were itinerant pedlars travelling between the various fairs or from one feudal household to another often in caravans for mutual protection—" a very poor mean set of people " as Adam Smith termed them, " like the hawkers and pedlars of the present time "[2]—in the course of time formed settlements, as lumbermen and trappers do to-day in North-West Canada. For settlement they might select the site of an old Roman town, by reason of its favourable situation at the junction of Roman roads, or they might choose the protecting walls of some feudal *castrum*, with its garrison, or be attracted both by the sanctuary and the custom of a monastery. Later, for more complete protection the trading settlement might build a wall, sometimes uniting the wall of this *burg* with the existing battlements of the *castrum*. This would give them a separate identity which they previously lacked and also a certain military advantage. Not infrequently such settlements, acquiring some size and influence, became the objects of special privileges and protection from the King, at the price of a money-payment or a loan, as was the case with German and Italian merchants in England ;   and these royal privileges generally gave them freedom, in varying measure, from seigniorial authority and impositions. At some stage of these developments the loose association of caravan days probably assumed the more formal dignity of hansa and gild ; and this organization tended to claim not only immunity from feudal jurisdiction but also a measure of control over local trade, which inevitably brought it into sharp conflict with the local lord.[3]

---

[1] Cf. Ashley, " Beginnings of Town Life ", in *Quarterly Journal of Economics*, vol. X, 375–7, 392, 402 seq. Although it never achieved the status of a chartered borough, Clare in Suffolk affords an example of a village growing for a time into a considerable town with a market. Burford, again, was still a village on a lord's estate when its lord procured for it one of the earliest recorded charters (R. H. Gretton, *The Burford Records*, 5 seq.) It sometimes happened that " the title of borough was given to small pieces of land, cut off from the surrounding manor, and having a few privileged inhabitants ". (G. A. Thornton in *Trans. Ryl. Hist. Society*, 1928, 85.)
[2] *Wealth of Nations*, 1826 Ed., 370.
[3] Ashley, *loc. cit.*, 389–92 ; Pirenne, *Belgian Democracy*, 15 seq., and *Mediæval Cities*, 117 seq. ; Carl Stephenson, *Borough and Town*, esp. 6 seq.

Fourthly, we have the explanation which associates the rise of towns with the right of *sauveté* or sanctuary granted by feudal authority. Though this is not necessarily incompatible with the previous explanation, it has a different emphasis, pointing to a distinction which may have been of crucial importance. According to this view, towns were less spontaneous growths than creations of feudal initiative itself for its own purposes. Feudal establishments with garrisons needed traders and craftsmen to minister to their needs, and hence would be a natural magnet to such loose elements of the population as were not subordinated to an overlord. Churches and monasteries, possessing the right of *sauveté*, were a natural asylum for pilgrims and fugitives of all kinds in a lawless age, who would come to constitute a separate lay population, engaged in subsidiary occupations for which the local establishment created a market. Sometimes, again, a lord would make an offer of special privileges to newcomers in order to institute a market for his own convenience ; and sometimes the *sauveté* was made the subject of a secular grant, bestowing a certain amount of immunity from feudal jurisdiction. Akin to this is the so-called " garrison theory " suggested by Maitland (and the parallel " military " theory of Keutgen in Germany) that towns were regarded as strongholds for purposes of emergency, to which inhabitants of surrounding places might retreat ; and that originally various lords kept houses there and a skeleton staff of retainers. For example, towns like Chichester and Canterbury in England at the time of Domesday had each between 100 and 200 houses attached respectively to 44 and to 11 different manors.[1]

With the limited knowledge in our possession, we shall probably have to be content for the present with an eclectic explanation of the rise of mediæval towns : an explanation which allows a different weight to various influences in different cases. Certain English towns may have had a purely rural origin, although their urban development was no doubt attributable to their position on a ford or near the estuary of a river, which caused them to become centres of trade. Manchester grew out of a village and seems to have remained consistently agricultural and non-commercial in character for some time even after it had secured the status of a borough.[2] Cambridge apparently arose, close to an older castle and camp, from a coalescence of villages (as did also Birmingham), but its position on a ford

[1] Lipson, *op. cit.*, 192.   [2] M. Bateson, *Mediæval England*, 395.

was no doubt responsible for its later growth, as was the case also with Oxford ; while Glasgow is said to have originated in the religious gatherings about the shrine of St. Ninian, because these afforded great opportunities for trade.[1] Norwich owed much of its position to Danish influence, to the settlement of Scandinavian traders there at an early date and to its position in the path of commercial intercourse with northern Europe.[2] Pirenne's explanation would seem also to fit the development of London (where it is said that German merchants had establishments in the reign of Ethelred) ; but the protection afforded by fortifications and religious establishments must also have played a part in attracting elements of the population that were unattached to the soil or were fugitives. The same would largely apply to continental towns such as Paris (which in the ninth century was no more than a small island enclosed by Roman walls) and Geneva, to cities on the Rhine like Cologne, which quite early had a colony of alien merchants, and to other German or Flemish towns like Bremen, Magdeburg, Ghent and Bruges. But there were many important centres where the urban community clearly originated in groups of traders and craftsmen who settled under the walls of a monastery or a castle, not only for the military protection that the latter gave or for its favourable situation on an existing trading route, but because certain privileges were offered to them in order that they should be available to cater for the needs of the feudal establishment. Thus, we find the abbey of St. Denis in France in the eleventh century attracting population around it by creating an area with the right of *sauveté*. " Four wooden crosses were set up at the corners of a tract of land large enough to hold a *burg* ; and King Philip I granted to the tract so marked out complete freedom from external jurisdiction, from toll and from military service." [3] In England towns like Durham, St. Albans, Abingdon, Bury St. Edmunds, Northampton, grew up round castles and monasteries, and on the borders of Wales the Norman baronage gave special privileges to attract traders and artisans to form town communities, as a means of settling and strengthening the frontier. At Bury, the Domesday Survey tells us, a community of bakers, brewers, tailors, shoemakers and so forth " daily wait

---

[1] Cunningham, *Growth* (Early and Middle Ages), 95–6 ; Maitland, *Township and Borough*, 41 seq., 52 ; Lipson, *op. cit.*, vol. I, 185–9 ; Carl Stephenson, *op. cit.*, 200–2 ; H. Cam, *Liberties and Communities in Mediæval England*, 3–10.
[2] Lipson, *op. cit.*, 194.　　　　[3] Ashley, *loc. cit.*, 374.

upon the Saint and the Abbot and the Brethren ", and there is some evidence here of commercial activity and the existence of a mint before the Norman Conquest.[1]

As to the reason for the revival of towns after their decline, and over many areas complete disappearance, between the eighth and the tenth centuries, the view has been advanced by Pirenne that the governing factor was the resurgence of maritime commerce in the Mediterranean, with its consequent stimulus to the movement of transcontinental trading caravans, and in turn to local settlements of traders. This maritime commerce had been earlier ruptured by the Islamic invasions ; but in the eleventh century the old commercial routes had been reopened, and expansion of this commerce with the East in subsequent years had followed close on the heels of the Crusades. Whether Pirenne's emphasis be justified, and whether the decline of trade and of towns prior to the year 1000 was as great as he supposes or not, there seems to be little doubt that a revival of Mediterranean commerce played a large part in reviving transcontinental trade and hence urban life in the eleventh and twelfth centuries. At the same time it is likely that the growing size of feudal establishments, with the increase in the number of retainers, by swelling the demand for products from a distance must have contributed substantially as a stimulus to the revival of trade and as a magnet to urban communities.

The possibility that towns may have arisen owing to the initiative of feudal institutions themselves rather than as groups of traders forming a semi-independent community (as is Pirenne's emphasis) indicates a distinction that may involve a point of some substance. Evidently if such a line can be drawn, the distinction must be an important one between towns which originated as " free towns ", independent of feudal society, either in the way that Pirenne suggests or by franchises to village communities as occurred in thirteenth-century France, and towns which, starting at the initiative of some feudal authority or early subordinated to the control of an overlord, grew up as elements of feudal society, serving seigniorial interests and owing feudal obligations individually or collectively. There would seem to be more significance attaching to such a distinction than to the differences between towns which grew from inflated villages or hugged the site of some Roman town or clustered round

[1] Lipson, op. cit., 190 ; M. D. Lobel, The Borough of Bury St. Edmunds, 1–15.

the nodal point of a trade route. No sharp line of demarcation can, of course, be drawn. A large number of towns were no doubt of intermediate type and would be hard to classify in either camp. In the course of time the boundary line would change; formerly dependent towns asserting themselves and securing a measure of independence, or the freedom of others being curtailed in favour of greater feudal control. Others which had all the appearance of independence seem often at the start to have been dominated by a few aristocratic families who possessed some land within the town (as was so frequent and important a characteristic of Italian cities).[1] It seems probable, if one may venture a tentative judgement, that a majority of towns originated on the initiative of some feudal institution, or in some way as an element of feudal society, rather than as entirely alien bodies. In England places like Bury, Abingdon, Durham, St. Albans and Canterbury were probably examples of the former. A curious survival of this status is the fact that until as late as the nineteenth century the dean and chapter of Peterborough continued to exercise the right to appoint the city magistrates. But on special locations, strategically suited to be important *entrepôts* of trade, towns may have had an independent character from the first, like some of the Hanse and Rhineland cities and possibly London; and the subsequent expansion of many others may have been chiefly, if not entirely, due to settlements of traders. Some that originated at much earlier times may have continued to maintain a more or less autonomous position throughout the mediæval period; and in parts of Europe that were newly settled or where feudal authority was weak, towns may have grown out of village-communities of more or less free peasants and developed as free communities of artisans and petty traders who banded together to resist the encroachments of an overlord. In Russia, for example, the older cities like Kiev and Pskov, Novgorod and Smolensk probably owed their origin to tribal settlements (*gorodische*), which thickened into towns, retained until a late period much of the democratic character deriving from their origin, and only gradually came under the political and economic sway of a land-owning and serf-owning *boyar* aristocracy. Again, many of the newer towns of north-east Russia between the Oka and Volga in the eleventh and twelfth centuries, like Suzdal, Rostov and Yaroslav, seem to have been founded as centres for

---

[1] Also of many towns in Eastern Europe, e.g. Poland, where the trading patriciate seems largely to have been recruited from the nobility (J. Rutkowski, *op. cit.*, 39).

craftsmen and for trade by feudal lords ; while Vladimir, by contrast, seems to. have originated as a free association of craftsmen, whose dependence the local *boyars* sought to enforce by war against it.[1] Lvov started as a fortress-town founded by the Prince of Galicz in the thirteenth century. Moscow itself grew out of a village on a small prince's estate.

Indeed, the extent to which feudal establishments, especially the Church, were interested in trade and themselves organized crafts on a considerable scale is a fact worthy of some emphasis ; and one must avoid the mistake of thinking of the feudal epoch as one in which trade disappeared entirely and to which the use of money was entirely alien. Hence it was natural that the control of towns and the foundation of them should be regarded as a valuable source of additional feudal revenue. As early as the eighth century agents for the French monasteries were active in Flanders purchasing wool for manufacture. In the wine trade of Burgundy it was the monasteries that were the important centres ; and abbeys on the Loire and Seine owned a fleet of river vessels for conducting their trade. In Florence the wool industry is said to have dated from the settlement of a monastic order, the Umiliati, in 1238 ; the work being done by lay brothers under the superintendence of priests.[2] In England the earliest establishment of German traders seems to have been an order of monks, " long engaged alternately in commerce and in warfare ", who came in ships to Billingsgate and secured royal patronage.[3] In Berkshire we find the chief market to have been that of Abingdon Abbey, from which the ships of the Abbot traded down the Thames to London, while in the thirteenth century there is indication that the Abbey was a centre of cloth manufacture.[4]

[1] Cf. B. Grekov and A. Jakubovski, *La Horde d'Or*, 170–2 ; P. Liashchenko, *op. cit.*, vol. I, 135–8. Grekov points out the significant difference that while towns like Suzdal had a walled Kremlin with the craftsmen's settlement *outside,* towns like Vladimir had a wall enclosing *both* Kremlin and town in one. He quotes an illuminating passage from the Chronicle of Nikon of 1177 to illustrate the attitude of the *boyars* of the neighbourhood to the artisan-settlement at Vladimir : " The town does not possess any sovereignty ; it is a *faubourg* which is our property and where our serfs live : our masons, carpenters, labourers and others." Curiously enough, Eck seems to take an exactly contrary view to Grekov. He speaks of Rostov and Suzdal as the scene of conflict between the princes and the communal urban democracies, while of Vladimir he speaks as " une ville princière par excellence, où la population était venue sur l'appel du prince et dépendait du prince " (A. Eck, *op. cit.*, 30).

[2] E. Dixon, " The Florentine Wool Trade ", *Ryl. Hist. Society, Trans.* NS. XII, 158. Cf. also Gertrude Richards, *Florentine Merchants in the Age of the Medici*, 39.

[3] G. Walford, " Outline Hist. of Hanseatic League ", *Ryl. Hist. Society Trans.*, IX (1881), 83.

[4] *V.C.H. Berks.*, vol. II ; 371, 388.

The Cistercians were everywhere actively engaged in the wool trade with Flemish and Italian merchants. In Yorkshire iron mining and smelting in the twelfth century were conducted mainly by religious houses, and we find the monks of Fountains Abbey sufficiently enriched by their commerce to lend money to Roger de Mowbray in the reign of Henry II.[1] Fairly extensively in Europe there were workshops on the larger estates, manned by serfs, and there were outhouses, called *gynecea*, where the women spun and wove under the superintendence of the wife of the lord.[2]

In fact, by the eleventh century on the Continent there seems to have existed a privileged semi-commercial upper class in episcopal establishments, which enriched itself by trade, usury and the profits of semi-slave labour, which purchased ecclesiastical preferments and was possessed of *lucri rabies* as surely as any Lombard or Jew. The line is, therefore, hard to draw between the dependent craftsmen and the lay brothers of monasteries, on the one hand, and the craftsmen and traders of the urban communities, on the other hand, who later built themselves a wall, outside the wall of the *castrum*, struggled for a measure of independence from their feudal overlord or " protector " and achieved for themselves a separate entity as a *burg*. Some have even suggested that it was the artisans of feudal establishments who formed the leaders of the insurgent town community which struggled for its autonomy. Of this there seems to be little direct evidence ; and in many cases there are signs that such artisans remained lay retainers of the abbot or lord, coming to constitute a class of *ministeriales* separate from the burgesses.[3] There may have been occasions on which the two elements made common cause and the line between them, doubtless, was often hard to draw. Examples of the burgesses themselves owing services to

[1] *V.C.H. Yorks.*, vol. II ; 342–3.

[2] In the ninth century, for example, the Abbey of St. Riquier was the centre of a town of 2,500, where dwelt artisans grouped in streets according to crafts, which were under a collective obligation to furnish wares to the Abbey. Even earlier we find the Abbey of St. Germain des Prés with a *gyneceum* where linen and serge were made, and the wives of abbey serfs were required to furnish stipulated quantities of cloth. It has been said that such establishments closely resembled " factories " based on slave labour during the classical period : " with rare exceptions these groups were mere aggregations of women ; no real organization of work was achieved by bringing them together. They worked side by side perhaps in a single room." (A. P. Usher, *Introd. to Ind. Hist of England*, 55–7.) Cf. *also* Bucher, *Industrial Evolution*, 102 seq.

[3] Cf. Ashley, *loc. cit.*, 378 ; also Pirenne, *Belgian Democracy*, 40–1. In Germany where the class of *ministeriales* assumed a much greater importance than elsewhere, they came to approximate in many cases to the petty nobility, being rewarded with land, emoluments and honours (J. Westfall Thompson, *op. cit.*, 324 seq.)

an overlord, like any feudal dependant, are fairly plentiful.   At Hereford the burgesses owed three days' reaping at harvest and periodic services at haymakings : services which they later managed to commute for a quit-rent ; and at Bury St. Edmunds the townsmen were under obligation to labour on the lord's demesnes at harvest : an obligation which the abbot was only persuaded into commuting under severe pressure.   In Domesday there are plenty of examples of burgesses owing villein services to lords, paying heriot and similar dues.[1]   Even as late as the eighteenth century Manchester was still bound to the use of the lord's mill and the lord's baking-oven.[2]   But it seems likely that the initiative in the struggle for urban independence came from those elements who were least subject to feudal domination initially, either because they were traders who had been attracted to the place from outside or were from the start endowed with a privileged status by some special grant or charter.   These elements would be inclined to lie uneasily within the body of feudal economy precisely because, while the holding of land within the burg was generally a condition of citizenship, their source of livelihood essentially consisted in trade—in making commodities for sale or acting simply as peddling intermediaries. It was they who would be most likely at a quite early date to form a hanse or gild among themselves—a gild merchant as it came to be called ; and to struggle for the right of this gild, or of the town government which the gild in fact dominated, to control the local crafts and the local market to its own advantage.

This struggle of the towns for autonomy, which extended over the thirteenth and fourteenth centuries in England, was in many cases a violent one, and in some continental cities (for example in Flanders and in Italy in the late eleventh and the twelfth and thirteenth centuries) took the form of a protracted civil war. But even in England the democratic struggle was far from being entirely peaceful.   At Dunstable at one time the burgesses, in face of the threat of excommunication, declared that they would " descend into hell all together " rather than submit to the arbitrary impositions of the prior.   In 1327 at Bury the townsmen made a forcible entry into the monastery and carried off the Abbot and monks to imprisonment until they should allow the grant of a gild merchant ; while in the same year at Abingdon

---

[1] Cf. Carl Stephenson, *op. cit.*, 78–80, 91.
[2] Lipson, *op. cit.*, 201 ; who adds : " the monasteries in particular clung tenaciously to the monopoly and could never be brought freely to relinquish its profits ".

a crowd, swollen by allies from Oxford, laid siege to the abbey and burned down its gates.   At St. Albans there was a ten-day siege of the monastery, because the Abbot refused the citizens the right to erect fulling mills of their own ;   at Norwich there was open war between town and cathedral and rioting in 1272 in course of which the cathedral church was set on fire ;   while urban disaffection " formed a considerable element in the Peasants' Revolt " of 1381.[1]   The economic crux evidently lay in the advantages which control of the local market could give— advantages not so much from the collection of tolls and dues, but from the ability by controlling market regulations to influence the terms of trade to one's own advantage.   The fact that feudal establishments themselves engaged in trade and often had nurtured a local market in order to supply themselves with a cheap source of provision was clearly a principal reason why the demands of the burgesses for autonomy were resisted so fiercely.

[1] Lipson, op. cit., 207 ; N. M. Trenholme in Amer. Hist. Review, VI, 652, 659, 663 ; Cunningham, Growth (Middle Ages), 210.

CHAPTER THREE

THE BEGINNINGS OF THE BOURGEOISIE

I

How far the town communities which eventually succeeded in winning partial or complete autonomy from feudal authority were at their inception egalitarian communities is not easy to determine. No doubt the position differed widely in different localities ; and in a large number of cases there must have quickly developed a distinction of economic means and perhaps also of social status between the original inhabitants, who were the owners of land within the town boundaries, and late-comers, immigrants from a distance or from the surrounding country-side, who bought land from some citizen of the older generation of burghers or for a period lodged with another or even squatted on waste land outside the walls of the town. In the larger continental cities it is clear that, in addition to the burghers proper, there dwelt inside the city a number of older aristocratic families, who were owners of land in the city and its immediate neighbourhood. These represented an element of feudal society that continued to exist inside the new urban society, sometimes retaining a separate identity, despite the accident of geographical contiguity, sometimes, as in Florence, being absorbed into the economic activities of the burgher body and dominating it.[1] In many Italian cities these feudal families seem not only to have dominated urban government, converting the city with the surrounding countryside into feudal-commercial republics, but to have used their feudal privileges to acquire exclusive rights in long-distance trade, especially in trade with the Levant : as for example, the five families who controlled Genoese trade in the twelfth century.[2] Their presence in these cases served to complicate the political struggle of the burghers against feudal authority, frequently converting this struggle into an internal class war within the town community as well as a contest against

[1] In Florence about a third of the bankers and the big export merchants of the society of the Calimala were apparently members of this urban nobility. (Cf. J. Luchaire, *Les Démocraties Italiennes*, 75–6.)

[2] Cf. E. H. Byrne on " Genoese Trade with Syria " in *Amer. Hist. Review*, 1920, pp. 199–201. Pirenne has suggested a contrast in this respect between the north and the south of Europe : in the latter the nobility continued to have residences in the towns ; in the former they retired to the country (*Mediæval Cities*, 169–171).

external authority. Even in some English towns we find traces of a distinction between a superior and an inferior stratum of burghers, and at a fairly early date. At Hereford some sort of higher status seems to have attached to the mounted burgesses, who formed a mounted guard on a visit from the King ; and the knights of Nottingham appear to have occupied a similar position. At Winchester, Huntingdon, Norwich and Derby the poor burgesses who dwelt outside the walls were evidently treated as being of inferior status,[1] while at Canterbury there are indications that precedence attached to the older land-owning families in and around the town.[2]   Again, in the struggle against the Abbot of St. Albans we find a distinction between the *majores*, or superior burgesses, and the *minores*; the latter counselling violent methods in 1327, while the former only dared to aid the revolt in secret and tried to settle the issue with the Abbot by the intervention of lawyers.[3]

Nevertheless, the inequalities that existed in English towns prior to the fourteenth century were not very marked.   While it may have been that the Gild Merchant generally contained no more than a section of the townsmen—those who engaged in trade on a substantial scale [4]—craftsmen do not appear to have been excluded from it, any citizen who traded retail or wholesale being eligible for admission on payment of an entrance fee.[5] Villein-status, it is true, was frequently a bar to Gild membership.[6] At the same time in many English towns the members of the Gild retained much of their agricultural status, and burgess-right, or the freedom of the town, was associated with the possession of a piece of land or a house within the civic boundaries.   In these cases trading was probably no more than an incidental source of income.   Among the crafts themselves there could have been

[1] C. W. Colby, " The Growth of Oligarchy in English Towns ", *Eng. Hist. Review*, vol. V (1890), 634.   Ashley suggests that " the hereditary possession of land would give an economic superiority to the old families when a class of landless freemen began to grow up in the town " (*Early Hist. of Eng. Wool Industry* in Publications of American Econ. Association, 1887, 18).

[2] Brentano in *English Guilds*, 2.

[3] N. M. Trenholme in *Amer. Hist. Review*, vol. VI (1900–1), 652–3.

[4] This does not seem, however, to have been the case with Bury St. Edmunds, for example, where there seems to have been " an elaborate fusion of the functions of merchant gild and borough community " (M. D. Lobel, *The Borough of Bury St. Edmunds*, 79).

[5] Cf. Gross, *Gild Merchant*, 107.   Ashley, however, expresses the opinion that all craftsmen except the richer ones would, in fact, have been excluded by the size of the entrance fee (*Surveys*, 216–17).   In Scotland the Gild Merchant seems to have been more exclusive than in England.

[6] Cf. H. S. Bennett, *Life on the English Manor, 1150–1400*, 301.   For London cf. Riley, *Memorials of London*, 58–9.

little differentiation between master and journeymen, and the disparity of earnings does not seem to have been great.[1] The journeyman worked alongside his employer in the workshop and often ate at the latter's table. His position was apparently rather that of a companion-worker than a hired servant, and one authority has gone so far as to state categorically that " it is impossible to find any distinction of status between a trader, a master and a journeyman " in. the early gilds.[2] If this is true, the lack of distinction is no doubt explained by the comparative ease with which the average journeyman, if he was thrifty and industrious, could himself eventually set up as a master, and by joining the gild could secure the right of having a workshop of his own and engaging in retail trade. This very prospect of advancement would have sufficed, not only very largely to identify the interests of journeymen with their masters, but also, through the influence of this upward mobility and the consequent competition within the ranks of master-craftsmen and traders themselves, to preclude any large disparity of earnings between the different ranks of urban society.

More important than the presence or absence of marked inequalities of income or of status is the method by which the citizens of these early towns acquired an income. Here, to begin with, there could have been little or no differentiation in most cases inside the urban community. In the course of time, as the town grew in population and in extent, the original owners of urban land no doubt enriched themselves from sales of lands or from leases at a high rent ; and this, as some writers [3] have stressed, probably formed an important source of capital accumulation in the thirteenth and fourteenth centuries. But at the outset it is evident that the essential basis of urban society lay in what Marx has termed the " petty mode of production " : a system, that is, where production was carried on by small pro-

---

[1] Cf. Mrs. Green, *Town Life*, II, 64. Also Pirenne : " Inequality of fortunes among the artisans seem to have been very rare ; and this organization deserves the title of non-capitalist " (*Belgian Democracy*, 90).

[2] R. H. Gretton, *English Middle Class*, 65. Cf. also : " A conflict of interests was generally unknown, the journeyman always looking forward to the period when he would be admitted to the freedom of the trade. This was, as a rule, not difficult for an expert workman to attain. . . . It was a period of supremacy of labour·over capital ; and the master, although nominally so-called, was less an employer than one of the employed. . . . The relations were in the main harmonious, and there was thus no wage-earning class as distinct from the employers or capitalists and arrayed in hostility against them " (E. R. A. Seligman, *Two Chapters on the Mediæval Gilds*, Publications of the Amer. Econ. Assocn., 1887, 90).

[3] In particular Sombart (*Der Moderne Kapitalismus*, vol. I, 643–50), and following him J. A. Hobson in his *Evolution of Modern Capitalism*.

ducers, owners of their own instruments of production, who traded freely in their own products. This was at any rate true of the handicraft body ; and even though from the earliest times there may have been some citizens who were exclusively traders, few of these in England could have been much more than pedlars travelling between the town market and neighbouring manors, and their activities could hardly have been extensive when the bulk of trade was local and took the form of an exchange of craftsmen's wares sold retail in the town market against country produce that the peasant brought to town to sell.[1] In such an economy there lay the basis for a modest prosperity, judged by the standards of the day ; but the margin for saving remained a narrow one, and there could have been little scope for capital accumulation, apart from windfall gains or the increment of urban land-values. The productivity of labour and the unit of production alike were too small. Evidently the source of capital accumulation has to be looked for, not within, but outside this petty mode of production which the urban handicrafts enshrined : in developments, which were very soon to disrupt the primitive simplicity of these urban communities. These developments took the form of the rise of a privileged class of burghers who, cutting themselves adrift from production, began to engage exclusively in wholesale trade. Here, in a wider and a widening market, lay rich opportunities of gain that far outshone the modest livelihood that a craftsman who worked with his hands and retailed his wares in the local market could ever have hoped to win.

The question at once confronts us as to what was the ultimate, as distinct from the immediate, source of this new burgher wealth. In feudal society the source of the riches of the aristocracy—of the sumptuous displays of feudal households, of the extravagant tourneys and festivals, of the military expenditure, of the munificent investments of the monastic orders and of the Church—is plain enough. It consisted in the obligatory labour of the serfs : it was fruit of the surplus labour, over and above what was allowed them for their own subsistence, of a servile class whose burdens were numerous and heavy and whose standard of life was extraordinarily depressed. And even though the number of labourers who served each master was

---

[1] The exceptions to this statement are, however, notable, at any rate by the thirteenth century, e.g. Laurence of Ludlow, *mercator notissimus*, and his father Nicholas, mentioned by Eileen Power in *The Mediæval Wool Trade in England*, 112–13.

relatively large, the productivity of labour was sufficiently low to have made the total surplus available a meagre one had not the share of the producers themselves been reduced to a miserable level and the burdens imposed on them been exceptionally severe. Again, in the developed capitalist production of a later epoch, the source of capitalist revenue and of continuing accumulation, while it is veiled in the form of contractual relationships and a free exchange of equivalents, is not difficult to find. In analogy with feudal society, it lies in the exploitation of a dependent proletariat—in their surplus labour over what is required to furnish the real equivalent of their own wages. But in this case it is a surplus that is enormously enhanced by reason of the augmented productivity of labour that modern technique renders possible. What, however, of the riches and the accumulation of the early bourgeoisie—that urban bourgeoisie of the fourteenth and fifteenth centuries which had no serfs to toil for them and had not as yet invested in the employment of an industrial proletariat? Their income, in whatever form it was immediately acquired, necessarily represented a share in the product of the peasant cultivator or the urban craftsman—a deduction from the product that would otherwise have accrued to the producers themselves or else as feudal revenue to the aristocracy. By what mechanism did this early merchant capital attract this share to itself—a share substantial enough to form the basis of those early burgher fortunes, of the burgher magnificence of fourteenth-century continental cities, of banking houses like the Lombard and the Florentine?

One answer that economists have never tired of furnishing since the days of Adam Smith is that this burgher wealth was in a true sense " produced " rather than " acquired "—" produced " by the very services that the spread of commerce performed for the direct producer or the aristocratic consumer. Commerce, by widening markets and making supplies, in greater variety, available in places or at seasons where they were never available before, served to raise the standard of life of the producer, and so derived its gains as a share of this general increase and not as an encroachment on an unchanged standard of consumption. It is true enough that the spread of commerce had an effect in raising the standard of communities that were previously confined within the narrow limits of a local market, just as at a later stage it created the conditions within production itself for an extended division of labour and hence a greatly enhanced productivity of labour, in the way that Adam Smith so forcibly described. By bringing salt and spices from a distance it enabled flesh to be eaten that might otherwise have rotted or been unpalatable ; by fetching raw material from afar it enhanced the quality of local cloth or even enabled cloth to be spun and woven where this was previously unobtainable ; by finding an outlet for crops when the season was bountiful and filling the hollows of an unfavourable year with outside supplies, it often helped to spare the cultivator the alternate tragedy of a glutted local market and of famine. All this is true ; yet it hardly affords an explanation of the vast fortunes and the great accumulations characteristic of the merchant class at this period. That commerce itself was useful, or augmented the sum of utilities, does not itself explain why the pursuit of commerce yielded such a handsome surplus whereas handicraft by itself could not : it does not explain why commerce was the basis of so large a *differential* gain. Windfalls, it is true, might be expected to be more plentiful in a novel and previously unadventured sphere. But windfall gains can hardly account for a persistent and continuing income on so large a scale : in the course of time one could have expected competition in this sphere, if it were unhindered, to bring the normal expectation of gain into line with that of urban industry.

The explanation which we are seeking is evidently twofold. In the first place, so much commerce in those times, especially foreign commerce, consisted either of exploiting some political advantage or of scarcely-veiled plunder. Secondly, the class of merchants, as soon as it assumed any corporate forms, was quick to acquire powers of monopoly, which fenced its ranks from competition and served to turn the terms of exchange to its own advantage in its dealings with producer and consumer. It is evident that this twofold character of commerce at this period constituted the essential basis of early burgher wealth and of the accumulation of merchant capital. The former belongs to what Marx termed " primitive accumulation ", to which more attention will be devoted at a later stage. The latter may be termed a sort of " exploitation through trade ", by dint of which a surplus accrued to merchant capital at the expense both of urban craftsmen and of the peasant producer of the countryside, and even at the expense of the more powerful aristocratic consumer, from whom a part of feudal revenue or feudal accumulation passed into bourgeois hands. Marx in a revealing passage speaks of commercial profit in this age as consisting essentially of " profit upon alienation ". In many cases " the principal gains were not made by the exportation of the products of home industries, but by the promotion of the exchange of products of commercially and otherwise economically un-developed societies and by the exploitation of both spheres of production. . . . To buy cheap in order to sell dear is the rule of trade. It is not supposed to be an exchange of equiva-lents. The quantitative ratio in which products are exchanged is at first quite arbitrary ".[1] It was precisely the lack of develop-ment of the market—the inability of the producers to effect an exchange of their products on any more than a parochial scale—that gave to merchant capital its golden opportunity. It was the separation of the raw material from the craftsman and the craftsman from the consumer at this period, and the fact that the resources in the hands of the producer were so meagre and their meagreness so straitly bounded his horizon in space and time which formed the source of commercial profit. It was the very co-existence of local gluts and local famines on which merchant capital thrived. Moreover, in conditions of primitive communications the existence of narrow local markets, each separate from others, meant that any small change in the volume of purchases or in the quantities offered for sale tended to exert a disproportionately large effect on the market price, so that the temptation to enforce regulations in the interest of those trading between these markets was very great. So long as these primitive conditions continued, so did the chances of exceptional gain for those who had the means to exploit them ; and it was only natural that the perpetuation of such conditions, and not their removal, should become the conscious policy of merchant capital. For this reason monopoly was of the essence of economic life in this epoch. For this reason also, while the influence of commerce as a dissolvent of feudal relationships was considerable, merchant capital remained nevertheless in large measure a parasite on the old order, and its conscious rôle, when it had passed its adolescence, was conservative and not revolutionary. Moreover, once capital had begun to accumulate,

[1] *Capital*, III, 387, 388. Marx goes on to point out that " continued exchange and more regular reproduction for exchange progressively reduces this arbitrariness. . . . By his own movements he (the merchant) establishes the equivalence of commodities ". To retard this levelling tendency was the essential aim of the commercial monopolies of the epoch of merchant capital. Elsewhere Marx says of the town at this period that it " everywhere and without exception exploits the land economically by its monopoly prices, its system of taxation, its guild organiza-tions, its direct mercantile fraud and its usury " (*ibid.*, 930).

whether from commercial profits or from urban land-values, a further vista of prosperous increase opened before it. This capital could now be fattened on the fruits of usury : usury practised on the one hand against the petty producers and on the other against decadent feudal society—against needy feudal knights and barons and the even less satiable needs of the Crown.

At first the control exercised by the merchant gild and the town administration over the market was no doubt exercised as a policy to benefit the town as a collective body in its dealings with the countryside, on the one hand, and with stranger-merchants, on the other. One aspect of the control over their own market that the towns won from feudal authority has been commonly stressed : it included the right to levy market-dues and tolls, which provided an important source of revenue to the town and relieved the burgesses of part of the heavy burden of *scot* and *lot* payments which they had to make as part of the collective liability for *Firma Burgi*, or for the price of charters and privileges. But another aspect of this control, which has had less stress, was in many ways more fundamental. Since the municipal authority had the right to make regulations as to who should trade and when they should trade, it possessed a considerable power of turning the balance of all market transactions in favour of the townsmen. If it could limit certain dealings, or at least give the priority in dealings, to its own citizens ; if it could put minimum prices on goods which townsmen had to sell and maximum prices on things which townsmen wished to buy ; if it could narrow the alternative sources of sale or purchase that were available to the surrounding countryside, and limit the right of stranger-merchants to deal with countryfolk direct or with anyone except themselves, then the town manifestly possessed considerable power of influencing the terms of exchange to its own advantage.[1] In fact, we find the towns in their regulation of the urban market trying to do all these things ; and in the regulations that they adopted there was a remarkable uniformity. In the first place there were the Assizes of Bread and of Ale

---

[1] Cf. Schmoller : " The soul of that policy is the putting of fellow-citizens at an advantage and of competitors from outside at a disadvantage. The whole complicated system of regulations as to markets and forestalling was nothing but a skilful contrivance so to regulate supply and demand between the townsman who buys and the countryman who sells that the former may find himself in as favourable a position as possible, the latter in as unfavourable as possible in the business of bargaining. The regulation of prices within the town is to some extent a mere weapon against the seller of corn, wood, game and vegetables from the country " (*Mercantile System*, 8–9). Cf. also Ashley, *Introduction*, 7 seq.

and Wine, which were contrived to cheapen the supply of commodities of which the town figured as consumer. " The town's chief concern with corn prices was to prevent them from being enhanced by interested parties. This was the underlying purpose in all of the regulations." [1] Sometimes things like wood, coal, hides, wool, tallow and candles were subjected to regulation as well. Not only were maximum prices imposed, but dealings in a particular commodity were commonly reserved to certain streets or a certain part of the town, and sales outside this area were prohibited lest these might provide a loophole for dealings at enhanced prices, with a consequent diversion of supplies. Most of the regulations concerning " forestalling " and " regrating " were inspired by a similar purpose. Strangers were generally precluded from buying until the townsmen had had the first offer ; as, for example, the Ordinances of Southampton, which laid down that " no simple inhabitant or stranger shall bargain for or buy any kind of merchandise coming to the town before burgesses of the Gild Merchant, so long as a gildsman is present and wishes to bargain for or buy it ", or the ordinances of the Butchers' Company of London, which forbade foreign butchers to purchase beasts at Smithfield before 10 a.m., freemen of the mistery being allowed to start buying at 8 a.m.[2] The laws of the Berwick Merchant Gild forbade anyone but a gild brother to buy hides or wool or skins and forbade butchers to go out of town and meet beasts coming in for sale.[3] In Paris there was a prohibition on anyone meeting a supply-convoy whether on land or on river with a view to making an advance contract outside a certain radius from the centre of the city.[4] " At Bristol when a ship came to port the town-traders assembled to decide ' what is to be done in that behalf for the weal of the said fellowship ', that is, they prevented competition by a preconcerted arrangement as to the prices at which the cargoes should be bought." [5] At times of special scarcity the town administration even adopted the expedient of collective purchase on behalf of its citizens, as at Liverpool where all imports had first to be offered to the Mayor for purchase on behalf of the town before they were exposed for sale.[6]

[1] N.S.B. Gras, *Evolution of the English Corn Market*, 68.
[2] A. Pearce, *History of the Butchers' Company*, 43.
[3] D. B. Morris, *Stirling Merchant Gild*, 43.
[4] Saint-Leon, *Histoire des Corporations de Métiers*, 153.   [5] Lipson, *op. cit.*, 245.
[6] Ashley, *Introduction*, Bk. II, 33-9 ; Cunningham, *Progress of Capitalism*, 67 ; Gross, *op. cit.*, 135-7.

Secondly, there were the regulations concerning strangers, the object of which was to prevent the latter from dealing direct with the surrounding countryside and force them exclusively to buy from and sell to town merchants as intermediaries. Most of the wares that stranger-merchants brought for sale were luxuries for the taste of well-to-do burghers or gentry of the neighbourhood, or else raw materials of some craft. Stranger-merchants were also at times purchasers from the local crafts, and might also have been buyers of local raw materials such as wool or leather from the villages, had this been permitted. Strangers were, accordingly, enjoined to deal exclusively with members of the Gild and to lodge with a host who was a citizen and a householder in the town and could be held responsible for seeing that no secret cabals and illicit deals took place on his premises. It was only at times of fair that a stranger was allowed to stake out a pitch and sell to all and sundry ; and the special prerogatives accorded by the Crown to groups of foreign merchants in London, which included the right to possess quarters of their own, such as the Steelyard, were regarded as exceptional and were a special ground of the aliens' unpopularity in that city. These aliens sometimes won from the Crown the right of retail as well as wholesale trade throughout the kingdom. But borough governments seem almost universally to have challenged the right of aliens to sell retail or to trade directly with the countryside or with other foreign merchants ; and the matter was a recurrent cause of conflict in the fourteenth century.[1] Ashley has said that " traders from outside were welcome when they brought with them foreign commodities which the burgher merchants could make a profit by retailing, or when they purchased for exportation the commodities which the burghers had procured for that purpose from English craftsmen and agriculturalists. They were welcome so long as they were ready to serve the interests of the burghers ; and when they sought to thrust these on one side they seemed to be violating the very conditions upon which their presence was allowed." [2]   A thorough example of this is afforded in Scottish towns. The charter given to Stirling in the thirteenth century laid down that stranger-merchants were forbidden either to buy or sell in

---

[1] Alice Beardwood, *Alien Merchants in England, 1350-77*, 39-40, 55-6.
[2] Ashley, *Introduction*, Bk. II, 14. Cf. also Mrs. Green, *Town Life*, II, 37-40 ; Schmoller, *op. cit.*, 11 ; Gross, *op. cit.*, 46-8. At one time in London there were complaints against foreign drapers that they bring cloths " and sell them in divers hostelries in secret " (Riley, *Memorials of London*, 551).

any part of the sheriffdom *outside* the borough and were under obligation to bring their merchandise into the town itself for sale. The general charter to all the burgesses of Scotland signed by the King of Scotland at Perth in 1364 is quite explicit about this burgher monopoly : " none shall sell but to the merchants only of such burghs within whose priviledge he resides. Whom we strictly charge to bring such merchandise to the Mercate and Cross of the burghs that the merchants may make purchase thereof, make an effectual monopoly of the same, without restriction." [1]

Thirdly, there were the various regulations of the gilds devised to restrict competition among the urban craftsmen themselves. In France there was a limitation on a competitor's right to call out his wares or to importune a customer when the latter was dealing at a neighbouring craftsman's stall. Similarly the London weavers made it an offence to entice away another's customer.[2] How common was the actual fixation of minimum prices for craftsmen's wares is not altogether clear. It was not generally admitted as one of the rights of craft gilds ; but was no doubt fairly widely practised, more or less openly in some cases and secretly in others. The minute regulation concerning quality, about which so much has been written, was also largely concerned (like demarcation-rules among craft-unions in the nineteenth-century trade union world) with preventing competition from taking the form of surreptitious changes in quality or the poaching of one section of a craft on the prerogative of another ; and to preclude the practice of undertaking work secretly for special customers and avoiding the eye of the official " searchers " under cover of darkness (as well presumably as in the interests of output-restriction), night-work and the sale of wares in a craftsman's house " by candlelight " were fairly generally forbidden. In the case of the London Cutlers a craftsman was forbidden to work " within any Aley, Chambre, Garet " and elsewhere than " in open Schoppe by the Strete side " ; and the Armourers and Brasiers forbade any sales " in innes and privy places ".[3] Sometimes citizens of a town were given the monopoly of purchase over some material essential for a craft. " With the object of preventing any advantage which could be secured to the town from falling to the inhabitants of the sur-

[1] D. B. Morris, *op. cit.*, 53, 63,
[2] Saint-Leon, *op. cit.*, 152 ; F. Consitt, *London Weavers' Company*, 83, 90.
[3] C. Welch, *History of Cutlers' Company of London*, vol. I, 142 ; S. H. Pitt, *Notes on the History of the Worshipful Company of Armourers and Brasiers*, 13.

rounding districts, it was sometimes ordered that certain commodities should not be sold at all to persons ' dwelling out of
the town '." [1] For example, the town butchers were sometimes
not allowed to sell their tallow to any but the town chandlers.

Such regulations would, of course, have exercised little effect
on the terms of trade between the townsmen and their customers
and providers if rival markets had been allowed to exist within
an easy distance, to which the villager could have resorted for
the exchange of his produce against urban wares. At any rate,
the proximity of these rival markets would have set strict limits
to the effect that gild policy could exercise on the terms of trade.
The right to possess a market without fear of rival within a certain
area was consequently a privilege that was zealously sought and
jealously guarded. A local monopoly of this kind was the crux
of the famous policy of the Staple ; and rivalry over Staple-
rights constituted throughout Europe a principal cause of conflict
between towns and of inter-civic wars.   " All the resources of
municipal diplomacy," says Schmoller, " . . . and in the last
resort of violence were employed to gain control over trade
routes and to obtain Staple rights : to bring it about that as
many routes as possible should lead to the town ; as few as
possible pass by : that through traffic, by caravan or ship, should,
if possible, be made to halt there, and goods *en route* exposed and
offered for sale to the burgesses ".[2]   One source of the constant
trouble between Bristol and the Lord of Berkeley was the
latter's claim to hold a separate market at Redcliffe Street.
At Canterbury it was the Archbishop's markets at Westgate
and Wingham that were the occasion of bitter conflict between
city and chapter. We find the Abbot of St. Edmunds protesting as strongly as any burgher when the monks at Ely set
up a market at Lakenheath, with threats that he would " go
with horse and arms to destroy the market " : threats that were
implemented by an expedition of 600 armed men at dead of
night.[3] The Prior of Rufford, in 1302, was restrained from
holding a market at Haddenham to the prejudice of Thame.[4]
The market at Lyme was condemned as being too near Bridport.
London tried to prevent its citizens from attending fairs or
markets outside the city ; London craftsmen being forbidden
to offer cloth for sale except within the city boundaries or any

[1] Ashley, *op. cit.*, 20.   [2] *Mercantile System*, 10.
[3] Lipson, *Economic History* (Middle Ages), 213.
[4] H. Liddell, *History of Oxford*, 553.

citizen to go south of the Thames to Southwark to buy corn, beasts or other merchandise " whereby market may be held there ".[1] Lynn merchants tried to monopolize the function of middlemen in the export trade in Cambridgeshire corn by preventing the merchants of Cambridge and Ely from selling to any but themselves ; and London fishmongers were free traders in Yarmouth where they went to purchase imported supplies, but were would-be monopolists in London whence they sought to banish the competition of Yarmouth merchants.[2] " The Stratford council employed men armed with cudgels to keep out the traders of Coventry. The Leicester glovers strove with might and main to prevent the glovers of Ashby and Loughborough from buying skins in their market."[3] " Ely was jealous of Cambridge, Bath of Bristol, Lynn of Boston, Oxford and Winchester—and indeed all the rest—of London."[4] In fact, generally " the mediæval towns of one and the same country regarded each other from a mercantile point of view with much more jealousy and hostility than different states now do ".[5] Abroad, the cloth Staple at Antwerp carried on a bitter struggle for a century against the wool Staple at Calais ; the rivalry of the Hanse with the merchants of Copenhagen led to a six years' war in 1546 between Denmark and Lübeck ;[6] and from 1563 till 1570 Lübeck, now in alliance with Denmark, warred with Sweden over the right to trade with Narva.[7]

At a more advanced stage this urban monopoly took the form of what may be termed a sort of " urban colonialism " in relation to the countryside. Even in England we hear quite frequently of towns extending their authority over the surrounding district, and thereby bringing pressure to bear on villages to deal only with the market of the town in question.[8] Scottish towns had rights of exacting tolls and enforcing the privileges of certain trades and crafts over large surrounding areas. The rights to levy tolls at gates and bridges in the neighbourhood were everywhere jealously regarded, since in canalizing or diverting traffic in a desired direction such tolls often played the same rôle that transport

[1] Lipson, op. cit., 212 ; H. T. Riley, Liber Albus, 238.
[2] Unwin, Finance and Trade under Edward III, 234, 237.
[3] Unwin in Commerce and Coinage in Shakespeare's England, vol. I, 315.
[4] A. Law, " English Nouveaux Riches of the Fourteenth Century," Trans. Ryl. Hist. Society, NS. IX, 51.
[5] Gross, op. cit., 51.
[6] C. Walford in Trans. Ryl. Hist. Society, NS. IX, 114.
[7] H. Zimmern, The Hanse Towns, 296.
[8] Mrs. Green, Town Life, vol. I, 3.

subsidies and the control of freight-rates play in the trade-policies of States at the present day.   On the Continent the tendency of wealthy burgher republics to dominate and to exploit a rural hinterland was much more developed ;   Italian communes, German imperial cities and Dutch and Swiss towns growing in this way into small principalities.   We find Ulm and Florence, for example, forcing all the cattle in the neighbouring districts to be brought into the city, and Cologne in the twelfth century barring Flemish merchants from access to the upper Rhine. We find Venice in the thirteenth century prohibiting Ragusa from dealing direct with the cities of the north Adriatic (unless this was for the purpose of importing foodstuffs to Venice), forcing Ravenna to abandon all direct imports from across the sea and even from north Italy and Ancona, and preventing Aquileja from exporting goods to the inland territory which Venice regarded as her special preserve.   Genoa prevented French merchants from trading beyond Genoa to the south ; and as early as the twelfth century Pisa and Lucca were engaged in bitter struggle over the claim of Lucca to have Staple rights over traffic between Pisa and the north.   Vienna was powerful enough to prevent merchants of Swabia, Regensburg and Passau from travelling down the Danube with their goods to Hungary and to compel them to offer their merchandise for sale to citizens of Vienna.   Rutkowski tells how " in the fourteenth century Cracow sought to prevent merchants of Torun from trading with Hungary, claiming the right of *entrepôt* for themselves, and to close the route to the east against merchants from Breslau ; while Lvov tried to monopolize trade with ' the Tartar lands ' to the east ".   The merchants of Novgorod prevented the Hanse merchants from trading further than their city, and themselves retained the right of acting as intermediaries between the foreign merchants and the towns of the hinterland.   The final struggle between Novgorod and Moscow, ending in the ruthless subjection of the former, largely turned on the prized monopoly of the *zavolochie* country—the area to the north-east extending to the Urals and beyond, rich in furs and metals.   Later, in the seventeenth century, the Russian merchant gilds were powerful enough to prevent English merchants generally from trading further south than Archangel, and Persian merchants from coming north of Astrakhan ;   while trading at Astrakhan was strictly limited to members of the trading gilds or *gosts*.   Thereby, they kept the monopoly of trade between northern Europe and Persia, and in particularly the highly prized silk trade, in their own hands ; and succeeded in maintaining the sale-price in Astrakhan for Russian products such as linen and furs at anything between 50 and 100 per cent. above their cost price including cost of carriage, and the price of silk at Archangel at more than 50 per cent. greater than at Astrakhan.[1] In Sweden the merchants of the Staple cities exercised a monopoly in the export of bar iron and prevented foreign buyers from penetrating to the iron districts to buy from the ironmasters direct. " The Hanseatic League ", says Heckscher, " endeavoured to cut off the inland cities from any direct connection with the Baltic and to deny to all other cities access to the inland markets " ; and the Electoral Council of Brandenburg in 1582 described the policy of Hamburg as being " concerned solely with extorting corn at low prices and on their own terms from the Elector of Brandenburg's subjects and selling it again afterwards as dear as they please ".[2]

II

There is every indication that these more ambitious policies were a product, not so much of the collective interest of the town, as of the class interest of a well-to-do section of wholesale merchants who had long since brought the urban government under their exclusive control. The system of market control and urban monopoly that we have described could be used with particular advantage by a group of specialized dealers whose gain consisted in the margin between two sets of prices : the prices at which they could buy local produce from the villager or the craftsman and the prices at which they could re-sell it to the stranger or the urban consumer ; or again the prices at which they could purchase exotic wares from a distance and dispose of them to local buyers. Where the regulations which had been

[1] In the sixteenth century English merchants had been granted the right of trading direct with Persia across Russia. But in the seventeenth century, under pressure from Russian merchant gilds, this privilege was revoked ; in 1649 the privileges of trading south of Archangel were cancelled ; and by the regulation of 1667 foreign merchants were forbidden to sell retail or to trade with any but Russian merchants. In 1619 the Tsar's government closed the sea-route to the Ob against all foreigners : the route by which English, Dutch and German merchants had been seeking a way into Mangazeia and the wealth of Siberia (cf. R. H. Fisher, *The Russian Fur Trade, 1550-1700*, 78).
[2] E. Heckscher, *Mercantilism*, vol. II, 60–76 ; Schmoller, *Mercantile System*, 13–14, 31 ; A. L. Jenckes, *The Staple of England*, 6–7 ; J. L. Sismondi, *History of Italian Republics* (ed. Boulting), 244 ; J. Rutkovski, *op. cit.*, 70–1 ; M. N. Pokrovsky, *History of Russia from the Earliest Times to the Rise of Commercial Capitalism*, 267–9.

framed in the interests of the craftsmen ran counter to the wholesale merchant's interest as a buyer of the products of local crafts,
his new-found power enabled the wholesaler to relax or to circum-
vent these regulations ; and where the restrictions aimed against
strangers shut him out from other markets, and narrowed his
field of enterprise, he could frequently secure a privileged status
for himself through treaties with the merchants of other towns
by which each agreed to relax restrictions on the other's trading
for their mutual benefit.   Such mutual trading concessions were
the basis, for example, of the Hansa of the north German
and of the Flemish cities.   When, indeed, the growth of merchant capital had reached this stage, the collective efforts of
wholesale or export merchants were apt to be directed towards
the weakening of the régime of urban monopoly, which had
nurtured their infancy, in the interest of strengthening the
monopoly of their own inter-urban organization.   At least, this
was the case with that part of the system of urban regulations
which served to protect the position of the craft gilds.   It
occurred, for example, in Flemish towns, where it led to a
veritable war between the town governments and the capitalist
interests of the Hansa which operated on a national scale and
sought to develop country industry in competition with the urban
crafts ; [1] while at Ulm the Fuggers contrived to have some of
the territory round Ulm detached from the control of that city
so that they could employ country weavers in competition with
the weavers' craft of the city.   But this part of the story belongs
to a later stage.

The beginnings of an organized trading interest in the towns,
distinct from the handicraft, almost universally assumed two
parallel forms.   First, a specifically trading element, frequently
drawn (at least in England) from the more well-to-do craftsmen,
separated itself from production and formed exclusively trading
organizations which proceeded to monopolize some particular
sphere of wholesale trade.   Secondly, these new trading organizations very soon came to dominate the town government, and to
use their political power to further their own privileges and to
subordinate the craftsmen.   In many areas on the Continent
as early as 1200 we already see this process unfolding.   In the
Netherlands the gilds of the larger towns, having asserted their
position against the Church and the nobility, were becoming
close corporations of the richer merchants, which sought to

[1] See below, pp. 152–6.

monopolize wholesale trade, levied an entrance fee which, as
Pirenne remarks, was " beyond the reach of the smaller men ",
and explicitly excluded from their ranks all those who weighed
at the *tron* or town weighing-machine—the retailers—and all
those with " blue nails "—the handicraftsmen.[1] At the same
time it is clear that political control in these same towns began to
pass into the hands of the richer burghers, who came to be known
as " the patriciate ". The office of *echevins*, to which election
had formerly been made by the whole burgher body, was now
filled by appointment by the patricians from among themselves ;
and these officers supervised the crafts, regulated wages and
controlled the town market. " Power passed insensibly into the
hands of the wealthiest. The form of government in these
centres of commerce and manufacture inevitably changed, first
from democracy to plutocracy and then to oligarchy ".[2]
Similarly, in the cities of north Italy power was in the hands of
a burgher plutocracy (commonly in alliance with the local
nobility). This ruling class that reigned over the city-republics
of Lombardy, Tuscany and Venetia drew their wealth from the
rich export trade with the Levant and from the valuable cloth
trade across the Alps into western and northern Europe.
Farming papal revenues formed a lucrative investment for
these rich burgher families, and in some cities, such as Florence,
banking and money-lending even excelled commerce in importance. In Florence the *Arti Maggiori* of bankers and export-
merchants (like the famous Calimala) controlled the government of the city from the middle of the thirteenth century, with
the exception of a brief victory of the *Arti Minori* between 1293
and 1295.[3] In east German towns in the fourteenth century
" aldermen were drawn from a few leading families of merchants,
clothiers or landowners and elected their own successors, the
craft gilds and the commons having no share in the government
of the town ".[4] In Paris the dominant position occupied
by the six leading *Corps de Métiers* bore a close resemblance
to the hegemony of the *Arti Maggiori* in Italian cities ; as did
also that of the *Herrenzünfte* at Basle.[5] As early as the thirteenth
century the government of Paris was apparently in the hands
of a Hanse of merchants—probably the *marchands de l'eau* who

[1] Pirenne, *Belgian Democracy*, 112 ; also Brentano in *Eng. Guilds*, cvii.
[2] Pirenne, *op. cit.*, 110 ; also Pirenne, *Histoire de Belgique*, vol. I, 369 seq.
[3] Sismondi, *op. cit.*, 237-9, 442, 564 ; Luchaire, *op. cit.*, 95-6, 108 seq.
[4] F. L. Carsten in *Trans. Ryl. Hist. Society*, 1943, p. 73 seq.
[5] Cf. Ashley, *Introduction*, Bk. II, 644-5, 647-51.

acquired privileges at the end of the twelfth century. By the middle of the fourteenth century we find the richer Parisian weavers forming themselves into the Drapers and subordinating both the craftsmen weavers and also the fullers and dyers to this new trading organization. Similarly the Parisian Saddlers became an organization of the trading interest which raised its entrance fees to exclude newcomers, claimed the exclusive right of buying any leather goods to sell again, and secured the right of control and inspection (the right of " search ") over the leather crafts.[1]

In English towns these developments seem to have occurred mainly in the fourteenth century ; and the growth of the " insignificant peddling traders of the eleventh, twelfth and thirteenth centuries " into " the important political plutocracy of the fourteenth " [2] is a remarkable feature of the time. Here the new development involved an actual usurpation of economic privileges and political control by the new burgher plutocracy, since in England there is some evidence of the existence of an earlier urban democracy which in the fourteenth century was abolished, and also evidence that trading privileges had been more or less open (*de jure*, at least, even if not *de facto*) to the general body of citizens. The actual forms that this usurpation took were various. In some cases the Gild Merchant, which may well have been composed originally of the majority of burgesses, including craftsmen, tended to become a close organization and to exclude craftsmen from the privileges of wholesale trade.[3] At Shrewsbury in 1363 we find manual workers being excluded from trading wholesale.[4] At Newcastle the Gild excluded anyone who had " blue nails " or who hawked wares in the street.[5] At Coventry the Gild Merchant (which was formed rather late) excluded all craftsmen and very soon became the governing body of the town. Here the Trinity Guild (as it was called), formed in 1340, " early arrogated to itself the power wielded by the municipal rulers " ; " it became the custom in very early times for the same man to serve in different years as

---

[1] Cf. Lespinasse et Bonnardot, *Les Métiers et Corporations de la ville de Paris*, iv ; Levasseur, *Hist. de Classes Ouvrières en France* (Ed. 1859), Tome I, 285 seq. ; Unwin, *Industrial Organization in Sixteenth and Seventeenth Centuries*, 24, 31 ; Wergeland, *History of Working Classes in France*, 32 ; Charles Normand, *La Bourgeoisie Française au XVIIe Siècle*, 153-6.

[2] A. Law, " English Nouveaux-Riches in the Fourteenth Century " in *Trans., Ryl. Hist. Society* NS., IX, 49.

[3] Ashley, *Introduction*, Bk. I, 80.

[4] Cunningham, " Gild Merchant of Shrewsbury ", *Trans. Ryl. Hist. Society*, NS. IX, 103.   [5] Gretton, *op. cit.*, 65.

mayor and master of the merchant fraternity " ; and " the few wealthy merchants who ruled the city were in no way responsible to their fellow-townsfolk for their actions and were said by the community to abuse their authority ". In the fifteenth century it becomes clear that the controlling group in the city consisted of mercers and drapers ; and that the latter used their power to subordinate the crafts engaged in cloth-making and cloth-finishing and to preclude the crafts from trading, either in their raw materials or their finished product, except through the drapers.[1] At Winchester, Oxford, Beverley, Marlborough and some other towns a clear distinction is apparent even at an early date between freemen of the town who could trade and weavers who were not freemen of the town and were forbidden to trade—whether because the latter were of villein status, or because they were late-comers to the town and lacked the means to purchase land and a house is not clear. Similarly at Leicester in the thirteenth century the Gild forbade weavers to sell to any but burgesses.[2] At Derby in 1330 there were complaints that the Gild had excluded the majority of citizens by the severity of their entrance fee and had prohibited townsmen from selling to any but its own members.[3] In Scotland the Gild Merchant seems to have been an exclusive body from its inception, and the Gild and the Borough organization to have been closely identified. As early as the twelfth century we find dyers, butchers and cobblers refused admission unless they abjured the exercise of their craft and left it to servants ; and in the thirteenth century fullers and weavers were already excluded from the Gild by the terms of its charter in Aberdeen, Stirling and Perth.[4]

In the majority of English towns, however, it does not seem to have been the original Gild Merchant that was the instrument of the new trading monopoly (as Brentano suggested) ; and, perhaps because so many English towns were scarcely distinguishable from villages at their inception, and hence were inclined to be more democratic and egalitarian in character, we do not find that continuity between the early trading gild and the later

---

[1] M. Dormer Harris, *Life in an Old English Town*, 88–93, 258–66.

[2] Ashley, *op. cit.*, 83. Ashley suggests that this may have been due to the fact that the weavers were aliens, and points out that the restriction later tended to disappear. Lipson, however, rejects this interpretation (*Econ. Hist.*, 323–4). Miss E. M. Carus-Wilson tells us that there is " positive evidence " that weavers were excluded (along with fullers) from the Gild Merchant, although dyers were members (*Econ. Hist. Review*, vol. XIV, No. I, 41–2).

[3] G. Unwin, *Finance and Trade under Edward III*, 234.

[4] Gross, *op. cit.*, 213 ; D. B. Morris, *op. cit.*, 54, 78 seq. ; cf. Cunningham, *Growth of Eng. Industry and Commerce* (Middle Ages), 348.

burgher plutocracy that is evident in continental towns and in Scotland. Curiously enough, in most cases the old Gild Merchant seems to have died about the time that the new monopoly of wholesale trade was beginning to harden. In the course of the thirteenth and fourteenth centuries in most cases it apparently lost its original function, and continued, if it did so at all, as little more than a name. At the same time we witness the formation of new mercantile gilds, or misteries, composed entirely of traders as distinct from craftsmen and endowed by their charters with exclusive rights over some particular branch of wholesale trade.[1] The concentration of trading rights in these bodies meant that the ordinary craftsman, for purposes other than retail sale from his stall or shop-front in the town, was compelled to deal exclusively with members of the appropriate mercantile gild. He was precluded from selling direct to any stranger-merchant, and he could not make any contract for exporting his wares outside the town except by using one of the limited circle of well-to-do wholesale traders in the town as intermediary. In some cases the old single Gild divided into a number of specialized companies. For example, at Andover there was a tripartition into Drapers, Haberdashers and Leathersellers, and at Devizes into Drapers, Mercers and Leathersellers.[2] More commonly a division occurred into a variety of gilds, both craft gilds and mercantile, the former possessing the monopoly of a certain line of production, the latter having exclusive rights over a certain sphere of trade. At Reading, for instance, the function of the original and unique Gild was apparently transferred to five companies.[3] Whatever their ancestry may have been, it is at any rate very common to find both general companies of merchants appearing in the towns of the fourteenth century, and also more specialized bodies of merchants. In London in the reign of Edward III the first of the famous Livery Companies secured incorporation. Of the twelve leading ones a half were at the outset composed exclusively of merchants, such as the mercers, grocers, drapers and haberdashers. But even those which included craftsmen were soon to come under the domination of the richer trading element ; as with the goldsmiths, where a minority of merchant goldsmiths took the nomination of

---

[1] Gross, op. cit., 116, 127–9 ; S. Kramer, *Craft Gilds and the Government*, 24; Cunningham, op. cit., 225 ; A. P. Usher, *Introduction*, 181 ; Gretton, op. cit., 67 ; Ashley in *Publications Amer. Econ. Assocn.* (1887), 36–7, 58–9 ; Kramer in *Eng. Hist. Review*, XXIII, 250–1.

[2] Gross, op. cit., 118–20.　　　　　　　[3] Gretton, op. cit., 67.

the wardens of the company into their own hands, against the protests of the craftsmen. Unwin tells us that this " control established by the merchants " and the " entire subordination of the artificers finds a close parallel in every one of the twelve great companies which had originated in a handicraft or included a handicraft element ".[1] Apparently their incorporation aroused considerable outcry among London citizens at the time, the allegation being made that prices had risen by one-third as a result of their influence.[2] Another example of the new tendency was " the affray " which took place in " Chepe and Crepelgate " in the reign of Edward III between Saddlers, on the one hand, and Joiners, Painters and Lorimers, on the other. The latter party alleged that the saddlers had designed, " by conspiracy and collusion ", to monopolize to themselves the trade in " any manner of merchandise that unto their own trade pertains " and to force the craftsmen in question to sell only to the saddlers. When the craftsmen refused, it was said that the saddlers attacked them with arms.[3] Whatever the truth about the dispute, it seems clear that the saddlers were the trading element, and were already beginning to stand in an employer-relationship to the craftsmen. Nor is this an isolated instance. The tendency for the poorer craft gilds to fall into subordination to a trading gild which begins to occupy the rôle of an *entrepreneur* to the industry is a fairly common occurrence at this period : for example, the Bladesmiths and Shearmen who come under the control of the Cutlers, and the Whittawyers and Curriers of the Skinners.[4]

Most striking of all was the case of the weavers, not only in London but also in other towns such as Winchester, Oxford, Marlborough, Beverley, who seem as early as the second half of the thirteenth century to have come into a position of economic subordination to the burellers. Whatever the precise origin of the burellers, they were men of some substance who occupied themselves in more than one branch of the cloth industry, buying wool and giving it out to be spun and woven, and probably supervising the dyeing and finishing of the cloth as well. By 1300 it is evident that they were a trading element which stood in a kind of employer-relationship to the weavers ; and eventually,

[1] Unwin, *Industrial Organization*, 42–4 ; also W. C. Hazlitt, *Livery Companies of London*, 68 ; Lipson, *op. cit.*, 379–81, who says : " in London and provincial towns a definite class of merchants was differentiating themselves from the craftsmen " (385).
[2] *Ibid.*, 383–4.   [3] Riley, *Memorials of London*, 156–9.
[4] Cf. A. H. Johnson, *History of Worshipful Company of Drapers*, vol. I, 24.

it would seem, they became organized with other cloth traders in the Drapers' Company. The weavers, who had been among the earliest of crafts, had previously occupied a fairly protected, if subordinate, position. Early in the fourteenth century we find a general attack made upon their rights, clearly at the instance of the burellers ; allegations being made by the latter that the Weavers' Gild was restricting the number of looms and raising prices by agreements among themselves. The weavers fought a stubborn rearguard action over several decades ; but by the middle of the century the privileges of the London Weavers had been drastically curtailed (including, significantly enough, their right to cease work in the event of a dispute between bureller and weaver), and the gild and its ordinances strictly subordinated to the authority of the Mayor. In 1364 the London Drapers were given the right to monopolize the trade in cloth, and weavers, fullers and dyers alike were enjoined to " keep themselves to their own mistery, and in no way meddle with the making, buying or selling of any manner of cloth or drapery ". The subjection of the craft to the trading element was complete. Not content with this, the London Drapers at the end of the fourteenth century instituted Bakewell Hall as a national *entrepôt*, with the aim of " prevent(ing) the country drapers from dealing directly with the customers of the London drapers and selling their cloth to them in detail ".[1] In other towns the weavers fared no better and even worse : they were " hampered in their trade by all sorts of oppressive regulations, forbidden to buy their tools or possess any wealth, or sell their goods save to a freeman of the city, while the status of villeins and aliens in the city courts was allotted to them ". [2]

Parallel with these developments went the concentration of political power in the towns into the hands of a burgher oligarchy : an oligarchy which seems to have been identical with the section of richer merchants that was acquiring the monopoly of wholesale trade. Even in more democratic days apparently it was customary for the richer and more influential burgesses to be elected to the committee of twelve which conducted the affairs

[1] W. J. Ashley, *Early History of the English Woollen Industry* (Publications American Econ. Assocn., 1887), 66–7.
[2] Mrs. J. R. Green, *Town Life*, vol. II, 142 ; also Consitt, *op. cit.*, 8–29 ; Johnson, *op. cit.*, vol. I, 206.   It seems quite clear that the increasing tendency to subordinate the craft gilds to the authority of the town government in the fourteenth century was promoted by the interests of the dominant trade gilds, and cannot be regarded as a subordination of producers in the interests of " the entire population of the town considered as consumers ", as Mrs. Green suggests (134–60).

of the city. But the right of election seems to have prevailed, all citizens participating in the borough elections; and even if the richer burghers ruled, they did so by consent of the whole city. Round about the year 1300 " an aristocratic select body usurped the place of the common council of the citizens ", and by the close of the reign of Edward III the burgesses at large " were entirely excluded from their right of suffrage in Parliamentary elections ".[1] At Beverley it is clear that an oligarchy had arisen by the fourteenth century ; by the fifteenth century Nottingham had become a close oligarchy ; and at York the Mercers had captured the government of the city.[2] At Winchester in the fourteenth century there were complaints " concerning oppressions inflicted by the twenty-four principal citizens ", who had usurped the election of the town bailiffs.[3] At the end of the previous century the burgesses of both Gloucester and Oxford speak of usurpation by the *divites et potentes*, and of the unjust taxation of the poor for the benefit of the rich. At Bury we find political power concentrated in the hands of the richer burgesses, and by the fifteenth century even the burgess body itself has become very small : a select body that acts as " a kind of standing council " to the aldermen.[4] At Lynn and Shrewsbury one hears of the rule of twelve ; at Newcastle the poorer burgesses complain of the power of the merchant gild, and at Scarborough of the transgressions of the *divites* who were excluding the mass of the citizens from any share in the government of the borough.[5] Quite commonly about this time a distinction of status appears between *potentiores*, *mediocres*, *inferiores* : a distinction evidently corresponding to the wealthy trading oligarchy, the more well-to-do craftsmen who possessed moderate means but still confined themselves to the local market, and the poorer craftsmen and journeymen who were soon destined to fall into economic dependence on one or other of the two wealthier grades of citizen.[6] In Cornish towns we meet a similar distinction (rather later than elsewhere, in the sixteenth century) between " capital burgesses " and " lesser townsmen ", the town government being concentrated in the hands of the former.[7] In London the original

---

[1] C. W. Colby, " Growth of Oligarchy in English Towns " in *Eng. Hist. Review,* vol. V (1890), 643, 648.
[2] Cf. Maud Sellers, *York Mercers and Merchant Adventurers,* xiii.
[3] Colby, *op. cit.,* 646-7.
[4] M. D. Lobel, *The Borough of Bury St. Edmunds,* 93.
[5] Colby, *op. cit.,* 644, 646, 648.
[6] Cf. Ashley, *op. cit.,* 133-4 ; also Hazlitt, *op. cit.,* 69.
[7] A. L. Rowse, *Tudor Cornwall,* 90.

method of election to the common council had been by the citizens in the various wards. For a brief period this was changed to election by the major gilds ; but probably on account of popular opposition a reversion was made to election by wards.[1] The City Aldermen, however, had to be " good and discreet " men, with goods of value of £1,000, and came to be appointed for life by the Mayor from four candidates nominated by the wards ; the Mayor himself being elected by the retiring Mayor and Aldermen from two Aldermen nominated in agreement with the Common Council and with the Masters and Wardens of the major Livery Companies. By the fifteenth century it had become common for the Aldermen to override the ward elections and for each to nominate a member of his ward to the council ; so that the Mayor and Aldermen virtually became a self-perpetuating body. At any rate, most of the Aldermen and Sheriffs and all the Mayors for a large number of years were invariably members of one of the twelve great Livery Companies, so that the latter can be said to have continuously monopolized the government of the city. As the historian of one of these companies has pointed out, the relationship between major gilds and the city was closely similar to that between the colleges and the university in Oxford or Cambridge.[2]

The connection between these political changes and the economic policy of the new trading class is sufficiently plain. It is true, of course, that in some cases the power was monopolized by one group of trading interests to the exclusion of others, and that here a certain section of the traders made common cause with the craft gilds to resist this usurpation. For example, at Beverley the drapers made common cause with the tailors, butchers and shoemakers in an insurrection in 1380 against the dominant clique ;[3] and in London in the fourteenth century drapers, mercers, tailors, goldsmiths and haberdashers were united in common opposition to the hegemony of the victualling gilds. Again, in certain cases the urban oligarchy may have been composed of the older landowning elements in the town, not of commercial *parvenus*. But in the majority of cases it is clear that this concentration of power in the towns in the

---

[1] In 1354, indeed, we find Parliament intervening in the government of London on the ground of its alleged notorious misgovernment by mayor, aldermen and sheriffs, who were mainly interested in preserving gild monopolies and raising prices. (Cf. G. Unwin, *Finance and Trade under Edward III*, 239.)

[2] A. H. Johnson, *History of the Worshipful Company of the Drapers of London*, vol. I, 27-8, 41, 52, 54-8 ; H. T. Riley, *Liber Albus*, 18, 35.

[3] *V.C.H. Yorks*, vol. III, 443.

fourteenth century represented the rule of merchant capital, and that one of its principal effects was to restrict the crafts to trading retail in the local market, and where the local market was not the main outlet for their products to subordinate the craftsmen to a close corporation of merchants with whom and on whose terms the producers had no option but to deal. Moreover, in many cases the regulations which had been devised to afford economic protection to the craftsmen were now turned to the latter's disadvantage. Sometimes the prices of craftsmen's wares were controlled,[1] while craftsmen were prevented from fixing minimum prices among themselves. In Coventry the Drapers who ruled the city prevented the fullers and tailors from acting on their charter, which awarded them certain rights as craft gilds, insisted in face of the opposition of the dyers' craft that drapers should be allowed to engage in the work of dyeing, and forbade dyers to dye any cloth that was not furnished by a local draper or shearmen to import any cloth from outside the town.[2] In Bristol there was trouble in 1317 accompanied by tumult and fighting in the town hall on account of the privileges that fourteen *de majoribus* had annexed to themselves in connection with the port and the market.[3] In some cases the new régime involved the decay of the old Assize of Bread and of the arrangements for privileged purchase of materials by the craftsmen. " Rich bakers and victuallers who rose to municipal offices turned the assize of bread and the inspection of cooking-houses into an idle tale " ; and the fine enacted by the regulations against offenders came to be treated by the well-to-do speculator as a licence-fee for the continuance of the practice—a fee which the merchant whose transactions were on a large scale could well afford, and which the poorer offender could not.[4] At Yarmouth in 1376 the " poor commons " petitioned that they be allowed to buy and sell their wares as of old ; and at Grimsby the ruling burgesses would not " suffer the poor men of Grimsby to partici-pate with them in the matter of purchase and sale according to the liberties granted to them ".[5] At Newcastle and at Hull alike

---

[1] Cf. Saltzmann, *Industries in the Middle Ages*, 201–10.
[2] M. D. Harris, *History of the Drapers' Company of Coventry*, 6–13.
[3] Colby, *op. cit.*, 649–50 ; John Latimer, *History of the Society of Merchant Adventurers of Bristol*, 8. The people of Bristol " made opposition, affirming that all the burgesses were of a single condition ". The fighting resulted in twenty deaths, and the popular rebellion lasted intermittently for more than two years. Latimer refers to 1312 as the year of " the great insurrection " of the commonalty.
[4] Mrs. Green, *op. cit.*, 49 ; Gretton, *op. cit.*, 53.
[5] Lipson, *op. cit.*, 321 ; Colby, *loc. cit.*, 645.

the craftsmen were excluded from trading abroad; at Exeter a similar restriction—against which the Tailors' Gild fought vigorously—applied to " adventuring beyond the seas "; at Bristol and Chester " men of manuell arte " and those who sold retail were excluded from wholesale trade with merchants who were not burgesses of the city.[1]

The new merchant aristocracy was not entirely a closed circle for those that had the money to buy themselves in; and in the fifteenth and sixteenth centuries there was a fairly constant infiltration into its ranks from among the richer master-craftsmen, who tended to leave handicraft for trade, and even to become employers of other craftsmen, as soon as they had accumulated sufficient capital to enable them to scan wider horizons than the retail trade of a local market afforded them. It was inevitable that the *parvenu* ambition of such men should find the exclusive privileges of the merchant companies irksome and cramping. Two roads of advancement lay open to them. They could purchase a position in one of the privileged companies and abandon their old calling; or they could struggle to secure for their own craft gild the status of a trading body. The former was frequently done in the case of London Livery Companies, admission to which was generally possible for a reputable burgess of the city on payment of the deliberately onerous entrance fee; and we find richer members among the fullers and shearmen and weavers and dyers securing admission to a company such as the Drapers'. An example of the latter tendency was the amalgamation of the fullers and the shearmen of London in 1530 to form the Cloth-workers as a merchant company trading in finished cloth in rivalry with the Drapers' Company.[2] Of such developments in the Livery Companies of London more will be said in the chapter which follows. When this type of thing occurred, however, in a provincial town where trade was more specialized and the ruling group more homogeneous in its interest, something like a revolution in the civic government was apt to occur, or at any rate a long-drawn battle over the spoils of office. For example,

---

[1] Kramer in *Eng. Hist. Review*, XXIII, 28–30. It appears that the principle of " one man, one trade " laid down by an Act of 1363, and perhaps intended by the feudal interests to curb the engrossing tendencies of the Grocers, was soon invoked by mercantile gilds like the Drapers " against the independence of the several handicrafts ". At any rate, in the year following the Act, the King proceeded to bestow charters on companies of wealthy wholesalers, like the Vintners, Drapers and Fishmongers, giving them each a monopoly of their several trades (Unwin, *Finance and Trade under Edward III*, 247–50).
[2] Unwin, *Industrial Organization*, 44–5.

at Exeter the richer master-tailors who controlled the tailors' gild wished by the end of the fourteenth century to have the rights of merchant tailors to sell directly to foreign traders. Accordingly they purchased a charter from the Crown which endowed them with the status of a trading company. This did not please the merchant oligarchy that held political control of the city ; and the Mayor proceeded to expel the tailors from the freedom of the city. Eventually a compromise was reached, by which the tailors shared both in the privileges of trade and in civic adminis-tration, " and the sorrows of defeat were left to the populace at large ".[1] This kind of compromise seems to have been surpris-ingly common in the fifteenth and sixteenth centuries in England, the mercantile oligarchy maintaining its position by admitting the richer craft gilds to a share in power and in economic privilege.

III

While there was some infiltration into the privileged ranks as capital accumulated among the crafts themselves, the monopolistic position of merchant capital in England was scarcely weakened thereby, and the increase of its wealth was not retarded. With the growth of the market, and especially of foreign trade, there was room for the numbers within the privileged ranks to grow without any serious overcrowding. Internally the market was expanding, not only through the growth of towns and the multiplication of urban markets, but also by the increased penetration of money economy into the manor with the growth of hired labour and the leasing of the demesne for a money-rent. Nevertheless it was foreign trade which provided the greatest opportunities for rapid commercial advancement, and it was in this sphere that the most impressive fortunes were made. Here for some time foreign merchants held the field ; their position being strengthened by special privileges from the English Crown. These were first the merchants of the Flemish Hanse, and later Italians, who purchased wool direct from monasteries and landowners, often advancing loans on the security of future wool deliveries. Before English merchants could enjoy the rich prizes of this sphere, the privileges of the foreign merchants had to be curtailed. This was not easy, since the English Crown was not only debtor to these foreign con-

[1] Mrs. Green, *op. cit.*, 173–81 ; cf. also B. Wilkinson, *The Mediæval Council of Exeter.*

cessionaires, but was under the recurrent necessity of new borrowing. There was a legend that the crusading Richard had bartered privileges to Hanse merchants against release from a German dungeon. At one time in the fourteenth century the royal crowns were in pawn to Cologne and Trier, and on another occasion the Queen and her child had to remain behind after a visit to Antwerp as pledges for a debt of £30,000. Until there were English merchants of sufficient substance to finance the King's expenditure, particularly his wars, and to farm his taxes, the privileged status of the foreign corporations could not be undermined.

Towards the end of the thirteenth century, and still more in the fourteenth, the Crown began to rely on revenue raised by an export tax on wool and on wool-loans from English wool-exporters ; and the English merchants who were organized in the Fellowship of the Staple were able to take advantage of the royal necessity to barter loans in exchange for monopoly-rights in the valuable export trade in wool. Professor Unwin and Professor Power have cogently demonstrated how this issue underlay the constitutional crisis of the fourteenth century and was entwined with the growth of Parliament. In 1313 a compulsory wool Staple was established in the Netherlands by royal edict : a Staple to which all wool for export had to be brought and offered for sale " at the orders of the Mayor and Company of Merchants ". This was regarded by the members of the English company as a weapon against their alien competitors in the export trade, and was strenuously opposed by the latter. But the Company which enjoyed the profits of this monopoly was a small and exclusive body. It apparently succeeded, not only in raising the price to foreign customers and in elbowing out foreign merchants from the export trade with Flanders, but in depressing the price of wool at home. There very soon arose a new demand for the repeal of the Staple privileges on a variety of grounds : both that they were too favourable to the Flemings and that they were unfavourable to those engaged in the internal wool trade in England. The wool-growing interest (which was powerfully represented in Parliament) would naturally have preferred the total abolition of Staple rights, since a free export trade would have given them a competitive price for their wool. Many of the smaller boroughs desired that alien merchants should attend their markets in order to increase their trade ; and in this respect were at variance with London and the port-towns. The merchants of the larger English towns, however, who wanted to have a footing in the lucrative traffic or to enjoy the rôle of middleman between grower and exporter, desired simply the replacement of the single wool Staple at Bruges by several Staples in a selected number of English towns. A principal ground of their complaint against the existing system was the old story that the merchants of Bruges were in a position to prevent wool buyers from having free access to the wool market of the city, and to prevent the traders of smaller Flemish towns from dealing directly with the English merchants who traded there with English wool. By contrast, it was argued that the transfer of the Staple to English ports would attract foreign buyers to the new Staple towns and give English merchants a direct access to a wider range of purchasers. At the same time, by prohibiting foreign merchants from buying wool except in the Staple towns, it was hoped to keep the middleman-trade of buying wool from abbeys and landowners and selling it for export in the hands of English wool-dealers.[1]

About the termination of the exclusive privileges of the Bruges Staple there was, accordingly, general agreement (except for a small circle of some thirty rich tax-farmers, like William de la Pole, who stood to gain from the privileges of a narrow export-monopoly) ; and the representatives of the shires and boroughs in Parliament united in petitioning the King to this effect. In the reigns of Edward II and Edward III policy was subject to frequent changes. Edward II had forbidden all save the nobility and dignitaries of the Church to wear foreign cloth. Edward III, in the course of a series of desperate attempts to finance a continental war by a wool subsidy and the proceeds of a wool monopoly, for two brief periods, in 1326-7 and 1332-4, substituted a number of English Staples for the Staple at Bruges, and even for a few years in the 1350's made the concession of permitting an open trade in wool for export and prohibiting the import of foreign cloth. But the triumph of the wool free traders was short-lived ; and in 1359 the Bruges Staple was restored,[2] and

[1] Cf. G. Unwin, *Finance and Trade under Edward III*, 213 ; A. L. Jenckes, *Staple of England*, 14 seq., 40 seq. ; Eileen Power, *Wool Trade in English Medieval History*, 91 ; Alice Beardwood, *Alien Merchants in England, 1350-1377*, 38-40, 55-6.

[2] Four years later, however, there was a fresh compromise—a shift of the Staple for English wool to Calais ; and at the end of the century the staplers became consolidated as the Company of the Staple of Calais. Their monopoly of export was not, however, quite complete, since certain Italian merchants were given licences to buy wool in England and to export it to Italy without going through Calais.

the privileges of the narrow circle of exporters organized in the English Merchants of the Staple were renewed. The persistence of this monopoly brought little profit to the main body of English merchants, and threatened to narrow the market for English wool, instead of widening it. Further progress had to rely on a flanking move : on a growing official encouragement to English cloth-making and to the development of the export trade in English cloth in rivalry with the Flemish industry. Indeed, as Eileen Power has pointed out, the very monopoly of the Staple by narrowing the channels of export and maintaining an " immense margin between the domestic and the foreign prices of wool " unwittingly assisted the growth of English cloth-making : " the low home prices meant that English cloth could be sold, not only at home but abroad, much more cheaply than foreign cloth, which had to pay an immensely higher sum for the same raw material ; and the export of cloth became increasingly more lucrative than the export of wool ".[1]   Nearly two centuries later we find the Merchants of the Staple criticizing alike the clothiers (because *inter alia* they caused a decay of husbandry) and the Merchant Adventurers, and joining in the demand that the cloth industry should be confined to corporate towns.[2]

In this new field of cloth export the first-comers seem to have been the Mercers, who began to establish factors (as, for example, the Mercers of York) at places like Bruges, Antwerp, and Bergen.[3] In 1358, the year before the restoration of the Bruges Staple, a body known as the Fraternity of St. Thomas à Becket, an offspring of the London Mercers' Company, managed to obtain certain privileges from the Count of Flanders and to establish at Antwerp a depot for its English cloth trade. This was taken as a grave challenge to the wool Staple at Bruges ; and a bitter warfare ensued between the English Adventurers and the Hanse for the trade of Flanders and the North Sea and between the Adventurers, claiming a monopoly in cloth, and the wool Staplers. In the fifteenth century " a great number of wealthy merchants of divers great cities and maritime towns in England, including London, York, Norwich, Exeter, Ipswich, Hull ", secured incorporation as the Company of Merchant Adventurers, and seem to have acquired exclusive rights to trade in cloth between England and Holland, Brabant and Flanders. This was the

---

[1] Eileen Power, *op. cit.*, 101.
[2] E. E. Rich, *The Ordinance Book of the Merchants of the Staple*, 24–5.
[3] Maud Sellers, *York Mercers and Merchant Adventurers*, xli.

lineal descendant of the Fraternity of St. Thomas à Becket, and its link with the Mercers was still close ; the Merchant Adventurers and the London Mercers sharing the same minute book down to 1526. So exclusive a body was it that only the richer members of the Mercers' and Drapers' Companies and some sons of gentry succeeded in securing admission to its ranks.[1] The trade war between the English cloth merchants and the Hanse was both protracted and bitter. English ships were attacked and taken as prizes and English merchants retaliated whenever they could. At one time the English settlement at Bergen was sacked. Such were the risks that accompanied the profits of monopoly : risks which arose, not from the natural order of things, but because the acquisition of monopoly was the *leitmotif* of all trade. Even as late as the middle of the sixteenth century English merchants at Dantzig were permitted only to trade on one day each week, and then with none but burgesses, and were successfully prevented from trading in any of the other towns of Prussia. It was said that English merchants were treated " worse than any other foreigners, the Jews only excepted " ; although this may well have been a partisan exaggeration. However, with the growing support of the Crown in the fifteenth and sixteenth centuries (a support which grew with the ability of English cloth merchants to rival their enemies in loans and bribery), the competitive position of the English cloth traders was progressively strengthened while at the same time the privileges of the foreigners in England were terminated. In the reign of Elizabeth the Steelyard merchants were first of all excluded from buying English cloth at Blackwell Hall (in 1576) and finally in the closing years of the century the Steelyard in London was closed. In 1614 the export of English wool was officially prohibited. This prohibition, which was a concession to the cloth industry, affected not only foreign merchants but also the English Staplers, who from that date ceased to be a company of wool-exporters, and turning their attention to the internal trade in wool were given the right in 1617 to be the sole middlemen in wool within the kingdom, the sale of wool being confined to certain home Staple towns.[2]

By the middle of the sixteenth century British merchants had ventured sufficiently far afield, both across the North Sea and into

---

[1] Cf. W. E. Lingelbach, " Merchant Adventurers in England ", in *Trans. Ryl. Hist. Society*, NS. XVI, 41–2.
[2] Cf. E. E. Rich, *op. cit.*, 77–86.

the Mediterranean, to inaugurate some five or six new general companies, each possessing privileges in a new area. The year 1553 saw the foundation of the Russia Company (which two years later received a charter giving it a monopoly) as the first company to employ joint stock and to own ships corporately. A number of members of the Merchant Adventurers were also members of the new company and may well have taken the initiative in its formation. In the same year as it obtained its charter from the English Crown, it was successful in negotiating, through its representative Richard Chancellor, an agreement with Tsar Ivan IV whereby it was to enjoy the sole right of trading with Muscovy by the White Sea route and to establish depots at Kholmogory and Vologda. In 1557 Jenkinson, a servant of the company, journeyed as far as Persia and Bokhara, and in 1567 the company obtained the right to trade across Russia with Persia through Kazan and Astrakhan. In the same year as the Russia Company was chartered the Africa Company was formed : a Company whose members were to grow fat on the lucrative enterprise which Nassau Senior later described as " to kidnap or purchase and work to death without compunction the natives of Africa ", about which " the English and the Dutch, at that time the wisest and most religious nations of the world, . . . had no more scruple . . . than they had about enslaving horses ".[1] In 1578 the Eastland Company was chartered " to enjoy the sole trade through the Sound into Norway, Sweden, Poland, Lithuania (excepting Narva), Prussia and also Pomerania, from the river Oder eastward to Dantzick, Elbing and Konigsberg ; also to Copenhagen and Elsinore and to Finland, Gothland, Barnholm and Oeland ". Among the powers assigned to it were " to make bye-laws and to impose fines, imprisonment etc. on all non-freemen trading to these parts ". Soon after its foundation it managed to make an important breach in the ramparts of the Hanse monopoly by securing the right to deal directly with the merchants of Elbing and with other Prussian towns.[2] The year before the foundation of the Eastland Com-

[1] Senior, *Slavery in the U.S.*, 4.
[2] Cf. A. Szelagowski and N. S. B. Gras in *Trans. Ryl. Hist. Society*, 3rd Series, VI, 166, 175. Prior to this the Merchant Adventurers had made a treaty with Hamburg to the same effect for a period of ten years from 1567 to 1577 ; and in 1564, after the closing of Antwerp to English merchants, the town of Emden (which was not a member of the Hanse League), admitted the Merchant Adventurers, who were able to use it as a port of transit to Cologne and Frankfurt. In 1597, however, there was a temporary setback : in retaliation for measures taken against Hanse merchants in England, the Hanse persuaded the Emperor to expel the Merchant Adventurers from the Empire as a company of monopolists.

pany, a number of members of the Merchant Adventurers founded the Spanish Company to monopolize the lucrative trade in wine, oil and fruit with Spain and Portugal, and to secure powers under charter to exclude competitors. Finally, in 1581 letters patent were granted by the Crown to four gentlemen, including a Sir E. Osborn and a Mr. Staper, and " to such other Englishmen not exceeding twelve in number as the said Sir E. Osborn and Staper shall appoint to be joined to them and their factors, servants and deputies, for the space of seven years to trade to Turkey . . . the trade to Turkey to be solely to them during the said term ". This was the origin of the Levant Company (incorporated in 1592 as a fusion of the earlier Turkey Company with the Venice Company), which numbered Queen Elizabeth among its leading shareholders and in 1600 begat the East India Company and in 1605 had its charter of monopoly renewed in perpetuity by James I.[1]

In varying degree these foreign trading companies were highly exclusive bodies. The Merchant Adventurers conducted a vigorous struggle against any interloping in its trade, so that this profitable intercourse might be preserved for the few and prices be fenced against the influence of competition. Similarly the Russia Company made strenuous (if far from successful) efforts to exclude interlopers trading through Narva ; and both the Eastlanders and the Spanish Company used their powers to control the trade. Centred in London, the powerful Merchant Adventurers Company had its replica in sister-companies in provincial towns like Newcastle and York and Bristol. Generally, however, while provincial merchants were awarded rights of trade, the bulk of the traffic passed through the hands of London merchants and it was Londoners that dominated the organization. Entrance to the ranks of the privileged companies was restricted by a limitation of apprenticeship and by entrance fees which tended to grow heavier in the course of time. By the beginning of the seventeenth century, for example, the entrance fee to the Merchant Adventurers had risen to the figure of £200.[2] Moreover, craftsmen and retailers were usually barred from membership : " the express desire

[1] Cf. C. Walford, " Outline History of Hanseatic League ", *Trans. Ryl. Hist. Society*, IX (1881), 128 ; M. Sellers, *op. cit.* ; Cawston and Keane, *Early Chartered Companies*, 15–22, 27–8, 61 seq. ; W. R. Scott, *Joint Stock Companies*, vol. I, 17–22, 103 ; I. Lubimenko, *Les Relations Commerciales et Politiques de l'Angleterre avec la Russie avant Pierre le Grand*, 23–34, 82, 114 seq. ; M. Epstein, *Early History of the Levant Company.*
[2] See below, p. 192 f.

to exclude " them being described by Unwin as " one common feature which characterizes the whole of the charters " of the foreign trading companies.[1] In addition, the quantities traded were carefully regulated, presumably in the interests of price-maintenance, by the control of shipping that the company exercised and the method of the " stint " by which the share of each participant was limited, as by the quota of a modern cartel. Whether, in addition, minimum selling-prices and maximum buying-prices were enforced on members as a general rule is not altogether clear. There is evidence that the Merchants of the Staple had employed price-fixing agreements in the fourteenth and fifteenth centuries, favouring a single foreign staple town in order to facilitate the enforcement of price-agreements ; [2] and the probability seems to be that the Merchant Adventurers used similar methods. In the reign of James I the Levant Company not only controlled the supply but fixed maximum buying prices for produce purchased in the Near East.[3] At any rate the clothiers and local traders who acted as intermediaries between the craftsman and the export merchant were under no illusions as to the effect of the monopolies ; for we hear a growing number of complaints from them in the sixteenth century that their sale outlets were narrowed and the price at which they could dispose of goods for export was abnormally depressed : for example, the complaint of certain clothiers to the Privy Council in 1550 that the Merchant Adventurers had by agreement fixed the buying-price for cloth so low that the manufacturers lost £1 a piece.[4]

This policy of exclusiveness was not without imitators in the less exalted ranks of urban society. By virtue of their apprenticeship regulations the crafts had always imposed a fairly strict control over admission. But in the fourteenth and fifteenth centuries there was a very general tendency towards a raising of the entrance requirements to a craft in the interest of limitation of numbers. Patrimony—the right of a son to succeed his father in the craft—had always been a means by which one whose family was established in the trade could avoid the onerous entrance-requirements and mastership could become an hereditary privilege. In the course of time it became increasingly difficult for any who were outside a certain circle of families

[1] *Studies in Economic History*, 173, also 181.
[2] Eileen Power, *op. cit.*, 89–90.
[3] M. Epstein, *Early History of the Levant Company*, 117–26, 130–1.
[4] *Studies in Econ. History : the Papers of George Unwin*, 148.

and who were not rich enough to buy a position in the gild to set up as a master. This exclusive tendency was remarkably widespread and was even more pronounced in the larger continental towns than it was in this country, where (as Pirenne has said) " in each town local industry becomes a restricted privilege of a consortium of hereditary masters ".[1] English craft gilds had early gained the right to exercise a virtual veto on any new entrants to their industry by means of the double provision that no one might set up as a master craftsman unless he had obtained the freedom of the city and that no newcomer might be admitted to the city's freedom (i.e. be made a full citizen) except on the recommendation and security of six reputable members of his craft.[2] Later it was frequently stipulated that the consent of the wardens of the craft gild was necessary for his admission.[3] Ashley states that " before the middle of the fourteenth century there are unmistakable traces of the desire to limit competition by diminishing the influx of newcomers ".[4] In 1321 the London weavers were accused of charging abnormal entrance fees to those wishing to enter the craft ; and ten years later we find general complaints being levelled at craft gilds that they charged apprentices " almost prohibitive fees for membership in the gilds ".[5] Mrs. Green even goes so far as to say that " when a man had finished his apprenticeship, cunning devices were found for casting him back among the rank and file of hired labour ".[6] To judge by legislation of two centuries later forbidding the practice (legislation of the 1530's), it had become the custom in some cases for journeymen and apprentices to be required by their masters to swear on oath that they would not set up as craftsmen on their own without the master's permission.[7]

---

[1] H. Pirenne in *La Fin du Moyen Age*, vol. 2, 147.
[2] In the case of London the latter enactment was made in 1319.
[3] Ashley, *Introduction*, vol. I, Bk. II, 77.
[4] *Ibid.*, 75 ; Gretton, *op. cit.*, 69-70.
[5] Kramer, *Craft Gilds and the Government*, 78-9 ; F. Consitt, *London Weavers' Company*, 21 seq. The weavers were also charged with restriction of output and of productive capacity ; the allegation being made that they had reduced the number of looms in London from 280 to 80 over the past thirty years. This was at the time when (as we have seen above) the weavers were fighting a losing battle against the burellers, who had become their employers ; and these charges against the weavers, originating in the enmity of the burellers, probably contained some propagandist exaggerations.
[6] Mrs. Green, *op. cit.*, 102 ; cf. also A. Abram, *Social England in Fifteenth Century*, 121.
[7] Unwin, *Industrial Organization*, 56 ; Kramer, *op. cit.*, 80 ; Hibbert, *Influence and Development of English Gilds*, 66-7. It is not clear why the latter writer should think that this practice exhibited the gilds " in a state of wholesale demoralisation " : all gilds in varying degrees attempted to secure a monopoly position for themselves and to restrict entry to a trade, as part of their essential function.

E

The result was an increasing tendency in Tudor times for journeymen who could not afford the expense of mastership to work secretly in garrets in a back street or to retire to the suburbs in an attempt to evade the jurisdiction of the gild : practices against which the gilds in their turn waged war, attempting both to widen the area of their jurisdiction and to increase the thoroughness of the official " searches ", through whose agency offenders against gild ordinances were brought to book. The London weavers in the fifteenth century introduced a prohibition on the hiring out of looms : a ban that was evidently intended to make it more difficult for poor journeymen to set up on their own.[1] Here, as we shall see, there was often a ground of conflict between the craft gild and the mercantile oligarchy of the town, since it was generally to the interest of the latter that the competition of craftsmen, willing to sell at cut-prices, as the garret-masters and suburban masters often were, should be multiplied. As for the mercantile gilds themselves and the livery of the greater London companies, these led rather than followed the fashion of exclusiveness ; and the raising of fees to the Livery had reached a level by the middle of the sixteenth century where (in the words of the historian of the London Drapers' Company) " the Livery was practically confined to men of considerable substance, and it was only the more wealthy of the Drapers who were able to take advantage of the openings offered ".[2] On the Continent Brentano tells us that often " the freedom (of the gild) became practically hereditary on account of the difficulty of complying with the conditions of entrance ". Sometimes there was a regulation that masters could not trade on borrowed money, which effectively excluded the man of small capital from securing a foothold. Sometimes in German towns journeymen were required to have travelled for five years before they could set up as masters. Expensive inaugural dinners, for which the new master had to pay, became the custom.[3] Quite widely in continental gilds the practice developed of requiring from an apprentice a *chef d'œuvre*, or masterpiece, before he could enter on mastership —a piece of work, both elaborate and perfect, on which it was necessary for him to work for a whole year or more. In France an edict of 1581 saw fit to denounce " the excessive expenses that the poor artisans are constrained to undertake to obtain the

---

[1] Consitt, *op. cit.*, 105.   [2] A. H. Johnson, *op. cit.*, vol. I, 193.
[3] Brentano in *Eng. Guilds*, cxxxviii, cl ; M. Kowalewsky, *Die Ökonomische Entwicklung Europas*, vol. V, 165–75.

degree of mastership ". In Paris the number of apprentices themselves was in the first place severely restricted. Generally there were two categories : *apprentiz-privez*, who were sons of masters and were exempt from the restrictions, and the *apprentiz-estranges*, who were usually limited to one per workshop. Not only was a considerable minimum period of service required of these *apprentiz-estranges*, but a price was charged to parents for apprenticing a son, and when parents were unable to meet this payment, the period of apprenticeship was prolonged by two years. As a result " access to mastership was obtained by strangers only by virtue of sacrifices, and considerable advantages were reserved to a child who followed his father's profession ", while for a growing number " the difficulties of mastership were insurmountable ".[1]

The result of these developments was, not only to fence off the profits of existing craftsmen from the levelling effect of the competition of newcomers, and by this means to provide a basis for a moderate accumulation of capital inside the more prosperous craft gilds themselves : it also had the effect of creating at the bottom of urban society a growing class of hired servants and journeymen who lacked any chances of advancement, and who, while nominally members of the gild in many cases, exercised no control over it and lacked any protection from it. On the contrary, both gild and town legislation generally imposed draconian regulations on the journeymen, controlling his wages, enjoining the strictest obedience on him to his master, and ruthlessly proscribing any form of organization or even meetings of journeymen (which were invariably denounced as " covins and cabals "). To the extent that this depressed class of hired servants existed, the possibility began to appear of profit being made, and capital in consequence accumulated, from direct investment in the employment of wage-labour. But until the later sixteenth century this apparently remained an unimportant source of capitalist income ; and the remarkable gains of merchant capital in the fourteenth and fifteenth centuries, while fruit of monopoly, were acquired by an exclusion of the mass of the producers from sharing in the benefits of an expanding volume of trade rather than by any actual depression of the general standard of life.[2] In

---

[1] Lespinasse et Bonnardot, *op. cit.*, c.–cx. ; H. Hauser, *Les Débuts du Capitalisme*, 34–6 ; Levasseur, *Hist. des Classes Ouvrières en France* (Ed. 1859), Tome I, 230.

[2] In these two centuries, indeed, there was probably a substantial rise in the standard of life both of the average villager and of the town craftsman, as Thorold Rogers suggested.

other words, the lavish profits of the new trading class owed their source to a relative, rather than an absolute, reduction in the income of the producers. But in the second half of the sixteenth century (and probably also in the seventeenth, at least during the first half of it) there is evidence that this ceased to be the case. In the century of what Lord Keynes has termed the great " profit inflation ", it is clear that real wages showed a catastrophic fall, not only in England but in France and Germany and the Netherlands as well. For this fact, the growth of a proletariat, robbed of other opportunities of livelihood and competing piteously for employment, was no doubt responsible.[1] But it seems also probable (although here there is much less evidence in quantitative form) that the standard of life of, at any rate, the poorer half of the peasantry and craftsmen declined in the course of this resplendent century.[2] To this must be added, as a source of bourgeois enrichment, the results of foreclosure and seizure of the property of others, both feudal property and the property of small producers, which will be the subject of fuller consideration below.

One feature of this new merchant bourgeoisie that is at first as surprising as it is universal, is the readiness with which this class compromised with feudal society once its privileges had been won. The compromise was partly economic—it purchased land, entered into business partnerships with the aristocracy, and welcomed local gentry and their sons to membership of its leading gilds ; it was partly social—the desire for intermarriage

---

[1] See below, pp. 237–8.

[2] For example, so far as export markets are concerned, Unwin has cited some evidence for the conclusion that, towards the end of the sixteenth century, as a result of the monopolistic activities of the chartered companies, not only were prices influenced to the disadvantage of handicraft products, but the *volume* of export of the products of home industry was reduced (*Studies in Econ. History*, 181–5, 198–204, 216–20).

It may be asked : how, in these circumstances, if the real consumption of the masses declined, could the price-level have risen and enabled the large profits of the period (depending essentially on the margin between price and money-wages, multiplied by the commodity turnover) to be successfully realized ? In other words, whence the expanding demand ? The answer apparently lies in the fact that it was the expenditure of the rich and the middling-well-to-do (i.e. the new bourgeoisie and the Crown, and also the rising class of provincial capitalists and larger yeoman farmers) that supplied the expanding market ; the increased expenditure of this section in a sense creating the conditions for profit-realization. Many of the expanding industries of the period catered for luxury-consumption of the more well-to-do. There was also an expanding investment in shipping, in building and (to a very small extent) in machinery and craft-implements, also in ordnance and military equipment. To this must be added the important effect of foreign trade— foreign trade conducted on highly favourable terms and balanced by an appreciable import of bullion into the realm.

and the acquisition of titles to gentility ; it was partly political —a readiness to accept a political coalition (as often happened in the government of Italian and other continental towns between the wealthy burghers and the older noble families) or to accept ministerial offices and a place at Court on the basis of the old State-form (as occurred with the Tudor régime in England). The degree to which merchant capital flourished in a country at this period affords us no measure of the ease and speed with which capitalist production was destined to develop : in many cases quite the contrary. Having previously existed, as Marx aptly remarked, " like the gods of Epicurus in the intermediate worlds of the universe ", merchant capital in its efflorescence between the fourteenth and the sixteenth centuries exercised a profoundly disintegrating effect. But in an important sense it continued to exist " in the pores of society ". It flourished as an intermediary, whose fortune depended on its insinuating cunning, its facility for adaptation, and the political favours it could win. The needs that merchants and usurers served were largely those of lords and princes and kings. These new men had to be ingratiating as well as crafty ; they had to temper extortion with fawning, combine avarice with flattery, and clothe a usurer's hardness in the vestments of chivalry. In the producer they had little interest save in his continuing submissiveness and for the system of production they had little regard save as a cheap and ready source of supply. They had as much concern for the terms of trade (on which their profit-margin depended) as for its volume ; and they minded nothing whether what they bartered was slaves or ivory, wool or woollens, tin or gold as long as it was lucrative. To acquire political privilege was their first ambition : their second that as few as possible should enjoy it. Since they were essentially parasites on the old economic order, while they might bleed and weaken it, their fortune was in the last analysis associated with that of their host. Hence the upper strata of these bourgeois *nouveaux-riches* took to country mansions and to falconing and cut capers like a gentleman without great embarrassment, and what remained of the old baronial families took these upstarts into partnership with a fairly cheerful grace. The merchant of Defoe's story retorted to the squire who told him he was no gentleman : " No Sir, but I can buy a gentleman ".[1] By the end of the sixteenth century this new aristocracy, jealous of its new-found prerogatives, had

[1] *The Compleat English Gentleman* (Ed. Buhlbring), 257.

become a conservative rather than a revolutionary force ; and its influence and the influence of the institutions it had fostered, such as the chartered companies, was to retard rather than to accelerate the development of capitalism as a mode of production.

CHAPTER FOUR

THE RISE OF INDUSTRIAL CAPITAL

I

Marx, in the course of his historical notes on merchant capital, has pointed out that merchant capital in its early stage had a purely external relationship to the mode of production, which remained independent and untouched by capital ; the merchant being merely " the man who ' removes ' the goods produced by the guilds or the peasants ", in order to gain from price differences between different productive areas. Later, however, merchant capital began to fasten upon the mode of production, partly in order to exploit the latter more effectively —to " deteriorate the condition of the direct producers . . . and absorb their surplus labour on the basis of the old mode of production "—partly in order to transform it in the interests of greater profit and the service of wider markets. This development, he suggests, followed two main roads. According to the first—" the really revolutionary way "—a section of the producers themselves accumulated capital and took to trade, and in course of time began to organize production on a capitalist basis free from the handicraft restrictions of the gilds. According to the second, a section of the existing merchant class began to " take possession directly of production " ; thereby " serving historically as a mode of transition ", but becoming eventually " an obstacle to a real capitalist mode of production and declin(ing) with the development of the latter ".[1]

Evidence that has accumulated in recent decades now makes it abundantly clear that the kind of transition to which Marx was referring was already in process in England in the second half of the sixteenth century ; and that by the accession of Charles I certain significant changes in the mode of production had already taken place : a circumstance peculiarly relevant to political events in seventeenth-century England, which bear all the marks of the classic bourgeois revolution. But the lines of this development

---

[1] *Capital*, vol. III, 388–96. Marx elsewhere dates " the capitalist era from the sixteenth century ", even though " we come across the first beginnings of capitalist production as early as the fourteenth or fifteenth century, sporadically, in certain towns of the Mediterranean " (to which he might have added Flanders and the Rhine district). (*Capital*, vol I, 739).

are far from clearly drawn. They are a complex of various strands, and the pace and nature of the development differ widely in different industries. The two roads of which Marx speaks do not remain distinct for the whole of their course, but often merge for a distance and in places intersect. As is specially characteristic of periods of transition, interests and loyalties are curiously mixed and social alignments change quickly. Yet, despite this complexity, certain broad tendencies stand out in clear relief : tendencies which represent a growing dominance of capital over production. In existing industries this development took the form which has been so fully elucidated by Unwin : namely, the growing dominance of a purely mercantile element over the mass of the craftsmen and the subordination of the latter to the former. In certain cases, an organization that was already very largely composed of a purely trading element (such as the Drapers or Haberdashers), and monopolized the wholesale trade in some finished commodity, brought the organizations of crafts-men under its control, or even absorbed them, while at the same time beginning to put out work to craftsmen in the countryside, where it was free from the regulations of the town craft gilds. In other cases, as with the Clothworkers, a mercantile element, constituting the Livery, came to dominate both the gild and the craft element that composed the lower rank in the company, termed the Yeomanry or Bachelors. As a later development, when this craft element had secured its independence from the merchants by incorporation as a new chartered body, as was the case with most of the Stuart corporations, the new company seems generally to have come under the control, in turn, of a small oligarchy consisting of the well-to-do capitalist section. At the same time in a number of new industries such as copper, brass and ordnance, paper and powder-making, alum and soap, and also in mining and in smelting, the technique of production was sufficiently transformed as a result of recent invention to require an initial capital that was quite beyond the capacity of the ordinary craftsman. In consequence, enterprises were here being launched by promoters on a partnership or joint-stock basis, and hired labour was beginning to be employed by them on a considerable scale.

Similarly, agriculture in the sixteenth century was under-going an important, if partial, transformation. It was a century, on the one hand, of extensive investment by city merchants in the purchase of manors ; and while most of this appears

THE RISE OF INDUSTRIAL CAPITAL

to have been either speculative in intention or with the object
of drawing rents from leases rather than of enjoying the profits
of farming the land, instances were not altogether uncommon
of capital being sunk in improvements and of the estate being
worked with hired labour as a capitalist farm. This was
particularly the case where land was used for pasture, and the
times saw many persons of substance who had become large-
scale graziers of sheep for the profitable wool trade. These
included some of the older squires who had been prompted by
the economic difficulties of the fifteenth century to improve the
demesne and to enclose the commons. At any rate the enclosure
of land into consolidated farms or holdings, about which there
was so much contemporary clamour, placed agriculture on a
new basis, even if the estate was leased out to tenants and its
new owner was no more than a rent-receiver. The victim of
the enclosure was generally the smaller cultivator, who now
dispossessed was doomed to swell the ranks of the rural proletariat
or semi-proletariat, gaining employment as a hired labourer if he
was lucky and being hunted by the cruelties of the Tudor Poor
Law if he was not. As Professor Tawney tersely comments,
" Villeinage ceases, the Poor Law begins ". On the other hand,
this century saw a considerable growth of independent peasant
farming by tenants who rented land as enclosed holdings outside
the open-field system. Among these there developed (as we
have seen in an earlier chapter) an important section of richer
peasants or yeomen,[1] who as they prospered added field to field,
by lease or purchase, perhaps became usurers (along with squire
and parson and local maltster and corn-dealer) to their poorer
neighbours, and grew by the end of the century into considerable farmers who relied on the hire of wage-labour, recruited
from the victims of enclosures or from the poorer cottagers.
It was by this class of rising yeomen farmers that most of the
improvements in methods of cultivation seem to have been
pioneered. Professor Tawney has told us that by the beginning
of the sixteenth century " small demesne tenancies had already
disappeared from many manors, even if they had ever existed on
them, and the normal method of using the demesne was to lease
it to a single large farmer, or at any rate to not more than three
or four ", while " the growth of large farms had proceeded so

---

[1] The word yeoman meant legally a 40/- freeholder. But it was popularly used
for any well-to-do farmer : as a contemporary definition has it, for " middle people
of a condition between gentlemen and cottagers or peasants ". (Cf. Mildred Camp-
bell, *The English Yeoman*, 22 seq.)

far by the middle of the sixteenth century that in parts of the country the area held by the farmer was about equal to that held by all the other tenants ", and in a sample of sixty-seven farms on fifty-two manors in Wiltshire and Norfolk and certain other counties " rather more than half have an area exceeding 200 acres and the area of rather more than a quarter exceeds 350 acres ".[1]   *(cf. landlord — entrepreneurs)*

The dividing line cannot, of course, be sharply drawn either between yeoman farmer of moderate means or handicraft small master and the *parvenu* capitalist employer or between the older mercantile monopolists of the fifteenth century and the later merchant-manufacturer and merchant-employer of the six-teenth and seventeenth centuries.   It is in each case a matter of quantitative growth which is at a certain stage sufficient to involve a qualitative change : in the former a growth in the resources of the small man sufficient to cause him to place greater reliance on the results of hired labour than on the work of himself and his family, and in his calculations to relate the gains of his enterprise to his capital rather than to his own exertions ; in the latter, a gradual shift of attention away from purely speculative gains, based on price-differences as the trader already finds them, towards the profit to be made by reducing the cost of purchase, which involved some measure of control over production.   To the first of these tendencies—the birth of a capitalist class from the ranks of production itself—the rapid price-changes of the sixteenth century, with their consequent depression of real wages and " profit inflation ", contributed in no small measure ; to which no doubt must be added substantial gains from usury at the expense of their poorer brethren.   The second tendency—the penetration of production by merchant-capital from outside—may well have been encour-aged by growing competition in existing markets, in consequence of the growing wealth and numbers of the trading bourgeoisie, tending to narrow the opportunities for purely speculative gains and to bring a closer approximation to the " perfect markets " of a later age.   This influence can hardly as yet have been a very strong one and probably operated little if at all in the sphere of export, where both expanding and highly protected markets were still sufficiently abundant (relatively to those privileged to enjoy them) to furnish lavish profits from exchange, and State policy imposed barriers enough between the market of purchase

---

[1] *Agrarian Problem in the Sixteenth Century*, 210–13.

and the market of sale. But in the sphere of internal trade, despite an expansion of the home market, the position must have been appreciably different ; and the dividing-line between the older group of merchant capital and the new very largely lay between those merchants of an older generation who had secured a dominating position in the export trades and those who, coming later into the field, found themselves shut out from the coveted and closely guarded realm of export and were constrained to confine their activities to wholesale trade within the national boundaries.

Even the older mercantile monopolies were not, of course, without their influence on the rate of exchange which prevailed between themselves and the producers in the local markets with which they traded. In other words, there probably was always here some element of exploitation of the producer. To the extent that the export trade in wool or in cloth was confined in the hands of a few, and new entrants were excluded by the restrictions against "interlopers", competition in the purchase of wool was reduced ; and this tended to make the price at which wool or cloth could be bought from grazier or craftsman in the local market lower than would have been the case if the number of buyers for export had been unrestricted. We have noticed, for example, at a quite early date the export mercantile interest upholding, and the sheep-grazing interests opposing, restrictions which precluded foreigners from coming into the country and buying wool direct in local markets ; while at the end of the sixteenth century we hear of London merchants trying to compel Norwich drapers to bring their cloth to Blackwell Hall in London for sale instead of selling it direct to foreign merchants.[1] We have seen that the essential purpose of gild monopoly had always been to create as far as possible a situation of excess supply in the market of purchase and of excess demand in the market of sale by maintaining a privileged bottleneck in between ;[2] and

[1] Unwin, *op. cit.*, 101.

[2] It might seem that, if the wholesale merchants had possessed sufficient resources, the mere competition among themselves, even though their number was limited, should have sufficed to establish "normal" competitive prices in the markets of purchase and sale. Actually, however, the demand of each buyer was probably limited fairly drastically by the liquid resources available to him at any one time (cf. the references to the continual cash difficulties of the wool merchants who bought from the Cotswold growers and sold to the Staplers in Postan and Power, *Studies in Eng. Trade in the Fifteenth Century*, 62, etc. ; also *Cely Papers*, xii–xv and xli, and for an example of barter transactions with cloth which may possibly have been due to this circumstance, cf. G. D. Ramsay, *The Wiltshire Woollen Industry*, 23). Moreover, with wholesale dealings confined to a close fraternity, customary agreements about poaching on private markets and price-cutting no doubt restricted price-competition among

this fundamental principle of the policies of the Gild and of the Staple the companies of export merchants were applying on a national scale. But this policy acquired a number of new, and significantly new, features when deliberate measures began to be taken to multiply the number of competitors among producers, or to exert direct pressure upon them with the object of developing new and cheaper sources of supply. The chief form that such attempts to cheapen supply assumed was that of establishing a private relationship of dependence between a private *clientèle* of craftsmen and a merchant employer who " put out " work for them to do. Supply could then be cheapened both by lowering the remuneration that the craftsman was willing to accept for his work and also by encouraging a better organization of the work (e.g. by an improved division of labour among the crafts). The dividing line between this and the " urban colonialism " of an earlier date cannot, of course, be drawn at all sharply. Both attempted to cheapen supplies by increasing the producers' dependence on one source of demand for their product as well as by widening the area from which supplies were compelled to flow towards a particular market. The difference consisted in the degree of control that the merchant-buyer exercised over the producer, and the extent to which such control influenced the number of producers, their methods of production and their location. When this control had reached a certain point, it began to alter the character of production itself : the merchant-manufacturer no longer simply battened on the existing mode of production and tightened the economic pressure on the producers, but by changing the mode of production increased its inherent productivity. It is here that the real qualitative change appears. While the growing interest shown by sections of merchant capital in controlling production—in developing what may be termed a deliberately contrived system of " exploitation through trade "—prepared the way for this final outcome, and may in a few cases have reached it, this final stage generally seems, as Marx pointed out, to have been associated with the rise from the ranks of the producers themselves of a capitalist element, half-manufacturer,

them pretty severely ; in the case of foreign trading companies such as the Merchant Adventurers and Merchants of the Staple there was a limitation of sales through a quota or " stint " and through control of shipping ; and there is evidence that in some cases the Gilds and Companies actually regulated prices (cf. Lipson, *op. cit.*, vol. I, 337–8, and vol. II, 224–5, 233, 237–9, 342 ; E. E. Rich, *The Ordinance Book of the Merchants of the Staple*, 90, 92, 149–52 ; W. E. Lingelbach, *The Merchant Adventurers of England*, 67–76, 90–8, and above, p. 116).

half-merchant, which began to subordinate and to organize those very ranks from which it had so recently risen.

The first stage of this transition—the turning of sections of merchant capital towards an increasingly intimate control over production—seems to have been occurring on an extensive scale in the textile, leather and smaller metal trades in the sixteenth century, when the larger merchants at the head of such companies as the Haberdashers, Drapers, Clothworkers and Leather-sellers started to encourage the establishment of craftsmen in the suburbs and the countryside. Since this constituted a challenge to gild restrictions which limited the number of craftsmen, the question of the apprenticeship regulations and their enforcement became everywhere a pivotal point of conflict between the mass of the craftsmen and their new masters. In many cases the merchant employers sought to subordinate the urban craft organizations to themselves, so that the enforcement of the craft restrictions was relaxed or even lapsed. In the case of the Girdlers' Company (to take a slightly later example) in the early seventeenth century we find the craftsmen of the company lodging complaints with the Lord Mayor and Aldermen of the City of London " that there was noe execution of the ordinances of this Company touching Girdling, whereby the poore artizans were undone ", including the ordinances touching those who " set on worke such as had not served 7 years at the art and also for setting foreigners and maids on worke ", and " that many Girdlers did exceed in taking of apprentices above their number, that many Girdlers set on worke forreyners, women and maids ". In this case for a time a not very stable compromise seems to have been reached whereby the artisan element shared in the Right of Search by which the regulations were enforced. But in 1633 we meet the charge that " of late divers merchants, silkmen and other trades being come into the Company, and bearing the chiefe offices thereof had put down the yeomanry and appropriated to themselves sole government of the Company, and . . . had neglected the suppression of abuses ".[1] Fairly widely attempts were made to prevent producers from selling their wares to rival buyers ; and sometimes the poorer craftsman was supplied by the merchant with his raw materials on a credit basis, so that the tie of indebtedness was added to his already restricted freedom of sale. At this

[1] W. Durnville Smythe, *A Historical Account of the Worshipful Company of Girdlers of London*, 84, 88, 90–2.

stage little change seems to have been effected in the methods of production themselves, except perhaps at the finishing end of the cloth trade, and still less change in the technique of production. The progressive rôle of the merchant manufacturer was here limited to *extending* handicraft production and breaking down the limits imposed by the traditional urban monopoly.

Even as early as the fifteenth century evidence of the rise of merchant-employers in the cloth industry is to be found in complaints that work was being put out to craftsmen who dwelt outside the town boundaries and hence were beyond the jurisdiction of the craft gilds with their limitation of apprentices and control of entry to the industry. We find a complaint of this kind made by Northampton in 1464 ; and we find Norwich and other cloth centres forbidding any burgess to employ weavers who dwelt outside the city boundaries. Whether the offenders were large London merchants or local cloth traders is not clear. But in face of new complaints from various towns in the sixteenth century, legislation was passed to prohibit the carrying on of the craft of weaving and clothmaking outside the traditional urban centres : legislation which seems, however, to have had no more than a temporary effect in stemming the rise of the country industry. In face of the complaints of Worcester that its prosperity was being ruined by the competition of country craftsmen, an Act was passed in 1534 to provide that no cloth should be made in the county of Worcestershire outside the boundaries of five principal towns, and by the Weavers' Act of 1555 this principle was extended to other parts of the kingdom by a limitation on any weaving and clothmaking and " the engrossing of looms " outside " a city, borough, town corporate or market town or else in such a place or places where such cloths have been used to be commonly made by the space of ten years ".[1] Further, the Act of Artificers of 1563 prohibited any from undertaking the art of weaving unless he had been apprenticed and any from being apprenticed unless he was the son of a £3 freeholder, " thus barring the access to the industry of fully three-quarters of the rural population ".[2]

But the clearest evidence of a general movement towards the subordination of craftsmen by a mercantile element is afforded

---

[1] Cf. Lipson, *op. cit.*, 487, 502–6 ; Froude, *History of England*, vol. I, 58. Froude spoke of this Act as shining " like a fair gleam of humanity in the midst of the smoke of the Smithfield fires ".
[2] *Studies in Econ. History : Papers of George Unwin*, 187.

by the development among the twelve great Livery Companies of London. Half of these had been composed purely of traders from the outset (like the Mercers and Grocers) ; and these generally continued to confine their activities to wholesale or to export trade. But those that originally had been handicraft organizations or contained a handicraft element came to be dominated by a trading minority which was using its powers to subordinate the craftsmen by the early decades of the sixteenth century. This occurred in the case of the Goldsmiths, the Haberdashers (which after absorbing the cappers and the hatter merchants assumed the title of the Merchant Haberdashers), the Merchant Taylors, the Skinners and the Clothworkers. In the case of the Girdlers we have cited a somewhat later example of the same tendency. Often the appearance of an exclusively trading element in a gild found expression in the tendency for leading members to acquire membership of kindred organizations, since this provided a means of evading the restrictions of their own gilds concerning the area of purchase and sale ; and sometimes this interlocking of interests between the trading element of kindred companies resulted in amalgamation. The Clothworkers' Company, for example, originated in an amalgamation between the fullers and shearmen, well-to-do members of which seem to have made a habit of taking up membership in the Drapers' Company, as did also weavers and dyers.[1] In such cases the upper rank of the Company, the Livery, came to be composed almost exclusively of the commercial element, and the governing body, the Wardens and Court of Assistants, were drawn from the Livery. Unwin remarks that " as considerable expense was involved in each stage of promotion [to the freedom, to the Livery and to the governing body], all but the wealthiest members were permanently excluded from office ", with the result that " the majority of freemen gradually lost all share in the annual choice of the four wardens ".[2] The historian of the Drapers' Company states that " the craftsmen proper, under the name of Bachelors or Yeomen, fell into a position of depend-

[1] An interesting foreign example of this tendency was the case of Andreas and Jakob Fugger. The chief Gilds in Augsburg were the Weavers' and the Merchants,' which in 1368 obtained a share in the government of the city, previously monopolized by aristocratic families. The father, Hans Fugger, had been a weaver who had also engaged in trade. His two sons were members both of the Weavers' and the Merchants' Gilds, and Jakob was Master of the former even though he had ceased to engage in weaving (cf. R. Ehrenberg, *Capital and Finance in the Age of the Renaissance*, 64).

[2] G. Unwin, *Industrial Organisation in the 16th and 17th Centuries*, 42.

ence ".[1] In the case of the Cutlers' Company, while the Yeomanry consisted of working cutlers, the Livery was " composed entirely of masters or of persons unconnected with the trade ". " None but the more substantial freemen could afford to enter the Clothing, for, in addition to the fees to the Company, Clerk and Beadle, the new Liveryman was expected to entertain the Court of the Company at a tavern, either wholly or in part at his own expense." [2] The government of the Merchant Taylors " was placed on a narrower basis " early in the sixteenth century. " Although for legislation affecting all the members a full assembly may still be needed, we find no trace of any such meeting being summoned, and the Master, instead of yielding up his receipts and payments after the expiration of his year of office openly in the common hall before the whole of the Fraternity, had only to do so to the Court of Assistants or to auditors appointed by the Court." [3] At about the same time there appears a division of the Gild into a Merchant Company and a Yeoman Company consisting of craftsmen. Since the records of the latter have been lost, the precise relationship between it and the parent company is not clear, but the relationship was presumably one of subordination rather than of complete independence.[4] And while a mercantile oligarchy controlled the Livery Companies, the leading Livery Companies in turn controlled the government of the City of London. " How completely the government of the City was now in the hands of the greater gilds is shown by the fact that most of the Aldermen and Sheriffs and all the Mayors for many years were members of one of the Greater Livery Companies. Thus by the close of the fifteenth century the Gild organization and that of the City had become amalgamated."[5]

At the same time, there is evidence that the mercantile oligarchy alike of the Merchant Taylors, the Clothworkers, the Drapers and the Haberdashers began to organize the domestic industry in the countryside. In doing so they were apt to come into rivalry with the clothiers and drapers of a provincial town : for example, the provincial clothiers who in 1604 complained to the House of Commons at " the engrossing and restraint of

---

[1] A. H. Johnson, *History of the Company of Drapers of London*, vol. I, 23, also 148–51. Cf. also Lipson, *Econ. History*, vol. I, 378–81 ; Cunningham, *Growth* (Middle Ages, I), 513 ; Salzmann, *Industries in the Middle Ages*, 177–8.
[2] C. Welch, *History of the Cutlers' Company of London*, vol. II, 79, 86–7.
[3] C. M. Clode, *Early History of the Guild of Merchant Tailors*, Part I, 153.
[4] *Ibid.*, 61 seq.   [5] A. H. Johnson, *op. cit.*, vol. I, 50–1.

trade by the rich merchants of London as being to the undoing
or great hindrance of all the rest ", or the Shrewsbury Drapers,
who " set on work above six hundred Persons of the Art or
Science of Shearmen or Frizers " within that town, and were for
a time successful in securing a prohibition on London merchants
sending agents into Wales to buy up Welsh white cloth that
would otherwise have flowed to the Shrewsbury market to supply
their own local cloth-finishing industry.[1] Like the Shrewsbury
Drapers, these local clothiers or cloth finishers were quite
commonly engaged in the employment of town craftsmen ; in
which case their interest lay in enforcing, and if need be reviving,
the local gild ordinances, and securing legislative sanction for
them, as under the 1555 Act, in order to stem the competition
of the country industry financed by larger capital from London.
To this extent the influence of these local capitalists was reactionary ; tending as they did to hold in check the spread of the new
domestic industry, and to limit the extension of the division of
labour between sections of the trade that seems often to have
gone with it.   In yet other cases the local clothiers seem at times
to have themselves become merchant employers of craftsmen
outside the town boundaries in the neighbouring countryside,
like the wealthy clothiers of Suffolk and Essex, of whom we hear
a weavers' complaint in 1539 that " the rich men, the clothiers,
be concluded and agreed among themselves to hold and pay one
price for weaving cloths ", or the Wiltshire clothiers who seem
to have successfully evaded the Act of 1555 and freely increased
the number of looms in the countryside.[2]   In this rivalry between
provinces and metropolis, between the smaller and the larger
capital, we have an important cross-current of economic conflict.
To some extent it resembles the rivalry between large and small
capitals, between metropolis and provinces, that later became an
important influence inside the Parliamentarian camp at the
time of the Commonwealth.   But between the earlier and the

---

[1] *Per contra*, the Welsh weavers were in favour of free trade and opposed to restrictions in favour of the Shrewsbury market.   At the time of the anti-monopolies agitation in the 1620's Parliament passed a Free Trade in Welsh Cloth Bill, in favour
of the London merchants. (Cf. A. H. Dodd in *Economica*, June, 1929.)   Another
example is that of the Coventry Drapers who, after a successful struggle with the
Dyers for hegemony, proceeded to subordinate both shearmen and weavers.   They
succeeded in prohibiting the former from taking employment or buying cloth from
" foreign " drapers ; but a complaint from the weavers that drapers and dyers
were themselves buying undyed Gloucester cloth was turned down by the town
authorities.   The Mayor who was a draper apparently rebuked the weavers' spokes-
man and " schooled the knave a little ". (M. D. Harris, *Hist. of Drapers Coy. of
Coventry*, 7-13, 21.)
[2] G. D. Ramsay, *The Wiltshire Woollen Industry*, 58-9.

later period there was an important difference. During the Tudor and early Stuart period the craft interest in the provincial gilds threw its weight against the extension of manufacture, and in particular of the rival country industry, while the mercantile interests, especially of London, had a contrary influence ; and the fact that Tudor and Stuart legislation showed a special regard for the restraining influence of the gilds was evidently a contributory factor in the gathering opposition of powerful merchant interests to the Stuart régime in the 1620's. By the middle of the seventeenth century, however, a section of the crafts themselves had become interested in the extension of industry and in evasion of the traditional gild restrictions. Even among the provincial organizers of country industry, whether they were richer craftsmen or members of local trading gilds, there were significant lines of division between large capitals and small : between the rich clothiers who bought direct from the wool-growers and the poorer clothier who had no alternative but to buy his wool from the wool stapler. While, however, it was in the cloth industry, England's leading industry of the time, that such tendencies were most strongly marked, they were not confined to this trade. The emergence of a similar class of merchant-employers is also to be seen at this time in the case of the Leathersellers, the Cordwainers (who subordinated the craftsmen cobblers), the Cutlers (who had already become employers of the bladesmiths and sheathers when they secured incorporation in 1415), the Pewterers, the Blacksmiths and the Ironmongers.[1]

The opening of the seventeenth century witnessed the beginnings of an important shift in the centre of gravity : the rising predominance of a class of merchant-employers from the ranks of the craftsmen themselves among the Yeomanry of the large companies—the process that Marx described as " the really revolutionary way ". The details of this process are far from clear, and there is little evidence that bears directly upon it. But the fact that this was the case seems to be the only explanation of events that were occurring at this time in the Livery Companies. The merchant oligarchy that formed the Livery in some cases appear to have transferred their activities exclusively to trade, their growing wealth and influence in the course of time presumably securing for them a foothold within the privileged ranks of the export trade, or at least as commission-agents on its fringe.

[1] Cf. G. Unwin, op. cit., 26–46.

Even where this was not so, their activities in relation to producers apparently became increasingly restrictive, tending to revert to the older emphasis of forming a close ring among themselves and excluding all outsiders from the trade rather than developing and extending the handicraft industry throughout the country, as they had shown signs of doing in the sixteenth century. The rise among the craftsmen of a richer, capitalist element who wished to invest their capital in the employment of other craftsmen and themselves to assume the rôle of merchant-employers represented a challenge to the close corporation of the older mercantile element. The control of the latter was exercised through their dominance over the company which possessed (by virtue of its charter) the exclusive right to engage in a particular branch of production.[1] The challenge to it, accordingly, took two forms : the struggle of the Yeomanry (dominated as this tended in turn to be by the richer master-craftsmen) for a share in the government of the Company, and in a number of cases the attempt to secure independence and a new status of their own by incorporation as a separate company. The latter was the basis of the new Stuart corporations, formed from the craft elements among some of the old Livery Companies : corporations which, as Unwin has shown, so quickly became subservient to a capitalist element among them, to whom the mass of the craftsmen were subordinated as a semi-proletarian class.

This is what occurred in the case of the Glovers' Company which (with the aid of Court influence to secure its incorporation) was formed by the leatherworkers who had previously been subordinated to the Leathersellers. A similar, but for some time less successful, attempt to secure their freedom was made by the feltmakers who were subordinated to the Haberdashers, by the pinmakers who had previously belonged to the Girdlers' Company, by the Clockworkers who separated from the Blacksmiths, and by the Silkmen who eventually secured their independence from the Weavers' Company. In a petition to James I in 1619 the leatherworkers complain against the Leathersellers that " once they put their griping hands betwixt the Grower and the Merchant and any of the said Trades, they never part with the commodities they buy till they

[1] In London, in contrast to what was apparently the case in other towns, any citizen (i.e. freeman) of the city had the right to engage in any branch of wholesale trade. But this freedom did not apply to crafts and to craftsmen.

sell them at their owne pitched rates without either regard or
care whether the workeman be able to make his money thereof
or no ".   Later they complain of the extent to which the ruling
group of the company had " long since changed to those that
know not leather, for generally the Master and Wardens and
Body . . . are men of other trades as braziers, hosiers, etc.".
At the time of the Commonwealth the working tailors of the
Merchant Taylors' Company refer in a petition to " divers rich
men of our trade " who " by taking over great multitudes of
Apprentices doe weaken the poorer sort of us " and show " an
intencion in the Company to exclude the Taylors members of
the Society from all office and place of auditt " ; the rank and
file of the Printers' Company declare that they are made " per-
petuall bondmen to serve some few of the rich all their lives upon
such conditions and for such hire and at such times as the Masters
think fit ", and many apprentices " after their Apprenticeship,
like the petitioners become for ever more servile than before " ;
and weavers allege that the governors of their company now
" gain by intruders " and have consequently dismissed the
officials of the Yeomanry whose function it was to search for
" intruders ". The feltmakers, who made an unsuccessful attempt
in the early years of James I to found a joint-stock company to
repair their deficiency in capital, seem to have been mainly
composed of the middle and smaller craftsmen.   In a manifesto
of the later sixteenth century they stated that, whereas " the
richest feltmakers do somewhat hold themselves contented for
that they with ready money and part credit do buy much (raw
material) and so have the choise and best ", the poorer craftsmen,
who have to be content with inferior wool at the price of the
best, " are daily and lamentably undone and are grown to such
poverty as they dare not show their faces ", and are indebted
to merchants who cut off their wool supplies altogether if they
show any tendency to complain.   In other words, the complaint
is that of small men against the inferior bargaining position to
which their lack of capital condemns them.   At another time
they complain of merchant haberdashers who " do kepe greate
numbers of apprentices and instructe wenches in their arte . . .
and do sell great quantity of wares unto chapmen altogether
untrymmed, whereby they saie a multitude might be sette on
work and relieved ".   But when finally under the Commonwealth the feltmakers succeeded in securing their charter of
incorporation, it is clearly the richer among them who are in

the forefront of the proposal. Reference is made to the fact that " many of the trade employ ten, twenty or thirty persons and upwards in picking and carding of wool and preparing it for use, besides journeymen and apprentices ", while the haberdashers in opposing the new company charge the latter with looking " not at all at the preservation of their poore members, but at the upholding of their better sorte ". As Unwin remarks, it is a good illustration of " the way in which the organizations set up to defend the small master against one kind of capitalist became the instrument of his subjection to another kind ". A less successful attempt was made by the artisan skinners to obtain certain rights within the Skinners' Company by " a surreptitious application in 1606 for new letters patent from the Crown without the consent or privity of the master and wardens of the guild ". Although the artisans obtained their charter, the governing body of the company refused to recognize it, and on appeal to the Privy Council managed to secure its cancellation. In the case of the Clothworkers the situation was again different. The mercantile element of the Livery had come by the end of the sixteenth century to be mainly engaged in foreign trade and accordingly less interested in the conditions of manufacture ; which may have partly accounted for the smaller resistance which they showed to the grant of a share of government in the company to the Wardens of the Yeomanry : a compromise that was finally reached during the Commonwealth. But this concession did not mean, as one might suppose, that the mass of small craftsmen were now to exercise a part-control in the administration of the company. On the contrary, it seems clear that by this time it was the interests of the richer craftsmen, themselves employing smaller craftsmen on a considerable scale, who were represented in the government of the Yeomanry; seeing that, as Unwin points out, " the wardens of the yeomanry were not elected by the rank and file of small masters and journeymen, (but) were nominated from above by the Court of Assistants out of the leading manufacturers ", and when a demand for universal suffrage was raised, the wardens of the Yeomanry in fact opposed it. Moreover, while these larger employers who had come to dominate the Yeomanry apparently tried to ignore the traditional apprenticeship regulations, in order to multiply the number of craftsmen employable by them, the smaller craftsmen, whose status was being undermined by this tendency, seem to have now made common cause with the mercantile element of the

Livery to uphold the old regulations : that very mercantile element to which large and small craftsmen alike had earlier stood opposed in the controversy over the export of undyed cloth in which the mercantile bigwigs of the Clothworkers had had a considerable interest.[1]

In addition to the " putting-out ", or *Verlag*-system, organized by merchant-manufacturers, there were also a few examples of factories owned by capitalists who employed workers directly on a wage-basis. But at this time these examples were rare in the textile trades, where the instruments of production were not yet sufficiently complex, outside the finishing end of the trade, to provide a technical basis for factory production. The instruments used were still within the competence of a craftsman of modest means ; they could be conveniently installed in a shed or a garret ; and since the work was highly individualized, the only difference between manufactory and domestic production was that in the former a number of looms were set up side by side in the same building instead of being scattered in the workers' homes. The location of production was concentrated without any change in the character of the productive process. There was little opportunity, at this stage, for subdivision of labour within the workshop itself or co-ordinated team work as a result of concentration. On the contrary, if work was given out to craftsmen in their homes the capitalist saved the expense of upkeep involved in a factory and the expenses of supervision. Except for the fulling-mill and the dye-house, factory production in textiles remained exceptional until the latter half of the eighteenth century. Even so, the cases that we find are significant as indicating the existence of considerable capitalists who were imbued with a desire to invest in industry as well as of the beginnings of an industrial proletariat. The best known of these manufactory-capitalists is John Winchcomb, popularly known as Jack of Newbury, who, being the son of a draper and apprenticed to a rich clothier, was farsighted enough to marry his master's widow. If the descriptions of him are true, he employed several hundred weavers, and owned a dye-house and fulling-mill as well.[2] In the same town we hear of Thomas Dolman, who from the accumulated profits of his establishment built Shaw House, costing £10,000. At Bristol there was Thomas Blanket, and in

---

[1] Unwin, *op. cit.*, 126–39, 156–71, 196–210 ; Margaret James, *Social Problems and Policy during the Puritan Revolution*, 205, 211–12, 219 ; J. F. Wadmore, *Some Account of the Skinners' Company*, 20.
[2] Johnson, *op. cit.*, vol. II, 48 ; *V.C.H. Berks*, vol. II, 388.

Wiltshire William Stumpe, the son of a weaver, who rented Malmesbury Abbey and in Oxfordshire Osney Abbey, installed looms and weavers in the empty monastic buildings and boasted that he could employ 2,000 workmen. Even where the cottage system prevailed, the finishing work was often done, at any rate in the West Country, in a large mill owned by the clothier.[1] In fact, this was at times a ground of conflict between the clothiers who had their capital invested in cloth finishing and the " pure " merchant capital of the City of London, which was concerned in cloth export, and hence was as willing to export unfinished as finished cloth, as was witnessed in the contest in 1614 over Alderman Cockayne's project to prohibit the export of cloth in an unfinished state.

But in a number of industries technical developments had already progressed sufficiently far to provide a basis for production of a factory type ; and in these enterprises even larger capitals than those of a Dolman, a Stumpe or a Blanket were concerned. In mining, for example, prior to the sixteenth century a capital of a few pounds usually sufficed to start mining operations on a small scale ; and coal was often worked by husbandmen on their own or on behalf of the lord of the manor. Even when worked by rich ecclesiastical establishments, as was frequently the case, a sum of £50 or £60 was a large amount to sink in drainage operations. But improved drainage early in the sixteenth century, resulting from the invention of improved pumps, encouraged the sinking of mines to greater depth (often to 200 feet), and was responsible for a big development of mining enterprise in the Tyne area. To sink mines at this depth and install pumping apparatus required a considerable capital, and many of the newer mines came to be financed by groups of adventurers, like the partnership of Sir Peter Riddell and others who financed a Warwickshire colliery about 1600 at a cost of £600, or Sir Wm. Blacket, a Newcastle merchant, who is said to have lost £20,000 in an attempt to drain a seam. A capital of £100 or £200 which had been common among Elizabethan adventurers began to be a thing of the past in the seventeenth century. We hear, instead, of more than a score of collieries on the south bank of the Tyne in 1638 producing nearly 20,000 tons a year each, and of one of them as having an annual value of £450, and of Woolaton near Nottingham producing 20,000 tons as early as 1598. We now hear of capitals running into several

[1] *V.C.H. Gloucester*, 2, 158.

thousands being commonly spent on pumping machinery.   Later
in the seventeenth century it was not thought very remarkable
that a sum of between £14,000 and £17,000 should be spent on
reopening the Bedworth Colliery; and between 1560 and 1680
the production of coal throughout the kingdom increased fourteen-
fold.[1]   In lead and silver mining in South Wales we hear of
Sir Hugh Middleton in the early years of James I leasing mines
in Cardiganshire at an annual rental of £400 : mines which in
1609 were said to be clearing a profit of £2,000 a month.   In
the first year of the Long Parliament an entrepreneur named
Thomas Bushell was employing 260 miners in Cardiganshire, and
during the Civil War could afford (from his mining profits
apparently) to lend £40,000 to the King, who had granted him
the valuable Cardiganshire concession.   Thirty years later, after
the Restoration, a company for working the mines in Cardiganshire and Merioneth was founded with a capital of £4,200 in
£100 shares, while in the closing years of the century a veritable
combine known as " Mine Adventure ", owning lead, silver,
copper and coal mines in South Wales, together with a dock
and canal and a smelting works and brick works was en-
deavouring to raise a capital of over £100,000 by public
subscription.[2]
     During Elizabeth's reign the method of saltmaking by dissolv-
ing rock salt came to replace the older method of evaporating
sea-water in pans or boiling liquid from brine pits and springs ;
and on the eve of the Civil War there was a saltworks at Shields
which probably produced as much as 15,000 tons a year, and by
the reign of Charles II saltworks in Cheshire with an output of,
perhaps, 20,000 tons a year.[3]   " During the last sixty years of
the sixteenth century the first paper and gunpowder mills, the
first cannon factories, the first sugar refineries, and the first
considerable saltpetre works were all introduced into the country
from abroad ", the significance of these new industries being that
" in all of them plant was set up involving investments far beyond
the sums which groups of master-craftsmen could muster, even

---

[1] J. U. Nef, *Rise of the Brit. Coal Industry*, vol. I, 8, 19–20, 26–7, 59–60, 378.
" When the enormous new demand for mineral fuel burst upon the Elizabethan
world it was the great landlords, the rich merchants and the courtiers who obtained
concessions.   Few peasants formed working partnerships to open pits without the
support of outside capital.   Where they did they were doomed to fail " (*ibid.*, 414).
[2] D. J. Davies, *Economic History of South Wales prior to 1800*, 71–4, 125–7.   At
various times in the century criminals were asked for and were sent to work in the
lead mines.   See below, p. 233.
[3] Nef, *op. cit.*, 174 seq.

if these artisans were men of some small substance ".[1] Powder-mills driven by water-power appeared in Surrey in the middle of the century ; at Dartford a paper mill was set up, one of the two water-wheels of which cost between £1,000 and £2,000 ; and by 1630 there were ten or more paper mills of a similar kind in various parts of England. In the reign of James I we even find a London brewery with a capital of £10,000.[2] In the iron trade " even in early times the apparatus of ironworks represented a volume of capital that few save landowners could command ".[3] Now we find blast-furnaces, often involving an outlay of several thousand pounds, replacing the older small-scale bloomeries or forges. In the Forest of Dean in 1683 it was estimated that to construct a furnace of up-to-date type and two forges, together with houses for workpeople and other appurtenances, an outlay of £1,000 was necessary ; such a furnace having an output-capacity of 1,200 tons a year. Many of these furnaces in the West Country seem to have been financed by local landowners and gentry. About the same time in the nail-making industry of the West Midlands the appearance of the slitting-mill was creating a class of small capitalists, often from among the ranks of well-to-do yeoman farmers or the more prosperous masters of handicraft nailmaking ; as was also the blade-mill, often driven by water-power, in sword- and dagger-making in the Birmingham district.[4] At the end of the sixteenth century two sister societies, corporations with large capitals, the Mines Royal and the Society of Mineral and Battery Works, were founded, the former to mine lead and copper and precious metals, the latter to manufacture brass. At one time the two companies together are said to have employed 10,000 persons. The wire works at Tintern, owned by the latter company, apparently alone involved a capital of £7,000 and employed 100 workers or more. In 1649 two capitalists spent £6,000 on a wire mill at Esher, which worked on imported Swedish copper. By the end of the seventeenth century a company called the English Copper Company had a capital of nearly £40,000, divided into 700 shares. But already before the Restoration " mining, smelting, brass-making, wire-drawing, and to a certain extent the making of battery goods, were all being carried out on a factory basis, the workers being brought together in comparatively large numbers, and con-

[1] Nef in *Econ. Hist. Review*, vol. V, No. I, 5.
[2] *Ibid.*, 7, 8, 11, 20.
[3] T. S. Ashton, *Iron and Steel in the Industrial Revolution*, 5.
[4] W. H. B. Court, *Rise of the Midland Industries 1600–1838*, 80 seq., 103 seq.

trolled by managers appointed by the shareholders or their farmers ".[1]

But these cases where technique had changed sufficiently to make factory production essential, while they were important as forerunners of things to come, did not at this period carry more than minor weight in the economic life of the country as a whole. In the capital involved as well as in the number of capitalists connected with them and the number of workpeople employed, they clearly remained of less importance than production under the " domestic system " ; while, as we shall see, they were largely captained by aristocratic patentees, whose enterprise was fostered by special grants of privilege from the Crown. Whether it was of equal or less importance than what Marx termed " manufacture "—production in " manufactories " or workshops where work was done, not with power-driven machinery, but with what remained essentially handicraft instruments [2]—is less easy to say. For one thing, some of the capitalist-owned establishments to which we have referred probably deserve to be classed as " manufactories " in the strict sense in which Marx used the term. This certainly applies to the textile workshops of a Jack of Newbury or a Thomas Blanket ; as it explicitly does to some of the textile " manufactories " that were started in Scotland in the middle of the seventeenth century, of which New Mills at Haddington is perhaps the best known.[3] But on the whole it seems evident that in seventeenth-century England the domestic industry, rather than either the factory or the manu-

---

[1] H. Hamilton, *English Brass and Copper Industries to 1800*, 85 ; also 13–17, 27, 60, 244. The average wage at the Tintern works in the sixteenth century seems to have been about 2s. 6d. a week, the minimum diet of a single person at the time being reckoned at about 2s. Both the Mines Royal and the Mineral and Battery Works had the power to impress workmen, and there is evidence of truck payment at some of their works and of female and child labour in their mines. (*Ibid.*, 319–23.) Also cf. Scott, *Joint Stock Companies*, vol. I, 31, 39–58.

[2] Cf. Marx, *Capital*, vol. I, p. 366 seq. Marx here expresses the view that the use of mechanical power need not be the sole or even essential difference between a " machine " and a " tool " and hence between " machinofacture " and " manufacture ". Rather does the crux of the difference lie in taking the tool which operates immediately on the material out of the hands of man and fitting it into a mechanism. But for exploiting these new possibilities at all fully power-driven mechanisms are, of course, necessary. See below, p. 258–9. Mantoux follows Marx in defining a machine as something which " differs from a tool, not so much by the automatic force which keeps it in motion, as by the movements it can perform, the mechanism planned by the engineer's skill enabling it to replace the processes, habits and skill of the hand " (*Industrial Revolution in the 18th Century*, 194).

[3] Cf. *Records of a Scottish Manufactory at New Mills*, ed. W. R. Scott. Reference is here made to a capital equivalent to £5,000 (English) laid out to purchase twenty looms and to employ 233 hands, with a yearly turnover about equal to the capital, and to the purchase of a number of " dwellings ", each capable of holding a broad loom and providing " accommodation beside for spinners " (*ibid.*, xxxiv, lvi, lxxxiv, 31).

facturing workshop, remained the most typical form of production ; and the " manufactory " seems to have been less common at this time in England than it was, for example, in certain areas of France.

The domestic industry of this period, however, was in a crucial respect different from the gild handicraft from which it had descended : in the majority of cases it had become subordinated to the control of capital, and the producing craftsman had lost most of his economic independence of earlier times. References become increasingly common at this time to craftsmen being " employed " or " maintained " by the merchant-manufacturing element, like the statement in a seventeenth-century pamphlet on the wool trade that there existed in England 5,000 clothiers and that " each of these do maintain 250 workmen, the whole will amount to upward of one million ".[1] The craftsman's status was already beginning to approximate to that of a simple wage-earner ; and in this respect the system was much closer to " manufacture " than to the older urban handicrafts, even if both domestic industry and " manufacture " resembled gild industry in the nature of the productive process and of the instruments employed, thereby sharing a common contrast with the factory-production of the industrial revolution.[2] The subordination of production to capital, and the appearance of this class relationship between capitalist and the producer is, therefore, to be regarded as the crucial watershed between the old mode of production and the new, even if the technical changes that we associate with the industrial revolution were needed both to complete the transition and to afford scope for the full maturing of the capitalist mode of production and of the great increase in the productive power of human labour associated with it. Since this subordination of production to capital was characteristic alike of the new domestic system and of " manufacture ", it is already true of early Stuart times that the former, like the latter, had nothing " except the name in common with the old-fashioned domestic industry, the existence of which presupposed independent urban handicrafts.

[1] *Reply to a Paper Intituled Reason for a Limited Exportation of Wool*, Anon.
[2] Cf. Marx : " Manufacture in its strict meaning is hardly to be distinguished in its earliest stages from the handicraft trades of the gilds otherwise than by the greater number of workmen simultaneously employed by one and the same individual capital. . . . An increased number of labourers under the control of one capitalist is the natural starting-point as well of co-operation as of manufacture in general " (*ibid.*, 311, 353).

. . . That old-fashioned industry (had) now been converted into an outside department of the factory, the manufactory or the warehouse." [1] Domestic production and " manufacture " were in most cases closely interlaced at different stages in the same industry, even sometimes with factory-production ; as, for example, the domestic weaver with his employer's fulling-mill or the handicraft nailer in the West Country with the slitting-mill ; and the transition alike of domestic industry into " manufacture " and of the latter into factory-production was a relatively simple one (once the technical conditions favoured the change), and was quite early bridged by a number of intermediate types. We frequently find the two systems mingled together even at the same stage of production : for example, in eighteenth-century Exeter the weaver rented his loom from a capitalist, sometimes working on his master's premises (unlike the spinner, who worked at home), and in the nearby Culm Valley the weaver's " independence had gone more completely, and he was compelled to live in the square of houses near the master's, and to work in the open court formed within this square ".[2] Sometimes, especially in the eighteenth century, we find a capitalist clothier simultaneously employing workers in their homes and workers assembled together in one place on looms that he had set up in a single workshop.[3]

Capitalist domestic industry, moreover, not only cleared the way for, but itself achieved, an appreciable change in the process of production ; and the growing hegemony of capital over industry at this period was very far from being merely a parasitic growth. Successive stages of production (e.g. the stages of spinning, weaving, fulling and dyeing in clothmaking) were now more closely organized as a unity, with the result that, not only was the division of labour extended between successive stages of production, or between workers engaged on a variety of elements to be assembled into a finished product,[4] but time could be saved in the passing of material from one stage to another, and a more balanced, because more integrated,

---

[1] Cf. Marx, vol. I, 464–5.
[2] W. G. Hoskins, *Industry, Trade and People in Exeter, 1688–1800*, 55.
[3] Cf. the cases, cited by Heaton, of James Walker of Wortley who employed twenty-one looms of which eleven were in his own loom-shop and the rest in the houses of weavers, and Atkinson of Huddersfield who had seventeen looms in one room and also employed weavers in their homes (*op. cit.*, 296).
[4] Marx, *op. cit.*, 327 seq. Marx refers to these two types of division of labour under the terms " heterogeneous " and " serial " manufacture. By the first half of the eighteenth century the worsted industry consisted of forty processes, each a specialized trade.

process could be secured. The potential importance of this can be gauged from the frequency of complaints in the textile industry about the results of lack of co-ordination between different stages, which involved the weaver especially in periodic waste of time waiting for work owing to absence of raw material.[1] Moreover, the capitalist clothier in woollen or worsted who controlled the product from raw wool to dyeing was in a better position to secure a uniform quality of spinning in preparation for weaving the particular grade of cloth he required ; whereas in cases where spinning was done by independent workers who were not directly employed by a clothier or his agents, complaints of poor and variable quality were common. Sometimes this consideration worked in favour of the " manufactory " rather than the putting out of work, and seems in fact to have been the chief technical advantage of the former system at this period ; production in a single workshop enabling a much closer super-vision of the work in process than was possible with the domestic system, even when the workers under the latter were dependent employées of a master-clothier. At the same time, the capitalist merchant-manufacturer had an increasingly close interest in promoting improvements in the instruments and methods of production : improvements which the craftsman's lack of capital as well as the force of gild custom would otherwise have frustrated. The very division of labour which is specially characteristic of this period prepared the ground from which mechanical invention could eventually spring. Division of labour itself begets a " differentiation of the instruments of labour—a differentiation whereby implements of a given sort acquire fixed shapes, adapted to each particular application ; . . . simplifies, improves and multiplies the implements of labour by adapting them to the exclusively special functions of each detail labourer. It thus creates at the same time one of the material conditions for the existence of machinery, which consists of a combination of simple instruments." [2]

The hosiery trade and the small metal trades afford two examples of transitional forms which are evidence of the close continuity between the capitalist domestic system and the manufactory and between both of these and factory production. One example belongs to the seventeenth and the other to the early eighteenth century. In the reign of Queen Elizabeth William Lee, a Nottinghamshire curate, "seeing a woman knit invented

[1] Cf. Lipson, op. cit., vol. II, 47–8.   [2] Marx, op. cit., 333.

a loom to knit ". The resulting loom or knitting-frame was, however, more complicated and more revolutionary in character than this simple description of the act of invention might imply ; and being a complicated mechanism it was too costly for at any rate a poorer craftsman to purchase and possess. In the words of a Petition of 1655, it involved " nothing different from the common way of knitting, but only in the numbers of needles, at an instant working in this, more than in the other, by a hundred for one, set into an Engine or Frame, composed of above 2,000 pieces of Smiths', Joyners' and Turners' worke ".[1] Apparently the frame was capable of doing 1,000 to 1,500 stitches a minute, compared with about 100 stitches a minute in hand-knitting. There is a mention of frames being made to the order of an Italian merchant at a price of £80 apiece in the money of the time. Evidently it was rarely possible for any but the most prosperous among the master craftsmen of the older industry to invest in this new instrument ; and the introduction of the new method does not seem to have been at all common until in 1657 during the Commonwealth a group of capitalists (many of them apparently merchant hosiers) secured incorporation for themselves as the Framework Knitters Company.[2] This Company appears to have been formed mainly on the initiative of fairly considerable merchants, and its constitution was such (at any rate after 1663) as to place control in the hands of " a close self-perpetuating oligarchy of officials ". One of its chief functions was to control the hiring out of frames to domestic craftsmen ; and although the domestic system continued despite the new machine, it continued on the basis of the ownership of the instruments of production by capitalists and the hire of these instruments to the individual producer. Between 1660 and 1727 the number of frames in the country is said to have grown from 600 to 8,000, mainly under the stimulus of a growing export-demand, especially from France. The frames were apparently leased out to workmen at rents equivalent to ten years' purchase or less ; and the larger capitalists used their influence over the Company to achieve a relaxation of apprenticeship restrictions in order to

---

[1] *Representation of the Promoters and Inventers of the Art, Mystery or Trade of Framework Knitting to the Lord Protector for Incorporation*, 1655. Another contemporary document, *The Case of the Framework Knitters*, speaks of the frame as " a most curious and complicated piece of mechanism, consisting of near 3,000 members or Pieces ", and refers to " 100,000 families and 10,000 frames employed in the Manufacture ".

[2] After the Restoration the company was reincorporated as the Worshipful Company of Framework Knitters in 1663. Apparently, even prior to 1657 a nucleus of such a company had been in operation for some years.

secure a plentiful supply of cheap labour.[1] In the latter part
of the eighteenth century a House of Commons Committee
(in 1779) reported on the " shameless exactions on the workmen
by their masters " in this trade. As a result of the employers'
monopoly extortionate frame-rents were being charged, so that
the net wage was no more than 6s. to 8s. weekly. It appears
that a workman who happened to own a frame for himself was
generally boycotted and starved of work until he agreed to rent
a frame from a member of the Company.

The second example has in many respects a modern flavour.
At the end of the seventeenth century a former ironmonger from
Greenwich, by name Ambrose Crowley, set up on the banks of
the Derwent a small industrial town, which was half-way between
a manufactory and a centre of domestic industry, engaged in
the production of nails, locks, bolts, chisels, spades and other tools.
In what had previously been a small village there was soon an
industrial community of some 1,500 inhabitants. The various
families lived and worked in their own houses, although these
were owned and rented by Crowley, as were also the tools and
materials with which the craftsmen worked. Each master-
workman had first to deposit " a bond for a considerable
amount ", which gave him the right to hold a workshop, where
he laboured with his family, probably employing in addition a
journeyman or two and an apprentice. Payment was made
for the work done on a piece-rate basis after a deduction for the
value of the materials supplied. The establishment even had
a kind of Whitley Council to deal with disputes : a tribunal
composed of two arbitrators appointed by Crowley and two by
the master-workmen, and presided over by the chaplain.
Knighted in 1706, Sir Ambrose Crowley later became M.P. for
Andover, by which time he could boast a fortune of £200,000.[2]
It is not unlikely that a similar type of organization was characteristic of other manufactories of the period : for example, the
New Mills in Scotland, in the records of which reference is made
to purchase by the management of a number of " dwellings " in
which to install looms ; a colony of linen weavers started in the
eighteenth century by a Captain Urquhart at Farres in Scotland ;

---

[1] Cf. J. D. Chambers in *Economica*, Nov. 1929 ; A. P. Usher, *History of Mechanical
Invention*, 240–5 ; W. Felkin, *History of Machine-wrought Hosiery and Lace*, 23 seq.
[2] *V.C.H. Durham*, vol. II, 381–7. On his death the business passed to his son, John
Ambrose, and at the end of the eighteenth century to his granddaughter. As for
the men, " Crowley's Crew ", as they were called, were at first Tories but in the
nineteenth century became keen Chartists.

and the cottages built at Newark in Northamptonshire by a
firm of clothiers to house a hundred weavers.[1] Both the sword
manufactory at Newcastle of which contemporary records
speak and the more famous Carron Iron Works probably
had a form of organization not very dissimilar from Crowley's
town.[2]

In the case of the Framework Knitters it was the growing
complexity and expense of the instruments of production that
was responsible for the craftsman's increasing dependence, as
it was also for the early transition to factory-production in copper
and brass and in branches of the iron trade. But in other cases
where fixed capital still played a relatively unimportant rôle,
it has been suggested that the governing reason for the dominance
of domestic industry by capital, where this occurred, was the
cost and difficulty for the craftsman of acquiring his raw material.
Thus in Yorkshire where local wool supplies were accessible, at
any rate for the coarser cloths, the weaver often retained a good
deal of independence, buying his wool supplies in the local market
and selling his cloth to merchants (commonly in the eighteenth
century from stands in the cloth halls of Halifax, Wakefield or
Leeds).[3] On the other hand, in cotton spinning and weaving
in Lancashire, in view of the reliance of the trade on imported
materials, capitalists like the Chethams of Manchester exercised
a fairly dominant influence from the early days of the industry.[4]
The same was true by the seventeenth century of woollen production in the south-west, where the capitalist clothier " owned
the raw material, and consequently the product, in its successive
forms ", while " those through whose hands this product passed
in the processes which it underwent were no more, in spite of their
apparent independence, than workmen in the service of an employer "; and similarly in Norwich the clothiers were " a real
aristocracy " who " affected the airs of gentlemen and carried

[1] Records of a Scottish Manufactory at New Mills, 31 ; S. J. Chapman, Lancs. Cotton
Industry, 23 ; Usher, Introduction to Industrial History of England, 348.
[2] Scrivenor, History of the Iron Trade, 75 seq.
[3] Cf. Cunningham, Growth (Mod. Times, I), 506 ; who explains the greater
independence of the Yorkshire weaver compared with other districts as due to the
fact that " the little grass farmers round Leeds who worked as weavers were able
to rely to some extent on local supplies ". Cf. also Lipson, op. cit., 70, 86–7, and
Lipson, Hist. of Engl. Wool and Worsted Industries, 71–8, 177. Schmoller speaks of
domestic workers possessed of other resources as being much better situated than
those whose " dispersion over the district, ignorance of the market, or inability to
take up other employment places them in absolute dependence on the market ".
(Principes d'Économie Politique, vol. II, 511–12).
[4] Wadsworth and Mann, Cotton Trade and Industrial Lancashire, 1600–1780, 36 seq.,
78 seq.

a sword ".[1] But in the case of the industry of the Cotswolds and Wiltshire difficulty of access to raw material supplies can hardly have been the reason ; and the probable explanation was rather (as has been stated in the case of Wiltshire) that " the time and expense of carrying (the cloth) to the distant market in London handicapped the independent small weaver and helped to put him ultimately in the power of the clothier who marketed his cloth ".[2] Again, the worsted manufacture of Yorkshire was in the hands of fairly large capitalist employers from the beginning, possibly for the reason that it had to go further afield for its raw material (for example, into Lincolnshire to buy the long-fibred wool of that county).[3]

But probably no more than a subordinate influence should in most cases be attributed to this access or non-access to raw material supplies or to markets. The fact that raw material had to be purchased from merchants who brought it from a distance instead of purchased locally, while it might sometimes mean that the selling market for the material was less competitive than it was in the alternative case, did not necessarily place the craftsman in dependence on the merchant from whom he bought his supplies as long as his own means were adequate and his need for credit did not cause him to become indebted to the purveyor of the material. Both in Yorkshire and in Lancashire the two classes of master-craftsmen, well-to-do independent and poor and dependent, seem to have existed ; many of the former being themselves employers of others, and acting as the middleman between the latter and the larger merchant in the principal market town. Alongside the small craftsmen of the Leeds and Halifax districts there existed (at any rate in the eighteenth century) the " manufacturing " clothiers who assembled a dozen and more looms in a single workshop, and in the cases described by Defoe combined carding, spinning, weaving and finishing under one roof.[4] The important influence in determining the degree to which the domestic producer became dependent was probably the producer's own economic status rather than the proximity or distance of the sources of raw material supplies. And here it is probably true to say that it was the possession of land that was

[1] Paul Mantoux, *Industrial Revolution in the 18th Century*, 63, 67.
[2] G. D. Ramsay, *op. cit.*, 20.
[3] Cf. Heaton, *Yorkshire Woollen and Worsted Industries*, 297-8. Worsted production generally needs long-fibred wool, whereas woollen production is served by short-fibred but heavily serrated wool.
[4] Cf. Heaton, *op. cit.*, 353.

the basis of such independence as the domestic craftsman in this first period of capitalist production retained.[1]   If he was a fairly prosperous yeoman farmer, who engaged in weaving as a by-employment, he could afford to provide his household with subsistence and with raw materials over a considerable interval, and hence, being independent of the credit and the favour of a merchant buyer, could afford to choose both the buyer and the time of sale and to wait if waiting gave him the opportunity of a better price.   He was not necessarily reduced to penury like his poorer neighbour when the " vent " was bad, and he could probably afford to travel farther afield in search of markets instead of accepting the first offer that came his way.   But the poor cottager who took to weaving as a necessity of existence enjoyed none of these advantages.   Not only did he lack ready money to lay out in purchase of materials some weeks ahead of sale of and payment for his cloth (which was at times considerably delayed), but for certain seasons of the year he may well have lacked the means to provide subsistence for his family unless he could mortgage his future output to a buyer.   In fact, he was already half a proletarian, and his relation to the merchant-buyer was consequently very close to that of a sweated home-worker of the present day.   The smallest adverse circumstance, affecting the accessibility of raw materials, the state of the market or the date of sale and payment, was sufficient to make his position desperate and so to create the condition for his future servitude. For one in his position a trifling incident, a minor shift in the situation, could exercise a decisive influence.   There seems little doubt that it was the poverty of this section of the crafts-men and his consequent need for credit that was responsible for the growing tendency for looms to fall into the capitalists' hands : the loom no doubt being pledged by the craftsman to his em-ployer in the first instance as security for a money advance.[2]

---

[1] Cf. Gaskell's division of weavers into " two very distinct classes ", " divided by a well-defined line of demarcation ".   " This division arose from the circumstance of their being landholders, or entirely dependent upon weaving for their support. . . . The inferior class of artisans had at all times been sufferers from the impossibility of supplying themselves with materials for their labour " (*Artisans and Machinery*, 26). In the serge industry of Devon it seems to have been the early appearance of " a considerable class of landless households " quite as much as the reliance of the industry on imported wool from Wales and Ireland and Spain that was responsible for the hold attained by Exeter and Tiverton merchants over the industry in the seven-teenth century and " the concentration of control in the hands of a comparatively few men " (W. G. Hoskins, *Industry, Trade and People in Exeter, 1688–1800*, 12–14).

[2] Cf. Mantoux, *op. cit.*, 65, who says : " From the end of the seventeenth century . . . this process of alienation, slow and unnoticed, took place wherever home industry had been at all impaired."

Domestic industry, and its incomplete subjection to capital, retained its basis so long as the sturdy independence of a class of middle-sized yeoman farmers remained.[1] In this way small property in land and petty ownership of the means of production in industry were yoked together. This basis to domestic industry was only finally undermined when the concentration of landed property had proceeded sufficiently far to sound the death-knell of this class.

II

In the Netherlands and in certain Italian cities these developments of capitalist production that we meet in Elizabethan and in Stuart England are to be found already matured at a much earlier date. This early appearance of Capitalism was no doubt connected with the early appearance in Flemish towns (as early as the twelfth century and even in the eleventh) of a roaming landless, depressed class, competing for employment—" a brutish lower class " of which Pirenne speaks.[2] In certain Flemish towns the capitalist merchant-manufacturer had already begun to make his appearance in the thirteenth century. Even by 1200 in many cases the gilds had become close corporations of the richer merchants, who monopolized wholesale trade, levied entrance fees that were beyond the reach of smaller men, and excluded from their ranks those who weighed at the *tron*, or town weighing-machine—the retailers—and those with " blue nails "—the handicraftsmen.[3] The latter could still sell his goods retail in the local market, and where the local market was a sufficient outlet for his wares, as in large centres like Hainault, Namur and Liége, the craftsman's interest was not so seriously damaged. But where he relied on an external market he was apt to find that the Gild monopolists were his only customers, and if he had also to resort to them to purchase the materials of his craft he was doomed before long to fall into a condition of dependence on the rich wholesaler. This at any rate is what seems to have occurred in the case of the Flemish wool-crafts and in the copper-working crafts of Dinant and the Meuse valley, where the craftsman depended both on foreign supplies of raw material and on markets outside the immediate locality. The result was a

[1] For the importance of the connection between weaving and land in Lancashire, cf. Wadsworth and Mann, *op. cit.*, 314 seq.
[2] Pirenne, *Mediæval Cities*, 160, also 117 seq.
[3] Cf. Pirenne, *Belgian Democracy*, 112 ; also Brentano in *English Guilds*, cvii.

fairly extensive "putting-out" system organized by capitalists
who gave out work to dependent craftsmen. A well-known
specimen of these early capitalists was Jean Boine-Broke, Draper
and Sheriff of Douai at the end of the thirteenth century, who
gave out raw material to a large circle of craftsmen and controlled
the finishing stages of clothmaking in workshops of his own.   It
is said that " he had reduced his employees to a condition of
helpless dependence.   They were most of them in debt to him,
many lodged in houses rented by him, and he had established
a kind of truck system." [1]   There were plenty of his tribe in
other towns like Dinant, Lille, Bruges, Ghent, St. Omer, Brussels
and Louvain ;   and since Flanders at this time was the great
entrepôt of traffic in northern Europe, there were rich gains to
be made by those who had the means and the position to engage
in this type of trade.   In the case of these men " the resources
at their disposal enabled them to buy by hundreds at a time,
quarters of wheat or tuns of wine or bales of wool. . . .   They
alone were in a position to acquire those precious English fleeces,
the fine quality of which assured the repute of Flemish cloth and
as owners of the raw material, of which they had in fact the
monopoly, they inevitably dominated the world of industrial
labour." [2]   As regards the lower ranks of semi-proletarian producers, an emissary of Edward III expressed his amazement at
" the slavishness of these poor servants, whom their masters used
rather like heathens than Christians, yea rather like horses than
men.   Early up and late in bed and all day hard work and
harder fare (a few herrings and mouldy cheese), and all to enrich
the churls their masters, without any profit unto themselves." [3]

The rise of this new power of merchant capital, sections of
which were already beginning to turn towards production even
at this early date, had important effects on municipal government in the leading Flemish towns.   Two connected tendencies
soon became apparent.   Political power in the leading towns
passed into the hands of the class of richer burghers to whom the
name of " the patriciate " came to be given.   The municipal
officials called *échevins*, whose function it was to supervise the
crafts, to regulate wages, and to control the town market, were
now appointed by this patriciate from among themselves instead

[1] A. H. Johnson, *History of the Company of Drapers of London*, vol. I, 76–7 ;   also
Pirenne, *op. cit.*, 97, 100.
[2] Pirenne, *op. cit.*, 98–9.
[3] Cit. Ashley, *Early History of Eng. Wool Industry*, Publications Amer. Econ.
Assocn. (1887), 43.

of being elected by the whole burgher body. At the same time, the patriciate of the various towns entered into mutual agreements for the exchange of privileges and formed a Hansa composed of the leading export merchants from the chief Netherland towns. The result of these changes was to cause municipal regulations that had been framed to give the townsman an advantage in his dealings with traders from other towns to be relaxed, and instead to strengthen the position of all Hansa merchants in their relations with craftsmen in the various towns where the Hansa was represented. Craftsmen were excluded from selling their cloth wholesale, and were therefore constrained to deal only with Hansa merchants ; and in the woollen industry the craft organizations were subordinated to the merchants, the control of the craft and its regulation being vested in the hands of the latter. The older urban localism had given way before the influence of a class organization which exercised a monopoly of wholesale trade. " On the banks of the Scheldt and the Meuse, as at Florence, the *majores*, the *divites*, the ' great men ', henceforth governed the *minores*, the *pauperes*, the *plebei*, the ' lesser folk '." [1] In German towns similar developments were taking place about the same time : for example, such was the dominance of a patriciate at Strasbourg that " some of the ruling families extorted from the craftsmen a yearly rent of from 300 to 400 quarters of oats ", while at Cologne " the craftsmen were almost serfs of the patricians ". [2]

It was not in all towns that power passed in this way entirely to a small bourgeois oligarchy. In episcopal cities like Liége and Arras, while a population of bankers, artisans and retail shopkeepers developed and were accorded certain privileges, considerable power remained in feudal hands, and the rise both of a burgher patriciate and of capitalist production was consequently retarded, even though it was not entirely prevented. Both here and in the more commercialized towns there was a certain amount of coalition, both social and political, between the older feudal and landowning families and the richer burghers. The latter bought land and house property, like their English counterparts, sometimes abandoning commerce to live as gentry on the revenues of land or of money-lending, earning for themselves the popular nickname of the *otiosi* ; while the princes' need

[1] Pirenne, *Belgian Democracy*, 110 seq. ; also Pirenne, *Histoire de Belgique*, vol. I 69 seq.
[2] Brentano in *English Guilds*, cix, cx.

of money soon brought them into a condition of indebtedness to this new moneyed class. Where this bourgeois patriciate ruled, there were plenty of outward signs of progress and of prosperity, even though the mass of the craftsmen were depressed and impoverished. It was an age, not only of a rapid growth of trade and of the cloth and copper industries, but of the construction of market halls, aqueducts, warehouses, wharves, canals and bridges ; and from this period date the reservoir of Dikkebosch and the Cloth Hall of Ypres and the founding of lay schools.

But already in the thirteenth century we find this hegemony of the larger capitalists challenged by a revolt of the crafts : a revolt which seems in some cases to have been aided and abetted by the Church (for example at Liége) and by sections of the feudal nobility and was joined by the producers in the newer capitalist-controlled industries. In 1225 there was a rising at Valenciennes, where the patrician magistrates were deposed and a commune was set up. This was, however, suppressed after a siege and the storming of the town. Twenty years later a further wave of strikes spread over Flemish towns ; there was a short-lived revolt at Dinant, and later several unsuccessful risings at Ghent which resulted in a secession of the craftsmen to form an independent community at Brabant. At this stage the patriciate was successful in maintaining the upper hand with the aid of severe repression. " The Hansa of the seventeen towns . . . seems to have lost any other object except to uphold the interests of the patrician government against the claims of the workers." [1] Weavers and fullers were forbidden to carry arms or to meet more than seven at a time ; and strikes were ruthlessly punished. But in the early fourteenth century the armed struggle broke out anew ; complicated now by the fact that Philip the Fair of France had lent support to the patricians while the craftsmen looked for support to the Count of Flanders, which gave the struggle the form of a national war of the Flemings against the French. War started with characteristic bitterness in 1302 with a general rising, in the course of which patricians and their French allies were impartially massacred (for example, at Bruges). It ended in 1320 with a Flemish victory at the battle of Courtrai. The result was in general a reassertion of the rights of the crafts in town government and a return to the old order of gild regulation and urban localism, with a consequent

[1] Pirenne, *Belgian Democracy*, 132.

setback to the development of capitalist production. In the
second year of the war at Liége (where the Cathedral chapter
had supported the people) the offices were divided between the
traders and the crafts ; and when the patricians organized a
rising, this was suppressed and membership of a craft was made
the qualification for magistrate's office. In Utrecht a democracy
was introduced on the basis of equal representation of the several
crafts. At Dinant the power was shared between the merchants,
the large craft of coppersmiths and nine smaller crafts. At
Bruges and Ghent the artisans regained partial control of the
échevins, and the crafts were made autonomous instead of being
subjected to the magistrates' authority. Gild regulations,
designed to limit numbers in a craft and to secure to gild members
supremacy in the local market, were generally strengthened ;
and attempts were made, not only to suppress the country industry in favour of the town but also to limit the freedom of trade
of the countryside in favour of the town market, for which Staple
privileges were jealously sought. Manufacture of cloth was
forbidden in the districts round Ghent and Bruges and Ypres ;
Poperinghe was made subservient to Ypres, and Grammont,
Oudenarde and Termonde to Ghent. The Hanse was deprived
of its exclusive monopoly, and certain of the craftsmen (presumably the richer among them) were given the right to engage in
wholesale trade.[1]

But the growth of Capitalism, while it was retarded by this
reassertion of gild privileges, was far from being completely
smothered. There were districts, such as Bruges and Dinant,
where the victory of the craftsmen was never more than incomplete ; and capitalist domestic industry in the villages was
able to evade the authority of the gilds in a number of places.
Moreover, in the fifteenth century an alliance of the larger
capitalists with the Princes and the nobility under the leadership
of Philip the Good of Burgundy (an alliance which drew upon
the support of the peasantry in their opposition to the trading
hegemony of the towns) proceeded to subordinate the autonomy
of the towns to a centralized administration. To this encroachment on their powers several cities opposed a fierce resistance.
But their sectional rivalries precluded them from any successful
degree of co-operation against the common danger, and their
internal position was weakened by the fact that the richer
burghers in each place, who had fingers in export trade or in

[1] Pirenne, *Histoire*, vol. I, 405 seq., *Belgian Democracy*, 128–71.

country industry, gave their allegiance to the House of Burgundy. Liége held out heroically against the Burgundian forces, but was finally subdued by the armies of Philip and ruthlessly sacked for its obstinacy. Ghent and Bruges were similarly beaten. Thenceforth the control of urban administration was shared by the Prince's officers ; the central government participated in the appointment of the town magistrates ; a right of appeal was established from town authority to a national tribunal ; urban domination over neighbouring towns and villages was broken, and special Staple privileges were abolished. The stage was cleared for a new rule of a bourgeois patriciate, favourable to at least a partial growth of capitalist production, even if the sub-ordination of the gilds and urban localism had been purchased by an alliance of merchant capital with the remnants of feudal power. After the war with Spain Pirenne tells us that " order was ultimately everywhere restored in the interest of the wealthy commercial class ". " The council, ' the law ' of the town, recruited from among quite a small number of rich families, monopolized the policing and the jurisdiction of the munici-pality ", and gild regulations and privileges fell into disuse. Both nationally and locally " the rich merchant class supplied the personnel of the administration and sat in the assemblies of the State ". The result of these new conditions was an impressive revival of the country cloth manufacture, some of it organized in " manufactories " and most of it pendent on Antwerp, the new cloth market and the capital. Capitalist enterprises in iron-smelting and coal mining began to appear in the Liége, Namur and Hainault districts ; and from the ashes of gild hegemony there arose a class of richer masters who gave employ-ment to their poorer brethren, in particular to the weavers and fullers, who had been virtually wage-earners for some time and being excluded from corporate rights were little more than " beggars working under compulsion ".[1]

The situation both in the cities of North Italy and in some of the Rhineland towns seems to have been not dissimilar ; with an important difference that in Italy the power of feudal princes, and particularly of the Church, was sufficiently great to prevent the bourgeois republics from ever achieving more than a con-ditional autonomy, and to secure that even inside these republics power was generally shared between the merchant oligarchy and the older feudal families who owned land and exercised certain

---

[1] Pirenne, *Belg. Dem.*, 188–238 ; *Histoire*, vol. II, 347 seq.

traditional rights in the town or its neighbourhood. From very early days these cities seem to have been ruled by an aristocracy, and " the great mass of the population, the artisans, the tradesmen, were altogether shut out " from the government.[1] Feudal obligations survived even inside the towns to an extent without any close parallel in England ; many of the artisans apparently remaining in semi-feudal service to bishops and noble families until quite a late date and the feudal class of *ministeriales* occupying a specially prominent position. As Mediterranean trade revived after the Crusades, the gilds of export merchants in the seaport towns growing rich and powerful came to form the aristocracy within the burgher body. They had retained in their hands a monopoly of the export trade and they proceeded to use their power to impose restrictions on the lesser gilds below them. The latter, in their turn, placed restrictions on apprentices setting up as masters and enacted maximum wages for workmen. It has been said that " practically the workman was the master's serf ".[2] Evidence not only of a fairly extensive capitalist-controlled " putting-out " system in the wool industry but also of manufactory-production is to be found in the early part of the fourteenth century. In Florence in 1338 there were said to be as many as 200 workshops engaged in cloth manufacture, employing a total of 30,000 workmen or about a quarter of the whole occupied population of the city ; and bitter struggles were waged over the workman's right of independent organization.[3] But in general for those who had both capital and a privileged position in the major gilds investment in the export trade to the Levant or across the Alps into France and the Rhineland, or farming the Papal revenues and granting mortgage loans on the estates of princes was more lucrative than the exploitation of dependent craftsmen and the development of industry.

As in Flanders, the rule of a mercantile oligarchy did not go unchallenged. The fourteenth century saw a number of democratic risings among the craftsmen and the lesser gilds ; and there was a period during which a more democratic régime prevailed in a number of cities. In Siena, for example, in 1371

[1] W. F. Butler, *The Lombard Communes*, 80 ; also E. Dixon in *Trans. Ryl. Hist. Society*, NS. XII, 160.

[2] J. L. Sismondi, *History of the Italian Republics*, ed. Boulting, 242 seq. ; also E. Dixon, *op. cit.*, 163–9, and Gertrude Richards, *Florentine Merchants in the Age of the Medici*, 41, who points out that the labourers were unable to leave their employment. Spinning was mainly a domestic industry put out to women in the home.

[3] Cunningham, *Western Civilization* (Mod. Times), 165 ; N. Rodolico in *History* (NS.) vol. VII (1922), 178–9.

there was a rising which resulted in a magistracy of craftsmen ; and in Florence in. 1378 a similar revolution was successful in transferring power from the Major to the Lesser Arts. There was even for a time a seizure of power by the *Ciompi*, wage-earners engaged in the wool industry, who in their turn had revolted against the dominance of the craft gilds that were their masters. As a rule, however, the close alliance of the mercantile and banking aristocracy of the towns with the feudal nobility proved too strong for the democratic movement. The former could draw on the support of feudal retainers and feudal cavalry ; and for the combined strength of feudal arms and financial wealth the more modest resources of the lesser gilds were scarcely a match.[1]

In a number of German towns we also hear of insurrectionary movements among the crafts in the fourteenth and fifteenth centuries following the rise of an employing capitalist element (for example, the *Tucher*) which sought to dominate the crafts. For example, such movements occurred in Cologne, Frankfurt, Augsburg, Halle, as they did at Florence or Bruges. The outcome seems frequently to have been a compromise in which the government was shared between the craft gilds and the patriciate of the older purely trading and land-owning families ; and this, in some cases, permitted a certain revival of urban monopoly to occur. But sometimes the alliance of urban patriciate and nobility resulted in a complete crushing of the craftsmen. In towns east of the Elbe there were prolonged democratic struggles against the urban patriciate extending over the fourteenth and fifteenth centuries, which drove the patricians to seek the alliance of the neighbouring margraves, and on the final crushing of the democratic movement resulted in " the establishment of the nobility as the ruling class in society ".[2] What later seems to have curbed this urban monopoly in those German cities where it still lingered on was, not the rise of a capitalist class whose interests lay in inter-regional trade and the promotion of a dependent country industry, but the power of the princes and squires, who asserted the rights of the country-side to buy and sell where it pleased and used their influence to deprive the towns of many of their Staple rights. The gild régime retained its hold within the town boundaries, but not

[1] Sismondi, *op. cit.*, 443-50, 564 seq. ; also cf. N. S. B. Gras, *Introduction to Economic History*, 147-8.
[2] F. L. Carsten in *Trans. Ryl Hist. Society*, 1943, 73 seq.

over a rural hinterland ; and stripped of their special trading privileges the prosperity of many of these towns faded, without, however, any vigorous country industry advancing to fill their place.[1]

While in most French towns anything that can be properly called capitalist production probably arrived much later than in Flanders and in North Italy, the subsequent development of the new economic order followed here more closely the English pattern than in other parts of the Continent. But even in the fourteenth century in places like Chartres and Paris we find evidence of an incipient class of capitalists, who gave out work to craftsmen, like the English clothier of the fifteenth and sixteenth centuries, and had secured a dominating position in the gilds, in a number of cases having succeeded in subordinating other craft gilds to their own. This tendency was specially prominent in the woollen industry, although it was not confined to this trade. In Paris it was evident alike in the textile, metal and leather gilds ; and in provincial towns like Amiens and Abbeville the gild of mercers in the fifteenth century seems to have secured control over other crafts, including the hatters and cappers. In Paris and Rheims there was apparently a prolonged struggle between the drapers and the mercers for supremacy, with an eventual victory to the former in the one city and to the latter in the other. Similarly in Strasbourg " a class of merchant-employers, known as *Tucher* or clothier, arose . . . and drew an increasingly sharp distinction between themselves and the working members, who were forbidden in 1381 to manufacture on their own account ", and were later prohibited from selling cloth altogether.[2] In fact, as Unwin has so painstakingly shown, developments inside the gilds of towns like Paris and Strasbourg at this time followed closely similar lines to those gilds and companies of London that have been described above. In newer industries like paper, silk, glass, printing, capitalist enterprise was found from a fairly early date, as in England ; and the temporary suspension of gild prerogatives by official decree in the sixteenth century may perhaps be regarded as an expression of the extent to which the influence of capital had already developed

[1] Cf. Brentano, on " Hist. of Gilds " in Toulmin Smith's *English Gilds*, cvii–cxx ; Schmoller, *Mercantile System*, 16–37.

[2] Unwin, *op. cit.*, 36–7. This prohibition was later relaxed, but apparently " only in favour of the few well-to-do trading weavers on payment of a fine to the clothiers, and four years after this the whole development received its consummation by the amalgamation of the two organizations into one body, which in the sixteenth century exercised control over all the crafts engaged in the manufacture of cloth ".

both in the new and in certain of the older trades and was exerting its influence to secure room for expansion. As Hauser says, " with the sixteenth century the era of capitalism has its true opening. All the new industries are centralized industries, which recruit their numerous workers from the continually growing army of unemployed ". In the following century, the century of Colbertian regulation, we find both a fairly developed system of dependent industry organized by merchant-manufac-turers (for example, at Sedan, Rheims, Rouen, Lyons and Elbeuf) and also of capitalist-owned manufactories, using considerable capitals and sometimes employing hundreds of wage-earners, in such centres as Montauban, Rheims, the Carcassonne district and Louviers. For example, half the looms in the Rheims district at this time were said to be in capitalist-owned manufac-tories. The substantial importance of a dispossessed and wage-earning proletariat in seventeenth-century France is attested by the number of decrees of the period which gave powers to recruit labour or which forbade workers to change their employment or which prohibited assemblies of workers or strikes on pain of corporal punishment or even death. (Even the Theological Faculty of the University of Paris saw fit to pronounce solemnly against the sin of workers' organization.) It is attested again by the revolts, amounting to insurrections, that broke out inter-mittently in Paris, Lyons and Normandy in desperate protest against what Boissonnade calls their " frightful misery " at this period.[1]

In the case of Italy, Germany and the Netherlands (and to a smaller extent in France) what is remarkable is less the early date, compared with England, at which capitalist production made its appearance, than the failure of the new system to grow much beyond its promising and precocious adolescence. It would seem as though the very success and maturity of merchant and money-lending capital in these rich continental centres of entrepôt trade, instead of aiding, retarded the progress of investment in production ; so that, compared with the glories of spoiling the Levant or the Indies or lending to princes, industrial capital was doomed to occupy the place of a dowerless and unlovely younger sister. At any rate, it is clear that a mature development of merchant and financial capital is not of

[1] Cf. Unwin, op. cit., 21, 25-36, 42-8, 80-1, 98-9 ; H. Hauser, Les Débuts du Capitalisme, 14-16, 22-3, 26-7, 42, 102-6 ; H. Sée, Modern Capitalism, 125-6 ; Bois-sonnade, Le Socialisme d'État, 124-30, 280-308 ; Renard and Weulersee, Life and Work in Modern Europe, 169 seq., 185-9, 200 seq.

itself a guarantee that capitalist production will develop under its wing, and that even when certain sections of merchant capital have turned towards industry and have begun both to subordinate and to change the mode of production, this does not necessarily result in any thorough transformation. When seen in the light of a comparative study of capitalist development, Marx's contention that at this stage the rise of a class of industrial capitalists from the ranks of the producers themselves is a condition of any revolutionary transformation of production begins to acquire a central importance.

III

It must be evident from what has been said that the breakdown of urban localism and the undermining of the monopolies of the craft gilds is one condition of the growth of capitalist production, whether in the manufacturing or the domestic form. And it is to this task that those sections of merchant capital which have begun to take control of industry bend the weight of their influence. But of scarcely less importance is a second essential condition : the need for nascent industrial capital itself to be emancipated from the restrictive monopolies in the sphere of trade in which merchant capital is already entrenched. Without this second condition the scope for any considerable extension of the field of industrial investment will remain limited, and the gains to be won by investment in industry, and hence the chance of a specifically industrial accumulation of capital, are likely to be modest, at least by contrast with the fortunes yielded by the carefully monopolized export trades. It is for this reason that the political struggles of this period assume such an importance ; as it is also for this reason that the social alignments that form the basis of these struggles are so complex and so changeable. Perhaps one should add a third condition, as deserving to rank with the other two. It is probably also necessary that conditions should be present which favour rather than obstruct the investment of capital in agriculture : not in the sense merely of mortgaging the estates of leading feudal dignatories or the purchase of a rent-roll, but in the sense of the growth of actual capitalist farming hand in hand with those forms of " primitive accumulation " that have generally been its accompaniment. Not only do such developments play generally an important rôle in creating a rural proletariat, but they are also a crucial factor in creating an internal market for the products of manufacture—a factor which was absent, for example, over most of France until the Revolution on account both of the feudal burdens on agriculture and of the restrictions which throttled any inter-local trade in the products of the soil.

In some respects the Tudor monarchy in England might perhaps be deemed comparable with the régime of Philip the Good in the Netherlands after the subordination of civic autonomy to a national administration.   But there remain some important differences between the two.   Although the ranks of the old baronial families in England were thinned, and the aristocracy had been extensively recruited from *nouveaux riches* commoners, the traditions and interests of a feudal aristocracy continued to dominate large areas of the country and to dominate State policy, which showed particular affection for the stability of the old order.   At the same time, landed property was extensively passing into the hands of the rich merchant class : a class which owed its position in the main to the privileges enjoyed as members of the few and exclusive companies which held the monopoly over certain spheres of foreign trade.   On them the new monarchy had come to rely alike for financial and for political support, and at times took up shares (as did Elizabeth and James I) in the more profitable of their trading ventures.   In return this *haute bourgeoisie* was endowed with titles and with royal offices which gave it a place at Court, where the real centre of political power at the time resided.

As we have seen, it was not an immediate interest of these grand merchants of the larger trading companies that urban monopoly and craft gild restrictions should be undermined. Generally they were neutral towards this issue and there was not an acute cleavage as in the Netherlands between urban crafts and inter-urban Hanse.   The attack on the restrictions of the craft gilds and the economic power of the town governments came from that newer generation of merchant capitalists and certain of the country squires who were undertaking the development of the country industry as employers of domestic craftsmen. It was also these merchant manufacturers who, when they could not secure admission to the privileged ranks of the export companies (which always remained their ruling ambition), came into acute conflict with the trading monopolies which limited their market and depressed the price at which they could effect a sale. This antagonism was particularly sharp between provincial traders or merchant-manufacturers and the export merchants of London, if only because of the greater difficulty that generally faced the former in securing admission to bodies like the Merchant Adventurers or the Eastland Company, both of which were ruled in the main by a close corporation of rich metropolitan traders, who were inclined to be sparing of admitting provincials to their ranks. In the cloth trade, for example, we hear of repeated and bitter complaints from provincial clothiers during the sixteenth century against the restrictions imposed upon them by the foreign trading companies, and in particular by the metropolitan notables at the head of these bodies ; and it is the verdict of Unwin that in the course of Elizabeth's reign " the Merchant Adventurers had contrived to make the channels of exportation narrower than ever before ".[1] We find East Anglian clothiers protesting against the monopolistic control of sales imposed by the Levant Company ; and we find clothiers of Ipswich who were outside the Eastland Company refusing the price offered for their cloth by the Company and claiming from the Privy Council a licence to sell directly to foreign merchants.[2] In the North of England we find a writer in 1585 in the course of lamentation on the stagnation of trade in the port of Hull complaining that " the merchants are tyed to companies, the heads whereof are citizens of London, who make ordinances beneficial to themselves, but hurtful and chargeable to others in ye country ". There was even at one time a movement on foot to boycott all dealings with Londoners on the ground that " by means of ye said companies all the trade of merchants is drawn to London ". For some years the merchants of Hull carried on a struggle with the Greenland Company which they denounced as a " monopolizing patent ", declaring that the Greenland trade should be free ;[3] and by the middle of the seventeenth century the encroachment of " interlopers " on the spheres of the export companies assumed considerable dimensions, to judge from the complaints of the latter, and was the occasion of perpetual conflict. Emboldened by the Commonwealth, the merchants of York convened a general meeting of their fellows in Newcastle, Hull and Leeds, to petition the Council for Trade that no London merchant " should come or send to

---

[1] *Studies in Economic History*, 185.
[2] Lipson, *Econ. History*, vol. II, 323, 342 ; *V.C.H. Suffolk*, vol. II, 265-6.
[3] *Cal. S.P.D.*, 1653-4, vol. LXV, 62-70.

keepe any fayres or mart on the north side of the Trent ", since " by these fayres the Londoner ingroseth almost all the trade of the northern partes " ; and in a letter to the M.P. for Leeds the merchants of York and Hull plaintively add : " Wee like little fishes are swallowed up by a great whale." [1]

On the whole the influence of the monarchy was on the side of the " great whale " with which it was so closely affiliated. At any rate little or nothing was done to give the little fishes greater freedom of movement. On the other hand, in the quarrel between the organizers of the new country industry and the authority of the town governments, the influence of the monarchy tended to be thrown in favour of the towns and of the old industrial régime. This no doubt was partly from principles of conservatism, from a desire to maintain stability in the social order and a balance of class forces, to which the organizer of country industry, like the enclosing landlord who uprooted village life, was a serious threat ; partly in the interests of maintaining a cheap and ready labour supply for squires' estates and yeomen farms, which the spread of country industry tended to disturb by offering to the poor cottager an alternative employment. But, whatever its primary motive, the significance of governmental policy in retarding the growth of capitalist production is none the less of outstanding importance.

The germs of a free trade movement accordingly lay in the immediate interests alike of enclosing landlords, of provincial drapers and clothiers and of those members of London Livery Companies who had a finger in the country industry. Here there must be no misunderstanding. The free trade that was sought was a conditional and limited free trade conceived, not as a general principle, as was to be the case in the nineteenth century, but as *ad hoc* proposals to remove certain specific restrictions that bore down upon the complainants. Neither in internal affairs nor in foreign trade did the movement against monopolies imply any general abrogation of control by the State or by trading and industrial companies. Often, in practice, it meant no more than the removal of the other man's privileges in order to supplant them with one's own. It only makes sense if it is regarded, not as a struggle for a general principle, but as an expression of a particular class interest.

[1] Cit. Heaton, *op. cit.*, 165–7 who adds : " During the seventeenth century this feeling rose to great heights of bitterness and was the cause of constant demonstrations of antagonism between the northern parts and the capital."

But antipathy to particular restrictions, damaging to a sectional interest, became transformed into a general movement against monopoly by the practice employed on an increasing scale by the Stuarts of selling monopolies for the starting of new industries. The practice had originated with Elizabeth who had bestowed valuable patents upon favourites and pensioners, upon servants of the Queen's household and upon clerks in lieu of salaries. But what his predecessor had started as an occasional expedient James I developed into a regular system. It is clear that the primary object of these grants was a fiscal one, to replenish a treasury depleted by the rising expenditures due to the price-revolution, and was not the fruit of a considered Colbertian policy of fostering industry. The result was a curious paradox. A practice, which on the face of it represented a bestowal of royal favour and protection upon industry, in fact aroused the opposition of industrial interests, and acted as a brake on the development of capitalist production. It is not to be denied that in certain directions, for example in mining, royal favour played a progressive rôle in stimulating industrial investment where, for want of that protection, this might have been absent ; or that certain of the industrialists of the time who were recipients of these favours remained loyal adherents of the monarchy even throughout the period of civil war.[1] The latter was no doubt to be expected, if only because the bulk of these industrial privileges were awarded either to persons at Court or to friends whom these courtiers sponsored. But in general the system of industrial monopolies was cramping and restrictive, both by reason of the exclusiveness of the patent rights that were granted and by reason of the narrow circle to which the grant of such rights was generally confined. Here there was considerable resemblance to Colbert's system of industrial monopolies in France. Resentment was naturally strongest among those who had interests in newer industries, and particularly among those richer sections of the craftsmen who were ambitious to launch out as investors and employers themselves. It was these men, as we have seen, who were the effective force behind the movement towards the new Stuart corporations, by means of which independence was sought from the trading oligarchy at the head of the respective Livery Company which was seeking to subordinate the industry to its own control.

[1] An example of this was Thomas Bushell, a privileged lessee of some of the Welsh mines of the Mines Royal. He was said to have financed the King to the extent of £40,000 during the Civil War.

But while these *parvenu* industrialists were eager enough to purchase royal charters as an instrument of their own independence, the condition of affairs which ultimately served their purpose was one where the possession of capital alone determined who should occupy the field. For this the Stuart régime of royal grants of monopoly substituted a system where influence at Court determined the distribution of economic rights of way. Not only was the system costly for the would-be industrialist, involving as it did both a payment to the exchequer and also the expenses incidental to obtaining the requisite influence at Court,[1] but from its nature it was heavily weighted against the man of humble social origins, against the provincial by contrast with the Londoner, and against the *parvenu*. This is well illustrated in the case of the pinmakers, who being persons of modest means and humble social station had to rely for their charter on the influence of gentlemen at Court, with the eventual result that the real control of the new company fell into the hands of the latter. And while in a few cases, like the Glovers, the Feltmakers, the Starchmakers and the Silkweavers, the rank and file of the producers themselves (or rather the capitalist element among them) secured some benefit from the system, the majority of monopolies awarded went directly to gentlemanly promoters, who enjoyed both wealth and influence, like the alum and glass monopolies, soap and playing-cards, the tin-buying monopoly, the patent to Sir Giles Mompesson for making gold and silver thread, and the case of the Duke of Buckingham's notorious " ring ", which proved to be a sufficiently unsavoury scandal for proceedings to be instituted against it by a Parliamentary Commission in the reign of James I.[2] It was through the influence of Lord Dudley that the patent for coal smelting was obtained by Dudley ; it was only by dint of lavish bribery to influential courtiers that Alderman Cockayne secured sanction for his famous scheme ; and it was no doubt because Cecil, Leicester and other prominent courtiers were interested as leading shareholders that the companies of the Mines Royal and the Mineral and Battery Works received such extended

[1] George Wood, a patentee in linen production, paid an annual royalty of £10 to the Crown and £200 a year as bribes to those who had obtained the privilege for him. The Feltmakers had to pay £100 to a Mr. Typper, M.P., to plead their case. The patentees for erecting lighthouses declared that to obtain the grant involved an initial cost of £600 plus an annual charge of £300. Scott comments : " The obtaining of a charter involved the bribing of prominent courtiers and in this way trade was subject to a high indirect taxation " (*op. cit.*, 170-6).

[2] Cf. W. Hyde Price, *English Patents of Monopoly*, 25-33.

privileges as they did.[1] Bourgeois interests in the provinces were
specially outraged by this Stuart policy of granting privileges to
corporations with a small and exclusive membership and with
power to control an industry throughout the country in the
interests of a small circle in the metropolis. The circle of
interests that were damaged by the system was a wide one. The
glass patent to Sir R. Mansell involved the suppression of rival
glass works, and was twice renewed in face of the strenuous
protests of the independent glassmakers. The salt monopoly
roused the anger of the fishing ports, because they declared that
it had resulted in a doubling of the price of salt. The monopoly
granted to the Society of Soapers of Westminster—" the odious
and crying project of soap ", as even Clarendon called it—
damaged the woollen industry ; and the monopoly of shipping
coal to London granted to the Newcastle Hostmen was said to
have raised the price of coal in the London market by 40 per cent.,
to the detriment of glass- and soap-makers, among others, who
relied upon this coal. Even the interests of some of the larger
London trading companies were touched by the system. The
tin-buying monopoly, which at one stage was granted to Sir
Walter Raleigh, encroached on what had previously been the
preserve of the Company of Pewterers. The tobacco-monopoly
hurt the Bermuda Society, and the suppression of the old soap-
boilers in the interest of the Westminster Soapers offended the
Greenland Company which had previously sold train-oil to the
older type of producer. Charles I was even so foolish as to annoy
the East India Company by sanctioning a rival company from
which he was to receive a share of the profits ; while persons so
anciently privileged as the Merchant Adventurers remembered
that they had recently had to distribute some £70,000 in bribes
in order to win a new charter.[2]

The opposition to monopolies waged its first Parliamentary
fights in 1601 and again in 1604 when a bill was introduced to
abolish all privileges in foreign trade. It was pointed out how
greatly the existing régime favoured London and starved the
remaining ports of trade ; [3] and it was suggested that foreign
trading companies should be open impartially to all persons on
payment of a moderate entrance fee. In supporting the Bill Sir

[1] *Ibid.*, 109 ; Scott, *op. cit.*, I, 40, 46, 143.
[2] Cf. Hyde Price, *op. cit.*, 73, 114–17 ; Scott, *op. cit.*, 145, 169, 203, 217, 219 ;
H. Levy, *Economic Liberalism*, 21 seq.
[3] The customs returns showed London with an import trade of £110,000 and the
rest of England only £17,000 (cf. Scott, *op. cit.*, 119–20).

Edwin Sandys declared that " merchandise being the chiefest and richest of all other and of greater extent and importance than all the rest, it is against the natural right and liberty of the subjects of England to restrain it into the hands of some few ". Apparently " the 200 families " were already an entity in Stuart times ; for the speaker added that " governors of these companies by their monopolizing orders have so handled the matter as that the mass of the whole trade of the realm is in the hands of some 200 persons at the most, the rest serving for a show and reaping small benefit ". After some intermittent skirmishing, in 1624 the opposition returned to the attack with a general anti-monopoly Act, from the provisions of which, however, the privileges of corporations, companies and boroughs were exempted, as was also " any manner of new manufacture within this realm " for a period of 21 or 14 years. But like similar legislation of more recent memory, this seems to have had little success in curbing the evil at which it was aimed. On the eve of the Commonwealth, in 1640, a speaker in Parliament could say : " better laws could not have been made than the Statute of Monopolies against Projectors, and yet, as if the law had been the author of them, there have been during these few years more monopolies and infringements of liberties than in any year since the Conquest " ; while Sir John Colepepper could make his famous denunciation of monopolies which " like the frogs of Egypt have gotten possession of our dwellings and we have scarcely a room free from them ; they sip in our cup ; they dip in our dish ; they sit by our fire ; we find them in the dye vat, the washing bowl and the powdering tub ; they share with the butler in his bar ; they have marked and sealed us from head to foot ; they will not bate us a pin ". Together with its denial of the right of arbitrary taxation and imprisonment, the challenge by Parliament to royal grants of economic privilege and monopoly can be said to have formed the central issue in the outbreak of the seventeenth-century revolution.

At the opening of the Long Parliament it seems that even the privileged members of the London trading companies leaned towards the Parliamentary side. A few aldermen were royalists, and in 1641 a royalist, Sir Richard Gurney, was elected Lord Mayor. But the Common Council was almost solidly Parliamentarian ; and when the King appointed as Lieutenant of the Tower Sir T. Lunsford, " a notorious desperado ", Sir Richard Gurney himself was constrained to appeal to the King to revoke the appointment, since otherwise the apprentices of London would storm the Tower.[1] Even the Merchant Adventurers made large loans to Parliament in 1641 and 1642,[2] but whether from enthusiasm for the Parliamentary cause or to propitiate a possible adversary remains obscure. At any rate, individual members of the greater London companies were numbered among Cromwell's supporters and even among his officials and advisers.[3] What is fairly clear, however, is that these circles were the chief strength of the extreme right-wing within the Parliamentarian camp, who, while they were not averse to bringing pressure upon the King to yield some part of his prerogative, never desired a complete break with the Crown, favoured negotiations with Charles after his rout at Naseby and in the years that followed (when the ways of Presbyterian and Independent were dividing) were stalwart opponents of the claims of the Army. Among the London Drapers, for example, there seems to have been a good deal of lukewarm support for the Presbyterians ; but the majority feeling among them was strongly hostile to the Independents.[4] It is evident that the ruling group which dominated the government of the City of London formed essentially the party of compromise and of accommodation and not the party of revolution. In Parliament itself the number of merchants and financiers was apparently small : no more than thirty in the Long Parliament and less than twenty in the first Parliament of the Protectorate.[5] The majority of members were lawyers or country gentlemen, the latter no doubt including some of the more considerable yeomen farmers as well as the enclosing squire and improving landlord.

But while London with its trade and industries was the central stronghold of the revolution—what Clarendon termed " the unruly and mutinous spirit of the City of London, which was the sink of all the ill humour of the kingdom " [6]—it was from the provinces that a large part of the mass support

[1] C. H. Firth on " London during the Civil War " in *History*, 1926-7, 26-7.
[2] Margaret James, *Social Problems and Policy during the Puritan Revolution*, 149. As a matter of fact there were two factions inside the company and there is some evidence that the majority one was royalist (cf. M. P. Ashley, *Financial and Commercial Policy under the Cromwellian Protectorate*, 122). Originally they had advanced £40,000 to Charles. But since they refused to pay tonnage and poundage, the King in retaliation deprived them of their monopoly on the outbreak of the Civil War ; after which they proceeded to lend sums probably totalling about £60,000 to Parliament between 1642 and 1649.
[3] Cf. M. P. Ashley, *op. cit.*, 5-10.
[4] A. H. Johnson, *History of the Drapers' Company*, vol. III, 215.
[5] M. P. Ashley, *op. cit.*, 7.
[6] *History of The Great Rebellion*, vol. VI, 264.

for the revolution was drawn ; and the rivalry that we have described between industrial or semi-industrial interests in the provinces and the more privileged trading capital of the metropolis was no doubt an important element in the antagonism that began to sharpen in the middle '40's between Presbyterian and Independent. Needless to say, the division of the country between the parties of King and Parliament followed fairly closely along economic and social lines. Centres of the woollen manufacture, in particular, were apt to be strongholds of the Parliamentary cause, as for example East Anglia, Gloucester and Cirencester in the West Country, and the manufacturing districts of the West Riding. A town such as Leicester was a stronghold of Puritanism, especially among those connected with the hosiery trade and among the shopkeepers (though not apparently innkeepers).[1] Clarendon took it for granted that " Leeds, Halifax and Bradford, the very populous and rich towns, depending wholly upon clothiers, naturally maligned the gentry ", whereas the gentry and the agricultural districts of Yorkshire were predominantly of the King's party. Interestingly enough, the small group of wealthier merchants in Leeds who dominated the town government seem to have been royalist, whereas the mass of the population of the town were solidly parliamentarian.[2]

Speaking generally, it seems true to say that those sections of the bourgeoisie that had any roots in industry, whether they were provincial clothiers or merchants of a London Livery Company who had used their capital to organize the country industry, were wholehearted supporters of the Parliamentary cause. The exceptions to this were a few royal patentees, who paradoxically were apt to be the proprietors of the most capitalistically advanced enterprises. On the other hand, those elements who were farthest removed from active participation in industry, who had invested in land and titles and become predominantly *rentier* and leisured, like the Flemish *otiosi* of an earlier century, felt their interests tied to the stability of the existing order and tended to give their support to the King. Thus the agricultural west and north of England, apart from the clothing towns and the ports, rallied to the Crown. These were the more backward parts of the country, where the newer capitalist agriculture was least in evidence and where the surviving remnants of feudal relationships were mostly to be

[1] R. W. Greaves, *The Corporation of Leicester*, 5.   [2] Heaton, *op. cit.*, 207, 227.

found.[1] But the new Cromwellian army and the Independents, who were the real driving force of the revolution, drew their main strength from the provincial manufacturing centres and, as is well known, from sections of the squirearchy and the small and middling type of yeoman farmer, who preponderated in the east and south-east. Cromwell himself was a gentleman farmer and Ireton, his chief lieutenant, was both a country gentleman and a clothier. Behind them were the rank and file of working craftsmen, apprentices, tenants and cottagers, with their dangerous " levelling " tendencies and their hatred alike of bishops and presbyters, projectors and monopolists, of " malignant landlords " and of tithes. The wife of one of Cromwell's colonels said that all were described as Puritans who " crossed the views of the needy courtiers, the proud encroaching priests, the thievish projectors, the lewd nobility and gentry " ; and Baxter, a leading Puritan divine, described the social composition of the two parties in the Civil War as follows : " A very great part of the knights and gentlemen of England . . . adhered to the King. . . . And most of the tenants of these gentlemen. . . . On the Parliament's side were the smaller part (as some thought) of the gentry in most of the counties, and the greatest part of the tradesmen and freeholders and the middle sort of men, especially in those corporations and counties which depend on clothing and such manufactures." [2]

There can be little doubt that the land question played a highly important part, if only as a background, in the disagreements internal to the Parliamentary cause ; and this may well have been chiefly responsible for the eventual compromise represented by the Restoration.[3] By the time of the civil war investment in land had become sufficiently extensive among the moneyed class to impose upon them a conservative bias and to render them timid of any measures that seemed likely to call a landlord's rights in question and to encourage the insubordination of tenants. Moreover, investment of capital in land-purchase, and to a less extent actual capitalist farming, had already progressed sufficiently to leave little change in the agrarian régime that the improving landlord or progressive farmer urgently

---

[1] For example, Cornish gentry who like Sir Bevil Grenvile threatened his tenants that if they did not grind at his mill he would " put them in suit " (cf. G. Davies, *The Early Stuarts*, 266).

[2] Cit. by Christopher Hill, *The English Revolution, 1640*, 18.

[3] Cf. Christopher Hill in *Eng. Hist. Review*, April 1940, where the opinion of Professor Archangelsky is quoted to this effect.

desired, apart from the abolition of feudal tenures which was carried through by Parliament in 1646. It is remarkable what strong opposition was shown, for example, not only by the House of Lords, but by the Presbyterian section in the Commons, and in particular by the leading merchants who composed the common council of the City of London, to the proposed sequestration of the estates of royalists and of bishops, and to the organized sales of delinquents' lands after sequestration had been already decided upon.[1] When later in 1656 Bills were introduced to control enclosures and to make fines for copyholders certain instead of arbitrary, these met with strenuous opposition.

But the tenant farmer and perhaps also the smaller freeholder, and certainly the poorer cottager, who were damaged by the enclosing or rack-renting landlord, were prepared to be much more radical ; and the poorer type of husbandman, according to Gregory King's estimate, composed about one-eighth of the population at this time. Evidently it is their voice that we hear in many of the popular pamphlets of the time, and their voice that soon began to spread dismay in propertied circles and to cause these to draw back in alarm. Thus we have displayed with remarkable clearness that contradictory feature that we find in every bourgeois revolution : while this revolution requires the impetus of its most radical elements to carry through its emancipating mission to the end, the movement is destined to shed large sections of the bourgeoisie as soon as these radical elements appear, precisely because the latter represent the small man or the dispossessed whose very claims call in question the rights of large-scale property. Before the Commonwealth has been long in being we hear of complaints from tenants against the new purchasers of sequestrated estates that " these men are the greatest Tyrants everywhere as men can be, for they wrest from the poor Tenants all former Immunities and Freedoms they formerly enjoyed " ; of the promotion of Parliamentary Bills " for the relief of tenants oppressed by malignant landlords " ; of organized opposition to enclosures and petitions for the abolition of tithes.[2]   Winstanley,

[1] Cf. Christopher Hill in *Eng. Hist. Review*, April, 1940, 224-34. The writer here speaks of this opposition as having " fought a steady rearguard action all through " on the question. The Army meantime were pressing for the sale of these estates. Cf. also the comment of another historian of this period : " The presbyterian was usually a man of property and detested and feared the radical views often expressed by the sectaries " (G. Davies, *The Early Stuarts*, 195).

[2] Margaret James, *op. cit.*, 87 ; *Cal. S.P. Dom.*, 1649, June 20 ; 1650, Jan. 21 and 28 ; 1650, April 13 ; vol. XXXIX, 88 and 91-2 ; vol. XLI, 2.

the Digger, was only expressing a widespread popular sentiment
when he complained that " in Parishes where Commons lie the
rich Norman Freeholders, or the new (more covetous) Gentry
overstock the Commons with sheep and cattle, so that the inferior
Tenants and poor labourers can hardly keep a cow but half
starve her ", that " the inferior Tenants and Labourers bear all
the burthens in labouring the Earth, in paying Taxes and Free-
quarter above their strength ; and yet the Gentry who oppress
them and live idle upon their labors carry away all the comfortable
livelihood of the Earth ", and that " England is not a Free People
till the Poor that have no Land have a free allowance to dig and
labour the Commons ".[1] So also was Lilburne when, with a
more urban bent, he fulminated against " Tythes, Excise and
Customs : those secret thieves and robbers and drainers of the
poor and middle sort of people and the greatest obstructors of
trade ", and against " all Monopolizing Companies of Merchants,
the hinderers and decayers of Clothing and Clothworking, Dying
and like useful professions, by which thousands of poor people
might be set at work that are now ready to starve ".[2] It is hardly
surprising to find a class-conscious landlord, on his side, declaring
that " if they get not some rebuke at first they will make a general
revolt for all landlords ",[3] or an anti-Leveller pamphleteer
roundly denouncing what he variously called " a design against
the twelve famous Companies of the City of London " and a
plot " to raise sedition and hurliburlies in City, Town and
Country " and " to raise the servant against the master, the
tenant against the landlord, the buyer against the seller, the
borrower against the lender, the poor against the rich, and for
encouragement every beggar should be set on horseback ".[4] In
more measured language Ireton made his reply in a debate on
universal suffrage : " If you admitt any man that hath a breath
and being . . . thus we destroy propertie. . . . Noe person
that hath nott a locall and permanent interest in the Kingdome
should have an equal dependance in Elections." [5] Earlier

[1] Winstanley, *Law of Freedom in a Platform* and *The True Levellers' Standard Advanced.*
[2] John Lilburne, *England's New Chains Discovered* (1648). Elsewhere Lilburne
denounced the " Patent of Merchant Adventurers who have ingrossed into their
hands the sole trade of all woollen commodities that are to be sent into the Netherlands " and also the monopoly of printing, " a great company of malignant fellows
invested with arbitrary unlimited Power ", adding that the men who formerly attacked
monopolies were now " setting up greater Patentees than ever the former were "
(*England's Birthright Justified against all Arbitrary Usurpation*).
[3] *Cal. S.P. Dom.*, vol. CCCCL, 27.
[4] *England's Discoverer or the Levellers' Creed* (1649).
[5] *Clarke Papers*, ed. C. H. Firth, vol. II, 314.

Edmund Waller had clearly summed up the Presbyterian point of view. " I look upon episcopacy as a counterscarp or outwork, which, if it is taken by this assault of the people . . . we may in the next place have as hard a task to defend our property, as we have lately had to recover it from the prerogative. If, by multiplying hands and petitions, they prevail for an equality in things ecclesiastical, the next demand may perhaps be *Lex Agraria*, the like equality in things temporal." [1]

Certainly among the people of both London and provincial cities—among the working craftsmen, the apprentices, the journeymen—the period of the Interregnum witnessed an extraordinary development of a democratic temper. It was said by a contemporary that " the citizens and common people of London had then so far imbibed the customs and manners of a commonwealth that they could scarce endure the sight of a gentleman, so that the common salutation to a man well dressed was French dog or the like ". [2]   Even after the return of Charles II it is clear that a strong republican opposition continued to exist, with extensive support among the working classes, both in London and provincial towns : an opposition which not only held meetings and demonstrations but was responsible for local risings, and the presence of which was evidently a powerful factor in forcing the ruling class to call in William of Orange and to unseat James II.[3]   In its economic policy the Commonwealth introduced a number of changes that were of substantial importance to the development of Capitalism. During this period the voice of provincial interests received much greater attention from the legislature than it had received before ; and the same was true of the voice of industrial interests. We find a marked increase in the number of democratic movements among the Yeomanry of the Livery Companies, some of which, like the Feltmakers, were successful in securing incorporation, thereby freeing themselves from the dominance of the merchant element. In the sphere of foreign trade, not only did the Navigation Act of 1651 give a powerful stimulus to English commerce and English shipping, but the privileges of the monopolistic companies were greatly reduced ; and, as the complaints of these companies to the Crown after 1660 are witness, it was a period when interlopers thrived and obtained important concessions.

[1] Cit. E. Bernstein, *Cromwell and Communism*, 54.
[2] *Reresby Memoirs*, cit. Beloff, *Public Order and Popular Disturbances, 1660-1714*, 32.
[3] Cf. Beloff, *op. cit.*, 34-55.

While the Levant Company was confirmed in its privileges (in return for a loan to the government), those of the Eastland Company were not renewed ; and new charters were only issued to the Merchant Adventurers and the Greenland Company after protracted negotiations in which attempts were made to reconcile the interests of interlopers with those of the Company. For a period of three years during the Protectorate the East Indies trade was actually free and open, to the delight of the enemies of chartered companies ; and even when, under threats from the Company to sell all its forts and stations in India, the charter of the East India Company was renewed in 1657, this renewal seems, again, to have been on the basis of a compromise between competing interests. There is some evidence that the net result of this relaxation of monopoly was that trade expanded and export-prices and the profits of the foreign trading companies fell.[1]

Some of these social and political changes disappeared with the Commonwealth. But by no means all of them did ; and the Restoration was very far from being a simple return to the *status quo ante*, as has sometimes been assumed.[2] Politically, the royal prerogative had suffered a mortal blow, and control of trade and finance, the judiciary and the army had been transferred into the hands of Parliament. With the abolition of the prerogative courts such as the Star Chamber, the Crown had lost an essential instrument of independent executive power. Feudal tenures, abolished in 1646 as the close to a chapter, were never restored. And when Charles II's successor forgot what Charles himself had been wise enough to remember, he was forced to go upon his travels again. Popular pressure was sufficient to defeat the aims of reaction, without a new civil war, to put a more tractable monarch on the throne and to tie him to Parliament by a contractual Bill of Rights. Court influence, even if it was not entirely unseated, was now subordinated to the sway of Parliament. " The commons had strengthened their hold on finance and they carried over from the revolutionary period a method of working which was to provide later the means by which they gradually increased their influence over the administration (the system of committees)." [3] The field of industry was no longer

[1] Cf. M. P. Ashley, *op. cit.*, 111–31.
[2] E.g. Durbin, *Politics of Democratic Socialism*, 196–7, where the seventeenth-century revolution is written off, *tout court*, as a failure and a " victory for the landed interest " over the bourgeoisie.
[3] G. N. Clark, *The Later Stuarts*, 11.

encumbered by royal grants of monopoly ; and, except for the East India Company, the exclusive privileges of the foreign-trading companies had been too much undermined for these bodies to regain their former position.[1]   In their place, the newer type of joint-stock company was coming into prominence, where capital was king.   Very far from all the sequestrated estates of royalist families were restored to their owners : the remainder were still held by their *parvenu* bourgeois purchasers.   While it is true that the bourgeois revolution in seventeenth-century England went only a relatively small distance in its economic and social policy, it had achieved enough to accelerate enormously the growth of industrial capital in the next half-century—a growth surpassing that of other countries which as yet lacked any similar political upheaval—and to set the stage for the industrial revolution in the century that was to come.

[1] By an Act of 1688 trade was thrown open and former monopoly-rights abolished except in the spheres of the Levant, Russia, Africa and Eastland Companies. One result was a big expansion of the trade of other English ports relatively to London.

CHAPTER FIVE

CAPITAL ACCUMULATION AND MERCANTILISM

I

To speak of a process of capital accumulation as an essential stage in the genesis of Capitalism might seem at first sight a simple statement which none could call in question. That capital must have been gathered between the fingers of a class of capitalists before any large-scale capitalist undertakings could be launched and Capitalism as a form of production could dominate the scene might seem to many too obvious to need much emphasis. Yet as soon as we begin to enquire as to the exact nature of the process by which this gathering together of capital could have occurred, the statement appears less simple, and a number of important questions arise. There are some, moreover, who have suggested that the existence of a distinct stage when capital was in some sense accumulating—a stage separate from and prior in time to the growth of capitalist industry itself—is a myth.

The first question that arises is one which economists are apt to put. Is accumulation to be conceived as an accumulation of means of production themselves or an accumulation of claims or titles to wealth, capable of being converted into instruments of production although they are not themselves productive agents? If the answer is that the reference in this context is to the former, then one is at once confronted with a further question. Why should the rise of capitalist industry require a whole period of *prior* accumulation? Why should not the accumulation of capital, in the sense of tangible objects, be synonymous with the growth of industry itself? There is no historical evidence of capitalists having hoarded spinning machines or looms or lathes or stocks of raw material in gigantic warehouses over a period of decades until in the fullness of time these warehouses should be full enough for factory industry to be started. Nor does reasoning suggest that this would have been a sensible, still less an essential, thing to do. There seems to be no reason why growth of equipment and growth of production should not have progressed *pari passu*; and if there is no reason why the growth of industrial

177

equipment should not have been financed, in the main, step by
step out of the profits of previous years (supplemented on special
occasions by credit), the problem about the need for some prior
accumulation as a prerequisite of capitalist industry seems to
evaporate into thin air.

If any sense is to be made, therefore, of the notion of a
" primitive accumulation " (in Marx's sense of the term) *prior
in time* to the full flowering of capitalist production, this must be
interpreted in the first place as an accumulation of capital
claims—of titles to existing assets which are accumulated primarily
for speculative reasons ; and secondly as accumulation in the
hands of a class that, by virtue of its special position in society,
is capable ultimately of transforming these hoarded titles to
wealth into actual means of production.   In other words, when
one speaks of accumulation in an historical sense, one must be
referring to the *ownership* of assets, and to a *transfer* of ownership,
and not to the quantity of tangible instruments of production in
existence.

But when this has been said, the task of clarification is still
incomplete.   If no more is involved than the process of transfer
of, say, debt-claims or precious metals or land from an old ruling
class, lacking enterprise or the taste for industry, to a new class,
practical in bent and fired with an acquisitive lust, the complaint
might justifiably be made that the word accumulation was being
misused : misused to denote a process more properly to be
described as a transfer of ownership-rights from one hand to
another than as a heaping-up either of claims or of the assets
themselves.   Behind this question of terminology lies a question
of substance.   If transfer of wealth is all that is involved in the
process, why should not a sufficient development of credit
institutions, as financial intermediaries between the old class
and the new, suffice to place the means for starting industry in
the hands of the latter ?   Why should one search for any more
complex historical process than this, let alone for a social revolution, as a pre-condition for industrial Capitalism ?

If there is an answer to this challenge, it must be that something *more* than a mere transfer is necessary : that there are
reasons why the full flowering of industrial Capitalism demands,
not only a transfer of titles to wealth into the hands of the
bourgeois class, but a *concentration of the ownership* of wealth into
much fewer hands.   It should become clear in what follows
that there are such reasons ; and this is a matter to which we

shall shortly return.   But if such reasons exist, they will evidently give a special character to capital accumulation as an historical process ;   and the term accumulation will from henceforth be used to denote a concentration, as well as a transfer, of the ownership of titles to wealth.

The various ways in which a class may increase its ownership of property seem to be reducible to two main categories.   Firstly, this class may purchase property from its former owners in exchange for the means of immediate consumption or enjoyment. In other words, this property may be sold against money or non-durable commodities.   In this case the old owners will increase either their consumption or their stocks of money, parting in exchange with their land or houses or other durable objects such as silver plate.   The new class will deplete its hoards of money or else lower its consumption below the level of its income, in order to build up its ownership of durable things ; and in the latter case it can be said to finance its purchases out of " saving ".   This method of acquiring durable wealth by saving out of income has frequently been regarded as the only form that accumulation can take, or at least has taken ; and from this assumption a number of theories derive which seek to explain the origin of Capitalism by some windfall gain of income accruing to the nascent bourgeoisie in the pre-capitalist period, such as profit-inflation due to monetary change, or swollen urban rents or the sudden opening of some new channel of trade.

But there is a second form in which the *parvenu* class may increase its holding of durable wealth ; and this has probably played the more important rôle of the two.   The bourgeoisie may acquire a particular sort of property when this happens to be exceptionally cheap (in the extreme case acquiring it by duress for nothing) and realize this property at some later period, when the market value of this property stands relatively high, in exchange for other things (e.g. labour-power or industrial equipment) which stand at a relatively lower valuation. Through this double act of exchange the bourgeoisie will acquire a larger proportion of the total wealth of the community.

The essential feature of this second form of concentration is that the result depends upon an increment in the capital-value of property, and not on current income or saving out of income. But for such an increment to occur on any extensive scale it is clear that very special circumstances must intervene.   The double transaction falls into two halves : a phase of acquisition and a phase of realization. What is necessary is the intervention of some circumstance sufficiently powerful to make the value of the property or properties in question *rise* between these two periods, *despite* the existence of a whole class of persons who are ready to purchase that property in the first phase and to dispose of it in the second. The presence of such a special circumstance would, indeed, be a necessity, although a weaker necessity, even for any considerable accumulation to occur by the process of saving out of income ; since without it the efforts of the bourgeoisie to acquire a certain type of property, for example land, would exert an upward pressure on its value,[1] and the subsequent attempt by the bourgeoisie to dispose of this property in order to invest in industry would exert a downward pressure on its value to their own detriment.   The attempt to accumulate would accordingly be self-defeating. The outcome would be a *de*crement, instead of an increment, in the property between the phase of acquisition and the phase of realization, and this loss in capital-value might go a long way to nullify the attempt of the bourgeoisie to enrich themselves by saving out of income. For this reason it seems unlikely that acquisition of property by saving out of income could have resulted, unaided, in any large amount of capital accumulation.

What was chiefly necessary therefore as the historical agency of the accumulation of wealth in bourgeois hands was some influence which would depress the value of whatever happened to be the object of hoarding by the bourgeoisie during the phase of acquisition and enhance its relative value during the phase of realization : for example, some influence which would place the former holders of land in urgent need, or else make them exceptionally spendthrift or addicted to money-hoarding, and hence ready to part with their land cheaply during the former period, and which in the latter period would cause the means of production (or some important element in them) to be abnormally cheap. This was unlikely to occur under normal conditions, and could be expected only as an accidental coincidence of fortuitous circumstances.   Least of all was it likely to happen under conditions approximating to free markets and perfect competition.   It

[1] One has to remember that these were days when the customary objects of hoarding had a strictly limited range.   As Professor Tawney has said, " the savings of the mass of the population, apart from land and the occasional purchase of annuities, consisted, according to their various stations, of corn, cattle, stocks of raw materials, furniture, plate, jewellery and coins.   It is these things which passed at death and which men showed their thrift in accumulating " (Introduction to Thomas Wilson's *A Discourse upon Usury*, 103–4).

might occur as a result of deliberate policy by the State, and it might occur as an incident in the break-up of an old order of society, which would tend to have the double effect of impoverishing and weakening those associated with the old mode of production and affording the bourgeoisie an opportunity of gaining some measure of political power, by means of which they could influence the economic policy of the State. If this be the case, we may well have the explanation of a crucial feature of the transition between feudal society and Capitalism of which mention was made in our first chapter : the fact that Capitalism as a mode of production did not grow to any stature until the disintegration of Feudalism had reached an advanced stage. If this disintegration itself had to be the historical lever for launching the process of capital accumulation, then the growth of capitalist production could not itself provide the chief agency of that disintegration. An interval had to elapse during which the petty mode of production, which was the legacy of feudal society, was itself being partially broken up or else subordinated to capital, and State policy was being shaped by new bourgeois influences in a direction favourable to bourgeois aims.[1] The new society had to be nourished from the crisis and decay of the old order.

When we examine the actual changes that were occurring in fifteenth- and sixteenth-century England, it is evident that economic distress at various periods both of large feudal landowners and of certain sections of smaller ones, placing them in the position of distress-sellers and involving them in mortgage and debt, must have played a major rôle in facilitating easy purchase of land by the *parvenu* bourgeoisie. Here force of circumstance and overt pressure often merged, as in the case of Sir Thomas More's poor husbandmen who " by covin and fraud " were " so wearied that they were compelled to sell all ". In addition to mortgages, there were at this period other kinds of debt-instruments, both private debt and State debt, available on fairly easy investment terms ; their significance in our present context consisting less in the income they yielded than in the opportunity they afforded to foreclose on the debtors' property or for speculative gain from subsequent resale of the debt when

---

[1] It is worth remarking that the political struggles of late Tudor times were largely occupied with the tendency of Tudor legislation to maintain the stability of existing rural society (e.g. against the pressure of enclosures and land speculation) and of the old urban handicraft economy : i.e. to stem the further disintegration of the old property-system.

the rate of interest had fallen. Especially as time went on, and
the new class added to its social status and its political power,
opportunities arose for the exercise of *force majeure* or astute
litigation or the employment of political favour and influence,
directed towards the acquisition of property on favourable terms.
Of this the dissolution of the monasteries by the Tudors is a
familiar example ; as is also, in the seventeenth century, the
sequestration and sale of royalists' lands under the Commonwealth. But there were also lesser instances of seizure of
property, or its cheap acquisition, under some kind of coercive
influence ; and in the case of overseas trade, and especially
colonial trade, as we shall see, there was a great deal of seizure
of property by force and simple plunder.

A special circumstance, to which an important influence in
the history of accumulation has been commonly assigned, was
the rapid increase in the supply of the precious metals in the
sixteenth century, and the price-inflation which resulted there-
from. The influence to which reference is usually made was
the rise in bourgeois incomes which this price-inflation must
have occasioned. While this was important, it was not the
sole effect that the monetary changes had upon the accumulation
of bourgeois wealth, and to a long-term view may not have been
the major effect. In addition, the price-inflation was no doubt a
powerful factor in facilitating the transfer of land into bourgeois
hands ; since, to the extent that existing owners of land were
inclined to acquire money as an object of hoarding or alternatively thought in terms of traditional land values, the price at
which land could be purchased tended to lag behind the rise in
other values.[1]

But of no less importance than the first phase of the process
of accumulation was the second and completing phase, by which
the objects of the original accumulation were realized or sold
(at least in part) in order to make possible an actual investment
in industrial production—a sale of the original objects of accumulation in order with the proceeds to acquire (or to bring into
existence) cotton machinery, factory buildings, iron foundries,
raw materials and labour-power. The conditions required to

---

[1] Marx spoke of " the increased supply of precious metals since the sixteenth
century " as " an essential factor in the history of the development of capitalist production ".   But he was here referring to the need for " a quantity of money sufficient
for the circulation and the corresponding formation of a hoard ", and adds that
" this must not be interpreted in the sense that a sufficient hoard must first be formed
before capitalist production can begin.   It rather develops simultaneously " (*Capital*,
vol. II, 396).

facilitate this final transition to industrial investment were in almost all cases the exact opposite of those which had cleared the path for the first stage. A growing volume of State debt or private spendthrift borrowing, or unusually favourable conditions of land-purchase and a tendency towards money-hoarding (tending to keep the rate of interest high)—the very conditions on which bourgeois accumulation had earlier thrived—now exercised a retrograde influence ; since in face of such conditions any widespread tendency to transfer wealth from these older forms into industrial capital would have promoted a sharp depreciation of the former and have either checked further transfer or resulted in considerable impoverishment of their *quondam* owners. A firm market—an elastic demand—for the assets with which the bourgeoisie were parting, and an elastic and cheap supply of the commodities they were now investing in was required. The latter condition may even be considered the more important of the two, since the existence of some positive inducement to invest in industry may have been more decisive at this period than the mere absence of deterrents upon the sale of other types of asset. Here the primary requirements were plentiful reserves of labour and easy access to supplies of raw material, together with facilities for the production of tools and machinery. Without these conditions, industrial investment would inevitably have been baulked and further progress arrested, however splendid the wealth and status of the bourgeoisie had previously grown to be. The marked preoccupation in the later seventeenth century with the evil of high wages, with the virtues of a growing population and the necessity for the employment of children of tender years,[1] and the increasing insistence of economic writers in the eighteenth century on the perils of State indebtedness [2] and on the advantages of freedom

[1] Cf. T. E. Gregory in *Economica*, vol. I, No. 1 ; E. Heckscher, *Mercantilism*, vol. II, 155 seq., who speaks of the " almost fanatical desire to increase population ", which " prevailed in all countries in the latter part of the seventeenth century ", in contrast with views prevalent earlier in the century (158). If one treats these views, not as related to any theory of general welfare, but as connected with class-interest, one does not need to share Professor Heckscher's surprise that the writers of the time should have failed to reconcile their advocacy of an abundant population with the existence of periodic unemployment.
[2] Cf. Adam Smith, *Wealth of Nations*, Bk. V, Chap. 3 : esp. " The public funds of the different indebted nations of Europe, particularly those of England, have by one author been represented as the accumulation of a great capital superadded to the other capital of the country, by means of which its trade is extended, its manufacturers are multiplied and its lands cultivated and improved. . . . He does not consider that the capital which the first creditors of the public advanced to the Government was, from the moment in which they advanced it, a certain portion

of trade seem to have been symptoms of a growing awareness of the requirements of a new situation.

The process by which a proletariat was created will be the subject of the next chapter. Without this process it is clear that a cheap and plentiful labour supply could not have been available, unless there had been a reversion to something closely akin to serf-labour. Labour-power would not have been " itself converted into a commodity " on a sufficiently extensive scale, and the essential condition for the emergence of industrial surplus-value as a " natural " economic category would have been lacking. That this process was so crucial to that full maturing of capitalist industry of which the industrial revolution consisted is the key to certain aspects of primitive accumulation which are commonly misconstrued. At the same time it affords an answer to a plausible objection that might be made to any separation of those two phases of accumulation which we have sought to distinguish : a phase of acquisition and a phase of realization (or of transfer of bourgeois wealth into industrial investment). We meet again the question with which we started concerning the very notion of accumulation as a distinct historical stage. Why, it may be asked, should these two phases be treated as consecutive rather than as concurrent ? Why should not the first bourgeois accumulators of land or debts be regarded, instead, as disposing of their properties to the next wave of bourgeois investors, and so on concurrently ? In this case there would always have been some sections of the rising bourgeoisie who were acting as buyers of a certain type of asset and some as simultaneously sellers of it ; and it would be otiose to postulate two separate stages in the process, each with its peculiar requirements, in the former of which the bourgeoisie exclusively invested, not in new means of production, but in the acquisition of titles to existing property such as land. It is, of course, true that in the search for essentials we have over-simplified the picture. To some extent the two phases doubtless overlapped ; most markedly

of the annual produce turned away from serving in the function of a capital to serve in that of a revenue ; from maintaining productive labourers to maintaining unproductive ones and to be spent and wasted generally in the course of the year, without even the hope of any further reproduction " (Ed. 1826, 879). Postlethwayt had also condemned the growth of public debt, and protested against the possession of the people by this " Stock-bubbling itch ".

As a matter of fact a large amount of the public funds in the eighteenth century was subscribed from Amsterdam, and the inflow of Dutch capital materially helped to keep down interest-rates in England despite Crown borrowing. On the retarding influence of a growing public debt on the development of Capitalism in France, cf. H. Sée, *Modern Capitalism*, 83.

in the seventeenth century. To some extent capital accumulation proceeded all the time by a direct ploughing back of current
profits into the financing of an expanded trade turnover and the
financing of domestic industry ; and some of the wealth that was
directed towards land by the bourgeoisie went not only into the
purchase of mortgages and the transfer of an existing asset but
also into land improvement. Nevertheless the overlap of the
two phases was apparently far from complete, and scarcely could
have been complete for a crucial reason. The reason is that the
conditions for profitable investment in industry were not fully
matured in earlier centuries. Other investments were preferable
to the difficulties and the hazards and the smaller liquidity of
capital devoted to industrial enterprise. The crucial conditions
necessary to make investment in industry attractive on any
considerable scale could not be present until the concentration-
process had progressed sufficiently to bring about an actual
dispossession of previous owners and the creation of a substantial
class of the dispossessed. In other words, the first phase of
accumulation—the growth of concentration of existing property
and simultaneous dispossession—was an essential mechanism for
creating conditions favourable to the second ; and since an
interval had to elapse before the former had performed its
historical function, the two phases have necessarily to be regarded
as separated in time.

The essence of this primary accumulation is accordingly
seen to consist, not simply in the transfer of property from an old
class to a new class, even if this involved a concentration of
property into fewer hands, but the transfer of property from small
owners to the ascendant bourgeoisie and the consequent pauperi-
zation of the former. This fact, which is so commonly ignored,
is the justification of Marx's preoccupation with phenomena
like enclosures as the type-form of his " primitive accumulation " :
an emphasis for which he has often been criticized on the ground
that this was only one among numerous sources of bourgeois
enrichment. Enrichment alone, however, was not enough. It
had to be enrichment in ways which involved dispossession of
persons several times more numerous than those enriched.
Actually, the boot of criticism should be on the other leg.
Those various factors in the process on which many writers have
laid stress, such as indebtedness, windfall profits, high rents and
the gains of usury, could only exert a decisive influence to the
extent that they contributed to the divorce of substantial sections

of small producers from the means of production ; and the
insufficiency of theories which seek to explain the rise of
Capitalism by the effects of monetary changes or the influence
of government finance (debts, armament orders, etc.) consists
in the fact that they emphasize only sources of enrichment and
provide no explanation of how from a society of small owner-
producers a vast proletarian army was born.

To the full maturing of industrial Capitalism certain further
conditions were also essential. In earlier centuries investment
in industry was evidently retarded (as we shall presently see),
not only by the deficiency of the labour supply, but by the
deficient development alike of productive technique and of
markets. It was retarded also, as we have previously seen, by
the survival alike of the régime of urban gild regulation and of
the hegemony of the big trading corporations. To some extent
a transformation of all these conditions was contingent upon a
dissolution of the previous mode of production, which centred
upon the small producer and the local market. Until in unison
all these conditions had changed, the soil for capitalist industry
to grow naturally, unhusbanded by political privileges and
grants of protection, remained limited in extent and diminutive
in yield.

II

On the importance of financial embarrassment, caused by
wars and economic crises, in driving landowners to mortgage
their property to city merchants we have already had occasion
to remark. The fall of land-values which had already occurred
by the end of the fourteenth century was followed by a period
of crisis of landlord estate-farming in the fifteenth century and
the decimation of families and the exhaustion of family fortunes
in the Wars of the Roses. In these centuries existing property
changed hands on a considerable scale and the bourgeoisie
acquired both novel forms of wealth and a measure of gentility.
We see the well-known wool-trading family of the Celys, who
turned over £2,000 of wool a year between the Cotswolds and
Flanders, spending their profits on hawks and horses and negotiating the marriage of their daughters to well-to-do gentlemen.[1]
Of them Professor Postan remarks : " It is very instructive to
watch the interests of the family shifted from Mark Lane to their

[1] *Cely Papers*, xv.

place in Essex. It is there that in the end we find the younger branches of the family all but merged into the county society, and all but absorbed in the pleasures of the hunt." [1] Even in *The Lives of the Berkeleys* we find after the early fifteenth century " sales of manors without rebuyings ", a growing number of them to commoners. In 1514 a petition was directed to the King which attributed the evils of the time to the many merchant adventurers, clothmakers, goldsmiths, butchers, tanners and other covetous persons who " doth encroache daily many ferms more than they can be able to occupye or maynteigne " ; and in the latter part of the sixteenth century there is a curious piece of legislation which is eloquent of the extent to which the transfer of landed property had taken place during that century and of the anxiety among the gentry about the social upheaval this would cause. Fearing the extensive land purchases of the time on the part of West Country clothiers, the country gentry of these districts secured the insertion of a clause in an Act of 1576 designed to limit future land-acquisitions by clothiers in Wiltshire, Somerset and Gloucestershire to 20 acres. [2] There is little evidence that any very effective attempt was made to enforce the clause, and it certainly did little to stem the tide.

The financial plight of the leading noble families was not unrepresentative of what was occurring very widely in the sixteenth century. The Duke of Norfolk became indebted to the amount of £6,000 to £7,000 (the equivalent of about six times that sum to-day), mortgaging three manors to his creditors. The Earls of Huntingdon and Essex were each indebted to an amount three times the size, the latter mortgaging four manors to three Vintners and a Mercer ; while the Duke of Leicester is said to have had debts amounting to £59,000. By the dissolution of the monasteries alone " land of the annual value of some £820,000, or capital value of £16,500,000, according to our money, was distributed among some thousand persons at once ; and of the remaining land, which was at first leased, most had been alienated by the end of the Tudor period ".[3] In the reign of Elizabeth, the Berkeley family repaired its fortunes by selling three manors for £10,000 to an Alderman of London ; and Professor Tawney

[1] M. Postan in *Econ. Hist. Review*, vol. XII, 6.   [2] 18 Eliz. c. 16.
[3] A. H. Johnson, *The Disappearance of the Small Landowner*, 78. " From the reign of Henry VII down to the last days of James I by far the better part of English landed estate changed owners and in most cases went from the old nobility by birth and the clergy into the hands of those who possessed money in the period of the Tudors, i.e. principally the merchants and industrials " (S. B. Liljegren, *Fall of the Monasteries and Social Changes*, 130-1).

has remarked that " the correspondence of Burleigh in the last decade of Elizabeth read like a receiver in bankruptcy to the nobility and gentry ".[1]   Half a century later, on the eve of the Commonwealth, debts owed to the City by Royalists alone reached a figure of not less than £2 million.[2]   Most of the investment in estates of this time by *parvenu* merchants was speculative in intention ; and where this was not so, social advancement or security seems to have been the dominant motive.   In some cases land was bought by city corporations ; as for example the Nottinghamshire manor of North Wheatley, the subject of a petition by its tenants to Charles I in 1629, where the owner " hath byn pleased to sell the said Mannor unto the Cittie of London, whoe has sold the same unto Mr. John Cartwright and Mr. Tho. Brudnell gent ".[3]   Many of such purchased estates, when they had been rack-rented and made an opportunity for enclosures were sold again by their new masters ; and in the case of North Wheatley, the fear which influenced the petitioners was that " the said Mr. Cartwright and Mr. Brudnell should take awae from your Tennants the said demeanes and woods after the expiration of their leases " and " your petitioners and Tennants be utterly undone ".   In the scramble for monastic lands, a regular tribe of land-jobbers appears and " alone, in couples or companies, buy large estates all over England and then sell parcels later on. . . .   There are found persons who secure lands from twenty or more monasteries in order to sell later."[4]   A continental parallel is found in Germany in that impoverishment alike of the knights and of large sections of the nobility which led to an extensive mortgaging of land to city merchants.   Similar tendencies appeared in the Netherlands after the Treaty of Cambrai in 1529.[5]   In France we hear of a certain butcher of Orleans who " was so enriched by moneylending that a great part of the houses of the town were pledged to him, and he bought ovens, mills and chateaux from the nobles ".[6]   The basis of the famous Fugger fortunes lay in the mortgaging of silver mines and of imperial estates ; and their fellow-townsmen the Welsers built their fortunes by speculating

---

[1] Tawney in *Econ. Hist. Review*, vol. XI, No. 1, 11–12.   [2] *Ibid.*
[3] *English Economic History : Select Documents*, Ed. Bland, Brown, Tawney, 259. Cf. also for mortgaging of estates, Tawney's Introduction to Thomas Wilson's *Discourse upon Usury*, 32–6.
[4] Liljegren, *op. cit.*, 118–19.
[5] Cf. Pirenne, *Economic and Social History of Medieval Europe*, 82 ; Schapiro, *Social Reform and the Reformation*, 59, 63, etc. ; J. Wegg, *Antwerp, 1477–1599*, 293.
[6] F. L. Nussbaum, *History of the Economic Institutions of Modern Europe*, 117.

in silver mines in the Tyrol, in copper in Hungary and in quick-silver in Spain.

Among the most powerful influences promoting bourgeois accumulation were the growth of banking institutions and the extension of Crown borrowing and State debt. On the Continent, Italian bankers had grown rich on exchange dealings, the farming of State taxes and city revenues, and the handling of debt. The famous *Casa di S. Giorgio*, for instance, originated from the funding of the Genoa city debt. These bankers " had no hesitation in squeezing the debtors . . . and not infrequently exacted interest of 50 per cent. and even over 100 per cent. from abbeys or individuals in distress ".[1] In Italy as early as the beginning of the fourteenth century one finds bishops borrowing in a single decade over 4 million florins from five Florentine banking houses ; and in the sixteenth century the Fuggers " made profits of from 175,000 to 525,000 ducats a year by advancing money to the Kings of Spain and collecting their revenues ".[2] It is a familiar story that spendthrift habits or economic ruin are always the best hosts for usury to fatten upon. In England, mercers dealt in bill-discounting, scriveners came to act as loan-brokers and to take deposits, and goldsmiths developed the habit of combining the receipt of deposits in precious metals with the issue of promissory notes and the making of loans. Already in the fourteenth and the fifteenth centuries borrowing by the English Crown had begun to assume impressive dimensions, and English merchants had begun to supplant the Jews and Lombards in the not invariably secure rôle of royal creditors. The Merchants of the Staple, for example, lent extensively to both sides in the Wars of the Roses,[3] and continued at intervals to lend to the Crown up to the years of the civil war.

But lending was not altogether a prerogative of *la haute bourgeoisie*, whether lending to the Crown or to private persons in distress. We find in 1522 a number of Wiltshire clothiers being assessed for a forced loan to the Crown of £50 each, and later in the century a number of clothiers being included among the seventy-five Wiltshire gentlemen who in 1588 answered the urgent royal appeal and loaned £25 to £50 apiece.[4] As Professor

---

[1] Pirenne, *op. cit.*, 132.   [2] Nussbaum, *op. cit.*, 119.
[3] Cf. Power and Postan, *Studies in English Trade in the Fifteenth Century*, 315.
[4] G. D. Ramsey, *op. cit.*, 47. Many provincial clothiers of the time were persons of substance. A clothier named Peter Blundell in the late sixteenth century left a fortune of £40,000, and a seventeenth-century clothier £100,000 (cf. Lipson, *A Planned Economy or Free Enterprise*, 95).

Tawney has written of the Tudor age : " At the bottom the tyrants of an underworld portrayed by the dramatists were the pawnbrokers who traded on the necessities of the poorer shop-keepers and the distressed artisans, and whose numbers and exactions—' a thing able only to stupefy the senses '—aroused astonished comment among writers on economic questions. At the top was the small aristocracy of great financiers, largely foreign, who specialized on exchange transactions . . . (and) took handsome commissions for helping to place Government loans. . . . Between these two poles . . . lay the great mass of intermediate money-lending carried on by tradesmen, mer-chants and lawyers. Mortgages, the financing of small business, investment in government loans, annuities, all were fish to its net. . . . It was through the enterprise of this solid bourgeoisie rather than through the more sensational *coups* of larger capitalists that the most momentous financial development of the next half-century was to be made." [1] In a single hundred of Norfolk alone there were to be found " three miserable usurers ", of whom two were worth £100,000 each, while " even in the little moorland town of Leek, far from centres of trade and industry, a money-lender could accumulate what was then the considerable fortune of £1,000 ". [2] Tax-farming was also from early times a lucrative by-pursuit of English merchants, scarcely distinguish-able from State loan-operations ; and both large export-mer-chants of London, Hull or Bristol and provincial clothiers took a hand in the game. As Marx observed of the growing financial needs of the State, " the public debt becomes one of the most powerful levers of primitive accumulation. As with the stroke of an enchanter's wand, it endows barren money with the power of breeding and thus turns it into capital, without the necessity of its exposing itself to the troubles and risks inseparable from its employment or even in usury." [3]

The reign of the last Tudor was essentially a period of transition ; and already before the closing years of England's Virgin Queen, the tide had begun to flow with some force in the direction of industrial investment. In seventeenth-century England conditions were to become considerably more favour-able to accumulation in this form. Capital investment in agri-cultural improvement began to be more common than it had been in Tudor times. The increasing popularity of the joint-

---

[1] Introduction to Wilson's *Discourse upon Usury*, 92.   [2] *Ibid.*, 89.
[3] *Capital*, vol. I, 779.

stock company and the growing practice of open selling of shares
(sometimes by auction) were witness both to the availability of
funds for investment and to the desire to invest in this form of
wealth. There even developed a tribe of projectors and stock-
jobbers, already sophisticated in the arts of dealing in margins,
of options and bear-sales; whose activities, however, (if their
contemporary critics are to be believed) were often of less advantage to the encouragement of permanent investment than they
were beneficial to their own pockets. In Paris similarly there
were the " project-mongers " who, Defoe tells us, " lurked about
the ante-chambers of the great, frequented the offices of State
officials and had secret meetings with the fair ladies of society ".
By 1703, the share capital of English joint-stock companies has
been estimated to have reached £8 million.[1] A large part of
this, probably at least a half, represented capital invested in
foreign trade and not in home industry ; but to this total must be
added the investments of individual undertakers in mining and
metal-working and of merchant-manufacturers in the organization of domestic industry. If the estimates of Petty and King
can be treated as comparable, the value of property in personalty
doubled in the twenty years after the Restoration. While real
wages showed a rising tendency in the course of the century,
they were at about their lowest point at its beginning, and
throughout the century remained substantially below the level
at which they had stood at the dawn of the Tudor age. While
there was a continued tendency to purchase landed estates on
the part of *nouveaux riches* elements in the towns, particularly
Crown lands and during the Commonwealth sequestrated
royalist estates,[2] the high price at which land and houses stood
in England in the latter half of the century acted as a not inconsiderable inducement to place money in industry and in joint-
stock enterprises, instead of in the land speculation that
had proved so attractive to *parvenu* wealth in the previous
century.[3]

At first sight it might seem as though the phenomenal gains
to be made from foreign trade in this age acted as a brake on
industrial investment by diverting capital and enterprise into

[1] W. R. Scott, *Joint Stock Companies*, vol. I, 161, 340–2, 357–60, 371. The £10
million may be compared with King's estimate in 1688 of the national income as
£45 million, the capital value of land and buildings as £234 million and the liquid
capital of the country including livestock as £86 million.
[2] Christopher Hill in *Eng. Hist. Review*, April 1940.
[3] Ehrenberg, *Capital and Finance in the Age of the Renaissance*, 364.

this more lucrative sphere. To some extent this was certainly the case, and afforded a reason why the new bourgeois aristocracy of the Tudor period devoted relatively little attention to the growth of industry, and fattening on the easy profits of foreign adventures so quickly became reactionary. Some of the profits of these overseas trading ventures are, indeed, astounding. Vasco da Gama is said to have returned to Lisbon in 1499 with a cargo which repaid sixty times the cost of the expedition ; Drake to have returned in the *Golden Hind* with booty that has been variously estimated at values between half and one and a half million sterling on a voyage that cost some £5,000 ; and the East India Company to have averaged a rate of profit of about 100 per cent. in the seventeenth century.[1] Raleigh even referred to a profit of 100 per cent. as " a small return ", compared with which it " might have gotten more to have sent his ships fishing ". In the African trade, with its lucrative slave-trade, a mere 50 per cent. was considered a very modest gain ; and a new company formed to monopolize the slave trade after the Restoration (in which the Duke of York and Prince Rupert participated) reaped profits of between 100 and 300 per cent. But it must be remembered that foreign trade in those days was monopolized in a comparatively few hands, and, despite the prevalence of interlopers, the opportunities for investment in this sphere by persons who stood outside a privileged circle were limited.[2] Outsiders generally had to be content with exploring opportunities of gain in internal trade or in manufacture. Had this not been so, the pressure of competition would no doubt

---

[1] Earl Hamilton in *Economica*, Nov. 1929, pp. 348-9 ; J. E. Gillespie, *The Influence of Overseas Expansion on England to 1700*, 113 seq. ; W. R. Scott, *op. cit.*, vol. I, 78-82, 87. In 1611 and 1612 the Russia Company paid 90 per cent. ; in 1617 the East India Company made a profit of £1,000,000 on a capital of £200,000 (*ibid.*, 141, 146).

[2] Entrance to the foreign trading companies, as we have seen, was usually closely restricted ; being possible only by patrimony, by apprenticeship (the number of apprentices being limited) or by purchase ; while retailers, shopkeepers or handicraftsmen were usually explicitly excluded. For the East India Company the entrance fee was £50 for a merchant, £66 for a shopkeeper, and for gentlemen " such terms as they thought fit " (cf. W. R. Scott, *op. cit.*, vol. I, 152). In James I's reign the entrance fee to the Merchant Adventurers rose to £200 (although in face of opposition it was subsequently lowered), and apprentices paid £50 for admission or more. In the case of the Levant Company no one residing within twenty miles of London other than " noblemen and gentlemen of quality " were admitted unless they were freemen of the City ; the entrance fee was £25 to £50 ; and high premiums had to be paid for apprenticeship, Dudley North paying £50, and at the end of the seventeenth century a sum of £1,000 sometimes being demanded (cf. Lipson, *op. cit.*, vol. II, 217, 341). It also often happened in practice, at any rate in the provinces, that leading members in a locality had a power of veto on the admission of new members from the district.

have sufficed before long to reduce the exceptional profits of the Levant or Indies trade to a more normal level. In the main this sphere was self-financing, new investment being drawn from the profits of previous trade. For this reason the glittering prizes of foreign trade were probably a less serious rival to investment in manufacture, at any rate for the *nouveaux riches*, than might have been supposed. Moreover, there were indirect ways in which the prosperity of foreign trade in the Tudor age aided industrial investment in the ensuing century. Some of the fortunes made by foreign adventurers no doubt eventually found their way into industrial enterprise ; while, as we shall presently see, the expansion of overseas markets, especially colonial markets, in the seventeenth century, to some extent acted as a lever to the profitability of manufacture at home.

But while there were some compensating advantages for industry from the activities of the foreign trading companies, it was not from them that the initiative in industrial investment was to come. Initiative in this new direction, as we have seen, lay, not with the upper bourgeoisie concerned with the export market, but with the humbler provincial middle bourgeoisie, in the main less privileged and less wealthy but more broadly based. Moreover, while it is doubtless true that bodies like the Merchant Adventurers and the Elizabethan trading companies in their pioneering days brought an expanding market for English manufactures, it was their restrictive aspect—the stress on privilege and the exclusion of interlopers—that came into prominence towards the end of the sixteenth and in the course of the seventeenth century. Their limitation on the number of those engaging in the trade and their emphasis on favourable terms of trade at the expense of its volume increasingly acted as fetters on the further progress of industrial investment and brought them into opposition with those whose fortunes were linked with the expansion of industry. The interests of industry, accordingly, as it developed came to be identified with an assault on monopolies and with the freeing of trade from the shackles of regulation. Yet this repudiation of monopoly was by no means unconditional. In England it is true that free trade, both internally and externally, was to become in the nineteenth century an essential part of the ideology of a mature Capitalism. But here conditions were in many respects peculiar ; and in other countries the doctrine of free trade was only accepted with substantial reservations. Even in the native land of *Smithian-*

ismus and Manchester liberalism, the tide was beginning to turn in favour of monopolistic privilege and regulation before the nineteenth century drew to its close. At the time of the industrial revolution, however, British industry required not only an expanding market for its products, if the field of investment in the newer forms of production was to be other than a very restricted one, but also an expanding supply of raw materials (a number of which came from abroad, most notably cotton), and also a cheap supply of foodstuffs as subsistence for its growing army of hired workers. Whereas England at the time, as an importer of corn and cotton and as a pioneer of the new machinery, who had everything to gain and nothing to lose by opening markets abroad to her manufactures, could afford to elevate freedom of foreign trade to the level of a general principle, other countries could seldom so afford. In particular, countries which relied on an indigenous agriculture, and not on import, for their food supply, such as Germany, and in the case of America also for their raw materials, inclined their affections towards a policy of differential protection for nascent industry. Where agricultural products both furnished the needs of home consumption and were exported, this policy had the significance, not only of excluding the competition of foreign industries from the home market, but of tending to raise the internal level of industrial prices while maintaining agricultural prices at the world level,[1] thereby turning the terms of trade inside the national boundaries to the advantage of industry ; just as within a system of metropolis and colonies the Mercantile System had previously done. In other words, Capitalism on the continent of Europe, in countries like Germany and France and later Russia, and also in U.S.A., looked in the direction of what may be termed an " internal colonial policy " of industrial capital towards agriculture before its interest in an export market for manufactures had been fully awakened.[2]

[1] Had there been mobility of capital and labour between industry and agriculture, such a result could not have endured as a long-term tendency. But in the conditions of the time, especially where agriculture was mainly peasant agriculture, any such mobility, even as a long-term tendency, was very small : in Taussig's well-known phrase, agriculture and industry constituted " non-competing groups ".

[2] This, of course, only retained its *raison d'être* from a capitalist point of view so long as Capitalism in agriculture itself was undeveloped, and agriculture remained primarily *peasant* agriculture whose exploitation in favour of industry was capable of widening the scope of profitable investment for capital. In England, however, Capitalism in agriculture developed appreciably in the seventeenth century. In Germany the conflict of interest between industrial capital and the large estates of East Prussia was an important factor in retarding the development of the former

A striking example of how the sweets of foreign trade and foreign loan business could be rival to the growth of industry is afforded by the Netherlands. Despite the precocious flowering of Capitalism in this early stronghold of the cloth industry, industrial investment in later centuries was to mark time ; and in the eighteenth century Holland was to be entirely eclipsed by England in the progress of capitalist production. The fortunes to be made from dealing in foreign stocks seems to have diverted capital and enterprise from industry. British securities became the chief object of speculation on the Amsterdam Bourse, ousting from this position even Dutch East India securities ; and " the Dutch capitalist could, merely by making contact with an attorney in London, collect his 5 per cent. on investments in English Funds, or by speculation in normal times win up to 20 or 30 per cent.".[1] Import and export merchants, whose interests lay in keeping open the door to foreign products, were powerful enough to prevent the protective tariff policy for which industry was clamouring ; [2] while scarcity of labour expressed itself in a relatively high cost of labour, which acted as a brake on industrial investment. At the same time, the Dutch linen industry was severely hit by the dwindling of its export trade in face of subsidized English competition (the output of the Haarlem bleaching industry being more than halved between the beginning and the end of the eighteenth century, and the number of its bleaching factories falling from twenty to eight).[3] " So far from stimulating Dutch industrial development ", says Mr. C. H. Wilson, " Holland's eighteenth-century loans almost certainly obstructed and postponed it, directly and indirectly. . . . (The) attitude of the Staplers and their allies the bankers . . . interfered with the free flow of internal capital, prevented what Unwin described as the fertilization of industry by commercial capital. . . . Dutch economic development was postponed by a leakage of capital into international finance." [4] The launching of a country on the first stages of the road towards Capitalism is no guarantee that it will complete the journey.

in the days of the monarchy, and in forcing that compromise between the capitalist class and the Prussian aristocracy which was the peculiarity of German development prior to 1918.

[1] C. H. Wilson, *Anglo-Dutch Commerce and Finance in the Eighteenth Century*, 62.
[2] It was not until 1816, after Dutch foreign trade had suffered decline, that protection was introduced for the benefit of the textile and metal trades.
[3] *Ibid.*, 61.
[4] *Ibid.*, 200–1 ; also cf. C. H. Wilson in *Econ. Hist. Review*, vol. IX, 113.

Of the importance for England of an expanding export market in widening the field of industrial investment from the middle of the eighteenth century onwards more will be said in a later chapter. Something of its importance can be judged when one considers how limited the home market for manufactures had been prior to this time. True, the development of a prosperous middle bourgeoisie of the towns itself provided a substantial market for the wares of handicraft industry ; and to this extent the growth of the bourgeoisie in numbers, as well as in wealth, was an important condition for the encouragement of industry, and a prosperous middle bourgeoisie was of greater moment than the splendour of a few merchant-princes. But this rising bourgeoisie was a thrifty class, and contributed considerably less in expenditure on the products of this industry than the real values which the income it drew from trade and industry represented ; and growth of its expenditure generally followed rather than led the growth of manufacture. At the same time the very limitation of the standard of life of the masses, which was a condition of the growth of capital accumulation, set fairly narrow bounds to the market for anything but luxury goods.

From the earliest days when woollen manufacture expanded beyond the confines of the gilds and the town economy, England's leading industry had been dependent on export markets in a high degree ; and the expansion of the frontiers of the clothmaking areas in England in the fifteenth and sixteenth centuries kept closely in step with the expansion of the market for English cloth in the Netherlands and Germany. Although the foreign market may have absorbed a smaller proportion of the country's total output than it has done in more recent times—in the early eighteenth century it may have absorbed only some 7 to 10 per cent.—nevertheless, as Mantoux observes, " only a negligible quantity of ferment is needed to effect a radical change in a considerable volume of matter ".[1] Of the manufactures which figured prominently in the Tudor age it is remarkable how many catered either for export or for the demand of the well-to-do : for example, the leather trades, whether they were concerned with shoemaking or saddlery, hat- and glove-making, hosiery, lace, sword-making, cutlery, pewter. It was the same with the leading industries that prospered in France in the seventeenth century under the Colbertian régime : like tapestries, glass,

---

[1] P. Mantoux, *Industrial Revolution in the Eighteenth Century*, 103.

silk, carpets, porcelain, they were pendent chiefly on the luxury demand of Court circles.[1] Until machinery had developed, and investment itself was proceeding on an appreciable scale, the metal trades had little scope, apart from government orders for purposes of war. The latter was an important stimulus to the brass and ordnance manufacture in later Tudor and Stuart times, as the expansion of woollen manufacture and its need for carding instruments seems to have been a principal ground of the contemporary prosperity of the trade of wire-making. Apart from this, the demand for metals sufficed to maintain nothing more grandiose than the West Country nailmaking craft, the manufacture of a few hand tools and the few staples of the blacksmith's art. The demand for ships, to which the Tudor navy in the sixteenth century and the Navigation Acts in the seventeenth so powerfully contributed, brought prosperity to the ports. To this extent the notion that government spending was the midwife to industrial Capitalism contains an element of truth. As a contributory influence (but no more) in creating conditions favourable to industrial investment, it had some importance : an importance which was often greater in the degree to which the social development of a country was backward ; as the powerful, though premature, influence of Peter the Great's armament orders on nascent Russian manufacture illustrates. The building of country houses in Tudor England and of a new type of farmhouse for the more well-to-do farmers (complete with staircase instead of only a removable ladder by the end of Elizabeth's reign) and the large amount of building in London in the twenty years after the Great Fire of 1666 must have afforded a stimulus, not only to the building trades, but indirectly also to other employments, to which these centuries had few parallels. It is true that the very growth of Capitalism served to develop its own market. This it did in two ways : by the profits it yielded and the employment that it encouraged ; and, scarcely less important, by its tendency to break down the self-sufficiency of older economic units, like the manorial village, and so to bring a larger part of the population and of its wants

---

[1] On luxury-consumption as an influence in early capitalism, cf. Sombart, *Der Moderne Kapitalismus*, I, 719 seq. The protectionist policy of Colbert seems to have been the product of a situation where investment in production was retarded both by narrowness of markets and by scarcity of labour. The latter half of the seventeenth century appears to have been a period of falling prices in France, largely due to hoarding of money by the peasantry and bourgeoisie (cf. Joseph Aynard, *La Bourgeoisie Française*, 296-300).

within the orbit of commodity-exchange.[1]   Here it was especially
that the rise of a capitalist agriculture in England in the sixteenth
century, and with it of a class of fairly prosperous yeoman farmers
who were linked with the market both as sellers and as consumers,
was of signal importance.   It is noticeable, for example, that
during this century the standard of comfort in well-to-do farm-
houses, as expressed, for example, in the quantity of household
furnishings, greatly increased in many parts of the country,
especially where sheep-farming flourished.   But in the early
days of manufacture, investment in new industries or the extension of existing industries was evidently hampered by the prevailing notion that the market for commodities was limited,
and that new enterprise only stood any chance of success if
either some new market was simultaneously opened abroad or
some political privilege was accorded to enable it to elbow
its way successfully into existing markets at the expense of
rivals.   For that mood of optimism to be born which was so
essential an ingredient of the pioneering activities of the industrial revolution, this notion of a rigid " vent " for the products
of industry and the commercial timidity essentially connected
with it had first to be banished ; and to provide room for the
immense growth in the productive powers of industry which the
industrial revolution occasioned, it was essential that an expansion of the market, larger in dimensions than anything witnessed
during the earlier period of handicraft, should occur.   But
until the vast potentialities of the new mechanical age, and of
the new division of labour introduced by machinery, had become
apparent, it was understandable that even the most enterprising
of the bourgeoisie should look to trade regulation and political
privilege for the assurance that his enterprise would prove profitable.

III

Concern with the importance of an expanding export market
may be said to have differentiated the economic spokesmen of
that second phase of primitive accumulation, which we have
distinguished, from the economic thought of the earlier phase

[1] Cf. Lenin's remark on the dependence of industry on the growth of a home
market in *The Development of Capitalism in Russia* in *Selected Works*, vol. I, 225 seq.,
297 ; e.g., " The home market for capitalism is created by developing capitalism,
which increases the social division of labour. . . .   The degree of development of
the home market is the degree of development of capitalism in the country."

in which industrial investment as yet held only a very modest place. At any rate, it was an emphasis that became more apparent in economic thought and writing as time went on. On the other hand, it was not this emphasis, but a different one, that distinguished the so-called Mercantilist school from their successors of the late eighteenth and nineteenth centuries. Adam Smith and his school, no less than their predecessors, regarded the expansion of markets as the pre-condition for the growth of production and of investment. The classical school were certainly more optimistic as to the capacity of the market to grow *pari passu* with the progress of industry and of the division of labour ; but of the importance of this growth they were more, rather than less, aware. What principally distinguished economic writers prior to the eighteenth century from those who followed after was their belief in economic regulation as the essential condition for the emergence of any profit from trade—for the maintenance of a profit-margin between the price in the market of purchase and the price in the market of sale. This belief was so much part of the texture of their thought as to be assumed rather than demonstrated, and to be regarded as an unquestioned generalization about the economic order with which they were familiar.

It was not only that to the bourgeoisie as a rising class in an age of primitive accumulation political influence appeared as a *sine qua non* of their own advancement, but that in a society based on the petty mode of production, with industry resting on the employment of hired labour still in its infancy, rent of land appeared as the only natural form of surplus : a notion which found its most explicit formulation in the famous doctrine of the French Physiocrats concerning productive and sterile labour. The productivity of labour was still low, and the number of workers employed by a single capitalist was seldom very numerous. It was accordingly still difficult to imagine any substantial profit being " naturally " made by investment in production. Interest was customarily regarded as an exaction from the small producer, at the expense of his penury, or else as deriving from the rent of land, and hence regulated by " the rent of so much land as the money lent will buy ".[1] If merchants or merchant-manufacturers were to be subjected to unrestrained competition, what source of profit could there be ? The margin between price of

[1] W. Petty, *Economic Writings*, vol. I, 48 ; cf. also Turgot, *The Formation and the Distribution of Riches*, sections lvii, lviii.

sale and price of purchase might suffice to cover the merchant's expenses, and if he were not too luckless secure him a bare livelihood as well.   But it was hard for contemporaries to see any source from which in conditions of unfettered competition even a modest fortune could be made.   Hence it is not surprising in this period that profit should have been regarded as fruit of successful speculation, in the sense of taking advantage of price-differences :   profit which would quickly disappear if too many persons were in a position to take a hand in the business of purchase and re-sale.   The trader of those centuries felt much like an industrial patentee to-day :   fearful lest those who emulate his example will too quickly snatch the fruit of his enterprise and enterprise be therefore discouraged.   Without regulation to limit numbers and protect the price-margin between what the merchant bought and what he sold, merchant capital might enjoy spasmodic windfalls but could have no enduring source of income.   Competition and surplus-value could not endure long in company.   It was natural to suppose that without regulation trade and industry would languish for lack of incentive to adventure money in such enterprise ;   and the bourgeoisie as a class could never come into its own.   Until the progress of technique substantially enhanced the productivity of labour, the notion could hardly arise of a specifically industrial surplus-value, derived from the investment of capital in the employment of wage-labour, as a " natural " economic category, needing no political regulation or monopoly either to create it or to preserve it.   Moreover, so long as surplus-value was conceived as reliant on conscious regulation to produce it, the notion of *economic objectivity*—of an economy operating according to laws of its own, independent of man's conscious will—which was the essence of classical political economy could scarcely develop.

All this, as we have said, was implicit rather than explicit in Mercantilist thought.   As regards the form in which their thought was expressed, the doctrines of these writers were evidently much less homogeneous than the classical economists, in their assault upon " the principles of the Mercantile System ", represented them to be.   The particular policies they sponsored were various ;   and some have gone so far as to deny, with Schumpeter, that " mercantilist policy embod(ied) any set of definite economic aims or purposes ".[1]   The common thread running through their writings, upon which attention has generally been focused, was the notion that money, if not synonymous with wealth, is at any rate an essential ingredient in the wealth of a nation : a notion which Adam Smith pilloried as a patent absurdity and which Lord Keynes has rehabilitated as an intuitive recognition of the connection between plenty of money and low interest-rates in stimulating investment and employment.[1] Here again, some writers have denied to Mercantilism even this element of unity, and Mr. Lipson has roundly stated that " the accumulation of treasure was not one of the fundamentals of Mercantilism " and that " the general body of mercantilist thought (1558–1750) was not built on a Midas-like conception of wealth ".[2]   That this emphasis on the advantage to a nation of possessing a large quantity of the precious metals was neither so central nor so universal an element in their doctrines as has been traditionally supposed is probably true, at any rate of the later Mercantilist writers as distinct from the older Bullionist school, who undoubtedly represented the attraction of " treasure " as the central advantage of foreign trade.   Nevertheless, the influx of gold and silver was an advantage to which they continued to make frequent appeals in the seventeenth century ; even if they claimed no more for money than the property of affording " radical moisture " to commerce (in Davenant's phrase), and

---

[1] As a matter of fact it was rather the landed than the mercantile interest which between 1650 and 1750 was agitating for lower interest-rates with the object of maintaining the value of land (a fact to which Marx draws attention in his *Theorien über den Mehrwert*). However, we have suggested above that the maintenance of high land-values was a condition favourable to the completion of the second phase of accumulation—the phase of realization of property previously acquired and a transfer into industrial investment. At the same time there were writers such as North and Petty who (in contrast to Locke) were beginning to preach that interest-rates depended not on abundance or scarcity of money but on the demand for and supply of industrial capital or " Stock ". North wrote : " It is not low Interest makes trade, but Trade increasing the Stock of the Nation makes Interest low . . . Gold and Silver . . . are nothing but the Weights and Measures by which Traffick is more conveniently carried on than could be done without them : and also a proper Fund for a surplusage of Stock to be deposited in " (*Discourses Upon Trade*, pp. 1, 4 and 16). Again, he speaks of " The Moneys Employed at Interest " as not being " near the Tenth part disposed to Trading People " but as being " for the most part lent for the supplying of Luxury and to the Expense of Persons, who though Great Owners of Land yet spend faster than their Lands bring in, and . . . mortgage their Estates " (*ibid.*, 67). John Bellers (who, being a Quaker philanthropist, is not to be regarded, perhaps, as altogether typical of the mercantile interest) wrote that " Mony neither increased nor is useful, but when it is parted with. . . . What Mony is more than of absolute necessity for home Trade is dead Stock to a Kingdom or Nation, and brings no profit to that country it's kept in " (*Essays about the Poor Manufacturers, etc.*, 1699, p. 13). Child also dissented from the view that the low interest-rates prevailing in Holland were due to abundance of money there (*New Discourse on Trade*, 9).

[2] *Econ. History* (3rd Edn.), vol. II, lxxx, lxxxvii. Mr. Lipson adds the remark that Mercantilist methods were " only the counterpart " of " the modern device of raising the bank rate in order to attract gold from abroad ", and that the imperfect development of credit placed a special premium on the possession of cash in trade transactions.

even if this had already ceased to be a major emphasis before the close of the century.

What seems most probable is that in appealing to the supposed advantage of attracting treasure into the realm they were using a conventional norm to justify measures which they regarded as advantageous on other grounds ; just as later economists used the alleged maximization of utility as the justification of a policy of *laissez-faire.* It seems clear that the main preoccupation which gave to the economic writings of the seventeenth century their element of uniformity was the creation of a favourable balance of trade, in the sense of an expansion of exports unbalanced by any equivalent intrusion of foreign goods into the home market. It was the expansion of exports as a net addition to the volume of sales on what was regarded as an inelastic and more or less limited home market that was the common objective of this school. A necessary condition of such a trade balance (in the absence of foreign investment) was an influx of precious metals. But the end they chiefly valued was the extra market for com-modities and not the metals, which were only the means.

Yet it is fairly clear that, while stating their theory in terms of a favourable *balance* of trade, they were equally if not more concerned with the advantages of favourable *terms* of trade—of buying cheap and selling dear ; and while honour was paid to the former, the latter was an important, and at times a major, preoccupation. The connection, if any, between the two was seldom discussed and never at the time made perfectly clear. But several writers stated that it was not the absolute amount of money in a country but its amount relative to that possessed by other countries which they regarded as important : for example, Coke who declared that " if our Treasure were more than our Neighbouring Nations I did not care whether we had one fifth part of the Treasure we now have ".[1] A favourable trade balance which drew gold into the country could have been expected to raise the level of internal prices, and similarly to depress the price-level of the country from which the gold had been drained, thereby lowering the price of the products which were purchased abroad for import and raising the price of exported commodities. Locke, for example, made it plain that for him this was the crux of the matter when he said that the disadvantage to a country of having less money than other nations was that " it will make our native commodities vent very cheap " and " make all foreign

---

[1] *Treatise,* III, 45 ; cit. Heckscher, *op. cit.,* 239.

commodities very dear " ; and earlier both Hales and Malynes
had indicated that not the *quantity* of exports, but the relation of
export and import *prices*, was their chief concern by demonstrating
the disadvantages of undervaluation of English money on the
foreign exchanges (due as Hales feared to debasement and as
Malynes thought to foreign exchange speculation) in making
English exports " too good cheap " and foreign commodities too
dear. In other words, the policy these writers were advocating
was not dissimilar to modern policies of currency overvaluation
(although Misselden at one time advanced a contradictory
proposal to overvalue *foreign* coins in order to tempt foreigners
to buy from England).

If, as a result of attracting money, wages as well as prices in
the home country had risen, then to this extent, of course, the
advantage to the merchant or manufacturer would have been
partly nullified by the consequent rise in cost of exported goods.
But Mercantilist writers seem to have presumed that State regulation could and would ensure that this did not occur. Little
attention, again, was paid to the possible effects of such a policy in
depressing the demand-price that the foreign buyer was able or
willing to pay for the goods exported to his markets, and thereby
provoking an inevitable reaction in the direction of an import
surplus. There is, however, a hint of recognition of this point in
a passage in Mun's *England's Treasure by Forraign Trade*. Here he
remarks that " all men do consent that plenty of money in a
Kingdom doth make the natife commodities dearer, as plenty,
which as it is to the profit of some private men in their revenues,
so is it directly against the benefit of the Publique in the quantity
of the trade ; for as plenty of money makes wares dearer, so dear
wares decline their use and consumption ".[1] Hales, in the course
of his dialogue, makes his " Doctor " reply to his " Knight " on
the subject of retaliation that English exports are indispensable
to foreigners ; which suggests that among writers of the time a
highly inelastic foreign demand for English products was taken
for granted. Mun elsewhere speaks of selling exports at a high
price " so far forth as the high price cause not a less vent in the
quantity ".

The reason why an inelastic foreign demand should have been
so easily assumed is not at first glance clear. A principal reason
why they imagined that exports could be forced on other
countries at an enhanced price without diminution of quantity

[1] *England's Treasure*, Pol. Econ. Club Ed. of Tracts on Commerce, 138.

was probably because they were thinking, not in terms of nineteenth-century conditions where alternative markets were generally available to a country, but of a situation where considerable pressure, if not actual coercion, could be applied to the countries with whom one did the bulk of one's trade. Their policy chiefly depended for its success on its application to a system of *colonial* trade, where political influence could be brought to bear to ensure to the parent country some element of monopoly ; and it is essentially as applied to the exploitation of a dependent colonial system that Mercantilist trade-theories acquire a meaning. Further point is given to their advocacy if we regard them as spokesmen of industrial rather than of merchant capital (or perhaps one should say of merchant capital that was already acquiring a direct interest in production). For the trade that they evidently had in mind consisted of an exchange between the products of home manufacture and colonial products which consisted chiefly of raw materials and therefore entered as an element into the cost of the former.[1] Any favourable turn in the terms of trade would, therefore, tend to lower industrial costs relatively to the prices of finished industrial goods and consequently to augment industrial profit.[2] That, when they spoke of stimulating exports, it was on manufactures that attention was focused, and that their concern to restrain import was not intended to apply to the import of raw materials

---

[1] The main English exports at the end of the sixteenth century were cloth and linen which were the most important ; and also lead and tin, including some wrought tin, hides and knives (to the Spanish West Indies), a little copper to Spain, some grain to France and Portugal, and some fish. Among imports were a variety of things such as wines from France and Spain, sugar and molasses from the West Indies, hemp and flax and hides and pitch and tar and tallow and furs from the Baltic ; cotton and silk, currants, skins and oils from the Mediterranean and farther east, and soap, oranges and spices from Spain.

[2] In so far as the difference between internal and external prices was maintained by a uniform import tariff, then the gain from the price-difference would, of course, accrue, not to importers or buyers in the home country, but to the State in revenue ; but if the limitation on import amounted to something like a quota-system, it would be the importer who would reap the gain. Actually, the restriction on import consisted of actual prohibitions in some cases and duties which were in effect prohibitive in others, while the duties themselves differentiated widely between different commodities. The effect of the differentiation was therefore to favour imported raw materials as against finished manufactures, and so to create price-divergencies inside the country between raw materials, which tended to be close to the world price, and the highly protected manufactured commodities. A subordinate motive for the differentiation against luxury-imports was apparently to encourage investment. Misselden referred to the contrast between expending income on luxury imports and investing it as " Stock " to employ the idle poor in the export trades. Mun, in admitting that an inflow of specie might raise prices, including the price of imports, argued that this damage could be prevented if increased income was not used for consumption, but was invested—and invested, he hoped, in ways which would tend to stimulate exports still further.

(but rather the contrary) is well attested by the statements of contemporary writers. Colbert defined " the whole business of commerce " as consisting in " facilitating the import of those goods which serve the country's manufacture and placing embargo on those which enter in a manufactured state ; " [1] part of Mun's defence of the East India trade and its licence to export bullion was that this trade brought in raw materials for manufacture ; and Coke declared that commodities imported could be more valuable than money if they were used in industry. John Hales had earlier deplored the export of raw materials and had advocated simultaneously a restriction on the export of wool and the freeing of corn-export in order to relieve agrarian distress.

Measures, not only of coercion applied to colonial trade in order that it should primarily serve the needs of the parent country, but also to control colonial production, became a special preoccupation of policy at the end of the seventeenth century and the first half of the eighteenth. A Report of the Commissioner for Trade and Plantations in 1699 declared that " it was the intent in settling our plantations in America that the people there should be only employed in such things as are not the product of England to which they belong ". Steps were taken to prohibit the colonial manufacture of commodities which competed with the exportable products of English industry, and to forbid the export of enumerated colonial products to other markets than England. Thereby, it was hoped, England would be given the pick of the colonial trade. For example, the American colonies were forbidden to export woollen goods by an Act of 1699, while tobacco and sugar were " enumerated " and could only be exported to England or to other colonies. During Robert Walpole's period of office as Prime Minister, not only were bounties given to encourage the export of manufactures such as silk, while import duties on raw materials such as dyes and hemp and timber were repealed, but colonial manufacture of hats was forbidden in the interest of English hatmakers, and Ireland was forbidden to export woollen goods lest they should compete in European markets with English cloth, or to trade with the other colonies except through London.[2] As early as

---

[1] Cit. Heckscher, *op. cit.*, 146.

[2] C. F. Brisco, *Econ. Policy of Robert Walpole*, 166, 185. The *Cambridge Modern History* refers to " bounties on exported manufactures which gave advantage to the merchant with the large purse over the merchant with the small " and helped " to enable well-grown industries to capture foreign trade " (vol. VI, 48-9). The King's Speech of 1721, while continuing to refer to the need for a favourable *balance*

1636 the Earl of Strafford had outlined his policy in Ireland as
being to " discourage all I could . . . the small beginnings
towards a clothing trade " which he found there, since " it might
be feared they would beat us out of the trade itself by underselling
us ", whereas " so long as they did not indrape their own wools,
they must of necessity fetch their own clothing from us " ; [1] and
the economic historian of seventeenth-century Ireland has said
that " the Irish sheep-farmer and wool merchant were supposed
by law to send their wool nowhere except to England ; thus,
legally speaking, the English were monopolist buyers and could
fix the price as low as it suited them ".[2]   In 1750, while the import
of pig-iron and bar-iron from the colonies was permitted for the
benefit of the English iron manufacturers, the erection of any
rolling mill, plating forge or furnace in the colonies was prohibited.

As one writer has said of it, this was the former " policy of the
town writ large in the affairs of State ".[3]   It was a similar policy
of monopoly to that which at an earlier stage the towns had
pursued in their relations with the surrounding countryside, and
which the merchants and merchant-manufacturers of the privileged companies had pursued in relation to the working craftsmen.
It was a continuance of what had always been the essential aim
of the policy of the Staple ; and had its parallel in the policy of
towns like Florence or Venice or Ulm or Bruges or Lübeck in
the thirteenth and fourteenth centuries, to which in an earlier
chapter the name of " urban colonialism " was given.   The aim
of reducing the costs of manufacture at home by keeping wages
down was, of course, maintained—the policy which Professor
Heckscher cautiously refers to as " wealth for the ' country '
based on the poverty of the majority of its subjects " and as
" approximating suspiciously closely to the tendency to keep

of trade, interpreted this as facilitating the import of raw material and expanding
the export of home manufactures.   Colonial trade is estimated to have accounted
for 15 per cent. of England's overseas trade in 1698 and 33 per cent. in 1774 (Lipson,
op. cit., vol. III, p. 157).

[1] *English Economic History : Select Documents*, Ed. Bland, Brown, Tawney, 471.

[2] G. O'Brien, *Econ. Hist. of Ireland in the Seventeenth Century*, 186.   On the other
hand, the Irish linen industry (largely though not exclusively in the north) benefited
in the eighteenth century from export bounties introduced in 1743 ; the intention
of these being (in words used by Sir William Temple some decades earlier) " to
wear down the trade both of France and Holland, and draw much of the money
which goes from England to those parts into the hands of His Majesty's Subjects
in Ireland, without crossing any interest of trade in England ".   There was always,
of course, a large amount of evasion of these colonial regulations by smuggling.
Cf., with regard to evasions in the American trade, A. M. Schlesinger, *Colonial
Merchants and the American Revolution*, 16-19.

[3] N. S. B. Gras, *Introduction to Economic History*, 201-2.

down the mass of the people by poverty in order to make them better beasts of burden for the few ".[1] But monopolistic regulation was now also to be directed externally in relation to colonial areas, which were to be kept as cheap suppliers of agricultural products for the benefit of the growing industry of the metropolitan economy. Its *raison d'être* lay in its influence to create enhanced opportunities of profit for industrial capital by raising the price-level of industrial products and depressing the price-level of agricultural products within the controlled economy of metropolis and colony : [2] an influence to which (as we have seen) the achievement of an export surplus from the metropolis might contribute by draining the colonial country of gold and increasing the flow of gold into the metropolis.   It is in the light of this tradition-scarred design of creating scarcity in markets of sale and cheapness and plenty in markets of purchase that the " fear of goods " and the conviction that " no man profiteth but by the loss of others ", which Professor Heckscher has stressed as prime ingredients of Mercantilist thought, acquire a meaning.

Like most projects of monopoly, the policy ran the risk of reducing the *volume* of sales while raising their unit-price. But whether or not this would be the result depended on how far economic and political pressure was successful in lowering costs in the colonies by making them work harder in order to give more goods in purchase of the same quantity as before.   This political pressure often sufficed, indeed, to make colonial trade forced trading and the profit on it indistinguishable from plunder. Tudor voyages of discovery (in Sombart's words) " were often nothing more than well-organized raiding expeditions to plunder lands beyond the sea ".   In France the same word was used for shipper and for pirate, and " the men who in the sixteenth century sent their argosies from Dieppe, Havre, Rouen or La

---

[1] *Op. cit.*, vol. II, 153, 166. Child almost alone of the economic writers of the time spoke against " retrenching on the hire of labour " as a policy " well becoming a usurer ".   But he was speaking as a champion of the East India Company against its critics among Whig merchants and industrialists.

[2] Cf. James Mill : " The mother country, in compelling the colony to sell goods cheaper to her than she might sell them to other countries, merely imposes upon her a tribute ; . . . not the less real because it is disguised " (*Elements of Pol. Economy*, 3rd Ed., 213), and J. B. Say : " The metropolis can compel the colony to purchase from her everything it may have occasion for ; this monopoly . . . enables the producers of the metropolis to make the colonies pay more for the merchandise than it is worth " (*Treatise on Pol. Economy*, Ed. 1821, vol. I, 322).   Cf. also Adam Smith, *Wealth of Nations*, Ed. 1826, p. 554 seq ; e.g. : " this monopoly has necessarily contributed to keep up the rate of profit in all the different branches of British trade higher than it naturally would have been, had all nations been allowed a free trade to the British colonies " (558).

Rochelle to Africa and America were shippers and pirates in one ".[1] As Alfred Marshall remarked, " silver and sugar seldom came to Europe without a stain of blood ". In the cruel rapacity of its exploitation colonial policy in the seventeenth and eighteenth centuries differed little from the methods by which in earlier centuries Crusaders and the armed merchants of Italian cities had robbed the Byzantine territories of the Levant. In India pressure was exerted on the peasant to cultivate raw silk for export ; and Burke denounced " the hand that in India has torn the cloth from the loom or wrested the scanty portion of rice and salt from the peasant of Bengal ". " The large dividends of the East India companies over long periods indicate plainly that they converted their power into profits. The Hudson's Bay Company bought beaver pelts for goods costing seven to eight shillings. In the Altai the Russians sold iron pots to the natives for as many beaver skins as would fill them. The Dutch East India Company paid the native producers of pepper about one-tenth the price it received in Holland. The French East India Company in 1691 bought Eastern goods for 487,000 livres which sold in France for 1,700,000 livres. . . . Slavery in the colonies was another source of great fortune " ; sugar, cotton and tobacco cultivation all resting on slave-labour.[2] Of Bristol it was said that " there is not a brick in the city but what is cemented with the blood of a slave ".[3] In seventeenth-century England, not only were convicts and pauper children and " masterless vagabonds " shipped to the colonies to swell their labour supply, but kidnapping for the same purpose became a profitable trade in which magistrates, aldermen and ladies at Court had a hand.[4] " The great trading companies . . . were not unlike their Genoese forerunners. They may be described

---

[1] Sombart, *Quintessence of Capitalism*, 70, 72.
[2] Nussbaum, *op. cit.*, 123. J. A. Hobson wrote : " Colonial Economy must be regarded as one of the necessary conditions of modern capitalism. Its trade, largely compulsory, was in a large measure little other than a system of veiled robbery, and was in no sense an equal exchange of commodities " (*Evolution of Modern Capitalism*, 13). He adds that " trade profits were supplemented by the industrial profits representing the surplus value of slave or forced labour ". Sombart similarly wrote that " forced trading is the proper term to apply to all barter between uncivilized people and Europeans in those days " (*op. cit.*, 74), and that " all European colonies have developed on the basis of forced labour " (*Der Moderne Kapitalismus*, I, 696 ; and on colonial slavery, 704 seq.). Some illuminating details of the methods of exploitation of India by the East India Company were given by Unwin in a paper to the Manchester Statistical Society, Jan. 9, 1924 ; since reprinted in *Studies in Economic History : Papers of George Unwin*.
[3] Cit. Eric Williams, *Capitalism and Slavery*, 61.
[4] J. E. Gillespie, *Influence of Oversea Expansion on England to 1700*, 23-7.

as semi-warlike conquering undertakings, to which sovereign rights, backed by the forces of the State, had been granted." [1] In short, the Mercantile System was a system of State-regulated exploitation through trade which played a highly important rôle in the adolescence of capitalist industry : it was essentially the economic policy of an age of primitive accumulation. So important was it thought to be in its time that in some Mercantilist writings we find an inclination to treat the gain from foreign trade as the only form of surplus, and hence as the only source both of accumulation and of State revenue (as the Physiocrats *per contra* laid a parallel stress on rent as the exclusive *produit net*). For example, Mun declared that if the sovereign " should mass up more money than is gained by the overbalance of his foreign trade, he shall not Fleece but Flea his subjects, and so with their ruin overthrow himself for want of future shearings ".[2] Again, Davenant stated that domestic trade did not enrich a nation, but merely transferred wealth from one individual to another, whereas foreign trade made a net addition to a country's wealth. Here Davenant evidently intended " a net addition to a country's wealth " to mean an increase of surplus ; just as did the Physiocrats when they contrasted the " productivity " of agriculture with the " sterility " of manufacture.[3]

In the attitude to this matter of regulated terms of trade we find a crucial difference of perspective between the economic thought of the time and later economic thought that was moulded in the " classical " tradition : a difference which modern commentators seem to have been slow to appreciate. Modern economists have been accustomed to deal in terms of supply-schedules and demand-schedules which are constant factors in their problem and are rooted in certain basic mental attitudes of rationally calculating and autonomous individuals; with the consequence that a raising of price against purchasers or a

---

[1] Sombart, *Quintessence*, 73.
[2] *England's Treasure by Forraign Trade*, 68.
[3] The doctrine of Mercantilist writers (like the doctrine of the Physiocrats) is often interpreted as though it denied that the volume of trade had any effect in increasing wealth. Even though they may not usually have been explicit about it, there seems little doubt that they had no intention of denying that trade increased wealth, in the sense of utilities. But with this they were not particularly concerned : their preoccupation was with profit or " net produce " (excluding wages). Their case rested on the assumption that (apart from lower wages) a change in the ratio of prices of imports and exports was the only way of increasing the rate of profit available to trade and manufacture. For example, Schrötter makes this plain in a passage quoted by Prof. Heckscher when he says that domestic trade makes people happy but not rich.

lowering of price against suppliers by monopolistic action has been generally taken to diminish respectively purchases or sales. True, in recent years there has been a growing amount of talk of " backward-sloping supply curves " (chiefly in the case of labour), of the possible " income-effect " as well as the " substitution-effect " of a price-change, and of possible shifts in consumers' demand-schedules as a result of advertising and high-pressure sales methods. Nevertheless, traditional habits of thought die hard. But the economic writers of the Mercantilist age were reared in a quite different tradition, and evidently conceived of supply and of demand conditions as being what might to-day be called " institutional products " and as very largely pliable in face of political pressure. To shift the conditions underlying the terms of trade to one's own advantage—to mould the market in one's own interest—accordingly appeared to be the natural objective of business policy and became a leading preoccupation of policy-makers. As regards the internal market, experience had presumably taught them that such measures could quickly reach a limit, especially when the field was already congested with established privileges and monopolistic regulations. Here there was little chance of a merchant expanding his stint save at the expense of another ; and internal trade was consequently regarded as yielding little chance of gain from further regulation. But in virgin lands across the seas, with native populations to be despoiled and enslaved and colonial settlers to be economically regimented, the situation looked altogether different and the prospects of forced trading and plunder must have seemed abundantly rich.

IV

Perhaps more revealing than what the writers of this school had in common are the differences that we can notice between writings that belong to an earlier and to a later period. An outstanding difference is in the attitude that was adopted towards import or export prohibitions at different periods, and particularly in the attitude towards different types of commodity. In the fourteenth and fifteenth centuries economic policy had regulated the export, not only of precious metals, but also of products such as corn and wool.[1] Certain imports (for example,

---

[1] The policy towards wool was subject to some fluctuation ; and wool export was permitted, subject to specific export licence. Although illicit trade continued,

wine which served the needs of the upper classes), on the other hand, were encouraged. Although some of these regulations, most notably the curtailment of wool export, were in part a concession to nascent home industry, the main emphasis of such regulation presented a contrast with later doctrine. Cheapness was at this period extolled as a virtue and export viewed with suspicion because it militated against plenty at home. This " policy of provision ", as he calls it, Professor Heckscher speaks of as a mediæval tradition deriving from the conditions of a " natural economy " which revealed the real object of exchange, plenty, unclouded by " a veil of money ". But it seems more reasonable to suppose that the emphasis on cheapness belonged to a period before the growth of capitalist manufacture, when England was primarily a producer of foodstuffs and raw materials and the interest of consumer (especially the urban consumer) and merchant alike lay in cheapness of the source of supply. Even when manufacture developed, it had at first more interest in cheapness of its raw material than in an expansion of markets abroad. While merchants had an interest in export, the more powerful of them, like the Staplers, could rely on acquiring special licence for the purpose and profited the more straitly that export was restricted for others.

Emphasis on the virtues of extended export waited on the emergence of a powerful manufacturing, as distinct from trading, interest ; since it was to the advantage of the maker that the market for his product should be as wide as possible, as it was also to his gain that the import of competing wares should be curtailed. True, he still had an interest in encouraging cheapness in his raw materials and in subsistence for labourers : a fact of which we have seen that Mercantilist doctrine took full account in reserving its advocacy of export for manufactures and confining its condemnation of imports to non-raw materials and to finished commodities that catered for luxury consumption. However, the weight of emphasis was shifted, and it was the sale of exports which grew to be the chief concern. For example, as cloth manufacture developed, the clothiers, while advocating a prohibition on wool export, had an interest in the development of cloth export ; just as later the cloth finishers (and the rivals

the tendency of State policy in the sixteenth century was progressively in the direction of restricting wool export in the interest of home cloth industry ; until under James I the export of wool was forbidden altogether. Prior to 1670, export of corn was permitted only when the home price fell below a certain level : a level substantially lower than the normal price.

of the Merchant Adventurers who formed the short-lived " King's Merchant Adventurers " in 1614 to export dyed cloth) fervently believed in export so long as this did not consist of an export of undyed cloth.   In the seventeenth century, while tanners and leather merchants petitioned against an embargo on the export of leather, the London Cordwainers' Company petitioned for a renewal of the embargo, on the ground that export " must ruin many thousand families that convert it into wares, there being a hundred to one more manufacturers than tanners and transporters ".[1]   Already in 1611 James I in the Book of Rates had announced a policy " to exempt and forbear all such merchandises inwards as serve for the setting of the people of our kingdom on work (as cotton wool, cotton yarn, raw silk and rough hemp) ", and at the same time to reduce duties on the export of native manufactures, while retaining the prohibition of export of certain raw materials.   In particular, a proclamation was issued restraining export of wool (although certain exceptions continued to be granted by a royal sale of licences as a fiscal expedient) : a policy that was continued by Charles I and Cromwell and embodied in an Act of Parliament at the Restoration.[2]   In 1700 cloth exports were exempted from all duties, and, after a duel with the East India Company over the charge that the Company was importing Eastern textiles to the damage of English manufacture, the import of Indian, Persian or Chinese silks or calicoes was prohibited.   Hostility towards corn export survived into the middle of the seventeenth century, presumably for the reason that the price of corn entered so directly into the price of labour. But after the Restoration, when capital investment in agriculture had begun to assume impressive dimensions, the policy of export restriction was replaced by a policy of import duties and even of encouragement to corn export.

Sixteenth-century writers, therefore, who preached freer export-facilities for manufactures were able to appear as progressive thinkers, emancipating thought from obsolete prejudices. This in large measure they were.   For one thing, Bullionist views had been difficult to reconcile with export-restriction, and writers

---

[1] Similar differences between the trading and the manufacturing element over the export of semi-finished products are found in other trades.   Thus, the London Pewterers in 1593 petitioned against the export of unwrought tin (cf. *Hist. of the Company of Pewterers*, vol. II, 21 seq.), and the handicraft and the merchant sections of the Skinners' Company for many years disputed over the export of undressed skins.
[2] Lipson, *op. cit.*, vol. III, 21–3.   One advocate of the wool-growers, championing free trade in wool, denounced the protectionist policy as " an evil legacy of the Great Rebellion " and " the work of the Commonwealth Party " (cit. *Ibid.*, 30).

who pointed out the contradition and demonstrated the connection between bullion-inflow and a commodity export-surplus were making a path-breaking contribution to a theory of foreign trade. It was natural for them to carry over the traditional assumption that " treasure " was desirable for its own sake, even if this had lost much of its plausibility now that the phase had passed when bourgeois accumulation had taken the form of the hoarding of money or of plate or land-purchase, and continued attachment to these older objects of accumulation was an obstacle to the industrial investment which was now becoming the bourgeois fashion. There was little to provoke them directly to a criticism of this assumption when it fitted so conveniently into an advocacy of protection of the home market and the unshackling of export.[1] Partly in consequence of their teaching, partly (perhaps more largely) at the insistence of the East India Company, the stringency of earlier policy with regard to the prohibition on bullion-export was relaxed. The essential argument was that imports involving bullion-export to pay for them might not be undesirable if these imports consisted of raw materials, which by encouraging manufacture would result in expanded exports and eventually draw more treasure back into the kingdom. But in the second half of the seventeenth century the assumption that abundance of money is to be desired for its own sake, rather than as incident to the promotion of more profitable terms of trade, increasingly drops out of the picture. In this connection a crucial qualification, as we have noticed, resided in the admission that, not the absolute amount of money in a country, but the amount relatively to what other countries possessed was the significant consideration. Although the view that at least a relative increase in a country's stock of money was an advantage was only in rare cases abandoned, the emphasis came gradually to be shifted. Davenant, for example, while paying his tribute to the Bullionist tradition by stating that an export " Overplus ", paid for in bullion, measures " the Profit a Nation makes by Trade ", had moved sufficiently far from the earlier standpoint to say of gold and silver that they were merely " the Measure of Trade ", and that " the Spring and Original of it is the Natural or Artificial Product of the Country ". " Gold and silver ", he declared, " are so far from being the only things that deserve

[1] When Mun, for example, argued that " moneys exported will return to us more than trebled ", he did not, in the form of his argument, go outside the traditional doctrine about money. But in making a statement of this kind he had completely shifted the focus of emphasis.

the name of Treasure or the Riches of a Nation, that in truth Money is at bottom no more than the Counters with which men in their dealings have been accustomed to reckon " ; and his principal concern was to emphasize the advantage of expanding exports by keeping home costs low.[1]

This is not to say that the views of writers of this period about the effects of trade policy did not remain in many respects confused. It is a characteristic of all ideology that, while it reflects and at the same time illuminates its contemporary world, this reflection is from a particular angle, and hence largely clouds and distorts reality. Certain relationships on which the historical setting of the writers in question causes thought to be focused are illuminated, at the same time as others escape attention and are obscured. The ideology of this period of nascent industrial capital could hardly base itself on the explicit assumption that the highest good consisted in maximizing the profit of a particular class. Hence this ideology appeared in the guise of the principle that trade must be subordinated to the general interests of the State ; and since the sovereign power was personalized in the Crown, it seemed reasonable to attach to the economic dealings of the Sovereign the analogy of the individual trader whose profit was measured by the balance in money that remained after all transactions of sale and purchase had been completed. The more realistic was his thinking, the more likely was a writer to be aware that this was not the real end of policy. Yet the assumption that it was had roots that were deep in the tradition from which his thought derived. Until sufficiently radical changes in the world of affairs had provoked a revolutionary departure in thought—an explicit repudiation of tradition—the path of compromise was a natural one for any mind that was child of its age to follow. To the bullion-fetish they continued to pay at least lip-service. As a consequence, though qualified by modern interpretation, the central contradiction remained for some time to breed fallacy and sow confusion : for example, the prevalent confusion between the terms of trade and the balance of trade, and between profit to a trader or a company of traders and gain to the nation, and the tendency to identify the addition to total profit due to foreign trade with the import of specie. Men continued to accept such corollaries of economic doctrine

---

[1] *Essay on the East India Trade*, 1697, 31, and *Discourses on the Publick Revenues*, 15–16. Cf. also the passages from other late seventeenth-century writers quoted by Lipson, *Economic History of England*, vol. III, 65–6.

as the statement of Napoleon that England would be damaged if goods were sold to her in war-time, provided that her exports could be stopped and gold consequently drained from the kingdom ; or Davenant's view that a war waged inside a country would impoverish it less than a war waged on foreign soil, since the expense of the former would not involve any export of bullion.

Entwined with the central protectionist issue were a number of subordinate themes. The usury question, for example, was a concern of a number of the writers of the time ; and at any rate the earlier writers apparently saw a causal relationship between plenty of money and lowness of interest-rates. Here they were successors to the early Tudor debate about the ethics of usury and the desirability of its prohibition ; but with this difference, that, while they shared the anxiety of writers like Thomas Wilson that interest should be lowered, they sought to do this indirectly by the measures they advocated rather than by legal prohibition.[1] As Professor Viner has remarked, " verbally at least they identified money with capital " and " much of their argument can be explained only if they regarded money and capital as identical in fact as well as in name ".[2] But in that age of nascent enterprise such an identification is not only understandable : it also mirrored a large element of truth. What the individual capitalist needed if he wished to be an economic pioneer was command over resources : what limited the field of his endeavours in an age of undeveloped credit was not only the non-availability of the requisite resources (e.g. labour-power or raw materials or mining-rights) but the non-availability also of the liquid means with which resources could be mobilized. Experience had taught him (or at least had deposited a strong impression on his mind) that " when money be plentiful in the realm ", not only was credit more plentiful, but markets were more brisk, and this meant better and quicker sales and a shorter period between production and sale for which provision had to be made. Yet this aspect of Mercantile policy seems rarely to have been uppermost in people's minds, and generally to have been subordinate to a preoccupation with the increased profit to be obtained from improved terms of trade. Among the more important writers

---

[1] Both Malynes and Misselden, for example, were agreed that " the remedy for usury may be plenty of Money ".

[2] *Studies in the Theory of International Trade*, 31.   Professor Heckscher also comments on the fact that they virtually treated money as a factor of production, interest being regarded as the rent of money, like rent of land.

of the late seventeenth century and after, any simple connection between money and interest-rates began to be explicitly denied ; emphasis being placed instead (and not only by Hume) on the growth of commerce and of a capitalist class, and hence on a growth of " stock ", as the surest way to make borrowing cheap.[1] Midway between these views stood the emphasis of some writers on hoarding (whether of actual coin or of plate) as tending to divert loanable funds from trade, and hence make credit for the merchant dear, and of others on luxury-expenditure and grand living—which, like hoarding, was regarded as a special sin of the aristocracy—as having a similar effect.[2]

Again, as a setting to their economic theorizing there was the embittered controversy over the East India Company and the Merchant Adventurers, in which the better-known Stuart pamphleteers were interested partisans. Misselden wrote as a propagandist for the original Merchant Adventurers' Company, of which he became a deputy-governor, in opposition to Malynes who had been in partnership with Cockayne in his ill-starred rival project, the so-called " King's Merchant Adventurers." In his first pamphlet Misselden, while defending chartered companies in general, criticized (by implication) the East India Company and its licence to export bullion : a view which he changed in his second pamphlet after the East India Company had taken him into its employ. Again, Mun, who was the son of a mercer and a director of the East India Company, in his *Discourse of Trade* developed what has been called the more liberal tendency of his doctrine (relaxation of control over bullion-export and his substitution of a theory of a " general balance " for that of " particular balances ") as a special plea for the activities of the East India Company against their critics ; and the same was true of what have generally been regarded as the " free trade " tendencies of late seventeenth-century writers like Child, Davenant and North, who were Tories (at a time when the East India Company was essentially a Tory corporation), as well as of the Tory critics of the Whig-owned *British Merchant* and its policy of prohibiting trade with France.[3]

[1] Cf. above, p. 201 f.
[2] Although there were, of course, certain writers of the time who defended luxury-expenditure, the weight of emphasis was on the other side ; which indicates that notions about " under-consumption " directly entered very little into Mercantilist doctrine.
[3] Cf. E. A. J. Johnson, *Predecessors of Adam Smith*, 57–62, 73–6, 145–9. In the 1660's and early '70's there was a good deal of anti-French feeling in connection with imports of French manufactures, and the Whig element in the House of Commons

Anyone contemplating Mercantilist writings through modern spectacles might perhaps be excused for concluding that their emphasis on a favourable trade-balance indicated a confused intention to increase the rate of profit by encouraging foreign investment. But such an interpretation has little evidence to summon to its support. Undoubtedly a certain amount of foreign investment occurred during this period, which aggregated over a century amounted to a considerable sum for those times ; and part of the profits of trade represented profits not only on working capital but on fixed capital sunk in the equipment and fortification of trading stations abroad and in ships, in bribes to purchase the goodwill of foreign notables (as in the East), and in plantations in the New World. Nevertheless, with a few exceptions, such as West Indian sugar plantations worked by negro slaves, such investment was an accessory to trading ventures rather than an independent enterprise, valued for its own sake ; and the preoccupation of practical men and of economic theorists alike was essentially with the terms of trade rather than with the conditions for investment abroad. Herein lay the crucial difference between the Old Colonial System of the Mercantile period and the colonial system of modern Imperialism : export of capital had not then assumed any considerable dimensions and did not hold the centre of the stage.

But in one respect it is true that an emphasis on investment began to appear in the writings of the late seventeenth century : for example, the Whig pamphleteers associated with the *British Merchant*. Properly appreciated, this emphasis furnishes us, I believe, with a key to the most significant difference between the doctrines of the later and of the earlier period. But the investment to which these later writers made implicit reference was the increased investment, not abroad, but at home, resulting from an expansion of export markets. In their hands the advocacy of a favourable balance of trade came to be interpreted, not so much as a balance of goods *simpliciter*, as of employment created by the trade. Trade should be so regulated that the things exported created more employment than the things imported created abroad ; which they considered would be the

showed hostility to the King for extending too much favour to France. " The Whigs were the nationalists of the epoch . . . as against an un-national monarch in alliance with the chief national competitor " (L. B. Packard in *Quarterly Journal of Economics*, May 1923, 435).

case if finished manufactures were exported and only raw produce imported.[1]

This new emphasis on employment is not really so surprising as at first it might seem.   The concern of Mercantilist writers had always been with the surplus or net produce which remained after the wages of labour had been paid ; and a carefully regulated colonial trade, serving the principle of " buying cheap and selling dear ", had been regarded by them as the leading method for enlarging this surplus, and enlarging it in greater proportion than any increase in the capital involved.   In an age when industrial investment was little developed, and the dominant interest consisted of the privileged " insiders " of the chartered trading companies, the monopoly-gain on a given trade turn-over was the natural focus of interest, and attention was accordingly focused upon favourable *terms* of trade.   But in the later seventeenth century, as we have observed, a shift of attention to the *volume* of export-demand for the products of home manufacture can be detected.   Greater export meant greater opportunity for the employment of labour in home manufacture ; and increased employment of labour (like increased cultivation of land in a plantation-economy) represented a widened scope for investment of capital in industry, since each additional labourer was a potential creator of additional surplus, and more employment meant more creators of surplus at work.   Whereas a change in the *terms* of trade (and hence presumably in the prices/cost ratio) tended to increase the *rate* of profit to be earned on a *given* capital, and so was retained as an object of policy (at least for a time), an expansion in the *volume* of trade, provided that it could be purchased without any unfavourable reaction on the terms of trade, would enable a *larger* volume of capital to be employed at a given rate of profit.[2]   Ultimately, of course, the focus of attention was to shift entirely to the volume of trade and its increase ; and the main ground of Adam Smith's assault on " the monopoly of the colony trade " was that this served to throttle any expansion of the market in the interests of establishing a set of monopoly prices.   Mandeville, indeed, writing in the

[1] Cf. the doctrine of " foreign paid incomes " preached during the controversy over the Treaty of Utrecht and Steuart's rather obscure distinction between the balance of " matter " and the balance of " labour ".

[2] Since, if the demand for manufactured commodities grew, and there was no accompanying fall in the price of these commodities and no rise in the price of raw materials, equipment or labour-power, the total surplus available to the capitalist would tend to grow *pari passu* with the increase of capital required to purchase the raw material, equipment and labour-power.

early eighteenth century, so far anticipated this later criticism as to maintain that " buying is bartering ; and no nation can buy goods of others that has none of her own to purchase them with ", and that " if we refuse taking commodities [of other nations] in payment for our manufactures, they can trade no longer with us, but must content themselves with buying what they want of such nations as are willing to take what we refuse ".[1] But for the time being even the rising industrial interest retained its affection for the system of regulation and protection. The colonial system was as yet unshaken by the American revolt and many of the potentialities of exploiting it appeared to remain untapped. Accordingly, the new emphasis on employment was merely grafted on to the structure of the older theory.

In this double element in later Mercantilist writings we touch the hem of a quite fundamental matter. Not at this period alone, but throughout the whole history of Capitalism we meet this crucial contradiction. In order to expand, in order to find room for ever new accumulations of capital, industry requires a continuous expansion of the market (and in the last analysis of consumption). Yet in order to preserve or to enhance the profitability of capital that is already invested, resort is had from time to time to measures of monopolistic restriction, the effect of which is to put the market in fetters and to cramp the possibilities of fresh expansion. The very depression of the standard of life of the masses that is a condition of profit being earned narrows the market which production serves. In the period of the system's adolescence, this contradiction was generally displayed in the form of a conflict between the interests of an older generation of capitalists, already entrenched in certain spheres of trade and usury where capital had earliest penetrated, and the interests of a new generation who had become investors in newer trades or industries or in newer methods of production. And it is to this fact that we must evidently look for a part of the reason why older and established sections of the bourgeoisie have always become so quickly reactionary and showed such readiness to ally themselves with feudal remnants or with an autocratic régime to preserve the *status quo* against more revolutionary change. In the seventeenth century the contradiction found expression in the conflict between rising industrial capital and the merchant princes with their chartered monopolies ; in the early nineteenth century in the challenge that the new class of factory-

[1] *Fable of the Bees* (Ed. 1795), 58 (Remarks on line 180).

capitalists threw down to the Whig aristocracy and the whole Mercantile System. In each case the complaint of rising industrial capital was not only that the existing régime of monopoly caused an undue share of the profits of trade and of manufacture to accrue to a privileged circle, but that it limited growth and expansion—set narrow frontiers to the industrial investment field.

Close on the heels of this new attention to the need for an expanding investment field came an awareness of a new possibility : that of *intensifying* the existing investment field by technical improvements which enhanced the productivity of labour. This possibility, once it was appreciated, was to have quite revolutionary consequences both in the realm of doctrine and in the realm of practice. In the seventeenth century we find no more than hints of such appreciation, and it again remained for the classical economists to appreciate both the possibilities and the implications of enhanced productivity of labour, and to expound these implications with clarity and deliberation. But the hints we find round about 1700 in writers who had caught the atmosphere of seventeenth-century scientific and technical discovery are indications of the prevailing wind : for example, the suggestion of writers like Grew or Postlethwayt that the surest road to riches lay in promoting inventions which caused an " œconomy in men's labour ". They are indications of the direction in which industrial capital was already beginning to look : indications that the epoch of industrial invention was at hand.

CHAPTER SIX

GROWTH OF THE PROLETARIAT

I

The rival merits of different types of colony formed a central topic of debate among early writers on colonial questions ; and chief among the differences discussed was that between colonies (like New England) consisting almost exclusively of small proprietors and colonies (like Virginia) where land-ownership was concentrated and there existed a wage-earning class. The latter reproduced the social structure of the mother country and was accordingly admired by writers of a conservative and aristocratic temper, whereas the former won the praise of apostles of *Liberté* and *Egalité* as models of a society of a new and ideal type. It was soon realized that the crux of the difference lay in the policy adopted by the ruling authority towards the sale and allocation of land. Where grants of land were made to settlers in small lots at a nominal price or on easy credit terms, the society that developed was one of small cultivators, where few were inclined to work for wages. By contrast, the sale of land in large blocks tended to create an economic society of large proprietors with a sharply defined class division between proprietors and propertyless. As Gibbon Wakefield pointed out in a familiar passage, " the plentifulness and cheapness of land in thinly-peopled countries enables almost everybody who wishes it to become a landowner . . . (and) cheapness of land is the cause of scarcity of labour for hire. . . . Where land is very cheap and all men are free, where every one who so pleases can obtain a piece of land for himself, not only is labour very dear, as respects the labourers' share of the product, but the difficulty is to obtain combined labour at any price." [1] It became clear to those who wished to reproduce capitalist relations of production in the new country that the foundation-stone of their endeavour must be the restriction of land-ownership to a minority and

---

[1] *A View of the Art of Colonization*, 325 ; *England and America*, vol. I, 247. Wakefield's view was that slavery was so common a basis of colonial economy because the plentifulness of land in such countries made free labour dear. Yet free labour was more productive. His remedy was for the government always to place a substantial price on all land. " If the land of the colony were of limited extent, a great importation of people would raise its price, and compel some people to work for wages " (*Art of Colonization*, 328).

the exclusion of the majority from any share in property. The apprehension of the same truth has in more recent times led colonial administrators in certain parts of Africa to reduce native tribal reserves and to impose taxation on natives who remain in the reserves, with the object of maintaining a labour supply for the white employer. It was evidently in the minds of many observers of those agrarian changes which accompanied the industrial revolution in England ; for we find the author of the Gloucestershire *Survey* of 1807 recording the forthright opinion that " the greatest of evils to agriculture would be to place the labourer in a state of independence [i.e. by allowing him to have land] and thus destroy the indispensable gradations of society ". " Farmers, like manufacturers," said another writer of the time, " require constant labourers—men who have no other means of support than their daily labour, men whom they can depend upon." [1]

To say that Capitalism presupposes the existence of a proletariat is nowadays a commonplace. Yet the fact that the existence of such a class is contingent on a particular set of historical circumstances has too seldom received attention in the past at the hands of writers who have devoted a wealth of analysis to the evolution of capital under its various forms and to the burgeoning of the capitalist spirit—perhaps because the stratagems of Lombard money-lenders and of Amsterdam stock-jobbers is a more resplendent tale to tell than that of paupers branded and hanged and cottagers harried and dispossessed. We have seen in the previous chapter that the process which created both Capital and Labour as joint products, the so-called " primitive accumulation ", appeared from one aspect as the concentration of property through the instrument of economic pressure and monopoly, usury or actual expropriation, and from the other aspect as the consequential dispossession of previous owners. One kind of property was born from the ashes of an older kind of property ; large property grew to adult stature by digesting the small ; and a capitalist class arose as the creation, not of thrift and abstinence as economists have traditionally depicted it, but of the dispossession of others by dint of economic or political advantage. For Capitalism as a system of production to mature, said Marx, " two very different kinds of commodity-possessors must come face to face and into contact : on the one hand, the owners of money, means of production, means of

[1] Cit. W. Hasbach, *A History of the English Agricultural Labourer*, 103, 136.

subsistence, who are eager to increase the sum of values they possess by buying other people's labour-power ; on the other hand, free labourers, the sellers of their own labour-power. . . . With this polarization of the market for commodities, the fundamental conditions of capitalist production are given. The capitalist system presupposes the complete separation of the labourers from all property in the means by which they can realize their labour. . . . The so-called primitive accumulation, therefore, is nothing else than the historical process of divorcing the producer from the means of production. . . . The expropriation of the agricultural producer, of the peasant, from the soil is the basis of the whole process." [1]

It may be that one reason for the common neglect of this aspect of the matter has been the implicit assumption that the appearance of a reserve army of labour was a simple product of growing population, which created more hands than could be given employment in existing occupations and more mouths than could be fed from the then-cultivated soil. The historic function of Capital was to endow this army of redundant hands with the benefit of employment. If this were the true story, one might have some reason to speak of a proletariat as a natural rather than an institutional creation, and to treat accumulation and the growth of a proletariat as autonomous and independent processes. But this idyllic picture fails to accord with the facts. Actually, the centuries in which a proletariat was most rapidly recruited were apt to be those of slow rather than of rapid natural increase of population, and the paucity or plenitude of a labour reserve in different countries was not correlated with comparable differences in their rates of population-growth. True, the industrial revolution in England coincided with an unusually rapid natural increase ; but it was also a period when other reasons for a swelling labour reserve were most in evidence : for example, the death of the peasantry as a class and the doom of the handicraft trades. It is certainly the case, as some writers have emphasized, that once industrial Capitalism was firmly established, its growing need of labour-power was supplied in the main by the natural rate of increase of the proletariat—by its own powers of reproduction. For example, during the nineteenth century the population of Europe increased by nearly

---

[1] Marx, *op. cit.*, 737–9. Elsewhere he says : " In order to make the collective labourer, and through him capital, rich in productive power, each labourer must be made poor in individual productive powers."

two and a half times. But over the three centuries in which capitalist industry was gaining a foothold (between the mid-fourteenth century and the time of Gregory King's estimate) the population of England probably grew by no more than 2 million from 3½ to 5½ million persons.[1] France had as large a " plague of beggars " in the sixteenth century as had England, and probably a larger. At the end of the fifteenth century there were said to be 80,000 beggars in Paris alone, and at the beginning of the seventeenth century a contemporary estimated that a quarter of the city's population were completely destitute. Later in the same century the Bishop of Montauban declared that " in my diocese of 750 parishes about 450 persons die every day from lack of food ".[2] Yet the population of France in 1700 probably remained at much the same figure as in the sixteenth and in the fourteenth centuries ; and the century noted for its " plague of beggars " may even have been one when the total population of the country was on the decline.[3] Clearly it is influences affecting the proportion of the population in different social classes with which we are here primarily concerned rather than influences affecting the size of the total population.[4]

The factors responsible for the growing army of the destitute in England in the century that followed the Battle of Bosworth are fairly familiar. The disbanding of feudal retainers, the dissolution of the monasteries, the enclosures of land for sheep-farming and changes in methods of tillage each played its part ; and while the absolute number of persons affected in each case may seem small by modern standards,[5] the result was large in

[1] On the accession of Henry VII it may have been no more than 2¼ million, so that from that date the population took nearly two centuries to double itself, and during the very period when Tudor unemployment was at its height the total population was no greater than it had been in the middle of the fourteenth century. Thorold Rogers suggests that the population may still have been no greater than 2¼ million at the end of Elizabeth's reign. If this was so, then the doubling of the population was confined to the seventeenth century, the very century in which the abnormal labour reserve of Tudor times was giving place to a certain tightness in the labour market in view of the revival of tillage and the expansion of industry.

[2] Cit. F. L. Nussbaum, *History of the Economic Institutions of Modern Europe*, 108.

[3] Cf. Levasseur, *La Population Française*, vol. I, 169, 202–6 ; G. D'Avenel, *Paysans et Ouvriers*, 370. Levasseur emphasizes that the unemployment and destitution of the sixteenth century was primarily due to " déclassement ".

[4] Cf. the remark of J. S. Mill, when he was speaking merely of the incomes of different grades among wage- and salary-earners : " The wages of each class have hitherto been regulated by the increase of its own population rather than of the general population of the country " (*Principles of Pol. Economy*, Bk. 2, Chapt. 14, Sect. 2).

[5] It has been suggested that between 1455 and 1607 the area enclosed amounted to some half-million acres (Gay's estimate) and that the number thrown out of employment between 1455 and 1637 was between 30,000 and 40,000 (A. H. Johnson,

proportion to the demand for hired labour at the time. It was the age when sheep devoured men ; the age of the " insatiable cormorants " who depopulated villages, when husbandmen were " thrust out of their own or by violent oppression put beside it, or by covin and fraud so wearied that they were compelled to sell all and depart away poor, silly, wretched souls " ; of " lords devising new means to cut them (their tenants) shorter, doubling, trebling and now and then seven times increasing their fines, driving them for every trifle to lose and forfeit their tenures " ; an age when desperate men took to highway robbery, and thieves and vagabonds alike were subjected to the brutalities of Tudor legislation with its brandings and whippings, its public hangings and quarterings.

What was happening over an important section of the country-side is well illustrated in two manors of Northumberland belonging to the same owner, a certain Robert Delavale. " There was [sic] in Seaton Delavale township," said a contemporary document, " twelve tenements whereon there dwelt twelve able men. . . . All the said tenants and their successors saving five the said Robert Delavale eyther thrust out of their fermholds or weried them by taking excessive fines, increasing of their rents unto £3 a piece, and withdrawing part of their best land and meadow from their tenements . . . by taking good land from them and compelling them to winne morishe and heatheground, and after their hedging heth ground to their great charge, and paying a great fine, and bestowing great reparation on building their tenements, he quite thrust them off in one yeare, refusing eyther to repay the fine or to repay the charge bestowed in diking or building." The holdings displaced were here fairly substantial ones, being " every one of them 60 acres of arable land ". In the manor of Hartley of the same Robert Delavale, " where there was [sic] then 15 serviceable men furnished with sufficient horse and furniture, there is now not any, nor hath been these 20 years last past or thereabouts " ; 720 acres of arable, former " free-holders' lands " with tenements, being converted into pasture " and made one demaine ".[1] While incidents such as this did

Disappearance of the Small Landowner, 58). Eden mentioned a figure of 50,000 as the number directly made destitute by the dissolution of the monasteries (*State of the Poor*, Ed. Rogers, 8). This may well have represented a figure of over 10 per cent. of all middling and small landholders and between 10 and 20 per cent. of those employed at wages in town and country ; in which case the labour reserve thereby created would have been of comparable dimensions to that which existed in all but the worst months of the economic crisis of the 1930's.

[1] Quoted in Tawney, *Agrarian Problems in the Sixteenth Century*, 257-8.

not characterize all the manors (far from it), or even all the counties of England, they were by no means isolated cases ; and the general tendency of the time over a substantial, if still minor, portion of the cultivated land of the country was in the direction of supplanting many small holdings by a few much larger ones. This process is seen at work (at least, there is strong *prima facie* evidence of it) in the sixteen sample manors examined by Professor Tawney, on eight of which two-thirds of the whole area and on another seven more than three-quarters had come into the hands of one individual, the farmer of the demesnes. Written on a 1620 map of one of these manors (in Leicestershire), like an epitaph, are the words " the place where the Town of Whatboroughe stood ".[1]   It is hardly surprising that the Tudor countryside should have been the scene of a pitiful host of refugees, the " vagabonds and beggars " of the official documents of the period : drifting into the boroughs to find such lodging and employment as they could or migrating to such open-field villages as would allow them to squat precariously on the edge of common or waste.   It was to the latter, perhaps more fortunate, part of the vagabond host that a seventeenth-century pamphleteer refers when he says that " in all or most towns where the fields lie open and are used in common there is a new brood of upstart intruders as inmates, and the inhabitants of unlawful cottages erected contrary unto law " ;   adding a common employer's grumble at his labour reserve that these were " loyterers who will not usually be got to work unless they may have such excessive wages as they themselves desire ".[2]   To render them entirely submissive in a master's hand required that these poor folk be further deprived even of the wretched parcel of ground to which they still clung.

The enclosure movement, while its consequences were probably less drastic in the ensuing century (since it coincided with some reversion from pasture to tillage), continued after 1600, until it reached a new peak in the orgy of enclosure bills which accompanied the industrial revolution.   By contrast with this peak of the movement in the eighteenth and early nineteenth century, the effects of Tudor enclosures on the concentration of ownership and on the numbers of the landless was a moderate one.   With these effects the beginnings of industrial Capitalism

[1] Quoted in Tawney, *Agrarian Problems in the Sixteenth Century*, 223, 259–61.
[2] *Considerations concerning Common Fields and Enclosures* (Pseudonismus ?, 1653). Cf. also W. Hasbach, *History of the English Agricultural Labourer*, 77–80.

which we meet at the end of the sixteenth century and in Stuart times are manifestly connected. But for a century following the Restoration complaint of labour shortage abounds, and the weak development of the proletarian army at this time must have exerted a retarding influence upon the further growth of industrial investment between the last of the Stuarts and the closing years of George III.

In the middle of the eighteenth century, however, the pace of dispossession quickens. " An admirer of enclosures, little inclined to exaggerate their evil effects, put the number of small farms absorbed into larger ones between 1740 and 1788 at an average of 4 or 5 in each parish, which brings the total to 40 or 50 thousand for the whole kingdom." [1] Whereas during the earlier wave of Tudor enclosures the percentage of land enclosed probably never touched 10 per cent. even in the four counties most affected, during the eighteenth century and the first half of the nineteenth in as many as fourteen counties " the percentage of acres enclosed by Acts enclosing common field and some waste rises as high as 25 per cent. to 50 per cent., and only falls below 5 per cent. in sixteen counties ; and whereas only twenty-five counties in all were affected at all in the earlier period, in the eighteenth and nineteenth centuries Acts were passed for thirty-six counties ".[2] Moreover, in the later period the total amount of land enclosed was some eight or nine times as large as that involved in the earlier period, and embraced about one-fifth of the total acreage of the country.[3] Small wonder that conscience should have goaded even the Earl of Leicester to the frank confession : " I am like the ogre in the tale, and have eaten up all my neighbours."

But this does not measure the full extent of the change in landholding in the direction of replacing many small holders by a few large ones. In addition to forcible eviction, many small holders, burdened by debt or in the later eighteenth and early nineteenth century cut off from their traditional by-employments in cottage industry or adversely affected by the growing competition of larger farms equipped with newer agricultural methods, requiring capital, must have surrendered their holdings to the more well-to-do peasant or to some improving landlord without any explicit act of eviction. In regard to leases, there was evidently a widespread tendency for landlords

---

[1] Mantoux, *Industrial Revolution in the Eighteenth Century*, 177.
[2] A. H. Johnson, *op. cit.*, 90.   [3] *Ibid.*, 90-1.

to encourage a few large tenancies in preference to a larger number of small. Arthur Young, for example, combined with his advocacy of higher rents the advice : " if you would have vigorous culture, throw fifteen or twenty (small) farms into one as soon as the present occupiers die off." In certain parts of the country a marked tendency begins to appear from about the second decade of the eighteenth century to replace leases for lives (copyholds) by leases for a term of years ; and on some estates " there are signs of an active attempt to buy out the interest of leaseholders for lives which almost reaches the magnitude of a campaign ".[1] It was chiefly the smaller tenant farmer who was affected by this process and by the rise in rents it entailed ; and " landowners in the early eighteenth century were quite clear as to what was a good estate. It was one tenanted by large farmers holding 200 acres or more." [2] Addington, writing in the middle of the eighteenth century, declared it not uncommon in various parts of the country to find half a dozen farmers where once there were thirty or forty. A modern historian of these agrarian changes, whom we have already quoted, has concluded that, on the basis of the available evidence, " there was a very remarkable consolidation of estates and a shrinking in the number of the smaller owners somewhere between the beginning of the seventeenth century and the year 1785, more especially in the Midland counties " ; and has found, for example, that in twenty-four Oxfordshire parishes, the number of freeholders and copyholders holding land of less than 100 acres diminished by more than a half in number and the acreage included in such holdings by more than two-thirds, while in ten Gloucestershire parishes the number " decreased to nearly one-third and the acreage to less than one-fifth ".[3] Goldsmith's " sweet smiling village, loveliest of the lawn ",

---

[1] H. J. Habbakuk, in *Econ. Hist. Review*, vol. X, No. I, 17.   [2] *Ibid.*, 15.

[3] A. H. Johnson, *op. cit.*, 132-3. A study made by Professor Lavrovsky of parishes not yet enclosed (or fully enclosed) by 1793 led him to the conclusion that " the independent peasantry had already ceased to exist, even in unenclosed parishes, by the end of the eighteenth century ". In sixty of these unenclosed parishes, only between a fifth and a quarter of the acreage remained in peasant ownership ; while of the total land occupied by the peasantry, whether freehold, leasehold or copyhold, three-quarters was in the hands of a comparatively few well-to-do peasant farmers (forming 11 per cent. of the total number), while small holders, cultivating less than thirty acres, and composing 83 per cent. of the total number of peasant holders, occupied no more than one-seventh of the total area of peasant land. There had been apparently a growth both of the *kulak* peasant and of the poorest smallholders, but the " middle peasantry " had become relatively insignificant. (Cf. review of Prof. Lavrovsky's findings by Christopher Hill in *Econ. Hist. Review*, vol. XII, Nos. 1 and 2, 93.)

where " rich man's powers increase, the poor's decay ", where

> Amidst thy bowers the tyrants hand is seen
> And desolation saddens all thy green
> One only master grasps the whole domain
> A half a tillage stints thy smiling plain

was no mere fancy ; nor was it exceptional in eighteenth-century England.

Coincident with the influence of enclosures in the Tudor age was the growing exclusiveness of the gilds which barred the way to any urban occupation except as a hired servant. The tightening of entrance requirements, the exaction of fees and payments as price of setting up as a master, the elaborate requirements of a " masterpiece ", all served to bar the man without means from ever rising above the rank of journeyman. Some towns even imposed obstacles and prohibitions upon the advent of newcomers and sought to drive away the mixed communities of unemployed and pedlars and would-be artisans that had settled as squatters outside the borough walls.[1] Said Cecil in a speech in 1597, " if the poor being thrust out of their houses go to dwell with others, straight we catch them with the Statute of Inmates ; if they wander abroad, they are in danger of the Statute of the Poor to be whipped ". Monopoly, since it implies exclusion, always has as its other face a heightened competition and a consequent depression of economic status in the unfenced zones. So it was that the régime of gild monopoly, while it was ultimately to prove an obstacle to capitalist industry, in its time performed the unwitting function for capitalism of swelling the ranks of those whose condition made them pliable to a master's will. Even when the gild régime had disintegrated or had been evaded by the growth of country industry and the dominance of the merchant-manufacturer, the ladder of advancement was but little widened for those on the bottom rungs. As the number of craftsmen was multiplied, so they lost their independence and became semi-proletarian in status, tied to a capitalist by

---

[1] In 1557 the Common Council of London ordered all occupiers of houses to put out of their houses any vagabonds or " masterless men ", and periodic searches for newcomers were instituted in London and other towns. In numerous towns there was an actual prohibition on new building. An Act of 1589 laid it down that only one family was to live in a house, and in London forbade the building of houses for persons assessed at less than £5 in goods or £3 in lands. Nottingham forbade anyone from the country to be received as a tenant without authority from the Mayor and ordered the removal of all foreign tenants who had entered the town during the past three years (Tawney, *Agrarian Problem,* 276–7 ; E. M. Leonard, *English Poor Relief,* 107–9).

inability to obtain working capital and progressively enchained by debt ; and the multiplication of apprentices that was everywhere encouraged by the growing dominance of capital over production served merely to increase the number of those who were destined for life to be wage-earners even if they had once cherished other ambitions. Eventually, with the growth of technique, the road of advancement to the journeyman or even the small master was all but blocked, without any deliberate restrictions on freedom of entry to a trade, simply by the size of the capital required to initiate production. For those who lacked the means to set up the plant, to purchase a credit-worthy reputation, business connections or the requisite training, such freedom remained purely nominal except in the very occupation that required none of these things—manual wage-earning ; and it was this occupation that the newly-grown freedom of the labour market served to fill with a superabundance of willing and empty hands.

It would be a mistake, however, to suppose that in either the sixteenth or the seventeenth century the proletariat constituted an important part of the population. Its numbers remained small, and its mobility was restricted, both by legal restrictions designed to protect the estates and the larger yeoman farms against the loss of their labour supply, and because so much of the work for wages was done by those who still retained an attachment to the land, even though a slender and precarious one. Professor Clapham has suggested a figure of about half a million as the size of the rural proletariat in seventeenth-century England : a ratio to freeholders and farmers of about 1·74 : 1.[1] It seems clear that, after the initial stimulus given to the growth of industry by the cheapness and plentifulness of labour in the sixteenth century, the growth of capitalist industry must have been considerably handicapped until the later part of the eighteenth century, despite the events of the Tudor period, both by the comparative weakness of the labour army and by its non-availability at those locations that were suitable for the concentration of industry. At the same time, the existence in the countryside of so large a number of small cottagers, still clinging to the soil but unable to gain a full livelihood from it, was evidently an important factor in the growth of the putting-out system, and in causing capital to be invested in the financing

[1] *Cambridge Historical Journal*, vol. I, 95. The total population of England and Wales at the end of the century was (according to Gregory King) about 5½ million.

of cottage industry rather than in concentrating production in the factory or manufactory. This tendency for the continued attachment of the peasantry to the soil to encourage village industry and to preclude the formation of a mobile labour supply largely serves to explain the persistence of more primitive forms of Capitalism and the retarded growth of factory industry in countries where primitive accumulation was undeveloped. Not until the period of the industrial revolution was this rural semi-proletariat to be finally uprooted from the land and the obstacles to labour mobility from village to town removed. Only then could capitalist industry reach full maturity.

A witness to the still backward state of development of a proletariat in these earlier centuries is the extent to which compulsion had still to be applied to maintain the supply of wage-earners. Preoccupation with the fear that the labour-reserve would be inadequate to meet the demands of farming and of industry is evident in the measures of coercion that were tacitly accepted as a normal constituent of public policy at this period. At times when the deficiency of labour for hire was most marked or when exceptional demands for manpower appeared, resort was had to special measures such as the impressment of labour. The most dreaded result, if the demand for hands should outrun the supply, was a rise in wages ; and ever since the Ordinance and Statute of Labourers in 1349 and 1351 had been hurriedly passed to deal with the alarming labour-shortage that followed the Black Death, the law had enacted maximum wages, or had empowered the local magistrates so to do, and had attached rigorous penalties, not only to any concerted attempt by labourers and artificers to better the conditions of their employment, but even to the acceptance by a worker of any higher wage than was statutorily ordained.[1] Not content with this, the statutes of this period provided that any able-bodied man or woman under 60, whether of villein status or free, if he or she lacked independent means of support, could be compelled to accept work at the prescribed wage, while the freedom of movement of the worker was at the same time curtailed.[2]

Two centuries later it is true that Elizabethan legislation instructed local magistrates to fix minima as well as maxima, and an Act of 1604 imposed a fine on clothiers who "shall

---

[1] The Statute of Apprentices in 1563, for example, imposed a penalty of ten days' imprisonment or a fine on an employer for paying wages above the prescribed level, but twenty-one days' imprisonment for a worker who accepted such a wage.

[2] Cf. B. H. Putnam, *Enforcement of the Statutes of Labourers* 71 seq.

not pay so much or so great wages . . . as shall be appointed "
and forbade master-clothiers to serve as magistrates on any
bench that was concerned with fixing wages in their own
trade. But this was at a time when the rapid price-inflation
had rendered the old statutory limits obsolete, and had lowered
real wages, particularly in the countryside, to such a level as
to threaten a drastic rural exodus (despite prohibitions upon
unlicensed migration) : an exodus calculated to have serious
consequences for that balance between industry and agriculture which Tudor policy was so anxious should not be disturbed.   For example, in the second decade of the seventeenth
century it was reported from certain areas of the West Country
woollen industry that wages had not risen during the past forty
years, although prices had almost doubled.[1] And over the
country at large it seems probable that in the sixteenth century
prices (in terms of silver) more than doubled while money wages
only rose some 40 per cent.[2] Moreover, this was a time when
the number of the landless and destitute had grown sufficiently
large to remove any serious danger that real wages would rise by
the unaided influence of demand and supply : it was a time
when officials raged against " the great number of idle vagabonds
wherewith the realm is so replenished ". Actually, the clauses
which dealt with minima, while they seem to have been enforced
in the letter, had apparently little effect in protecting the labourer
against a worsening of his condition, since in most cases the
magistrates, having once established a scale of money wages,
did little more than reissue these same scales year after year,
despite a continued rise in the cost of living.[3] Thorold Rogers
described the Statute of Artificers of 1563, which re-enacted the
control of wages, made service in husbandry compulsory on all
persons not otherwise employed, and forbade servants to quit

[1] G. D. Ramsay, op. cit., 69.
[2] Earl J. Hamilton in Economica, Nov. 1929, 350–2 ; Georg Wiebe, Zur Geschichte
der Preisrevolution des XVI und XVII Jahrhunderts, 374 seq. According to the index
compiled by Prof. D. Knoop and Mr. G. P. Jones (Econ. History, vol. II, 485–6)
wages doubled over the century, but so also, according to their price-index, food
prices rose equivalently more—namely, by more than four times (and wheat-prices
by about six times)—so that the net result is the same in the case of this index as
with Wiebe's : namely, a fall in real wages by more than a half over the century.
The difference between the two sets of indices is accounted for by the fact that Wiebe
measured prices in terms of silver and the data used in the other case were in terms
of coin.
[3] Cf. Lipson, op. cit., vol. III, 258, 276. An example cited by Lipson is that of the
Wiltshire wage-assessments, which remained unchanged from the accession of
James I till the Commonwealth except for one change in 1635 in the assessment for
agricultural labourers.

their town or parish without a written licence, as " the most powerful instrument devised for degrading and impoverishing the English labourer " : a degradation which, a century later, the Act of Settlement consummated and " made him, as it left him, a serf without land, the most portentous phenomenon in agriculture ". [1] " From 1563 to 1824 ", the same writer declared in a deservedly famous passage, " a conspiracy, concocted by the law and carried out by parties interested in its success, was entered into, to cheat the English workman of his wages, to tie him to the soil, to deprive him of hope, and to degrade him into irremediable poverty. . . . For more than two centuries and a half the English law, and those who administered the law, were engaged in grinding the English workman down to the lowest pittance, in stamping out every expression or act which indicated any organized discontent, and in multiplying penalties upon him when he thought of his natural rights." [2]

When, even under these conditions, the supply of labour for any new enterprise was insufficiently plentiful, for example in mining, it was not uncommon for the Crown to grant the right of impressment to the entrepreneur or to require that convicts be assigned to the work under penalty of hanging if they were refractory or if they absconded. This was done in the case of South Wales lead mines leased to royal patentees in Stuart times ; from which apparently numerous convicts ran away, despite the threatened penalty, declaring that " they had better have been hanged than be tied to that employment ". [3] Throughout this period compulsion to labour stood in the background of the labour market. Tudor legislation provided compulsory work for the unemployed as well as making unemployment an offence punishable with characteristic brutality. A law of 1496 enacted that vagabonds and idle persons should be placed in the stocks

[1] *History of Agriculture and Prices*, vol. V, 628 ; *Six Centuries of Work and Wages*, vol. II, 433. The Act of 1563 had empowered the justices to fix the rate of wages of artificers, handicraftsmen, husbandmen and other labourers whose wages had in times past been rated ; but the Act of 1604 extended this to all workmen or workwomen, thereby, as Eden remarked, "frequently afford(ing) master manufacturers ample means of domineering over their workmen " (*State of the Poor*, Ed. Rogers, 24).

[2] *Six Centuries*, vol. II, 398. Cf. also the verdict of two continental historians : " The existence of this reserve army of labour [in the sixteenth century] always at hand and semi-gratuitous, in addition to the workmen in regular employment, naturally lowered the position of the whole wage-earning class. . . . Elizabethan wage legislation . . . delayed and hindered the considerable rise which would have been necessary to maintain the workers in the same degree of real comfort " (Renard and Weulersee, *Life and Work in Modern Europe*, 93–4).

[3] D. J. Davies, *Econ. Hist. of S. Wales prior to 1800*, 81.

for three days and three nights, and on a second offence for six days and nights. Vagabonds in London in 1524 were ordered to be " tayed at a cart's tayle " and " be beten by the Sheriff's officers with whippes " and have " round colers of iron " affixed to their necks. The notorious Statute of Edward VI decreed that anyone refusing to labour " should be branded with a red-hot iron on the breast " and " should be adjudged the slaves for two years of any person who should inform against such idler ", the master being entitled to drive his slave to work " by beating, chaining or otherwise in such labour, however vile so ever it be " and to make him a slave for life and brand him on cheek or forehead if he should run away. Elizabethan legislation provided that begging should be punishable by burning through the gristle of the right ear and on a second offence by death ; the former penalty being humanely modified in 1597 to one of being stripped naked to the waist and whipped until the body was bloody.[1] After the Restoration, when labour-scarcity had again become a serious complaint and the propertied class had been soundly frightened by the insubordination of the Common-wealth years, the clamour for legislative interference to keep wages low, to drive the poor into employment and to extend the system of workhouses and " houses of correction " and the farming out of paupers once more reached a crescendo.[2]

On the Continent legislation in these centuries was, if any-thing, more draconian. In Flanders and in France alike (and the same was true of Germany) the sixteenth century was one of acute destitution and a redundant army of labourers, as it was also a century of falling real wages. Government inter-vention endeavoured, more deliberately it would seem than in England, to maintain money wages at their old level in face of a doubling of prices. Combination among workers was visited with brutal punishment ; flogging, prison and banishment were the penalties for strikes. Workers were bound for long terms of service, often extending over several years, and were hounded down like military deserters if they left their employment. In the following century, which was one of greater labour scarcity, Colbert waged a war against the destitute of a callousness even more remarkable than that of the Tudor régime in England ; persons without a means of livelihood being given the alternative

[1] E. M. Leonard, *Early History of English Poor Relief*, 25 ; F. M. Eden, *State of the Poor*, Ed. Rogers, 10–18.
[2] Cf. T. E. Gregory, in *Economica*, No. I, p. 45, on the advocacy at this time of workhouses as a means of lowering wages outside.

of expulsion from the kingdom or condemnation to the dreaded slavery of the galleys. " Vagabond-hunts " were organized alike in the Netherlands and in France to supply crews, and pressure was brought to bear on the Courts to make condemnation to galley-slavery a common punishment even for trifling offences. There was frequently forced recruitment of labour for privileged establishments of all kinds, and parents who did not send their children into industry were threatened with heavy fines. " Houses of correction " for the workless were multiplied as virtual convict establishments for forced labour, their occupants being frequently hired out to private employers ; in other cases the institution itself being leased to a contractor.[1]

If the formation of a proletariat by the methods we have outlined played the rôle in the growth of Capitalism that we have assigned to it, one would expect to be able to trace a fairly close connection between the main stages in this process and the condition of the labour market, as reflected in the movement of real wages, and consequentially between this process and the growth of industry. Such a connection is not difficult to find. It is a familiar fact that during the two centuries of labour scarcity prior to the events of the Tudor age real wages in England rose considerably, and by the end of the fifteenth century stood at a relatively high level. Estimates suggest that between the early decades of the fourteenth century and the end of the fifteenth real wages may have increased by about a half, or in terms of wheat more than doubled. But after 1500 the reverse movement sets in ; and what wage-earners over two centuries had previously gained, within a century they were to lose, and more than lose.

In recent years a good deal of prominence has been given to the so-called price-revolution of the sixteenth century as a powerful agency in the transition from the mediæval to the modern world. Professor Earl Hamilton has attributed to the influx of gold and silver from America to Europe in this century " the greatest influence that the discovery of America had upon the progress of Capitalism " ; and Lord Keynes, in a frequently quoted passage, has called the authors of the *Cambridge Modern History* to book because they " make no mention of these economic factors as moulding the Elizabethan

<hr />

[1] Cole, *Colbert*, vol. II, 473 ; G. Rusche and Kirchheimer, *Punishment and Social Structure*, 41–5 ; 53–4, 84–5 ; P. Boissonnade, *Colbert, 1661–83*, 256–269, 276–8 ; P. Boissonnade, *Le Socialisme d'État : L'Industrie et les Classes Industrielles en France, 1453–1661*, 303–8.

Age and making possible its greatness ".[1] On whether the
emphasis often given to these events is exaggerated opinion has
been divided. But that they exerted a powerful influence few
will be prepared to deny. What is important for our present
purpose, however, is less the size of that influence than the fact
that the precise character of the influence which this price-
revolution exercised was very largely determined by the state
of the labour market—the size of the labour reserve—at the
particular time or place when these monetary events occurred.
It is a commonplace that a price-revolution which touched all
prices equally would have no significant effects upon the economic
order : at any rate, none of the epoch-making effects of which
these writers speak. What gave the Tudor price-inflation its
special significance was the influence it had either upon the
relative incomes of different classes or upon the value of property.
Some part, as we have seen, was no doubt played by its tendency
to impoverish the older landed interest, whose rental claims in
money tended to be fairly rigid (or at least to be sluggish in their
upward adjustment to a rising price-level) and who consequently
tended to part with their property at a low valuation to the rising
bourgeoisie. This particular influence may have been partly
counteracted by the growing demand during this century for
wool, and the advantages to be derived by landlords from
enclosure,[2] which tended to have a favourable effect on the
value of land. But this influence nevertheless must have
remained an important one. Scarcely less important, however,
was the effect of monetary change upon the movement of real
wages ; and it is undoubtedly upon this effect that the historical
rôle of the price-revolution very largely depended. To the
extent that money-wages failed to rise as the commodity price-
level rose, all employers and owners of capital were abnormally
enriched at the expense of the standard of life of the labouring
class : the price-revolution generated that " profit inflation " of

[1] Earl J. Hamilton in *Economica*, Nov. 1929, 344 ; J. M. Keynes, *Treatise on Money*,
vol. II, 156. Between about 1520 and 1620 Mexican silver production increased
about four and a half times. In 1519 the first Aztec spoils reached Spain ; but
the largest increase came from the exploitation of the Potosi mines after 1545. In
Spain prices (in terms of silver) seem to have risen by as much as 400 per cent. within
the century, and in Britain by about 300 per cent. between 1550 and 1650. Cf.
also Sombart, *Der Moderne Kapitalismus*, I, 529–33, 554 seq.
[2] Contemporaneous complaints of a lag of rents behind prices were, however, not
uncommon : for example, the complaint of the Knight in Hales' *Discourse* (quoted
by Prof. Hamilton), that " the most part of the landes of this Realme stand yet at
the old Rent ". Prof. Hamilton quotes this lag of rents as an argument against
Sombart's view that rent was a major source of capital accumulation at the time.

which Lord Keynes has spoken as being responsible for those " golden years " when " modern Capitalism was born " and as " the fountain and origin of British Foreign Investment ".[1]   The crucial question, therefore, was whether money-wages tended to move in sympathy with prices or to lag behind.

In this respect the effects of monetary inflation were far from uniform.   In Spain, while real wages at first seem to have fallen under the impact of the price-revolution in the first half of the sixteenth century, they later rose, and by 1620 were actually *higher* than they had been in 1500.   By contrast, in France and Britain real wages continued to fall throughout the sixteenth century and remained throughout the seventeenth century below the level at which they had stood in 1500.[2]   Both Professor Earl Hamilton's estimate (based on the figures of Thorold Rogers and Wiebe) and the index compiled by Professor Knoop and Mr. Jones suggest that real wages in 1600 in England were less than a half what they had been a century before.[3]   To quote again Lord Keynes : " The greatness of Spain coincides with the Profit Inflation from 1520 to 1600, and her eclipse with the Profit Deflation from 1600 to 1630.   The rise of the power of England was delayed by the same interval as the effect of the new supplies of money on her economic system which was at its maximum from 1585 to 1630.   In the year of the Armada Philip's Profit Inflation was just concluded, Elizabeth's had just begun." [4]

If the monetary factor had such diverse influence according

---

[1] *Op cit.*, 155-9.

[2] In France, there seems to have been a short-lived break in the first two decades of the century.   The subsequent fall, and the continuance of real wages at a very low level throughout the century (whereas in England there was some recovery) seems to have been due to the repressive legislation that the first signs of labour-scarcity at the beginning of the century evoked.   In England, however, the revolutionary events of 1640-60 gave some scope to democratic movements among journeymen, artisans and tenants.

[3] Earl Hamilton, *American Treasure and the Price Revolution in Spain, 1501-1650* ; Thorold Rogers, *Hist. of Agriculture and Prices*, vol. IV; Wiebe, *Zur Geschichte des Preisrevolution des XVI u. XVII Jahrhunderts*, p. 374 seq. ; Knoop and Jones, *loc. cit.* Lord Keynes, and also Prof. J. U. Nef, express the opinion that the estimate of real wages falling by more than a half must be an exaggeration.   But if we were to judge by wheat-prices, and to measure wages in terms of wheat, the fall would appear to be greater still.   This is the period to which Thorold Rogers referred as " the long cloud that was coming over the long sunshine of labour ".   The masses, he wrote, were " to exchange a condition of comparative opulence and comfort for penury and misery, unhappily prolonged for centuries. . . . From the Reformation till the Revolution the condition of English labour grew darker and darker.   From the Revolution to the outbreak of the War of American Independence its lot was a little lightened, but only by the plenty of the seasons and the warmth of the sun " (*op. cit.*, vol. IV, vi-vii).

[4] Keynes, *op. cit.*, 161.

to the circumstances upon which it impinged, the presumption is that conditions in the labour market must have played the decisive rôle in determining the outcome : that, as Weber has said, " the tendency that will result from an inflow of precious metal depends entirely upon the nature of the labour-system ".[1] And if we look in this direction for a reason, we find a very simple one to hand. The state of the labour market in sixteenth-century England, when it received the impact of the price-revolution, was one of surplus labour, following those events which we have described and which made the reign of Elizabeth the age of the " sturdy beggar ", of the vagabond and the dispossessed, whom a barbaric legislation condemned to branding or to public hanging. A similar plethora of labour, evidenced in the abnormal army of roaming vagabonds, was a characteristic of France and Germany in this century, largely as product of the oppression and eviction of peasantry and the restrictiveness of the gilds.[2]   In Spain, by contrast, there was a much greater demand for labour by feudal establishments and the Church ; as mercenaries there were possibilities of emigration to the new world ; the population had recently been reduced by the expulsion of the Moors, and was to be further reduced at the end of the sixteenth century by pestilence.   Moreover, the process of primitive accumulation in this still-feudal country had not begun.   True, in the first half of the ensuing century the labour reserve in England was also to be depleted, and with the growth of industry in the age of the Stuarts and some slackening of the process of enclosure and the engrossing of farms, a period of actual labour-scarcity was to ensue : a scarcity which lasted until the Georgian enclosures and the industrial revolution. This was also the case on the continent of Europe, if for different

[1] M. Weber, *General Economic History*, 353.   Schumpeter goes so far as to say that " all the durable achievements of English industry and commerce can be accounted for without reference to the plethora of precious metals ", and that in Spain the influx of precious metals actually retarded the growth of capitalism (*Business Cycles*, vol. I, 232).   This seems an overstatement.   Monetary inflation *per se* no doubt had an effect in *facilitating* a fall in real wages, which might otherwise have been tardier and smaller.   What we are claiming here is simply that (a) such effect as monetary change had was principally *via* its effect on real wages, which depended on the condition of the labour market, and (b) that probably *most* of the fall in real wages which took place would have occurred in the absence of monetary inflation.

[2] Cf. Rusche and Kirchheimer, *Punishment and Social Structure*, 11–14 ; E. Levasseur, *La Population française*, vol. I, 189 ; E. M. Leonard, *Eng. Poor Relief*, 11–13.   The previous century, the fifteenth, had, however, been one of depopulation in France, following the Hundred Years War and the Black Death, as it had been in England.   After the sixteenth century the population of France seems to have remained stationary for the next century, and in the seventeenth century a new period of labour shortage set in (Levasseur, *op. cit.*, 202–6).

reasons. For example, in Germany the devastating effects of the Thirty Years War on the population was to aid in throttling economic activity for some time. But it was precisely during this period that real wages were stabilized, although at a lower level than at the end of the fifteenth century; and during the seventeenth century they even showed a tendency to rise, both in England (during the Commonwealth), and in France (during the first few decades of the century, before oppressive legislation reduced them again). Finally in England with the new and more powerful wave of enclosures in the latter part of the eighteenth century, dislodging as it did the army of cottagers from their last slender hold on the fringes of the commons, a tendency appeared for a further decline in real wages between about the 1760's and the end of the Napoleonic Wars : [1] a tendency which coincided with a new epoch of industrial expansion.

Of the replacement of many small properties in land by a few large ones England provides the classic example ; and with the radical nature of this change the comparatively early transition to industrial Capitalism in this country is evidently connected. But if it were the case that only by this classic method of dispossession could a proletariat arise, the growth of industrial Capitalism in certain other countries of Europe, if tardier there and less assured in its beginnings, would be hard to explain. In certain parts of the Continent, but not in all, some parallel to the English situation could be found by the beginning of the nineteenth century. In certain districts of France by 1789, including Picardy, Artois, and the Île de France, there existed (mostly on church lands) large farms of the type that was coming to predominate in eighteenth-century England. " A few French landlords had thrown farm to farm and had let the consolidated holdings to men of substance." [2] But even in these districts probably no more than a fifth of the land was farmed in this way ; and over most of France " the nobility, almost without exception, let out their land in scraps to wretched little farmers from the

---

[1] Hasbach, op. cit., 116–31, 174–6. Arthur Young's figures show a doubling of the price of wheat between 1770 and 1812 against an increase of wages of about 60 per cent. The prices of meat and milk and butter more than doubled. Prof. Clapham, using the price-estimates of Silberling, thinks that between 1794 and 1824 rural real earnings may have risen slightly, but if so very little (*Econ. Hist. of Modern Britain*, vol. I, 127–31). It is to be noted that *earnings* and not simply wage-rates are being referred to here ; and that the rise was in the north where demand for labour was growing. In the south of England there was a fall.

[2] J. H. Clapham, *Economic Development of France and Germany*, 17.

lower ranks of the peasantry ".[1] Few of the labourers who hired themselves for wages were completely landless, outside Flanders and Normandy, Picardy, Burgundy, Brittany and the neighbourhood of Versailles. They were mostly poor peasants : a semi-proletariat, still possessing a scrap of land, which, though insufficient to maintain a family, was generally enough to save them from utter destitution.[2] In parts of northern France between 60 and 70 per cent. of the peasantry owned less than one hectare of land, and between 80 and 90 per cent. held less than five hectares (five hectares being generally considered the minimum size that could support a peasant family) ; while at the same time there existed a small minority of well-to-do large peasant farmers.[3] Even the extensive purchase of church lands and of confiscated estates of the nobility by the bourgeoisie and by what Sée calls " the peasant aristocracy " during the revolution did not result in enclosures on the English model. A bourgeois became the *rentier* instead of cleric or gentleman ; but the actual leasing and working of the estate remained generally unimpaired.

In Schleswig-Holstein and in Denmark there had been an enclosure movement of the English type in the late eighteenth century, in the latter case supported by the government ; and a similar development had occurred in southern Sweden. " The old framework of village life gave way before a deliberate attack from above." [4] But in western Germany conditions were much closer to those prevailing over the greater part of France. While there had been some tendency towards eviction and the consolidation of land into the landlord's hands, this tendency was relatively little developed, partly owing to the weakness of the knights, and partly because the princes were inclined (like the Tudors in England) to legislate against such tendencies in the interests of maintaining the traditional economic order. In the countryside there was no distinct landless class as yet ; but there existed, as in France, a semi-proletariat of those unable to live from their holdings, who worked for the richer peasants and performed supplementary labour for wages on the lord's estate. In the east, the home of the powerful *Junkers*, things were very

---

[1] J. H. Clapham, *Economic Development of France and Germany*, 17.

[2] *Ibid.*, 18 : " The more peasant holdings there were in any province, the less room there was for a landless class."

[3] H. Sée, *Economic and Social Conditions in France during the Eighteenth Century*, 2–6, 17–21.

[4] Clapham, *op. cit.*, 32.

different; and the tendency of *Junkers* to dispossess peasants and to enlarge their own holdings had in many districts progressed apace. " In parts of Pomerania things had gone so far that the true peasant who lived by his holding had almost disappeared." [1] When serfdom was abolished in Prussia under the edicts of Stein and Hardenberg, the most privileged type of serf (roughly the equivalent of the English copyholder) had to sacrifice a part (sometimes a third, sometimes a half) of his holding to the lord in compensation; while the lowest ranks of the peasantry, cottagers and virtual tenants-at-will, were in effect dispossessed and became a labour-reserve for the Junker estates.

In the Russian Baltic States emancipation in the reign of Tsar Alexander I was accompanied by the dispossession of the peasantry, so that the former serfs now constituted a landless proletariat, still forbidden to migrate and accordingly obliged to work for the landowners on what was now nominally a free wage-contract. In the remainder of Russia, the Emancipation of 1861 provided for the retention by the peasants of the land they had previously occupied; and no sweeping dispossession such as occurred in Prussia and the Baltic States took place. The serf-owners were compensated by redemption-payments from the State which were to be collected from the peasantry by annual payments spread over forty-nine years.[2] As these redemption-arrangements worked out, however, they resulted in a decrease in the area allotted to the peasantry as compared with the area occupied by them on the eve of the Emancipation : a decrease which was small when averaged out over the whole country, but which reached as high as 25 per cent. in the black earth belt east of the Dnieper, where holdings in many areas had previously been exceptionally small. At the landowners' instigation, an amendment had been introduced by which a peasant who wished to be absolved from the redemption payments could choose instead to receive only a quarter of the standard land-allotment; and in areas where land was valuable the landowners encouraged this form of settlement, and the so-called " poverty lots " were numerous. This resulted in the immediate creation in these districts of a semi-proletariat, forced by the insufficiency of their holdings to take hired employment on the nearby estate or in local industries, or driven to that " hunger-renting " of additional

---

[1] *Ibid.*, 37. Cf. also F. A. Ogg, *Economic Development of Modern Europe*, 203.
[2] Those payments outstanding were cancelled in 1905 as a concession to the revolutionary movement of 1905–6.

land at inflated rents or in return for labour performed for the owner (the *otrabotnik* system) which characterized the half-century following the Emancipation : a tendency accentuated by subsequent developments in the economy of the Russian village in the later nineteenth and early twentieth centuries which will be discussed below. One section of the former serfs, the household serfs or *dvornie lyudi*, were emancipated without land, and being completely landless became forthwith " the recruiting ground for the new industrial army ".[1]

II

There is another method by which a proletariat may come into being, tardier perhaps and certainly less obtrusive than the classic English method of eviction and engrossment of farms as a policy initiated from above, but nevertheless extensively found. It consists of the tendency to economic differentiation which exists within most communities of small producers unless special institutions prevail which are capable of preventing inequality. The chief factors in this differentiation are differences that arise in course of time in the quality or quantity of land-holding and differences in instruments of tillage and of draught animals ; and the agency of eventual dispossession is debt. In this connection, two examples illuminate very clearly the essentials of the process by which the small producer became a servant of capital and a proletarian.

This process is, perhaps, nowhere more clearly depicted than in the case of those mining communities which were anciently characterized by the practice that is known as " free mining ". The example they offer is of special significance because both law and custom were in their case devised to give the maximum stability to such communities of small producers and to preserve the rights of the small man. Yet despite this, the forces making for economic differentiation and the final disintegration of these communities eventually prevailed. The districts in England

---

[1] G. T. Robinson, *Rural Russia under the Old Régime*, 89, also 83–92. In the west and particularly in Poland (for political reasons) the treatment of the peasantry at the Emancipation was most favourable. Moreover, peasants on State and Imperial lands (who had paid money-dues before) came off better than on private estates. On the latter, " in the black-soil belt where the land was well worth keeping, the landlords cut the peasants off with reduced allotments, to be redeemed at a moderate premium ; in the north the allotments were more ample, but the price upon them was nearly doubled for redemption purposes. North and south the scales were weighted against the peasant " (*ibid.*, 88).

where the right of " free mining " existed—a customary right generally confirmed by royal charter—comprised the Forest of Dean, the tin-mining areas of Cornwall and Devon, known as " The Stanneries ", and the lead mines of Derbyshire, the Mendip Hills and of Alston Moor, in Cumberland. The custom was that any inhabitant of the area, whether villein or gentleman, had the right, known as " bounding ", to stake out a claim for himself, and on payment of a fee to the Crown or to the local possessor of seigniorial rights was free to start mining. This right once established was only liable to forfeiture if its owner failed to work his claim or transgressed the mining code. So long as there were available ore deposits, this institution of " bounding " prevented the ownership of minerals from becoming the monopoly of a few. The size of any single holding was explicitly limited, and it was " open to the poorest villein to become his own master simply by laying out a claim and registering its boundaries in the proper court ".[1] The mining law of the Mendips provided that after procuring a licence the prospective miner should be " at hys fre wylle to pyche wythyn the seyd forest of Mendip and to brecke the ground where and yn what place he shall think best himself ". The size of the claim was determined either by a throw of the axe or by setting up " a payre of styllings wythyn 24 hours ".[2] In Cornwall and Devon the independence of the miner was safeguarded by the explicit provision of rights of free access to running water to wash his ore and of procuring faggots for his smelting forge. In Derbyshire he was allowed to cut wood and timber from the King's forests, and in Somerset and Cumberland it was expressly stipulated that he should be free to smelt his ore wheresoever he pleased.[3]

In some respects there is a parallel between these mining communities and the town gilds. Like a gild their rights were generally enshrined in a charter, and they exercised certain judicial functions in trade matters, possessing from an early date a mining court, which largely dealt with technical questions, and in the Stanneries possessing a parliament to legislate on matters concerning mining law and usage. The essential difference was the absence in the mining communities of restrictions against

---

[1] G. R. Lewis, *The Stanneries*, 35. Mr. Lewis states his opinion that " had the mines remained attached to the ownership of the soil, perhaps nothing could have saved the Stanneries from a régime of capitalism ".

[2] *V.C.H. Somerset*, II, 367.

[3] Saltzmann, *Industries in the Middle Ages*, 46 ; *V.C.H. Cornwall*, I, 526 ; *Somerset*, II, 368 ; *Derby*, II, 326.

newcomers ; anyone being free to engage in operations, provided that room for new claims remained unoccupied. There was apparently no actual corporate organization, apart from the mining courts and the Stanneries' parliament, and there is no evidence that the free miners engaged in any corporate action. Only in the case of the Forest of Dean was there anything approaching a closed corporation, with collective regulations and collective functions. Here, in matters of sale there was a species of collective bargaining, and a fixing of minimum prices, under the control of " bargainers " appointed by the miners' court. Unlike other districts, entry was here restricted to sons of free miners or to those who had served an apprenticeship. At the same time, to preclude any concentration of power into the hands of a few, no miner was allowed more than four horses or to have a wagon or to become the owner of a forge ; and presumably to safeguard the community from dependence on middlemen the carrying of coal and ore was confined to miners.[1]

Despite these egalitarian regulations, there must always have been some tendencies to inequality internal to these mining communities. Firstcomers or those fortunate enough to have staked out good diggings for themselves must always have possessed substantial advantages. But as long as there were new diggings available and access to them remained free, the differential advantages of the favoured few could hardly have formed the basis for class differentiation, since, so long as self-employment was open to all, the basis for a class of persons who were willing to labour for others because they lacked any alternative was absent. These differential advantages may have formed the ground for the growth of a small *kulak* class ; but had it not been for the impact of external forces, inequalities would probably have remained relatively small and the free mining districts would have retained their character as fairly homogeneous communities of not very sharply differentiated small producers. What seems to have been of crucial importance, if only as the initial wedge of a series of disrupting influences, was the rise in the fourteenth century of the so-called " cost agreement " system, under which one of the associates of a mining group was excused from actual labour in return for a monetary payment. Despite enactments to the contrary, many of those possessing mining claims sold them or sold shares in them to local gentry and clergy and merchants of neighbouring

[1] Lewis, *op. cit.*, 168–73 ; *V.C.H. Gloucester*, II, 233–4.

towns. As a result we soon find in the coinage rolls persons like Thomas the Goldsmith, Richard the Smith and Thomas the Pewterer, the Vicar of Bodmin and the Rector of St. Ladoce, the clerk of Lostwithiel, the priors of Tywardratch and Mount St. Michael and sundry merchants recorded as " producers " of tin. As a later development we meet the " tribute system ", under which the owners of a claim, when they were unwilling to work the mine, leased it to a group of workmen or to a small master in return for a share of the product.[1] But he e again, so long as free diggings were available and trade in tin was unobstructed, the possibility that a class which drew income from ownership-claims and not from productive activity would fatten on this system remained limited, since the lessees of a mine could exact from the tributers no more than the equivalent of the superior productivity of their mine over an available " marginal " digging : otherwise the tributers would presumably have pre-ferred to dig an inferior claim for themselves. In other words, the only surplus that could appear was the equivalent of differen-tial rent.

In the fourteenth century, however, one hears of a certain Abraham the Tinner employing as many as 300 persons and of " certain of the wealthy tinners of Cornwall " who " had usurped stanneries by force and duress and compelled the stannery men to work in these, contrary to their will, for a penny for every other day, whereas before they worked twenty pence or more worth of tin per day, and for a long time had prevented tinners from whitening and selling their tin worked by them ".[2] As yet such cases were exceptional ; but it is clear that other influences were at work to deprive the free miners of their economic independence. Of these influences the most import-ant was the growing economic advantage enjoyed by smelters and ore-dealers and buyers of tin : advantages which brought the mine-worker into a position of increasing dependence. From the earliest records we find that the sale of tin was confined to two coinage days in the year, when tin could be stamped at the appointed coinage towns and the appropriate dues paid, as required by law. At the beginning of the fourteenth century we hear complaints from the tinners that the staple for tin had been fixed at Lostwithiel, a town some distance from the mining areas.[3] The infrequency of sales and the distance of the trading

[1] Lewis, *op. cit.*, 189–90 ; *V.C.H. Cornwall*, I, 539, 556.
[2] Lewis, *op. cit.*, 189–90.   [3] *Ibid.*, 210, 212 ; *V.C.H. Cornwall*, I, 558–9.

centre combined to place the tinner of small means at considerable disadvantage. He lacked the means with which to finance
his operations over the intervening six months before he could
market his tin, and he might be unable to bear the cost of carting
his product to the distant coinage town ; whereas the owner of
a mining claim who possessed some capital, or drew an income
from other sources, could more easily do both these things.
The result seems to have been to place the poor tinners and
tributers in a position of increasing dependence on gentlemen
tinners or on middlemen, who could advance them capital and
arrange the transport of their tin to the coinage towns ; and
the free trade in tin which was a necessary complement to free
mining began to disappear. The system of money-advances to
tributers, known as " subsist ", became increasingly common
and laid an increasing load of debt on the shoulder of the mine-
worker who held no other property than his mine, thereby
augmenting the bargaining disadvantage under which he
laboured as well as exacting profit from his necessity. By the
sixteenth century the tributer appears to have become involved
in a mire of dependence, into which he tended to sink ever more
deeply. His plight was further worsened by the custom of
truck-payments, and his income was reduced to a mere starvation wage. The tribute system, in its turn, eventually yielded
place to " tut-work ", under which the owner simply auctioned
the working of the mine to gang-leaders for a piece-work wage,
knocking it down to the lowest bidder.[1]

This sorry state Henry VII made a move to better by appoint-
ing two extra coinages, " because the poor tinners have not been
able to keep their tin for a good price when there were only
two " ; and an ordinance of 1495 provided that " no persone,
neyther persones, having possession of lands and tenements
above the yerely value of £10 be owners of eny tynwork, with
the exception of persons claiming by inheritance or possessed of
tynworks in their own freeholds." But these measures seem to
have had little lasting influence in checking the tendencies we have
described. Perhaps the measures came too late, when dependence had already fastened its shackles too firmly on the miners
and too many persons of property could claim the possession of
tinworks by inheritance. Apart from these early Tudor enactments, Mr. Randall Lewis has said that " with true *laissez-faire*
spirit the English mineral law left the unorganized tinners . . .

[1] L. L. Price, *West Barbary*, 37.

unprotected, and handed them over to the tender mercies of the middleman and regrator ".[1]

But there was to be a further burden loaded on to the producer's back. With the declared object of providing a steady market for tin and a means of advancing capital to the industry, a monopoly was established in the buying of the metal : a monopoly which aroused the protests of the London Pewterers' Company as well as of the tin producers. Whether or not the middle layer of tin-interests—the local dealers and the smelters and the rich tinners—were benefited, no benefit was apparent to the mine-workers. On the contrary, the monopoly evidently had the effect of lowering the price received by the producer at the same time as it raised the sale-price of tin to the pewterer ; and the buying price of tin seems to have remained at this low level in face of rises in the export-price. During the Commonwealth the monopoly was suspended, with the result that the buying-price of tin rose as much as from £3 to £6 per hundredweight ; and this, combined with a decline of the coinage system, with its limited number of days of sale, seems to have caused the wages of tributers and tut-workers to rise to a level of 30s. per month.[2] But with the Restoration both the buying-monopoly and the coinage rules were reimposed, and wages fell by a half. There followed riots in Falmouth and Truro ; the miners demanding free sale of tin and the removal of the monopoly : a demand which it is interesting to note that the rich tinners opposed.[3] But the resistance of the miners was ineffectual, and by the end of the seventeenth century the producer's subordination to capital appears to have been complete. Two stages of usury marked this subordination. At the top were the merchant monopolists, who advanced credit to the tin-masters, dealers and smelters, and by the lowness of the price at which they purchased the tin exacted a profit-margin of something like 60 per cent. In turn the tin-masters and dealers and smelters advanced money to the tributers and tut-workers, and not infrequently enjoyed in their turn a profit-margin of 80 or 90 per cent. By 1700 the owners of smelting houses, instead of advancing money to groups of workers, had frequently become " adventuring tinners " directly employing miners at a piece-

[1] Lewis, *op. cit.*, 211. By this time the Stanneries Courts and Parliament seem to have been composed almost entirely of gentlemen tinners and ore dealers and merchants.

[2] *Ibid.*, 220 ; *V.C.H. Cornwall*, I, 558–9.

[3] Lewis, *op. cit.*, 220.

wage.[1] Exploitation through usury was passing, and the capitalist wage-system was succeeding to its place.

For other free-mining areas the information we have is more scanty, and the governing factors in the transition from free mining to wage-labour are less easy to detect. Nevertheless, the main outlines of the story remain fairly clear. In the Forest of Dean breaches in the protective regulations with which the miners had fortified themselves seem to have become increasingly common in the course of time. The custom grew, in imitation of the town gilds, of electing gentlemen of means to be free miners ; and, despite explicit prohibitions, claims were leased by their owners to outsiders. But the most potent factor in disintegrating the old community appears to have been the growth of monopoly in the smelting of ore. In the late sixteenth century licences were given by the Crown to capitalist adventurers to erect blast-furnaces in the Forest. These supplanted the old-fashioned bloomeries ; and their introduction was responsible for riots among the free miners, who complained of " frequent assaults upon the privileges of the miners by royal patentees ".[2] In 1640 these privileges were to suffer a more sweeping encroachment in the shape of a grant by the Crown of all mines and mineral rights in the Forest to a Sir John Winter at an annual royalty of £10,000 to £16,000. Further riots, followed by prolonged litigation, ensued ; but so far as can be gathered the miners were unsuccessful in upholding their claims ; and in the course of the next few decades these claims had to be drastically abated. In 1678 the prohibition on carting of coal and ore by outsiders was abandoned, and nine years later the miners surrendered their right to control selling-prices. The encroachment of the capitalist, able to mine with improved methods and to market the product more easily, progressively increased until free mining was no more than a memory.[3] But the mining law while it lasted must have had a considerable effect in delaying the intrusion of the capitalist undertaker ; and it is significant that the latter was not fully established in this district until the late seventeenth century.

In the Mendips the growth of monopoly in the smelting of ore seems, again, to have been the paramount influence in the disintegration of the system of free mining. The clauses in the

[1] Lewis, 214–16 ; H. Levy, *Monopoly and Competition*, 9.
[2] *V.C.H. Gloucester*, II, 225 ; Lewis, *op. cit.*, 208.
[3] *V.C.H. Gloucester*, II, 225–8.

mining law which secured to the miner freedom to smelt his ore where he pleased came to be progressively disregarded by the lords of the soil, and " the more powerful lords used every effort to ensure that the lead ore raised on their own lands should be smelted at the furnaces of the lordship ".[1] Towards the end of the sixteenth century we find speculators and adventurers from outside advancing capital to miners in return for " parts " or shares, and, on the other hand, miners who were in difficulties mortgaging their mines for ready cash. We are told that " Bristol merchants, neighbouring gentlemen, local publicans, all took a hand in the game ". Those who had capital to invest could sink deeper shafts and reach richer deposits. Perhaps they were also in a better position to evade the smelting monopoly and to handle the marketing of the metal. At any rate, the poor miner, who lacked the advantages bestowed by capital, was gradually ousted, probably to become, as elsewhere, the employee of the new class of owners. But about this development the available records do not seem to afford us any details.[2]

In the silver mines of Saxony one can trace a development that affords some quite remarkable parallels with the English case. Here it had been the custom for seigniorial lords, where for any reason they did not wish to work the minerals themselves with serf-labour, to lease the mining rights to associations of free workmen. These associations worked the minerals co-operatively, somewhat after the manner of a Russian *artel* ; and since payment was generally made to the lord in the form of a given proportion of the product, certain privileges and a measure of protection were given to these mining associations by the lord. In some cases these associations were granted immunity from feudal law like urban communities ; and where they prospered they were sometimes raised to the dignity of a special mining town, possessing a certain degree of autonomy and the right to have a local court and a local law of its own. Whether in origin these mining associations were privileged serfs or peasants and artisans who were not members of the servile class is not clear ; probably they were the latter. But by the fourteenth century a number of them had become both prosperous and exclusive, and many of them had sold claims or shares in the association to outsiders, such as local squires or clergy or town merchants. To aid the rapid exploitation of the mine, the seigniorial lords encouraged the development of the tribute system, and apparently

---

[1] *V.C.H. Somerset*, II, 368.   [2] *Ibid.*, 374–6.

stipulated that the tributers to whom the mine was leased should be labourers without property and that landowning peasants should be excluded. These tributers were furnished with certain materials ; and since, being propertyless, they had no alternative means of livelihood, they were ready to surrender a large proportion of the product of their labour to the association. In this way a fairly sharp line of division came to be drawn between the associates owning the mine, who were purely *rentiers* drawing income from their claims to mineral exploitation, and the tributers who leased the mine and worked it but retained only a part of its product. This tribute-system, accordingly, as in the English Stanneries, represented a half-way house to the wage-system ; the latter, as time went on, tending to displace the former " owing to the increasing disparity in bargaining power between the two parties concerned ".[1]

In Saxony, as in the Forest of Dean and the Mendips, another factor was to intervene to complete the process by which the tributer was degraded to the position of a wage-earner ; and this factor which completed the transition was again the growth of monopoly among smelters and ore-purchasers. The monopolistic rights of smelting capitalists were rooted in concessions to build smelting works which were purchased from the seigniorial lords ; and in the fifteenth century " the records give abundant evidence of the increasing difficulties in selling, and the complaints of the tributers rehearse in no uncertain terms the straits to which they were reduced by the oppressions of the ore-purchasers and smelters ".[2] To ease their plight the Emperor Maximilian, in response to appeals, erected a competing smelting-house to take the tributers' ore, and Ferdinand took similar action in the Black Forest. But these cautious remedies seem to have given no more than temporary alleviation. We hear for a time of the miners resisting by forming gilds and by calling strikes ; but in the course of the sixteenth century their status steadily deteriorated. Piece-work, and sometimes even time-work, supplanted the tribute system ; and at the end of the sixteenth century it became common for leases to be given directly to capitalist lessees who employed hired hands to work the mines. " This continued until, in the course of time, we find the lessee taking on more and more the character of a captain of industry, relieving the associates of . . . the whole of their claim."[3]

The main lines of this story of the mining communities can,

---

[1] Lewis, *op. cit.*, 180, also 74.   [2] *Ibid.*, 180.   [3] *Ibid.*, 181–3.

indeed, be traced in the history of many peasant communities of recent memory ; to which it seems likely that the largely unrecorded story of the English peasant community in earlier centuries affords a close parallel. In the case of the Russian village there was much discussion in social-democratic circles at the close of the nineteenth century concerning the actual tendencies at work inside the village economy with its roots in the traditional *mir* or village commune. Writers of the Narodnik or Populist school had argued that the *mir* represented the germ of the Socialism of the future, and that by preserving the traditional features of the village economy the development of Capitalism could be avoided. The Marxists, on the other hand, and in particular Lenin, argued that village economy was destined to disintegrate in face of the influences of the market and was already well advanced on the road towards capitalist agriculture, with the growth of class differentiation among the peasantry. In this development usury (together with various forms of semi-usurious loan-contracts in kind or in labour) appears to have played a leading rôle. The peasant who, from good fortune or good management, was better supplied with ready cash than his neighbours could rent additional land from the landowner and provide working cattle and instruments of tillage. But the poorer peasant was not in a position to do the same. He was less well equipped, and if he rented land, this probably had to be either on the *métayage* system, under which he often had to yield as much as a half of the produce to the landowner, or else on the labour-rent system, whereby he undertook to pay for the extra land by means of a given amount of work on the owner's farm. Unlike the purchase or hire of additional land by the rich peasant, this renting of land by the poor was a sign of poverty—of inability to scratch together sufficient for the subsistence of his family from his existing holding with the methods of cultivation available to him. Consequently, he was generally forced into paying an exorbitant rent under these forms of leasing. This was the " hunger renting " of which we hear so much in the Russian agrarian literature of the time. Indeed, as Lenin pointed out in his *Development of Capitalism in Russia*, the very cheapness with which the landlord and the well-to-do peasant could get work performed under these transitional forms of exploitation served as an obstacle to the introduction of improved methods of cultivation, and in particular of machinery.

But often what the poorer cultivator hungered for even more than for land [1] was draught animals and equipment or seed-corn with which to till his existing holding ; and it was frequently deficiency of capital which set a limit to the amount he could farm, and which was the immediate occasion of his economic dependence on some more prosperous neighbour. It had been the custom in most villages (except in west Ukraine and White Russia) for the land of the commune to be periodically redistributed according to the amount that each could till. One might have expected such an institution to have precluded the growth of inequality. But if he lacked equipment or seed-corn, this periodic redivision brought little help to the poorer peasant. Consequently the largest shares were generally claimed by the more well-to-do cultivators, who proceeded to lease them out to poorer neighbours on a *métayage* basis. When such leases were made, the poorest could not even work the land with his own animals and implements, and had to hire these as well, which relegated him to the position of a hired labourer, supplementing the yield of his scanty holding by working on another's land and receiving payment in kind from the product. Moreover, as Stepniak observed, the rich peasants, or *kulaks*, had " the great advantage over their numerous competitors in the plundering of the peasants " that they were " members, very important members, of the village commune ", and hence were often in a position to use " the great political power which the self-governing *mir* exercises over each individual member ".[2]

But payment in kind in return for land-leases was not enough : at certain seasons of the year money was needed to meet the burden of taxation or perhaps to purchase seed. Confronted with this need for ready-money, which recurred at regular intervals, the poorer villager had resort to the richer as a money-lender ; and to the existing dependence of the former on the latter for the loan of equipment and probably also for trading in his corn was added the dependence of debtor to creditor. This relationship of dependence held a cumulative tendency, the end of which was apt to be the final alienation of the peasant holding in favour of the creditor. It used to happen " about twice a year during the collection of taxes and at sowing-time " that " the peasant, hard pressed for money or seed, (was) willing

---

[1] The hunger for land was greatest in the more thickly settled regions of the Black Earth east of the Dnieper, where the peasant had come worst out of the redemption settlement after the Emancipation of 1861.

[2] Stepniak, *The Russian Peasantry*, 55.

to pledge anything to save his household from flogging.   Within a few years the peasant (was) usually turned into a homeless proletarian." [1]   As a next stage, the *kulak* who had added field to field, and had become successively a leaser of land and of implements, local corn-dealer and village money-lender, instituted village *kustarny* industries and began to employ his moneyless clients and debtors on the putting-out system.   Later these new *kustarny* capitalists often grew rich enough to move into the town and become owners of up-to-date factories ; and many of them (like the Artamanovs of Gorki's *Decadence*) were to supply the sinews of the Russian capitalist class.   Meanwhile, their poorer neighbours tended to sink progressively into dependence, until burdened by debt and taxation and no longer able to maintain themselves on their meagre holdings, as whole families they joined the ranks of the rural proletariat, or at least supplied part of the family as semi-proletarians to eke out the income from the family-holding by wage-employment in the nearby mines or factory towns.[2]

These examples of the growth of class differentiation and the transition to a wage-system, which can find their parallel in peasant communities in almost any region of the world, are instructive for a number of reasons.   They illustrate that the disappearance of free land, while it may be of outstanding importance in primitive communities, is not the only factor, and need not be the main factor, in creating a dependent wage-earning class, as has sometimes been maintained.[3]   Even where free land exists, other factors such as debt or monopoly may rob the small producer of his independence and eventually occasion his dispossession.   At the same time it is clear that economic inequalities are unlikely to create a division of society into an employing master class and a subject wage-earning class, unless access to the means of production, including land, is by some means or other barred to a substantial section of the community.   These examples further illustrate how unstable an economy of

[1] N. I. Stone in *Political Science Quarterly*, XIII, 107 seq.

[2] Cf. *Ibid.* ; also Lenin, " Development of Capitalism in Russia " and " The Agrarian Question in Russia ", in *Selected Works*, vol. I ; L. A. Owen, *Russian Peasant Movement, 1906–1917*, 88 seq. ; G. Pavlovsky, *Agricultural Russia on the Eve of the Revolution*, 107–8, 199–206.   Lenin quoted figures to show that in some districts at the time almost a half of the villagers who worked for wages were employed by the local *peasant bourgeoisie* (*op. cit.*, 285).   At the end of the nineteenth century about a quarter of the male peasant population in the Black Earth belt worked as agricultural labourers for wages (Pavlovsky, *op. cit.*, 199).

[3] For example, Achille Loria in *Economic Foundations of Society*, 1–9, and *Analyse de la Propriété Capitaliste*.

small producers can be in face of the disintegrating effects of production for a market, especially a distant market, unless it enjoys some special advantage which lends it strength or special measures are taken to give it protection and in particular to give protection to its poorer and weaker members. It is here that political influence and the interference of the State may be of outstanding significance for the outcome. Finally, they afford a vivid illustration of the part played alike by monopoly and by usury in causing the simultaneous enrichment of a privileged class and the progressive subjection of a dependent class. In the epoch of primitive accumulation usury always has two faces : the one turned towards the old ruling class—towards the knight, the baron, the prince or the monarch, whose financial embarrassments drive him in search of cash at any cost ; and the other face turned towards the more defenceless victim of the two, the needy small producer. It is hard to say whether the extravagances of the one or the penury of the other is the greater source of enrichment to the usurer. But while the first type of transaction, by effecting an eventual transfer in the ownership of the pledged assets from the old ruling class to the new, is a powerful lever in the accretion of bourgeois wealth, the second type of transaction not only is this, but also serves to beget the very class whose existence is a crucial condition if this new bourgeois wealth is to find a field of investment in production. This class, once it is begotten, has a very convenient quality which gives it an important advantage, as a permanent object of investment, over others. The endowments of Nature are limited ; mineral resources are exhaustible ; usury, like leeches, is apt to bleed the source on which it feeds ; even slave populations appear to have a tendency to die out. But a proletariat has the valuable quality, not merely of reproducing itself each generation, but (unless the present age prove an exception) of reproducing itself on an ever-expanding scale.

CHAPTER SEVEN

THE INDUSTRIAL REVOLUTION AND THE NINETEENTH CENTURY

I

When one reaches the period of the Industrial Revolution, a major problem of scale and of perspective confronts any study of this present kind. One is faced with raw material, in the shape of factual records to hand, which are immensely rich ; much (though not all) of this material already sorted and classified by hands expert in such field-work. The well-worked canvas is so crowded with detail that an intruder who approaches it, desirous of making a manageable and impressionist representation of the scene, is baffled by a serious dilemma. Either he may achieve no more than a few trival strokes of the brush that retain little of the qualities of the original, or he may become so immersed in the depiction of detail of which he is no proper master as to produce merely an inferior copy of what others have done. Even were this dilemma to be adequately solved, and the work of abstraction competently handled, the form of this work would necessarily depend on some principle of selection about which perhaps no two persons could be expected to agree.

About the main shape of economic events in nineteenth-century England—or, indeed, in Western Europe or America—very little probably remains to be said that has not been said already and much better. Gaps doubtless remain in the chronicle which, when filled, will illuminate corners that are still dark. But the century of cheap printing and the spread of almost universal literacy has bequeathed to us documentary sources of an abundance so far exceeding that of any previous century as to leave us in little doubt about the main outlines of the story, or about the essentials of the picture of economic and social life with which we should have been confronted, had we lived in any given social *milieu* in the days of Pitt or Peel or Gladstone. Yet the difficulty of the contemporary economist who turns to the material of a hundred years ago for illumination is not primarily one of *embarras de richesse*. Strangely enough, the difficulty is in some respects the opposite : a poverty of material of the kind he most needs. When he passes from description to analysis, from the main incidents of the story to its motivation, and from the detail of the picture as it stands at each point of time to its movement, he is apt to find himself very much more in the dark. He is in the dark partly, no doubt, because the questions that he needs to ask have too seldom been formulated sufficiently fully or correctly for the economic historian to have sorted the material that is relevant to their answer. But in certain directions it is apparently because the data required to find answers to those particular questions are not yet to hand. At first one is tempted to think that it is simply because the events of this century are so close to our eyes, and hence its wealth of recorded detail enables us to adopt a quite different level of vision, that our search for the causal story of this period is particularly exacting in the questions it asks. But fuller reflection suggests that the explanation more probably lies in the objective situation confronting us in this period : in the fact that the economic system which emerged from the industrial revolution had so grown in complexity, and was moreover so different in its essence from its appearance, as to render the task of interpretation itself more formidable.

If we stand back from our canvas and let the scene as a whole shape itself to our eyes in a distinctive pattern, we must immediately be impressed by two outstanding features. First, and most familiar, is the fact that in the nineteenth century the *tempo* of economic change, as regards the structure of industry and of social relationships, the volume of output and the extent and variety of trade, was entirely abnormal, judged by the standards of previous centuries : so abnormal as radically to transform men's ideas about society from a more or less static conception of a world where from generation to generation men were destined to remain in the station in life to which they had been appointed at birth, and where departure from tradition was contrary to nature, into a conception of progress as a law of life and of continual improvement as the normal state of any healthy society. In Macaulay's phrase, economic progress from 1760 onward became " portentously rapid ". It is evident—more evident than in any other historical period—that interpretation of the nineteenth-century economic world must essentially be an interpretation of its change and movement.

Second is the fact that the economic scene in the nineteenth century (or at least in the first three-quarters of it in England) affords a combination of circumstances quite exceptionally favourable to the flourishing of a capitalist society. An age of technical change which rapidly augmented the productivity of labour also witnessed an abnormally rapid natural increase in the ranks of the proletariat,[1] together with a series of events which simultaneously widened the field of investment and the market for consumption goods to an unprecedented degree. We have seen how straitly in previous centuries the growth of capitalist industry was cramped by the narrowness of the market, and its expansion thwarted by the low productivity which the methods of production of the period imposed ; these obstacles being reinforced from time to time by scarcity of labour. At the industrial revolution these barriers were simultaneously swept away ; and, instead, capital accumulation and investment were faced, from each point of the economic compass, with ever-widening horizons to lure them on.

It is hardly likely that in their simultaneous appearance on the scene these novel and propitious circumstances affecting supply of labour, productivity and markets were unconnected. As to the precise nature of the connection between them few would probably deem the available evidence sufficient to warrant a complete answer. But they were clearly the product in large measure of the stage of development which Capitalism in Britain had already reached, and not the fortuitous result of circumstances external to this process of development. The increase in population is now known to have been due to a fall in the death-rate rather than to a rise in the birth-rate. The improvements in medical attention and public health which occasioned this smaller mortality may have been in part a reaction to the labour scarcity of the earlier eighteenth century ; as the labour-saving inventions of the eighteenth century also probably were. Expansion of the market was itself a joint product of invention, of extended division of labour, of heightened productivity and of population-increase (as the now discredited Say's Law had at least the virtue of emphasizing). But whatever the degree to which and whatever the form in which these factors were connected in their singular arrival, there was no valid reason (except perhaps according to the more extreme versions of Say's Law) to

---

[1] Arnold Toynbee spoke of the " far greater rapidity which marks the growth of population " as " the first thing that strikes us about the Industrial Revolution—a decennial increase of round 10 per cent. at the close of the eighteenth century and of 14 per cent. in the first decade of the nineteenth century, as against 3 per cent. as the largest decennial increase before 1751 " (*Lectures on the Industrial Revolution of the Eighteenth Century*, 87).

regard their continued association as part of the natural order of things or as destined indefinitely to survive. Yet this was what many, if not most, nineteenth-century writers seem implicitly to have assumed. The last quarter of the nineteenth century was already casting doubts on such an assumption : shadows of doubt which the twentieth century was to deepen ; until in the period between wars an exactly opposite opinion was to crystallize. This opinion, startling when first uttered, would probably to-day command a wide measure of assent. It is that the economic situation of the hundred years between 1775 and 1875 was no more than a passing phase in the history of Capitalism, product of a set of circumstances which were destined, not only to pass, but in due course to generate their opposite—that, in the words of one recent writer, it " has been nothing else but a vast secular boom ".[1]

It is now a commonplace that the transformation in the structure of industry to which the title of the industrial revolution has been given [2] was not a single event that can be located within the boundaries of two or three decades. The unevenness of development as between different industries was one of the leading features of the period ; and not only do the histories of different industries, and even of sections of an industry (let alone of industry in different countries), fail to coincide in point of time in their main stages, but occasionally the structural trans-formation of a particular industry was a process drawn out over half a century. The essence of the transformation was that change in the character of production which is usually associated with the harnessing of machines to non-human and non-animal power. Marx asserted that the crucial change was in fact the fitting of a tool, formerly wielded by a human hand, into a mechanism ; from that moment " a machine takes the place of a mere implement ", irrespective of " whether the motive power is derived from man or from some other machine ". The important thing is that " a mechanism, after being set in motion,

[1] J. R. Hicks, *Value and Capital*, 302 f.
[2] The first use of this description has often been ascribed to Arnold Toynbee in his *Lectures*, published in 1887 ; and it has been said that " the general currency of the term " dates from their publication (Beales in *History*, vol. XIV, 125). Actually Engels used the term in 1845 in his *Condition of the Working Class in England in 1844* (1892 Ed., pp. 3 and 15), where he speaks of it as having " the same importance for England as the political revolution for France and the philosophical revolution for Germany " ; and the origin of the term has been credited to him (cf. Mantoux, *The Industrial Revolution in the Eighteenth Century*, p. 25). The phrase seems, however, to have been current among French writers as early as the 1820's. (Cf. A. Bezanson, *Quarterly Journal of Economics*, vol. XXXVI, p. 343.)

THE INDUSTRIAL REVOLUTION

performs with its tools the same operations that were formerly done
by the workman with similar tools ". At the same time he
points out that "the individual machine retains a dwarfish
character so long as it is worked by the power of man alone ",
and that "no system of machinery could be properly developed
before the steam-engine took the place of the earlier motive-
power ".[1] At any rate, this crucial change, whether we locate
it in the shifting of a tool from the hand to a mechanism or in
the harnessing of the implement to a new source of power,
radically transformed the production-process. It not only
required that workers should be concentrated in a single place
of work, the factory (this had sometimes occurred in the previous
period of what Marx had called "manufacture "), but imposed
on the production-process a collective character, as the activity
of a half-mechanical, half-human team. One characteristic of
this team-process was the extension of the division of labour to
a degree of intricacy never previously witnessed, and its extension,
moreover, to an unimagined degree within what constituted,
both functionally and geographically, a single production unit
or team. A further characteristic was the increasing need for
the activities of the human producer to conform to the rhythm
and the movements of the machine-process : a technical shift
of balance which had its socio-economic reflection in the growing
dependence of labour on capital and in the growing rôle played
by the capitalist as a coercive and disciplinary force over the
human producer in his detailed operations. Andrew Ure in his
Philosophy of Manufactures triumphantly announced as the "grand
object " of the new machinery that it led to "the equalization
of labour ", dispensing with the special aptitudes of the "self-
willed and intractable " skilled workman, and reducing the task
of work-people "to the exercise of vigilance and dexterity—
faculties, when concentrated on one process, speedily brought to
perfection in the young ".[2] In the old days production had
been essentially a human activity, generally individual in
character, in the sense that the producer worked in his own time
and in his own fashion, independently of others, while the tools

---

[1] *Capital*, vol. I, pp. 308, 378. "The machine which is the starting point of the
industrial revolution supersedes the workman who handles a single tool by a
mechanism operating with a number of similar tools, and set in motion by a single
motive-power, whatever the form of that power may be " (*ibid.*, 370-1).
[2] *The Philosophy of Manufactures*, Ed. 1835, 20-1. Ure defined a factory as "a
vast automaton, composed of various mechanical and intellectual organs, acting
in uninterrupted concert . . . subordinated to a self-regulated moving force "
(*ibid.*, 13).

or simple implements he used were little more than an extension of his own fingers. The tool characteristic of this period, says Mantoux, was " passive in the worker's hand ; his muscular strength, his natural or acquired skill or his intelligence determine production down to the smallest detail ".[1]   Relations of economic dependence between individual producers or between producer and merchant were not directly imposed by the necessities of the act of production itself, but by circumstances external to it : they were relations of purchase and sale of the finished or half-finished product, or else relations of debt incidental to the supply of the raw materials or tools of the craft.   This remained true even of the " manufactory ", where work was congregated in a single place, but generally as parallel, atomistic processes of individual units, not as interdependent activities requiring to be integrated as an organism if they were to function at all.   Whereas in the old situation the independent small master, embodying the unity of human and non-human instruments of production, had been able to survive only because the latter remained meagre and no more than an appendage of the human hand, in the new situation he could no longer retain a foothold, both because the minimum size of a unit production-process had grown too large for him to control and because the relationship between the human and mechanical instruments of production had been transformed.   Capital was now needed to finance the complex equipment required by the new type of production-unit ; and a rôle was created for a new type of capitalist, no longer simply as usurer or trader in his counting-house or warehouse, but as captain of industry, organizer and planner of the operations of the production-unit, embodiment of an authoritarian discipline over a labour army, which, robbed of economic citizenship, had to be coerced to the fulfilment of its onerous duties in another's service by the whip alternately of hunger and of the master's overseer.

So crucial was this transformation in its several aspects as fully to deserve the name of an economic revolution ; and nothing that has subsequently been written in qualification of Toynbee's classic description of the change is sufficient to justify that abandonment of the term which some worshippers of continuity seem to desire.   Its justification lies less in the speed of the technical change itself than in the close connection between technical change and the structure of industry and of economic

[1] *Op. cit.*, 193.

and social relations, and in the extent and significance of the effects of the new inventions upon the latter. It is true that the transformation came very much earlier in some industries than in others ; and while those events which we describe as a revolution are properly to be treated as a closely inter-connected set, the timing of this set of events in different lines of production did not show any close relationship. Nor could it reasonably have been expected to be so in view of the very different character of different branches of industry and the quite different technical problems that each had to solve before power-machinery could take the field. What is perhaps more remarkable is the stubbornness with which the old mode of production continued to survive and to hold a not-inconspicuous place for decades, even in industries where the new factory industry had already conquered part of the field.

In Arnold Toynbee's view, it was " four great inventions " that were responsible for revolutionizing the cotton industry : " the spinning-jenny patented by Hargreaves in 1770 ; the water-frame invented by Arkwright the year before ; Crompton's mule introduced in 1779, and the self-acting mule, first invented by Kelly in 1792 " ; although " none of these by themselves would have revolutionized the industry ", had it not been for James Watt's patenting of the steam-engine in 1769 and the application of this engine to cotton-manufacture fifteen years later. To these he adds as crucial links in the process Cartwright's power-loom of 1785 (which did not come at all widely into use until the 1820's and 1830's), and as affecting the iron industry the invention of coal smelting in the early eighteenth century and " the application in 1788 of the steam-engine to blast-furnaces ".[1] Engels had also instanced Hargreaves' jenny as " the first invention which gave rise to a radical change in the state of the English workers " ; coupling this with Arkwright's introduction of " wholly new principles " in " the combination of the peculiarities of the jenny and throstle ", with Cartwright's power-loom and Watt's steam-engine.[2] To this chain of crucial innovations it is now customary to add as earlier links : on the one hand, Kay's flying shuttle of 1733, described by Usher as " a strategically important invention " solving a difficulty that the great Leonardo had seen as crucial,[3] and having what Mantoux describes as " incalculable consequences ", and Paul

[1] *Op. cit.*, 90–1. [2] *Op. cit.*, 4–6.
[3] A. P. Usher, *History of Mechanical Inventions*, 251.

and Wyatt's spinning machine of the same year (which was not dissimilar from Arkwright's but was not a practical success and remained very little known) ; on the other hand, Dud Dudley's patent for making iron with pit coal as early as 1621, the work of the Darbys at Coalbrookdale in smelting with coal in the early decades of the eighteenth century, and Cort's puddling process (patented in 1784) and rolling mill. Similarly Watt's steam-engine had as its forebears Newcomen's atmospheric engine of 1712, in which " the active source of pressure was the atmosphere, but the actual operation turned upon the production of steam ", and Savery's engine of 1698, which was based on the principle of a vacuum created by condensing steam. But both of these earlier inventions in their practical use were confined to pumping in mines and waterworks.[1]

We have previously mentioned that in certain spheres the changes which we associate with the industrial revolution had already appeared as early as the end of the Tudor period.[2] While still exceptional, these cases were by no means unimportant, as the writings of Professor Nef have recently demonstrated. But the newer technical methods of this period had as yet no application to what were still (so far as their influence on employ-ment and social structure was concerned) the major industries of the country. These early enterprises of a factory type constituted little more than rather isolated outposts of industrial Capitalism, even if as outposts their weight was more considerable than used to be supposed. A number of them relied on State protection and political privilege rather than on their own economic vigour for survival. The workshops of a Jack of Newbury or a Stumpe in the textile trades were scarcely " factories " in the nineteenth-century " machinofactory " sense, even if they have been so called : rather were they of the type of Marx's " manufactories ". They were, moreover, rather rare examples in an industry which remained individual, small scale and scattered so far as its production-process was concerned, even if its economic relationships were becoming capitalist in character under the merchant manufacturer and the putting-out system.[3] Even William Lee's remarkable invention of the stocking-frame in 1598 did not lead to factory production, but only to capitalist relations (in the sense of the economic dependence of the producer on the capitalist) on the basis of

[1] A. P. Usher, *History of Mechanical Inventions*, 307–9.   [2] See above, pp. 139–42.
[3] See above, pp. 145–50.

individual production in the home, under the frame-rent system that has earlier been described. Rather more than a century later Lombe's silk-throwing machine of 1717, by contrast, precipitated a transfer to factory production, " with its automatic tools, its continuous and unlimited production and the narrowly specialized functions of its operatives ".[1] But even so, the extent of its influence was limited. As Mantoux emphasizes, Lombe's machine " was the point of departure of no new invention " ; John and Thomas Lombe remained " precursors rather than initiators ", and " the industrial revolution had been heralded, but not yet begun ".[2] In the iron industry again, it is true, Tudor and Stuart times saw some large furnaces, involving the investment of sums of capital which ran into four figures : they saw forge hammers and furnace-blowing engines worked by water-mills and automatic rolling and slitting mills. But so long as charcoal smelting prevailed, the economic sovereignty of the small furnace, scattered among the woods and forests, was not seriously undermined. Availability of fuel was a limit on size as well as on location ; and until the technical problem of smelting with coal had been solved, a larger and more modern type of ironworks could not become an economic proposition, and in turn the expansion of metal production in its various branches was hampered by the scarcity of pig-iron.[3]

It is now recognized that the speed with which the revolution conquered the main field of industry, once the crucial set of inventions had provided the means of conquest, was less rapid than used to be supposed. In primary iron production the passing of the old small-scale charcoal furnaces was almost complete by the end of the eighteenth century (although in 1788 they were still yielding about a fifth of British pig-iron) ; and by the 1820's Cort's new methods of puddling and rolling were well established in the English iron districts, and the Nasmyth steam-hammer was arriving to complete the process. Whereas in 1715 the Coalbrookdale works had been valued at £5,000, by 1812, " according to the estimates of Thomas Attwood, a complete set of iron works could not be constructed for less than £50,000 ; and in 1833 one with a productive capacity of 300 tons of bar

[1] Mantoux, op. cit., 199.   [2] Ibid., 201.
[3] Ibid., 195. Prof. Usher has emphasized that " for many sixteenth-century and seventeenth-century industries the obstacle to the use of more power was cost and physical availability quite as much as the mechanical difficulty of applying power " ; with the result that inventions at this time tended merely to supplement the work of men and animals and " had little influence upon the general structure of industry " (op. cit., 298).

iron a week would cost anything from £50,000 to £150,000 ".[1]
But the finishing metal trades were much more backward.   The
Black Country nailmaking industry in the '30's was still in the
hands of small masters in small workshops and continued largely
to be so even in the '70's, with a nailmaster owning warehouses
from which he distributed rods and orders to domestic nailers,
or renting space in shops adjoining his warehouse to nailers who
had no forges of their own.   Of the Birmingham metal trade
generally, in 1845 a contemporary writer remarked that " like
French agriculture " it has " got into a state of parcellation ".
Here in 1856 " most master manufacturers employed only five
or six workers ", and " during the first sixty years of the nineteenth
century " in the whole of this district " expansion of industry
had meant . . . an increase in the number of small manufacturers rather than the concentration of its activities within
great factories ".[2]   In gun-making, jewellery, the brass foundry,
saddlery and harness trades the '60's still witnessed a remarkable
coexistence of highly subdivided processes of production with the
small production unit of the shop-owner, putting out work to
domestic craftsmen.   Even the coming of steam power failed in
many cases to transfer these small industries on to a proper
factory basis ; " factories " being divided into a number of
separate workshops, through each of which shafting driven by
a steam-engine was projected, and the workshops being rented
out to small masters who needed power for certain of their
operations.[3]   While the first cutlery factory in Sheffield was
started in the 1820's, as late as the '60's most even of the " large
cutlery men " had part of their work done by outworkers ; and
many of those who worked in the so-called factories were in fact
working on their own account, hiring the power which the factory
provided and in some cases working for other masters.[4]   In
view of facts like these, Professor Clapham has even declared
that in the England of George IV outwork was " still the predominant form " of capitalist industry ; since although it was
" losing ground on the one side to great works and factories, it
was also gaining on the other at the expense of household production and handicraft ".[5]   In cotton it was not until the 1830's,

[1] T. S. Ashton, *Iron and Steel in the Industrial Revolution*, 163.
[2] G. C. Allen, *Industrial Development of Birmingham and the Black Country, 1860–1927*, 113–14.
[3] *Ibid.*, 151.
[4] J. H. Clapham, *An Economic History of Modern Britain : the Railway Age*, 33, 99, 175.
[5] *Ibid.*, 178.

more than half a century after the inventions of Arkwright and Crompton and almost a half-century after Cartwright's power-loom, that the power-loom was in widespread use and the older spinning-jenny was definitely in decline.   In the woollen industry power-machinery only won its victory in the course of the 1850's ; and even in 1858 only about half the workers in the Yorkshire woollen industry worked in factories.   Hosiery in 1851 was still predominantly based on the system of small master-craftsmen (some 15,000 of them, with 33,000 journeymen), employed by capitalist hosiers on a putting-out system.   The power-driven rotary knitting-frame and Brunel's circular knitter were then only just beginning to make serious inroads upon the industry.   In cotton at the same date a quarter of the firms, but in woollen and worsted no more than a tenth of the firms, employed over 100 workers ; while in trades like tailoring and shoemaking production was overwhelmingly in the hands of small firms employing less than ten workers apiece.   It was not until the last quarter of the century that boot and shoe production, with the introduction from America of the Blake sewer and other automatic machinery such as the closing-machine, shifted from the putting-out or manufactory system to a factory basis.[1]

The survival into the second half of the nineteenth century of the conditions of domestic industry and of the manufactory had an important consequence for industrial life and the industrial population which is too seldom appreciated.   It meant that not until the last quarter of the century did the working class begin to assume the homogeneous character of a factory proletariat.   Prior to this, the majority of the workers retained the marks of the earlier period of capitalism, alike in their habits and interests, the nature of the employment relation and the circumstances of their exploitation.   Capacity for enduring organization or long-sighted policies remained undeveloped ; the horizon of interest was apt to be the trade and even the locality, rather than the class ; and the survival of the individualist traditions of the artisan and the craftsman, with the ambition

[1] *Ibid.*, 33–5, 94–5, 143, 193.   In 1871 there were 145 recorded boot and shoe " factories " but with no more than 400 h.p. of steam in all.   Power was only used for heavy work such as cutting butts or stiff sewing, and several of the processes in boot-making were still done by outworkers.   Lasters and makers often worked in the factory, side by side on benches ; but nearly all the finishing was done at home. In 1887 there were in the town of Northampton some 130 shoe manufacturers employing some 17,000 to 18,000 workers (cf. A. Adcock, *The Northampton Shoe*, 41–5). In the early '90's we find the trade union claiming that its two largest branches had finally removed sweating by securing the abolition of outworking.   (Monthly Reports of the National Union of Boot and Shoe Operatives, March 1891.)

to become himself a small employer, was for long an obstacle to any firm and widespread growth of trade unionism, let alone of class consciousness. The differences within the Chartist movement had reflected very clearly the contrast between the factory workers of the northern towns, with their clogs and " unshorn chins and fustian jackets " to whom Feargus O'Connor directed his appeals, and the artisans of London skilled trades who followed Lovett and the small master craftsmen of the Black Country. By this heterogeneity of a still primitive labour force the dominion of Capital over Labour was augmented. By the primitive character of the employment relation, which remained so common, and the survival of traditions of work from an earlier epoch, both the growth of productivity was hindered and a premium was placed on the grosser forms of petty exploitation associated with long hours and sweated labour, children's employment, deductions and truck and the disregard of health and safety. As late as 1870 the immediate employer of many workers was not the large capitalist but the intermediate sub-contractor who was both an employee and in turn a small employer of labour. In fact the skilled worker of the middle nineteenth century tended to be in some measure a sub-contractor, and in psychology and outlook bore the marks of this status.

It was not only in trades still at the stage of outwork and domestic production that this type of relationship prevailed, with their master gunmakers or nailmasters or saddlers' and coach-builders' ironmongers, or factors and " foggers " with domestic workers under them. Even in factory trades the system of sub-contracting was common : a system, with its opportunities for sordid tyranny and cheating through truck and debt and the payment of wages in public houses,[1] against which early trade

---

[1] As in the Birmingham domestic industries factors were sometimes called " slaughtermen " because of their habit of beating down workers' wages, and in nailmaking " the trucking fogger, often a publican, paid in bad dear goods and undersold the honest master ", so also " truck of a corrupt sort was still practised (in the early '70's) by some of the mining butties and doggies of the Midlands and the South-West " (Clapham, *Econ. Hist.* (Free Trade and Steel), 456). Paying wages at long intervals was another evil, leading to the indebtedness of workers to sub-contractors or innkeepers or to company shops which gave credit but charged high prices in return. At Ebbw Vale about this time cash wages were only paid monthly and sometimes at Rhymney only every three months (*ibid.*, 457). Marx remarked that " the exploitation of cheap and immature labour-power is carried out in a more shameless manner in modern manufacture than in the factory proper. . . . This exploitation is more shameless in the so-called domestic industry than in manufactures, and that because the power of resistance in the labourers decreases with their dissemination ; because a whole series of plundering parasites insinuate themselves between the employer and the workman ; because poverty robs the workman of the conditions most essential to his labour of space, light and ventilation " (*Capital*, vol. I, 465).

unionism fought a hard and prolonged battle. In blast-furnaces there were the bridge-stockers and the stock-takers, paid by the capitalist according to the tonnage output of the furnace and employing gangs of men, women, boys and horses to charge the furnace or control the casting. In coal-mines there were the butties who contracted with the management for the working of a stall, and employed their own assistants ; some butties having as many as 150 men under them and requiring a special overseer called a " doggie " to superintend the work. In rolling mills there was the master-roller, in brass-foundries and chain-factories the overhand, who at times employed as many as twenty or thirty ; even women workers in button factories employed girl assistants.[1] When factories first came to the Birmingham small metal trades, " the idea that the employer should find, as a matter of course, the work places, plant and materials, and should exercise super- vision over the details of the manufacturing processes, did not spring into existence " ; [2] and even in quite large establishments survivals of older situations persisted for some time, such as the deduction from wages of sums representing the rent of shop-room and payment for power and light. The workers on their side often continued the habits customary in the old domestic work- shops, " played away " Monday and Tuesday and concentrated the whole week's work into three days of the week.[3] Here it needed the arrival of the gas-engine (rendering obsolete the old system of hiring steam-power to sub-contractors), the growth of standardization, and the supersession of wrought iron by basic steel (lending itself to manipulation by presses and machine- tools) as the staple material of the metal-working trades to complete the transition to factory industry proper, and to effect " an approximation of the type of labour employed in a variety of metal manufactures owing to the similarity of the mechanical methods in use ".[4]

Many of those who have sought to depict the industrial revolution as a continuing series of changes which even out- lasted the nineteenth century, rather than as a once-for-all change, seem to have employed the term as synonymous with a purely technical revolution. In so doing they have lost sight of the special significance of that transformation in the structure of industry and in the social relations of production which was the consequence of technical change at a certain crucial level.

[1] Allen, *op. cit.*, 146, 160–5.   [2] *Ibid.*, 159.
[3] *Ibid.*, 166.   [4] *Ibid.*, 448.

If we focus our attention on technical change *per se*, it is both true and important that, once launched on its new career, this change was a *continuing* process. Indeed, one has to regard this fact that, once the crucial transformation had come, the industrial system embarked on a whole series of revolutions in the technique of production, as an outstanding feature of the epoch of mature Capitalism. Technical progress had come to be an element in the economic cosmos that was accepted as normal, and not as something exceptional and intermittent. With the arrival of steam-power, previous boundaries to the complexity and the mass of machinery and to the magnitude of the operations which machinery could perform were swept away. To a certain extent, even, revolution in technique acquired a cumulative impetus of its own, since each advance of the machine tended to have as its consequence a greater specialization of the units of its attendant human team ; and division of labour, by simplifying individual work-movements, facilitated yet further inventions whereby these simplified movements were imitated by a machine. With this cumulative tendency were joined two further ones : towards a growing productivity of labour, and hence (given stability, or at least no comparable rise, of real wages) a growing fund of surplus-value from which fresh capital accumulation could be derived, and towards a growing concentration of production and of capital ownership. As is nowadays accepted as a commonplace, it was this latter tendency, child of the growing complexity of technical equipment, which was to prepare the ground for a further crucial change in the structure of capitalist industry, and to beget the large-scale, monopolistic (or semi- or quasi-monopolistic) " corporation capitalism " of the present age.

The genetic history of that crucial series of inventions between the seventeenth century and the nineteenth century still contains many dark places. Yet, while we do not know enough about the origins of these inventions to be dogmatic about their causation, we have no right to regard them as fortuitous events, unrelated to the economic situation in which they were planted— as some *deus ex machina* which need have no logical connection with the preceding section of the plot. Indeed, it is now widely recognized that industrial inventions are social products in the sense that, while they have an independent lineage of their own, each inventor inheriting both his problem and some of the aids to its solution from his predecessors, the questions that are posed to the inventor's mind as well as the materials for his projects are shaped by the social and economic circumstances and needs of the time. As Mr. Beales has aptly said, nowadays " the inventor is seen as a mouthpiece of the aspirations of the day rather than as the initiator of them ".[1] While the inventions of the eighteenth century doubtless owed part-parentage to the scientific ferment of the seventeenth century, a remarkable feature of them was the extent to which they were the products of practical men, groping empirically and keenly aware of the industrial needs of the time. For example, while it is true that the researches of Boyle and others into the primary laws of pressure in gases provided one of the essential conditions for the invention of the atmospheric and steam-engines, the practical problem of smelting with coal, on the other hand, was solved before the chemistry of metallic compounds was properly understood. The problems these men of industry and invention put to themselves were formulated, not *a priori*, but out of the fullness of their own experience. Moreover, for a successful invention—an invention that will have significance for economic development—the mere solution of a problem in principle is not enough. Examples are plentiful of the gap which is frequently to be observed between discovery of the principle and its translation into actual achievement, as are also examples of the gap that is apt to exist between the completion of a project and the adoption and launching of it as a commercial proposition. We have not only to remember what Usher has called " the complexity of the process of achievement ", due to the fact that successful invention generally comes only as the climax of a whole series of related discoveries, sometimes independent of one another at first and depending for their solution on different hands ;[2] we have also to remember that the qualities and experience needed for successful synthesis and application are often those of an industrial organizer rather than of a laboratory worker. Unless the economic *milieu* is favourable—until economic development has reached a certain stage—neither the type of experience and quality of mind nor the means, material or financial, to make the project an economic possibility are likely to be present, while the problem will probably never be formulated in the concrete form which evokes a particular industrial solution. Although Wyatt and Paul both planned and built a

---

[1] *History*, vol. XIV, 128.

[2] On the inventions of steam, of the gas-engine and petrol-engine and on inventions in textiles as a *successive* development cf. R. C. Epstein on " Industrial Invention " in *Quarterly Journal of Economics*, vol. XI, 242-6.

spinning machine, it was not until thirty-five years later that there appeared a similar machine on the same lines which was destined to have an economic future ; and this was probably due to the fact that Arkwright possessed the practical business sense which the earlier men had lacked. Even so, Arkwright was seriously handicapped for lack of funds in the early stages, although he was less unfortunate in this respect than Wyatt and Paul had been. Dud Dudley by 1620 seems to have dis-covered how to smelt iron with coal (if his own account can be relied upon) ; but it was not until a century later that the Darbys put it to successful use. Brunel's invention in the hosiery trade was made in 1816, but was not introduced effectively until 1847. Moreover, the development of the steam-engine waited upon a sufficient qualitative improvement in the technique of iron-production to enable boilers and cylinders to be made that were able to withstand high pressures ; and the making of machines of sufficient simplicity and accuracy to serve their purpose was limited by the existence of machine-tools capable of fashioning metal parts with sufficient precision.[1] At the same time, while the prevailing state of industry restricted the type of discovery that could be made, conditions of industry also prompted and guided the thought and the hands of inventors. The discovery of coal-smelting was a direct answer to a problem that had been posed for some time by the growing scarcity of wood-fuel. Kay's invention of the flying shuttle came as a solution of the difficulty that previously the width of the material which could be manu-factured was limited by the length of a weaver's arms (throwing the shuttle from one hand to the other). In the 1760's inventors received the explicit encouragement of the offer of two prizes by the Society for the Encouragement of Arts and Manufactures, " for the best invention of a machine that will spin six threads of wool, flax, cotton or silk at one time and that will require but one person to work it and to attend it ", in order to overcome the lag of spinning capacity behind the needs of weavers and of merchants' orders, especially at the season " when the spinners are at harvest work " and " it is exceedingly difficult (for the

---

[1] We learn that Smeaton had to tolerate errors in his cylinders amounting to the thickness of a little finger in a cylinder 28 inches in diameter, and that Watt was handicapped by having to work with an early cylinder which had an error of three-quarters of an inch. It was only with improvements in boring-machinery by Wilkinson round 1776 that Boulton and Watt were able to secure delivery of adequate cylinders. Similarly the balance-beam in steam-engines persisted because it was not possible to make surfaces accurate enough to attach cross-head to crank (Usher, *op. cit.*, 320).

manufacturers) to procure a sufficient number of hands to keep their weavers employed ".[1] The inventions which ushered in the modern world were not only closely interlocked with one another in their progress : they were also interlocked with the state of industry and of economic resources, with the nature of its problems and the character of its personnel in the earlier period of Capitalism from the soil of which they grew.

It is sufficiently obvious that, until these inventions had arrived, the state of industry was not such as to provide an attractive field for capital investment on any very extensive scale. Usury and trade, especially if it was privileged trade, as was generally the case in those days, held the attraction of higher profits even when account was taken of the possibly greater hazards involved. It would, of course, be quite wrong to regard this period of technical innovation as standing entirely alone and as succeeding centuries of completely stationary technique.[2] The later Middle Ages witnessed the fulling-mill and the water-wheel. The sixteenth and seventeenth centuries saw a crop of discoveries which laid a technical foundation for the earliest examples of factory industry : improvements in the vacuum pump, which facilitated deep mining ; scientific studies of the flight of projectiles and of the pendulum and Huygen's study of circular motion, which had its practical application in clock-making and similar mechanisms. Nevertheless, even within the lineage of inventions themselves, the epoch of the steam-engine surpassed all these, because the marriage of the steam-engine to the new automatic mechanisms opened up a field of investment in the " abridgement of human labour " which in its extent and richness had seen no parallel ; while at the same time the newly-won knowledge of the practice and theory of mineral compounds laid a material basis such as had not previously existed for the

[1] Cit. Mantoux, op. cit., 220.

[2] The Executive Secretary of the official United States Temporary National Economic Committee in his Final Report had occasion to enumerate the " major industrial inventions " of the various centuries, with the following result :

10th century	.	.	.	6	" major industrial inventions "
11th "	.	.	.	4	" " "
12th "	.	.	.	10	" " "
13th "	.	.	.	12	" " "
14th "	.	.	.	17	" " "
15th "	.	.	.	50	" " "
16th "	.	.	.	15	" " "
17th "	.	.	.	17	" " "
18th "	.	.	.	43	" " "
19th "	.	.	.	108	" " "
20th century (up to 1927)			27	" " "

(*Final Report*, p. 105.)

equipment of industry with a stock of mechanical instruments of growing number, magnitude and intricacy.

As a result of the change, the old mode of production, based on the petty production of the individual craftsman, even if it was often stubborn in survival, was destined to be uprooted ; the factory proletariat was swollen from the ranks of that class of small producers who had had this petty production as their livelihood ; and the economic gulf between the master class and the employed, between owners and ownerless, was significantly widened by the new economic barrier which the initial outlay now involved in starting a production unit imposed against passage from the latter class into the former.   It is small wonder that the economists of the time should have regarded the slowness of capital accumulation, not any boundaries to its field of investment, as the essential limit on economic progress, and should have postulated that, given an adequate supply of capital and a sufficiently all-round development of the various branches of industry, only the interference of governments with trade or inadequacy in the supply of labour could suffice to freeze progress into economic stagnation.   Characteristic of the optimism of the time was the retort which Ricardo made when Malthus emphasized the dangers of over-production and gluts due to " deficiency of effective demand ".   Ricardo's answer was that the situation which Malthus envisaged (where a rapid capital accumulation occasioned a fall in the value of commodities relatively to the value of labour power and a consequent fall of profits) was essentially one in which " the specific want would be for population " : [1] a want which, as Malthus himself had preached, could never fail to be satisfied if only food supplies were adequate to keep down the death-rate.

This " want for population ", by which, of course, Ricardo meant a proletarianized population willing to hire itself to the new factory-kings, was a vital want for the new expanding Capitalism ; and without both the developments that have been sketched in the previous chapter and the greatly quickened rate of natural increase of the proletariat, this want could not have been met.   Although the effect of the inventions of the time was towards an " abridgement of human labour ", the

---

[1] Ricardo, *Notes on Malthus*, p. 169.   In his *Principles* Ricardo wrote that " the general progress of population is affected by the increase of capital, the consequent demand for labour and the rise of wages " (p. 561).   In other words, an increased demand for labour had no difficulty in evoking its own supply, provided that trade (including import of food) was free.

immense impetus that they gave to the expansion of investment promoted a considerable net increase in the demand for labour. We have noticed that the death-rate fell in the later decades of the eighteenth century, and the birth-rate remained at a high level during the crucial years of the industrial revolution. Moreover, the industry of the north-west factory towns was able at this time to draw on a plentiful supply of starving immigrants from Ireland : an important labour reserve which fed alike the need for unskilled building labour in London in the middle eighteenth century, the expanding factory towns of the industrial revolution and navvy-labour for railway construction in the 1840's and 1850's.[1]   After reaching its lowest point round 1811, the death-rate, however, proceeded to rise from about the end of the Napoleonic Wars and continued to do so until the late 30's ; and this despite a shift in the age-composition of the population that was favourable to a low death-rate.   This rise, most marked as it was among infants in the large towns, was clearly product of economic distress and of the conditions in the new factory towns of this period, with their insanitary hovels and fetid cellar-dwellings, breeding-grounds of " low and nervous fevers " and " putrid and gaol distempers " and of cholera, about which Mrs. Gaskell and others later wrote.   Towards the end of the '30's the birth-rate began to fall, and despite a recovery between 1850 and 1876 never regained (as an average over a decade) the levels at which it had stood in the last decades of the eighteenth century.[2]   By the close of the century, with the prospect of a slackened rate of natural increase, and with the epoch of " primitive accumulation " long since passed, the optimism of classical political economy that the ranks of the proletarian army would always expand in the degree that capital accumulation required was to find itself built on shifting sand.

While in the heyday of the industrial revolution natural increase of population so powerfully reinforced the proletarian-

[1] In the middle of the nineteenth century nearly 10 per cent. of the population of Lancashire was Irish-born.   (Cf. J. H. Clapham in *Bulletin of the International Committee of Historical Sciences*, 1933, 602.)

[2] Cf. Clapham, *op, cit.*, 53–5 ; T. H. Marshall in Econ. Hist. Supplement No. 4 to *Econ. Journal*, Jan. 1929 ; G. T. Griffith, *Population Problem in Age of Malthus*, 28,36. In 1751 the population of the United Kingdom had been approximately 7 million ; seventy years later, in 1821, it was double that figure ; and by the 1830's it was more than 16 million.   Clapham gives as reasons for the fall in the death-rate at the end of the eighteenth century such things as the mastery of the ravages of smallpox and the disappearance of scurvy, the conquest of aqueish disorders by better drainage, and a reduction of infant and maternal disorders and the beginnings of trained midwifery. Cf. also Dorothy George, *London Life in the Eighteenth Century*, 1–61.

izing of those who had previously enjoyed a meagre livelihood on the land or in domestic handicrafts, a mere increase of numbers of itself was not sufficient to the needs of industry. The commodity labour-power had not merely to exist : it had to be available in adequate quantities in the places where it was most needed ; and here mobility of the labouring population was an essential condition. With starvation as a relentless goad to employment, and with labour unorganized, many of the factors to which comment is so often directed to-day as retarding mobility had no place ; and economists were able to maintain that if only the labour market were unfettered and free from the unwarranted interference of legislators or charity-mongers, a rising demand for labour, wheresoever it arose, would generally evoke the supply to satisfy it within a reasonably short interval of time. It has always, of course, to be borne in mind that, when they spoke of plenty in connection with supply, both economists and factory-kings had in mind not only quantity but also price ; and that they required the supply to be, not merely sufficient to fill a given number of available jobs, but in sufficient superabundance to cause labourers to compete pitilessly against one another for employment so as to restrain the price of this commodity from rising with its increased demand. Once the Laws of Settlement had been repealed and the older provisions for regulation of wages by the local justices had fallen finally into disuse, such conditions were approximately fulfilled. The very concentration and venom of the attack on the Speenhamland system is witness to the fact that this remained, in the period following the Napoleonic Wars, the only serious obstacle to the attainment of that perfectly elastic supply of labour to industry that was so much desired. Apart from this, with the coincidence of enclosures and the ruin of village handicrafts to cause extensive rural over-population, England was exceptionally well placed in the possession of that favourable condition of the urban labour market which industrial Capitalism required. While the conflict of interest between landed property and industrial capital showed itself in the struggle over the corn laws (" this expiring act of feudal despotism ", as Andrew Ure called them), the Law of Settlement (called by Adam Smith " this ill-contrived law " and " an evident violation of natural liberty and justice ") was early amended to exclude those who were not actually chargeable on the parish, and the Speenhamland system remained as the only instance of any serious attempt to maintain a labour reserve in the countryside and to restrain its movement into the towns. In 1834 this system was itself to give place to " the new Poor Law ", which set the seal on unfettered free trade in the labour market.

In other countries such restraints on the movement of labour sometimes proved a quite serious brake on the growth of factory industry. Of this two foreign examples should suffice to stress the contrast. We have earlier cited the case of the Baltic States, where, following the emancipation of serfs, emancipated peasants were precluded from moving away from the locality, in order that they might remain as cheap labourers for the large estates. In other parts of the Russian Empire after 1861 the institution of the village commune, with its collective obligation for taxes and the obstacles in the way of transfer of the holding of a peasant household—obstacles which remained until the Stolypin legislation after 1905—served to retard the flow of labour from village to town and from regions of surplus labour to regions of growing demand for labour in mill or mine. In Prussia, where the landed estates were farmed on a large scale by their owners, complaint of labour-shortage tended to be chronic throughout the later nineteenth century and the early part of the twentieth, and repeated efforts were made by the political spokesmen of the *Junkers* to impose checks upon this " land-flight of the labourer ".[1] A measure of the obstacles in such countries to the movement of the rural labour reserve into the towns is the discrepancy between the price of labour in the rural districts and in the areas of expanding industry. In Tsarist Russia, for example, it was apparently not uncommon for the difference in wages between the more remote rural districts and the larger industrial centres to approach a ratio of 2 : 1 (the difference proving an important factor in the survival of the rural *kustarny*, or handicraft, trades in competition with factory industry). Similarly, the difference in daily wages in West and East Germany at the turn of the present century approximated to a ratio of 1·9 to 1·15.[2]

---

[1] Cf. W. H. Dawson, *Evolution of Modern Germany*, 266 seq. Among the measures urged by the Conservatives upon the Prussian Diet were severe restrictions on the operations of employment agencies and a prohibition on any offering of work by them to agricultural labourers, a strengthening of the law regarding breach of contract, a restriction of the issue of workmen's tickets on railways, and a prohibition on young people under 18 leaving home for other districts without express permission from parents or guardians.

[2] *Ibid.*, 273. The difference here may exaggerate a little the effectiveness of the restrictions on mobility, since wages in the east were kept down by the influx of Polish labour across the border and by the assignment of soldiers to harvest work to supplement the *Junkers*' labour supply at periods of peak demand.

Compared with such cases, Capitalism in England in the first half of the nineteenth century was favoured by an unrestricted labour market. Seldom can the conditions for a buyers' market have been more fully and so continuously sustained.

But regarding the rôle played by abundance and cheapness of labour-power in the industrial revolution we meet an apparent contradiction. There is a good deal of evidence for the conclusion that the invention and adoption of the new machinery, which offered so great an " abridgement of labour ", was accelerated by the comparative dearness of labour in the eighteenth century ; and that it has often been in places where labour was abnormally cheap that the older methods of handicraft production in small workshops or the out-work system have been able to survive. It is clear that many eighteenth-century inventors were conscious of labour-saving as a primary objective. Wyatt, for example, put in writing as a leading advantage of his spinning machine the fact that it would reduce the labour required in spinning by one-third and thereby enhance the profit of the manufacturer ; [1] and it is well known that it was scarcity of spinners, rendering the supply of yarn insufficient to meet the weavers' demands, which prompted the first introduction of spinning machinery. In the year 1800 a meeting of merchants was held in a Lancashire town with the purpose of devising improvements in the power-loom in view of the shortage of weavers ; and a contemporary pamphleteer (in 1780) gave it as his opinion that " Nottingham, Leicester, Birmingham, Sheffield, etc., must long ago have given up all hopes of foreign commerce if they had not been constantly counteracting the advancing price of manual labour by adopting every ingenious improvement the human mind could invent ".[2] Perhaps this influence does not deserve to have major stress laid upon it amid the other factors which in combination produced the industrial revolution, and is to be regarded rather as affecting the precise timing of technical change and the point of its initial introduction.[3] But whatever the emphasis that we give it, the contradiction is no

---

[1] Mantoux, *op. cit.*, 217.

[2] Cit. Lilian Knowles, *Industrial and Commercial Revolutions in the Nineteenth Century*, 31–2. Dr. Knowles assumed it to be " obvious that this scarcity (of labour), combined with the growing foreign demand for the goods, was one of the great impulses to the adoption of machinery ".

[3] As we have seen, Ure, for instance, seems to have regarded the main advantage of the machine as the supersession of " intractable " by more tractable labour, and the employment of women and children, thereby imposing a new discipline on the productive process.

more than apparent. An economic revolution results from a whole set of historical forces, poised in a certain combination : it is not a simple product of one of them alone. The presence of some mineral element (to use an analogy) in minimum quantities may be necessary to the production of the distinctive qualities of a certain metallic alloy ; yet at the same time the presence of it in excess of some crucial proportion may radically alter the qualities of the compound. It can be simultaneously true that the availability of a proletarian labour-supply at a price below some crucial level is a necessary condition for the growth of capitalist industry and that the presence of this necessary element, cheap labour, in a degree disproportionate to the other essential ingredients of the situation may serve to retard that change in technique which is destined to precipitate the new economic order. It may well have been the case that the lag of labour-supply behind other factors in the process of capitalist development in the first half of the eighteenth century precipitated those changes of technique which were to open up vistas of a new advance. But unless by the dawn of the new century labour had been as plentiful as it was then coming to be, the progress of factory industry once started could not have been so rapid, and might even have been halted. There would seem to be fairly general agreement that, whether influenced by the wage-level or not, the technical change of this period had a predominantly labour-saving bias : a feature of technical change which probably characterized the whole of the nineteenth century. If true, this conclusion is evidently of the greatest importance ; since, in the degree that invention bore this character, Capitalism as it expanded was able to economize on the parallel expansion of its proletarian army : capital accumulation was thereby enabled to proceed at a considerably faster rate than the labour-supply was increasing.

It is a familiar fact that, while the capital to finance the new technique largely came from merchant houses and from mercantile centres like Liverpool, the personnel which captained the new factory industry and took the initiative in its expansion was largely of humble origin, coming from the ranks of former master craftsmen or yeomen farmers with a small capital which they increased by going into partnership with more substantial merchants. They brought with them the rough vigour and the boundless ambition of the small rural bourgeoisie ; and they were more inclined than those who had spent their time in the counting-house or the market to be aware of the detail of the production process, and so to be alive to the possibilities of the new technique and the successful handling of it. Among the new men were master clock-makers, hatters, shoemakers and weavers, as well as farmers and tradesmen.[1] The yeoman farmer who had previously engaged in weaving as a by-employment had the modest good fortune to possess some capital and an acquaintance with industry and also land which he could mortgage or sell to raise additional funds. Many of the new names of the early nineteenth century were of this class : Peel, Fielden, Strutt, Wedgwood, Wilkinson, Darby, David Dale, Isaac Dobson, Crawshay, Radcliffe. While Cartwright was a gentleman's son and a Fellow of Magdalen, among his fellow inventors Hargreaves was a weaver, Crompton came of a family of small landowners and Arkwright started with very modest means, although his second wife brought him a little money. Of this renowned quartet none of the first three, however, founded a big industrial concern. But although it is true that there was a strongly democratic strain in the pioneers of factory industry, which differentiated their interests sharply from the older Whig families and the merchant monopolists, sheltering behind trade regulations and economic privilege, one must avoid falling into that exaggeration of their rise from humble origins by dint of enterprise and industry to which their contemporary admirers like Samuel Smiles were prone. It was rare for a man to rise unless he had some capital at the outset. Radcliffe had organized the putting-out of work to village weavers, at one time giving employment to as many as a thousand hand-looms ; and Dale, father-in-law of Robert Owen, by dint of being clerk to a mercer, had found the means similarly to organize the domestic weaving industry before he became the founder of the New Lanark Mills. Remarkably few came from the ranks of journeymen or wage-earners ; and those who did owed their start to some accident of fortune or to patronage. Even those who started with the advantage of some capital and trade connections were frequently handicapped by the difficulty of acquiring sufficient means to launch out on the scale which the new technique demanded (as

---

[1] Cf. Cunningham, *Growth* (Modern Times, II), 619 ; Gaskell, *Artisans and Machinery*, 32–3, 94–5 ; Radcliffe, *Origin of Manufacturing*, 9–10 ; S. J. Chapman, *Lancs. Cotton Industry*, 24–5 ; Marx, *Capital*, vol. I, 774. To some extent these new men were aided by the rapid growth of the " country banks " ; and it seems probable that the Scottish banking system contributed to the early spread of the new industry in Scotland.

was the astute Arkwright, for example) ; and in sectors where expansion of the market was less rapid and scope for new men less ample the man of small means was much less common. In the West Riding of Yorkshire the new factory owners seem mostly to have been drawn from the class of capitalist merchants ; [1] the small master-weavers having to content themselves with running mills on some sort of co-operative basis. In the iron and machinery industries the man of small means faced formidable obstacles, to judge by the complaints about the difficulty of raising capital by borrowing, which seem in this case to have been unusually loud. Boulton, for example, wrote to a certain Peter Bottom, who had asked that his brother should be taken as an apprentice : " I do not think it an eligible plan for your brother, as it is not a scheme of business that will admit of a mediocrity of fortune to be employed in it. It even requires more than is sufficient for a considerable merchant, so that a person bred in it must either be a working journeyman in it, or he must be possessed of a very large fortune." [2] This Boulton had learned from his own hard experience. Having sold part of the property inherited from his father and raised £3,000 on his wife's estate, he had been under the necessity of borrowing £5,000 from a well-to-do friend in addition to other smaller loans ; and at one time he was in serious difficulties about meeting the interest-charge on funds borrowed in this way.[3]

Of the twenty-eight of whom precise details are given among the successful " men of invention and industry " immortalized by Samuel Smiles, fourteen came from small property-owners or yeomen farmers, master-weavers, shoemakers, schoolmasters and the like, six came from quite prosperous middle-class circumstances, and only eight seem to have had any trace of working-class origin.[4] Of the eight out of the twenty-eight who became capitalists of any importance, only one, Neilson, was of working-class origin, and " he had to part with two-thirds of the profits of his invention (to partners) to secure the capital and influence necessary to bring it into general use ".[5] The other seven were men who belonged to the lower middle or middle class. Of the

[1] Cunningham, op. cit., 618 ; Mantoux, op. cit., 271.
[2] J. Lord, Capital and Steam-Power, 91 ; also 108.
[3] E. Roll, An Early Experiment in Industrial Organization, 10–11.
[4] Men of Invention and Industry and Industrial Biography. Of the engineers cited in Smiles' Lives of the Engineers, Stephenson, Metcalf and Telford came of working-class families ; Edwards, Smeaton, Brindley and Rennie were sons of farmers or squires. The rest, five in number, were from the middle or upper class.
[5] Smiles, Industrial Biography, 159.

workmen of whom Samuel Smiles wrote, very few had any startling achievements, *qua* captains of industry, to their credit.
Henry Cort died in poverty, and his invention was adopted by
Richard Crawshay ; thereby demonstrating, as Smiles ingenu-
ously adds, that " as respecting mere money-making, shrewdness
is more potent than invention, and business faculty than manufacturing skill ".[1]   Joseph Clement by dint of hard work and
saving secured employment in London, received promotion to the
post of superintendent, and died as master of a small workshop
employing thirty men.   Fox was the son of a butler who had
the good fortune to interest his father's employer in his inventions
and so to secure the capital with which to start a small business ;
Murray, a blacksmith's apprentice, was promoted to be senior
mechanic of a Leeds engineering firm as a recompense for
improvements he had made, and later went into partnership in a
small machine factory in the town ;   Richard Robert became the
mechanical partner in a firm of which a certain Mr. Sharp
provided the capital ;   and Koenig, son of a German peasant,
borrowed money to start a printing business in England, but failed
and died poor.   The most colourful story of the series is that of
Bianconi, who well illustrates the mixture of luck and sharp
practice and the astute employment of windfall gains which
contributed to the successful rise of a capitalist of the time from
humble origins.   Apprenticed to an itinerant print-seller bound
for Ireland, and then setting up in business on his own with some
money that his peasant family in Lombardy had left him, Bianconi
astutely used such spare means as he had to buy up guineas
from villagers at a time when gold was at a premium.   Trading
on the ignorance of countryfolk about tendencies in the gold
market proved to be a lucrative pursuit ;   and with the gains
acquired in speculating in guineas he started a two-wheeled car
service in the neighbourhood of Waterford to attract the custom
of villagers who could not afford to travel by coach.   Finally
he made a minor fortune at an election in Waterford by hiring
his cars to one of the parties and then transferring them to the
rival party half-way through the election, thereby contributing
to a sudden turn of fortune for the latter, and winning for himself
a gift of £1,000 from the victorious candidate whom his abrupt
volte-face had aided.   Thenceforth, being no longer short of
capital, he could " command the market both for horses and
fodder ", and he died a prosperous and respected figure.[2]

[1] Smiles, *Industrial Biography*, 114.   [2] Smiles, *Men of Invention and Industry, passim.*

Of the capital for the cotton industry the major part seems to have come from already established merchants. Arkwright raised capital for his invention at first by borrowing from a local Nottingham bank, and later by loans from two rich merchant-manufacturers in the hosiery trade. Radcliffe, one of the most prominent of the new captains of industry, only managed to make a firm start when he had gone into partnership with a Scottish merchant, trading with Frankfurt and Leipzig ; and even he " came to grief in his later years and was dependent on the capital of others ".[1] Quite widely " the merchant who imported cotton enabled the young manufacturer to set up for himself by giving him three months' credit, while the exporting merchant rendered similar assistance by paying for the manufacturer's output week by week. It was in this way, by a flow of capital inward from commerce, that most of the early industrial enterprises of Lancashire got started and the immense expansion of the cotton industry was rendered possible." [2] Sometimes merchant capitalists themselves set up as industrialists in Lancashire as in Yorkshire. Nathan Rothschild, trading between Manchester, Frankfurt and the East, with a capital of £20,000 derived from his father engaged in manufacturing and in dyeing as well as in the supply of raw materials to other manufacturers ; and, having trebled his capital in less than ten years, transferred his attentions to the London money market. With gains such as these before them, it is hardly surprising that neither industrialists nor economists of the time were much troubled by the fear that industrial investment might outrun the expansion of the investment-field.

II

If we revert to the character and consequences of technical change in the nineteenth century, a crucial question presents itself for answer : how, if at all, can technical change *per se* be said to occasion a deepening of the investment-field, in the sense of providing opportunity for investment of capital at an enhanced rate of profit ? The fact that it can properly be said to do so has often been disputed ; and in probing this question we immediately reach the core of the problem of the momentum of capitalist progress, about which the economists of the last century for the most part held such optimistic opinions.

[1] G. Unwin in Introduction to G. W. Daniels, *Early History of the Cotton Industry*
xxx.   [2] *Ibid.*

To some it might seem that there could be no sufficient reason for expecting technical change, however labour-saving its character, to enhance the profitability of investment. While technical change, which increases the productivity of labour, will (in Ricardian language) augment riches (or the total of utilities), it will not necessarily enhance the values created, since the labour required to produce the larger aggregate of commodities will now be no greater than what was previously required to produce a smaller aggregate. In other words, the effect of the improvement will be to lower costs, and hence prices ; and while the quantity of output will be increased, its price per unit, and the profit to be earned per unit of output, will be equivalently smaller. To many this denial that improvements in the productivity of labour will necessarily increase the rate of profit has appeared as one of the most perverse corollaries of Ricardian doctrine. But the argument, so far as it goes, is a valid one ; and it seems to have been the ground for the notion implicit in classical thought that technical change *per se* need be assigned no place among the factors governing profit on capital. According to this view (as we have seen) the field for capital investment was defined essentially by the labour supply, and this in turn by the conditions of food supply to provide subsistence for the army of labourers. Obsessed as were the classical school with the threat of diminishing returns on land (in the absence of free import), they tended to focus attention on the limiting influence of this factor to the exclusion of any other : on the danger of a rising cost of subsistence as the population grew, bringing a rise in the cost of labour-power and a fall in profit as its relentless consequence.[1]

It is in the setting of this discussion that we have to view Marx's famous demonstration that there was a purely technical reason for a fall in the rate of profit, and hence a self-defeating tendency inherent in the process of capital accumulation itself. This was the simple fact, previously noticed by some economists (for example, Senior and Longfield) but assigned by them no

[1] Cf. Ricardo : " No accumulation of capital will permanently lower profits unless there be some permanent cause for the rise of wages. If the funds for the maintenance of labour were doubled, trebled or quadrupled, there would not long be any difficulty in procuring the requisite number of hands to be employed by these ; but owing to the increasing difficulty of making constant additions to the food of the country, funds of the same value would probably not maintain the same quantity of labour. If the necessaries of the workman could be increased with the same facility, there could be no permanent alteration in the rate of profit or wages, to whatever amount capital might be accumulated " (*Principles*, 398-9).

central importance and scarcely woven by them into the general corpus of doctrine, that the tendency of technical change was to raise the ratio of " stored-up to living labour " : of capital equipment (measured in value-terms) to labour of current production. With a given " rate of surplus-value ", or ratio of product-value to the value (expressed in wages) of the labour-power directly engaged in the creation of that product, the tendency would be for the profit rate on the *total* capital (both what was advanced to pay the wages of these direct workers and that embodied in the capital equipment) to fall.

But at the same time as he enunciated this principle, Marx emphasized the possibility of another and quite opposite effect of technical improvement. Technical improvement, if it affected the production of the workers' subsistence as well as other lines of production—if it cheapened wage-goods as well as non-wage-goods—would tend to cheapen, not only the products of industry, but labour-power itself. It was true that, with a given labour-force at his disposal, a capitalist might find himself in possession of a product of the same total value after the improvement as before (since each unit of product had been cheapened by the change). But if money wages had at the same time fallen because the workers' food had been cheapened, labour-power would absorb a smaller proportion of that produced value, and both the proportion and the quantity available to the capitalist would consequently rise. " In order to effect a fall in the value of labour-power," said Marx, " the increase in the productiveness of labour must seize upon those branches of industry whose products determine the value of labour-power, and consequently either belong to the class of customary means of subsistence or are capable of supplying the place of those means. . . . But an increase in the productiveness of labour in those branches of industry which supply neither the necessaries of life, nor the means of production for such necessaries, leaves the value of labour-power undisturbed." Elsewhere he says : " The value of commodities is in inverse ratio to the productiveness of labour. . . . Relative surplus value is, on the contrary, directly proportional to that productiveness. . . . Hence there is immanent in capital an inclination and constant tendency to heighten the productiveness of labour, in order to cheapen commodities, and by such cheapening to cheapen the labourer himself." [1]

[1] *Capital*, vol. I (Unwin ed.), 304–5, 577.

It is, therefore, in *this* case, where technical change effects a universal cheapening of commodities, that one can properly speak of an *intensification* of the investment-field in consequence of mechanical improvement. But unless it has the effect of cheapening labour-power relatively to the total value of its product,[1] there will be no such consequence. Two observations are clearly relevant here. This effect is likely to grow weaker (i.e. so far as the *proportional* effect on profit is concerned) as the productivity of labour rises. When labour-productivity is low, and wages swallow a relatively large share of the net product, an improvement in the arts of industry which cheapens commodities, and with them labour-power, by a given amount will increase the surplus available as profit to the capitalist by a relatively large proportionate amount. But at a higher stage of productivity, where the amount of surplus yielded by each unit of labour is much larger, a given cheapening of commodities, and with them of labour power, will increase that surplus by a much smaller proportionate amount—until in the limit (as Marx observed [2]), where workers need no wages because wage-goods have become free goods, improvements in productivity can exercise no further effect on the size of the surplus. Hence, one would expect this influence to operate less strongly—i.e. the possibility of what we have termed an intensification of the investment-field to be less—at an advanced stage of industrial Capitalism than at an earlier and more primitive stage when the productivity of labour was smaller.

Secondly, there is no Lassallean " iron law " by which a cheapening of the things which enter into the workers' subsistence necessarily and always results in an equivalent fall in the cost of labour-power to an employer. Whether it does so or not will evidently depend on the state of the labour market at any given time and place. The situation most favourable to the operation of such a tendency will naturally be one in which the supply of labour is very elastic—where a large surplus of labour exists or is in process of being created. In the first half of the nineteenth

---

[1] It should be noted that what is stated here is a lowering of wages relatively to the *total value* of what is produced by that labour (thereby increasing the difference between these two quantities). This is *not* the same thing as a cheapening of labour-power in greater proportion than the cheapening of the product (i.e. than the fall in its value *per unit*). If both labour-power and the product fall in price in the *same* proportion, the difference between total wages and total value-produced will nevertheless increase, because the invention has increased output per worker.

[2] *Capital*, vol. III, p. 290.

century, with its unorganized labour market and workers at a continual bargaining disadvantage in face of an employer, it was no doubt a reasonable assumption to make that this would be the case ; at any rate so long as the supply of labour outran the demand (a demand which in a labour-saving age progresses at a slower rate than capital accumulates), and a reserve army of labour continued to be recruited to exert a continuous downward pressure on the price of labour. But in the degree that these conditions change, in particular as labour becomes organized for collective bargaining, the net consequence of technical improvement may be altogether different. A cheapening of wage-goods may result in no equivalent cheapening of labour-power ; and a part or even a large part of the consequence may be, not to increase the profitability of capital, but to cause real wages to rise. In the last half-century or three-quarters of a century in advanced industrial countries like Britain and U.S.A. the process that we have termed an intensification of the invest-ment-field, consequent on technical change which enhances the productivity of labour, may have been of very little account. At least it must have played a very much humbler rôle than it did in the heyday of capitalism during the first half of the nineteenth century.

Although it might seem to be elementary to distinguish investment from the object of investment, discussion of this type of question has often been clouded by a failure to separate the effects of technical improvement as such from the effects of simple capital accumulation : i.e. the effect of a change in technical knowledge, with capital in some sense given as to quantity, and the effect of increased capital accumulation in a given state of technique. True, it may seldom or never be possible in practice to separate the two types of change. Yet a failure to make the distinction for purposes of analysis can evidently result in gross confusion of thought. There is the further difficulty that even the assumption of " a given state of technique " is not free from ambiguity : it may refer either to a constant state of technical *knowledge*, with its application subject to variation, or to a con-stant state of the technical *methods* actually in use. If technique is assumed to be constant in the latter sense, then it follows that increased capital accumulation has no option but to take the form of a simple multiplication of plants and of machines of a given type—a process which is sometimes referred to nowadays as a " widening " of capital, and which Marx called " an increase of capital with a constant technical composition of capital ".[1] As machines are multiplied, so is the need for labour to man them ; and unless the labour supply can expand concurrently with the expansion of capital, this widening process must at some stage be brought to a halt. A point will be reached where new plants have insufficient labour to staff them ; and the effect of further investment will be simply to bid up the price of labour until profit disappears and a crisis intervenes. Here we seem to have something like the classical picture. The progress of industry is essentially limited by the rate of expansion of the proletarian army. Conversely, unemployment (short of market difficulties, such as might be precipitated by a sudden interruption of the investment-process—a matter we shall come to in due course) could be regarded as symptom of an absolute shortage of capital.

But, even if we leave the problem of market demand on one side for the moment, it can reasonably be doubted whether this is a very realistic picture of the situation, at any rate in a mature capitalist country like nineteenth-century England ; and it is questionable whether we can find much in the economic crises of the nineteenth century to correspond to it at all precisely. In the depression of the 1870's, as we shall see, there are signs that something like this may have characterized the investment-situation ; but on other occasions in the nineteenth century and subsequently anything corresponding to it at all closely is harder to discern. Perhaps it more often applies than present-day economists, with their bias towards continuous variation, are apt to imagine. But it has commonly been argued that the entrepreneur is generally faced at any particular time, not with a unique technical form in which it is practicable to invest, but with a choice between several technical forms. In other words, he is confronted with some range of technical alternatives, the actual choice between which will be determined by calculation of the prospective rates of profit to be derived from investing in each of them in the given situation. It may well be that the practicable alternatives that confront him are generally much smaller in number than economists have tended to suppose, and his choice more limited. It may be that at times when technical change is proceeding by what (economically speaking) are considerable " leaps ", and every innovation is a substantial landmark, the difference in physical productivity of different methods is so great as in practice to leave the entrepreneur little

[1] *Capital*, vol. I, 625–35.

or no choice ; in which case the method that industry adopts at any one time will be simply determined by the step that history has reached on the ladder of invention. But in periods when change proceeds more gradually by minor improvements and modifications of a machine-process, the general structure and basic principles of which have been established for some time, the range of practicable choice for the entrepreneur will be widened. Even when the industrial revolution was in full cry at the end of the eighteenth century, the spinner could use either the jenny or the mule, or in the early nineteenth century either the water-loom or the steam-power loom ; and it can be argued that the difference in physical productivity of the alternatives, though considerable, was perhaps not so great that a difference between cheap labour and dear labour could have failed to affect the choice.

If this be the case, it follows that it is less unrealistic to picture capital investment proceeding in face of a constant state of technical *knowledge* (i.e. of a given range of alternative methods) than with a given technical method in use in each industry. In such a situation capital investment would at first move in the direction of *widening*—of multiplying the number of plants of a type which in existing conditions proves to be the most profitable. It will continue to do so, as the line of least resistance, so long as there is a sufficient surplus of labour (or a sufficiently rapid expansion of labour) to permit the building of new plants and the hiring of labour for manning them to proceed *pari passu*. But as soon as labour becomes scarce—as soon as the surplus is exhausted, or its rate of increase falls behind the increase of capital—and there are signs of this scarcity exerting an upward pressure on its price, there will be a tendency (it has been argued) for the entrepreneur to take an alternative road : to choose another among the range of technical alternatives in front of him. It will follow that this shift in the direction of his choice is likely to be towards a technical method that is more labour-saving than the one in use before : a method which was in the old situation less profitable, but which now, when labour to operate it is dearer, has become the preferable alternative. This shift of direction has been called, by contrast with " widening " of capital, a shift towards " deepening " capital ; and the change of technical method involved has been described as being " induced " by the growth of capital seeking investment and by a change in the cost of labour, rather than " autonomous " in the sense of being the result of an addition to our existing fund of knowledge.[1] It can be shown that in this new position the rate of profit will probably be smaller than it was originally, before the " widening " had proceeded so far or so fast as to cause wages to rise. But while movement along the line of " deepening " will reach a position that is more profitable than if the " widening " has been proceeded with, and in this sense represents a partial evasion of the " squeeze " exerted by dearer labour, both positions will tend to be positions of lower profitability than the original one (i.e. before the investment-process had gone so far and labour had become scarce). This is, therefore, the situation *par excellence* where Marx's " tendency of the rate of profit to fall " overpowers the " counteracting influence " of a " rise in relative surplus-value " ; and in so far as the actual dynamic of events approximates to this abstract model, the process of capital investment can be expected progressively to exhaust its opportunities, except in so far as possibilities of intensifying the investment-field (in the way that we recently discussed) are provided for the capitalist by the " autonomous " creations of the inventor—creations which must be applicable to the production of things that enter into the workers' budget.

There are, however, two difficulties about this analysis as we have just described it. In the first place, the validity of the argument that a *general* rise in wages will prompt the general adoption of more labour-saving methods rests on a special, and commonly unnoticed, assumption : namely, that not only do wages rise but also the rate of interest chargeable on borrowed capital at the same time falls. If all that occurs is a rise in the cost of labour, then, provided that this rise applies to the making of machines as well as to the operation of them, the initial cost of the more complex labour-saving machine will rise (and hence the capital charges to be debited to it) in the same degree as the costs of operating the less labour-saving machine. If the obstacle to installing the former before consisted essentially in its greater cost of construction, then this obstacle will remain undiminished, since the construction cost will have increased in the same measure as the cost of the labour of operation which its introduction would spare. Only if in the meantime the rate of interest has fallen,

---

[1] Cf. J. R. Hicks, *Theory of Wages*, 125 seq. Prof. Hicks here writes : " A change in the relative prices of the factors of production is itself a spur to invention, and to invention of a particular kind—directed to economizing the use of a factor which has become relatively expensive. The general tendency to a more rapid increase of capital than labour which has marked European history during the last few centuries has naturally provided a stimulus to labour-saving invention " (124–5).

will the more complex machine (involving a greater initial capital outlay against which interest has to be debited) rise in cost in *smaller* proportion than the rival method.

To economists of the classical mould this latter assumption was apparently so congenial as to be tacitly accepted ; the Ricardian dictum that " if wages rise, profits fall " probably leading them to conclude that a fall in profit-expectations must necessarily result fairly soon in a downward adjustment of interest-rates. Modern doctrine, however, has been inclined to challenge this necessity, and to raise the doubt as to whether in such circumstances there is any reason to expect interest rates to fall. If this be the case, then this way of escape from such a situation into more labour-saving methods is barred to Capitalism ; and if the investment-process and its hunger for labour outruns the resources of the industrial reserve army, thereby precipitating a fall of profit, the only result can be an economic crisis and a paralysis of the investment-process, until some quite new invention appears to augment the productivity of labour, and to create new openings for the profitable investment of capital. The chance that periods of more or less chronic stagnation may set in is accordingly strengthened.

The second difficulty concerns the line drawn between technical change, " induced " by an increase in invested capital, and an " autonomous " change in technical knowledge, which alters the whole range of technical choices available. Is it really possible, even for purposes of analysis, to draw a line between the two ? When conditions change, the entrepreneur will not simply take a blue-print of a new machine from his drawer, where it had previously rested awaiting a situation favourable to its economical use : he will more probably set his mechanics to work, or nowadays his research and designs department, to explore the possibility of some new model, or some appropriate modification of existing models, which would permit the requisite economizing of labour at the smallest additional cost.[1] Indeed, it is probable, as we have seen, that a number of the early epoch-making inventions were made under some such impetus as this. In the actual process of historical change with which we are confronted, neither is invention an autonomous process, unyoked to the progress of capital invest-

---

[1] Professor Hicks, indeed, appears to have this in mind when he suggests a distinction within the category of " induced " inventions between those newly discovered methods which, if they had been known before, " would have paid even before prices changed ", and those which would not (*ibid.*, 126).

ment, nor is the process of capital investment separable from its effects on the growth of invention, which in turn reacts on the investment-process through its influence on profitability. The distinction we have cited is useful in unravelling the parts played by two elements in a conjoint process so far as they can be separated without too serious a distortion of reality. But it must not lead us into thinking that in actuality the two are anything but interdependent and that their consequences can generally be treated as anything but a joint product.

This means that it is less easy than has sometimes been supposed to postulate *a priori* what will be the long-term effect either of technical change or of capital accumulation. So much will depend on the precise composition of the elements of the conjoint process ; and only the empirical study of actual situations can throw light on what this is. As an initial simplification, enabling us to hold certain essentials of the actual process in thought, the kind of distinction of which we have been speaking no doubt has importance. But all that seems possible to say, at this level of analysis, is that the expansion of Capitalism will be constantly conditioned by a conflict and interaction between expansion of capital seeking investment, on the one hand, and the conditions of its profitable employment on the other ; that the latter will turn upon the character of technical change, the rate of increase of the proletarian army and upon the supply of natural resources (or on import possibilities) to afford food for workers and raw materials for the industrial process, each of which will to some extent react upon the others in the manner we have described ; and that there are reasons, which we have mentioned, to expect the possibilities of expanding the opportunities for profitable investment to get narrower as capital accumulation proceeds.

In this initial simplification of the factors on which change depends no mention has been made of markets. Yet to plain common sense it would appear that the expansion of markets must be, in several senses, a crucial limit upon the rate at which Capitalism can expand. Even Adam Smith, father of the classical school, gave central importance to the size of the market as the factor controlling the extent of the division of labour (and hence, by implication, the development of machinery). But is there not a different and more direct sense in which the field of investment for capital is limited by the extent of the market : namely that the profit to be earned on a given quantity of invested capital depends on whether the demand for the products of industry is great or small?[1] As soon as we admit this consideration, it becomes evident that there is a further sense in which technical change may widen the field of investment for capital : a sense quite distinct from, if apt to be confused with, what we have talked of above. This is the sense in which the invention of power-looms created a new field for investment of capital in expanding the manufacture of steam-engines, or in more modern times the invention of the aeroplane created a new field for investment in aeroplane factories.

It is self-evident that, if markets were to expand *pari passu* with the growth in the stock of invested capital, they could exert no limiting influence on the development of Capitalism (although, of course, the configuration of demand would influence the way in which a given total of capital was distributed, and hence the relative growth of different industries). Again, the economists of the Ricardian school were able to eliminate this factor from their reckoning by virtue of a particular assumption. Thereby, indeed, they were enabled to regard consumption as itself always dependent on production, instead of the other way round. This was the implicit assumption (or something equivalent thereto) that all income received, whether by labourer, capitalist or landlord, was spent in some form within each unit-period of time ; so that, even with a growing income-stream, income and expenditure, receipt of money and its outflow, kept more or less in step, with only a negligible time-lag. Spending in this context referred to direct expenditure on consumption goods (sometimes called " unproductive consumption ") and also to what was customarily called " productive consumption "[2]—

---

[1] This effect on profits will be expressed through changes in the quantity of labour employed per plant : i.e. through changes in the *number* of workers who can be employed in the existing state of demand, and not through changes in the rate of surplus-value per worker.

[2] The use of these terms was apt to vary, chiefly according as the consumption of food by labourers was included in " productive consumption " or excluded. Mountifort Longfield defined " unproductive consumption " as " where the value of the commodity consumed is destroyed, and is not transferred to some other commodity. In such consumption consists all the enjoyment that man derives from wealth " (*Lectures on Pol. Economy*, L.S.E. Reprints No. 8, p. 164). Senior defined " productive consumption " as " that use of a commodity which occasions an ulterior product ", and included the necessities of a worker and his family (*Outline of the Science of Pol. Economy*, 1938 Ed., 54). J. S. Mill declared that " the only productive consumers are productive labourers " ; but added that " that alone is productive consumption which goes to maintain and increase the productive powers of the community ; either those residing in its soil, in its materials, in the number and efficiency of its instruments of production or in its people " (*Principles*, Bk. I, Chap. III, § 5).

expenditure by capitalist entrepreneurs in the hire of additional labour and in the purchase of new capital goods. In such circumstances the demand alike for consumption goods and for capital goods would advance in step with any increase in industrial equipment ; and any problem of demand that could exist must be, not one of any absolute deficiency of demand, but only of the proper balance or proportion in which the new industrial equipment was distributed between these two main categories of industry, or between their various constituent branches.

The introduction of this assumption into the structure of Ricardian doctrine was one of those ingenious simplifying devices which often fetter subsequent thought as much as they serve as crutches to the first limping stages of analysis. But it was not quite the trickster's sleight-of-hand that to unsophisticated common sense it often appears to have been. It had at least a certain amount of justification in the circumstances of its time. True, when we look at the real world, either then or now, we can find abundant reasons why this crucial condition may not hold. The capitalist system includes no mechanism by which people's decisions to save a part of their income (in the sense of refraining in a unit-period of time from spending all their income on consumption, and hence increasing, or rather trying to increase, their holding of money) is co-ordinated with the decisions that entrepreneurs are simultaneously making to enlarge their plants and build up their stocks of raw materials or goods-in-process with the object of expansion. Although it used to be thought that the rate of interest provided the required mediating instrument between the two sets of decisions, economists nowadays fairly widely recognize that this is at best a very imperfect instrument for the purpose, even if it can be regarded as such an instrument at all. Another way of stating the problem, which is fashionable to-day, is that there is no mechanism whereby investment (and thereby the income and consumption of those given employment by this investment) is maintained at a level sufficient to create a demand that will maintain the working of existing industrial equipment at full capacity. Hence, from time to time and possibly most of the time, there may well be— in fact, *probably* will be—a lag of demand behind the growth of productive equipment. Thereby this equipment is precluded from being fully utilized, and from realizing the profit that the situation could otherwise have yielded. As we shall see, there are reasons for thinking that in the modern age such a condition of excess productive capacity has become more or less chronic. Yet in the first half of the nineteenth century the situation was very different ; and there were a number of circumstances which explain, once again, the bias of the classical mind towards an optimistic view. This period happened to be one that was exceptionally rich in influences which were buoyant towards the demand both for consumption and for capital goods. The situation at the time was such that the intervention of factors continually tending to expand the market came to be regarded as normal, and as permanent features of the new age which had dawned with the coming of *laissez-faire*. Chief of these buoyancy-factors was the rapidity of technical innovation itself, which was creating, not only a whole new race of mechanisms of which the like had not been seen before, but a whole new industry, or set of industries, of machine-making to beget and to service these new mechanical creatures. Reinforcing this was the exceptional situation of the export trade of Britain at the time and also the effects on demand of a population, moreover an increasingly urbanized population, that was multiplying at an unexampled speed.

In the century or two prior to the industrial revolution the demand for capital goods was small, both relatively and absolutely, and the dimensions of anything that could be called a capital goods industry were correspondingly slender. Investment activity, as we have seen, was largely confined to ordinary building, which only assumed any considerable volume at special periods such as the rebuilding of London after the Fire, and shipbuilding. Normal building activities consisted of current repairs—thatching, for example, must have constituted a significant, though small, local industry of the countryside—and the building of cottages to house the increase of the population. To this was added those bursts of country-house building, and earlier church building, and the construction of yeoman farmsteads and their spacious barns, which characterized the more prosperous years of Tudor and Stuart England. In the eighteenth century growing urbanization, and particularly the growth of London, initiated something of a secular building boom. There was a certain amount of tool-making and of trades like the nailmaking industry of the West Country, most of this the work of domestic craftsmen or artisan mechanics. But few, if any, of these things provided scope for the investment of capital. The early machines were mostly made of wood and were constructed as far as possible in the immediate locality by the men who used them and by craftsmen working directly to their order ; only the more essential metal parts being ordered from a distance. Artisans such as carpenters, locksmiths or clockmakers turned their hand when required to wheelwork or the setting up of a jenny or a loom. As machinery grew more complicated and the early factories arrived, that versatile artisan, the millwright, acquired a position of key importance : a trade which (according to a contemporary account) " was a branch of carpentry (with some assistance from the smith) but rather heavier work, yet very ingenious ".[1] Iron-making itself was very limited in scale— in 1737 there were some fifty-nine iron furnaces scattered over eighteen counties producing some 17,000 tons annually [2]— and a large part of its market consisted of demand for ordnance. Indeed " wood was the raw material of all industry to an extent which it is difficult for us now to conceive ".[3] Conveyances and containers were made of wood, and also ships and bridges, and the carriages of cannons and a large part of every house ; and wood-working was in major part the preserve of the old type of artisan working with the simplest of traditional tools. The home market for manufactured articles of general consumption, as again we have earlier remarked, was a narrow one ; and the export market, so important for the woollen industry, remained cramped and restricted under the conditions of the Mercantile System. In 1700 the tonnage of outgoing vessels at English ports amounted to no more than 317,000 registered tons, or between 1 and 2 per cent. of the present-day traffic in the port of Liverpool alone.[4]

With the approach of the Industrial Revolution, this situation became radically transformed. By the middle of the eighteenth century the recorded tonnage of outgoing vessels was about double what it had been at the beginning of the century. There- after, the export trade showed a quite remarkable increase ; and so far as the textile trades were concerned, there is every sign that the rise of export-demand went ahead of productive capacity and was a principal spur to technical change in the latter half of the century. By 1785 recorded export tonnage had passed the million mark ; and in the two decades at the end of the century the figure was nearly trebled. Valued in pounds

[1] Cit. Mantoux, *op. cit.*, 221.
[2] L. W. Moffit, *England on the Eve of the Industrial Revolution*, 147.
[3] J. U. Nef, *Rise of the British Coal Industry*, vol. I, 191.
[4] Mantoux, *op. cit.*, 102.

sterling, exports at the end of the century were three times what they had been in the middle and five times what they had been at the beginning.[1] Of the total export values in 1800 the combined exports of wool and cotton constituted nearly 30 per cent. By 1850 all textile yarns and fabrics combined constituted 60 per cent. of a total of export values which had doubled over the half-century. As the early machinery became harnessed to steam-power, and productive equipment grew in mass and in the amount and complexity of its metal parts, not only was there a need for the erection of special buildings to house them, and sometimes of dwellings for workers in the neighbourhood of the new plants, but the demand arose for specialized machine-making firms. Prior to 1800 the only firm of this kind was the Soho enterprise of Boulton and Watt, which by that date had made nearly 300 engines in all ; more than a third of these being for textile factories and between a fifth and a sixth of them for mining. But it was not until the 1820's that professional machine-making firms began to appear in any number either in London or in Lancashire.[2] The key inventions of new machine-tools by Bramah and Maudslay just before the turn of the century, in particular the screw-cutting lathe and the slide-rest, laid the basis for further specialized branches of industry to make machines for making machines ; and the chief " external economy " of each particular industry at this period, on which the development of these several industries so largely depended, consisted in this novel growth of specialized mechanical engineering. In turn, the mounting output of machinery and its upkeep laid new claims on the iron industry and on the mining of coal and of ore. Iron production touched a million tons by 1835, and trebled within the next twenty years. Coal production, which stood at about 6 million tons at the end of the eighteenth century, reached 20 million by 1825 and some 65 million by the middle 1850's.[3] As regards the home demand for consumption goods, this also was inevitably enlarged by the growth of population and its increasing urbanization, even if this growth was precluded from being as spectacular as one might have expected by reason of the wretched conditions and the meagre earnings of the mass of the population. But if the factory proletariat had few pence to spare beyond the barest needs of subsistence, there was an inevitable modicum of things which they now had to buy in the market, whereas previously such things could to a large extent

---

[1] *Ibid.*, 103-4.   [2] Clapham, *op. cit.*, vol. I, 152-3.   [3] *Ibid.*, 425, 431.

be made at home. Not only did homespun decline in favour of the factory product, but the mere increase in numbers brought an increase in the shawls and clogs which each family needed to have.

There can be little doubt that in the period following the Napoleonic Wars the combined influence of these factors was expansionist in a quite unparalleled degree. But in the '40's and '50's of the century there arrived on the scene a novel activity which, in its absorption of capital and of capital goods, surpassed in importance any previous type of investment-expenditure. Even when we label these decades of the mid-nineteenth century " the railway age ", we often fail to appreciate to the full the unique strategic importance which railway-building occupied in the economic development of this period. Railways have the inestimable advantage for Capitalism of being enormously capital-absorbing ; in which respect they are only surpassed by the armaments of modern warfare and scarcely equalled by modern urban building. This is not to say that they were the only source of demand for iron at this period. Other grandiose projects of the time were children of the iron age, such as pier-building on cast-iron piles ; an example of which in the early '40's was Southend pier which we find described in a contemporary account as " of extraordinary length, stretching out as it does over the shallow bay a distance of a mile and a half ".[1] But the 2,000 miles of railway line opened in the United Kingdom in 1847-8 must have absorbed nearly half a million tons of iron for rails and chairs alone, or one quarter of the iron output of that date; and, according to Tooke, railway expenditure gave employment to 300,000 "on and off the lines" in the peak year.[2] By 1860 some 10,000 miles of railway had been laid in Great Britain and Northern Ireland : a figure which was to increase by half again between 1860 and 1870.

Railway building at home was by no means the whole of the story of the importance of railways for investment and for heavy industry in Britain. Although we generally have in mind the '80's and the decade prior to 1914 when we speak of capital export, it must not be forgotten that foreign investment played a far from negligible rôle in the middle of the nineteenth century. Foreign investment at this time chiefly took the form of lending to governments, and not of direct investment as was later to be the case. But this foreign investment was ultimately directed to

[1] *The Times*, Oct. 3, 1844.   [2] Tooke and Newmarch, *History of Prices*, Vol. V, 357.

railway construction in a very large measure, and served the double function of providing a profitable outlet for capital and also stimulating the export of British capital goods. Close on the heels of the British railway boom of the '40's came continental railway building ; and following this there yawned the even larger maw of American railroad construction. Between 1850 and 1875 there was an average annual export of capital from this country of £15 million, in addition to the reinvestment of the net earnings on past investments, which by the 1870's had attained a level of £50 million.[1] The '50's witnessed a considerable rise in the export of capital goods ; iron and steel exports doubling in value in the first three years of this decade and in the early '70's reaching a level five times that of 1850. Between 1856 and 1865 £35 million of railway iron was shipped abroad, and between 1865 and 1875 £83 million ; [2] and already by 1857 products of iron, copper and tin amounted to one-fifth of British exports. Between 1857 and 1865 there was some shift of British capital towards Indian railways and public works, and the iron for Indian railways was almost exclusively supplied from British orders.[3] Railway building in Russia and in America continued, however, to create a strong demand for British railway iron in the '60's ; and although German railway building was more or less at an end by 1875, Russian railway building only reached its peak in the '90's, when some 16,000 miles of road were constructed, while American building proceeded spasmodically into the last quarter of the century, and in 1887, in a revived burst of activity, 13,000 miles of track were built in the United States.[4] Indeed, over the whole period of 1865 to 1895 American railway mileage multiplied four or five times ; although as the century drew to a close an increasing proportion of American railway equipment was supplied from American and not from British sources. Taking U.S.A., Argentine, India, Canada and Australasia together, the length of railway track in these countries rose from about 62,000 miles in 1870 to 262,000 miles in 1900 ; and even in the seven years prior to 1914 British capitalists provided £600 million for railway construction in overseas countries—countries, incidentally, which

[1] L. H. Jenks, *Migration of Capital*, 332 and 413.   [2] *Ibid.*, 174.
[3] *Ibid.*, 207 seq.   This author states that in 1869 there were about 50,000 English share and debenture holders, holding an average of about £1,500 of Indian Guaranteed railway securities.   " The India Office was the real fiscal agent for the railway companies, and actually advanced sums to cover their capital needs when the market was temporarily tight " (220).
[4] D. L. Burn, *Economic History of Steelmaking*, 78.

were mainly concerned in the production of raw materials and foodstuffs.[1]

But such factors of market-buoyancy as we have outlined are by nature transitory. Their effect will be a once-for-all and not a continuing effect, in the sense that there is a limit to the amount of railways that are likely to be wanted over any given area of the world's land surface, and that a particular set of inventions which creates the need for an industry to make a new type of machine can bring about the foundation of that new industry once, but does not go on continually calling new industries into existence. It has sometimes been argued that such factors only appear to be transitory if we focus attention on each separate example of them ; and that there is no obvious reason why they should not have a permanent line of successors and hence exercise a continuing expansionist influence on conditions of demand. Why should not one set of inventions breed children and in turn grand-children, each generation requiring a larger and more complex machine-making industry than the one before, or at least by their new technical creations maintaining the demand for the machine-making industry that already exists ? Even if railway building progressively approaches saturation-point, does not economic progress make it likely that railway building will be succeeded by newer objects to stimulate investment and heavy industry, such as the electrical industry, the ringing of continents with oil pipe-lines or the building of *autobahnen* ? [2] To this riddle about probabilities it is hard to see that there is an answer apart from our observation of what has actually occurred over a series of decades : a matter to which we shall later return. Whether such events are likely to reproduce their kind obviously depends on the whole changing complex of interdependent historical processes—depends on the changing total situation of which they are part, and is not to be deduced from their own characteristics as a genus.

But there is a special reason for thinking that the sort of golden age for Capitalism that we have been describing is bound to be transitory. This reason is connected with the essential nature of what we mean by investment in productive equipment : the simple fact that each act of investment leaves the stock of productive equipment larger than it was before. As Dr. Kalečki has

---

[1] A. K. Cairncross, *Home and Foreign Investment in Great Britain, 1870–1930* (an unpublished Ph.D. dissertation, in the University Library, Cambridge), p. 333.
[2] Cf. the argument of Schumpeter in *Capitalism, Socialism and Democracy*.

aptly put it : crises under Capitalism occur because " investment
is not only produced but also producing. . . . The tragedy of
investment is that it causes crises because it is useful." [1] If we
suppose investment to proceed at a steady annual rate, under the
continuing inspirations of such factors as we have been discussing, the result must be a comparable increase in the productive equipment of industry, including presumably the industries
which produce articles of final consumption.[2] To enable this
growing capital equipment to be fully occupied, and to prevent
the profits earned by its owners from falling because it cannot be
fully utilized, consumption must not merely be maintained but
must continually expand in like degree. If this does not happen,
the influence of sagging markets is bound sooner or later to put
a brake upon the investment process. In a class society where
the consumption of the mass of the population is restricted by
their poverty, while increases of surplus income above wages go
predominantly into the hands of the rich whose consumption
already approaches the saturation point or who have a thirst
for accumulation, it is obvious that such a lag of consumption
behind the growth of capital equipment will operate as a
powerful tendency. Accordingly, for this tendency to be
counteracted, those counter-stimuli that we have termed
buoyancy-factors in the market (whether new export-demand or
the excitation of the consumption of the rich by new wants) [3]
must not merely persist, but must continually grow in potency
—they must not merely reproduce their kind, but each generation
of them must beget a succeeding generation larger than its own.

[1] *Essays in the Theory of Economic Fluctuations*, 148–9.
[2] This is taken here to mean that investment proceeds as a constant absolute
amount per unit of time. In these circumstances the market for capital goods will
only expand to the extent that replacement-demand grows as the stock of capital
equipment grows. With a constant rate of investment, there will be no reason,
ceteris paribus, for total income to grow ; and unless the proportion of total income
spent on consumption *increases*, the profit realizable by capitalists cannot increase,
and the effect of the growing amount of capital equipment must be to reduce the
profit realized by each unit of this equipment (by causing the intensity with which
each unit of equipment is utilized to fall, and the ratio of equipment both to labour
employed and to output to rise). What we have loosely termed " buoyancy-factors "
will, therefore, have to exert, not merely a constant, but an *increasing* influence in
order to counteract the increasing difficulties of raising consumption as a proportion
of income as this proportion rises. Alternatively, in the case where the rate of
investment and total income are both rising, the effect of growing capital equipment
will be progressively to retard investment, unless the factors stimulating the rise of
investment (either directly or *via* a rise in consumption) increase so as to counteract
the retardation.
[3] These stimuli may, of course, operate, not on consumption, but on investment
directly ; stimulating an *increasing* rate of investment (to balance the lag of consumption) by virtue of an ever-accelerating pace of technical innovation, instead of the
constant rate of investment that we have assumed above.

Such a course of events there seems to be no sufficient ground
to expect.

III

What has become known as the Great Depression, which
started in 1873 and, broken by bursts of recovery in 1880 and
1888, continued into the middle '90's, has come to be regarded
as forming a watershed between two stages of Capitalism : the
earlier vigorous, prosperous and flushed with adventurous
optimism ; the later more troubled, more hesitant and, some
would say, already bearing the marks of senility and decay. This
was the period of which Engels spoke his well-known phrase
about " the breakdown of . . . England's industrial monopoly ",
in which the English working class would " lose its privileged
position " and " there (would) be Socialism again in England ".[1]
About its character and significance as well as its causes there
has been a good deal of controversy. That it was far from being
uniformly a period of stagnation has been particularly emphasized by recent commentators : that judged by production indices
and technical advance it was in fact the contrary, and that for
wage-earners who retained their employment it was a period
of economic gain rather than of loss.[2] But the fact that it was
a period of gathering economic crisis, in the sense of a sharpening
conflict between growth of productive power and of business
profitability, has not been seriously denied ; and all the signs
suggest that, in the case of British Capitalism at least, certain
quite fundamental changes in the economic situation were
occurring in this last quarter of the nineteenth century.

In our estimate of its significance much necessarily depends
upon our diagnosis ; and while certain superficial features of
the Great Depression, and of the sequence of events associated
with its onset, are clear enough, there are a number of more
fundamental questions about it to which the answers remain
obscure. A question on which a great deal evidently turns is one
concerning the relative weight in its causation of the various
factors limiting the investment-field which we have been dis-

[1] Preface to 2nd Edition of *The Condition of the Working Class in England.*
[2] A fact which, incidentally, does much to explain the stubborn opposition at
the time of the so-called " Old Unionism " to the militant tendencies of the " New
Unionism ", leading to a rift in the ranks of Labour ; just as a somewhat parallel
phenomenon (as we shall see below) goes to explain the strong survival of an
" aristocracy of labour " tradition in the British Labour movement in the 1920's
and the '30's.

cussing above. What occurred cannot, of course, be attributed exclusively to any one of them alone, and must be regarded as the work of all of them in combination. The investment-field, as we have seen, is a thing of several dimensions ; and if one speaks of it as cramped or inelastic, this inelasticity must refer to all its dimensions and not only to one. Nevertheless, it may be appropriate to speak of some one limit as the crucial one, in the sense that no practicable expansion in other directions could compensate for its narrowness ; and it is of some significance to determine (if this can be done) the relative importance of various factors as immediate causes of the depression. For example, how far, if at all, could the economic *malaise* of the '70's be attributed to a partial saturation of investment opportunities in the first of the senses in which we have discussed it—to a fall in the rate of profit due to the rapidity of capital accumulation as such, which had gone ahead of the possibilities of augmenting the mass of surplus-value capable of being extracted from the process of production, even if the demand for commodities had expanded *pari passu* with production and no serious limitation of markets had emerged ? [1]   Or how far was it due to the failure of effective demand to keep pace with the expansion of production—to a waning influence of those buoyancy-factors of which we have spoken ; and in particular to the failure of consumption to expand *pari passu* with the expansion of productive power directed towards the output of consumption goods ?

There is probably some evidence of the existence of the first type of situation in the fact that the real wages of labour were rising in the middle decades of the century ; since this could be taken as a *prima facie* indication of the fact that demand for labour was beginning to outrun the expansion of the proletarian army, and that the situation which the Ricardians had feared was coming to pass. According to Professor Bowley's estimates, money-wages rose from 58 in 1860 (1914 = 100) to 80 by 1874,

---

[1] The " rapidity of capital accumulation " referred to here applies to the growth over time of the *stock* of capital relatively to the growth of other factors such as the labour supply or appropriate changes in technique ; resulting in what would be called by many writers to-day " a fall in the schedule of the marginal efficiency of capital ".   It is not intended to refer to any possible effect on profit-margins due to the rate of investment *per unit of time* being high or low.   An attempt is being made to distinguish here the operation of factors which would cause a decline in profitability even though the market-situation initially (i.e. before the depression started) placed no hindrance in the way of full-capacity working, and, on the other hand, of factors which affect profitability primarily because they make full-capacity working of existing equipment impossible.

and real wages from 51 to 70.[1] Most significant for investment, building labour costs are estimated to have risen between 1860 and 1875 by nearly 50 per cent., and much faster than the cost of prime materials.[2] To this rise of wages the growing organization of skilled labour as a result of the national amalgamated unions of the '50's and '60's no doubt contributed. The 1860's were a period of abnormally rapid capital investment and of very great expansion of the productive equipment of industry. For example, between 1866 and 1872 the world output of pig-iron had increased from 8·9 million tons to 14·4 million, of which increase Great Britain had been responsible for two-fifths. In the Cleveland district about thirty new blast-furnaces had been built between 1869 and 1874 alone, increasing the productive power of this area by 50 per cent. In the hæmatite area of Cumberland and North Lancashire there was an expansion of about 25 per cent. in the early years of the '70's, and Lincoln-shire in four years increased its furnaces for utilizing phosphoric ores from 7 to 21.[3] Altogether the capital invested in iron works is estimated to have trebled, and in mines to have doubled between 1867 and 1875.[4]

Moreover, in the two years which immediately preceded the crisis there was a particularly sharp rise of wages,[5] and the unemployment figure (according to the incomplete data of the time) in 1873 was down to scarcely more than 1 per cent. Interest rates throughout the '70's were exceptionally low. Discount rates, in particular, in the winter of 1871 were (according to *The Economist*) " far below the level " at which they could

---

[1] *Wages and Income in the United Kingdom since 1860*, 34.
[2] G. T. Jones, *Increasing Returns*, 89.   [3] D. L. Burn, *op. cit.*, 21.
[4] D. H. Robertson, *A Study in Industrial Fluctuations*, 33. Colin Clark estimates that real capital in the United Kingdom grew by 50 per cent. between the decade of the '60's, and the period 1875–85, and doubled over the three decades between the '60's and the '90's (*Conditions of Economic Progress*, 393 and 397). Saving as a percentage of the national income in the '60's he estimates at 16 or 17 per cent.
[5] Between 1871 and 1873, according to available data, money-wages rose by some 15 per cent. The mineral price index rose from 86 to 131, indicating the appearance of bottlenecks at early stages of production ; from which Mr. W. W. Rostow concludes that " rising labour and raw material costs began to eat into the profitability of trade " (*Econ. Hist. Review*, May 1938, p. 154). Sir Lothian Bell in his evidence before the Royal Commission on the Depression of Trade and Industry said : " The price of labour rose with the price of iron to such an extent that I say that the cost of pig, and I may say of all kinds of iron, rose to double what it was in former years " (2nd Report of Ryl. Commission, p. 40, Qu. 1,923). Mr. D. L. Burn, however, takes the view that " the statement of costs gave no support to the view that, in the immediate crisis, wages disproportionately high for prices could be held at fault for the difficulties of the iron trade ", wages having moved in harmony with prices and not ahead of them (*op cit.*, 41).

have been expected to stand in view of the expansion of trade : [1] a phenomenon which Alfred Marshall attributed to the fact that " the amount of capital seeking investment has been increasing so fast that, in spite of a great widening of the field of investment, it has forced down the rate of discount ".[2] Technical change had been rapid, absorbing a larger quantity of capital to set a given amount of labour in motion ; but despite this, the absorption of labour into production (about the size of which no reliable statistics are available) must have proceeded at a very considerable rate.

There is a great deal to be said for the view, expressed by some contemporary writers on the Depression, that the fall of prices in the '70's and '80's, on the contrary to being occasioned by monetary influences connected with the supply of gold, as economists have so widely held,[3] was the natural consequence of the fall in costs which the technical changes of the past few years had brought about. D. A. Wells, writing in the late '80's and speaking both of U.S.A. and of Britain, estimated that the saving in time and effort involved in production in recent years had amounted to as much as 70 or 80 per cent. " in a few " industries, " in not a few " to more than 50 per cent. and between one-third and two-fifths as a minimum average for production as a whole.[4] It is possible that over manufacturing industry in general in this country the real cost in labour of producing commodities fell by 40 per cent. between 1850 and 1880. At any rate, there seems to be sufficient evidence that this fall of prices was not of *itself* a sign of sagging demand. On the other hand, if the fall in price was wholly to be interpreted in terms of technical improvement and fall in costs, the ensuing fall in profit and mood of depression remain unexplained.

In this connection it is important to bear in mind again the distinction between the two directions along which an increase in the stock of invested capital may proceed, and their distinct

---

[1] *Economist*, Jan. 27, 1872.　　　　[2] *Official Papers*, 51.

[3] Of the monetary explanation it has recently been said : " None of the major characteristics of the Great Depression can be traced to a restricted response of the banking system. The prevailing tendencies in the short-term capital market, on the contrary, were towards abundant supply " (W. W. Rostow on " Investment and the Great Depression " in *Econ. Hist. Review*, May 1938). Sir Lothian Bell before the Royal Commission on the Depression of Trade and Industry stated : " Want of purchasing power is not due to the want of money, because bankers and others have large sums lying unemployed " (Qu. 1,998, in answer to Prof. Price). *The Economist* at the time was a strong opponent of the view that the fall of general prices was due to monetary causes (cf. esp. issue of July 31, 1886).

[4] D. A. Wells, *Recent Economic Changes*, 28.

effects. In the first place, the increase may take the form of financing technical innovation which raises the ratio of " stored-up to living labour " and enhances the productivity of labour. Let us assume that in this case selling-prices have fallen in the same degree as the fall in real cost measured in terms of labour. Then the rate of profit would decline as a net result of the change, unless the price of labour-power had also fallen by enough to augment the surplus available as profit in a degree sufficient to offset the rise in what Marx termed the " organic composition of capital " (i.e. the rise in the ratio of machinery, etc., to direct labour occasioned by the progress in technique).[1] In the second place, the increase of capital could take the form simply of a multiplication of plants and equipment of production, expanding the employment of labour and hence output without necessarily lowering costs. In this case a decline of profitability would result if, but only if, the expansion either of the market or of the labour supply failed to keep pace with the expansion of productive capacity ; and a fall in selling-prices would in *this* case be presumptive evidence that productive capacity had in fact outrun the growth of demand. What makes our present task specially difficult is that investment during this period obviously took both these forms, in proportions that can hardly be calculated.

If the productivity of labour had been augmented during this period in such a striking degree, one would expect to find that there had been at least some compensating increase in Marx's " relative surplus value ". We have seen, however, that money-wages, instead of falling, actually rose considerably between 1860 and 1874 ; and even after 1874, when selling-prices were launched on their spectacular descent, the degree to which money-wages fell was comparatively small. There does not therefore seem much evidence that this compensating factor had any considerable importance prior to 1873, or even subsequently. It is true that between the '70's and the '90's there occurred a considerable cheapening of foodstuffs relatively to manufac-

---

[1] If selling-prices had not fallen as a result of increased output, or at least had not fallen in any comparable degree to the fall in real costs in terms of labour, then, of course, there might have been no reason for profitability to decline, even though wages had remained unchanged, or even though wages had risen somewhat. But given the fall in selling-price and the rise in the productivity of labour, the crucial variables on which the result depends will be : the proportionate change in the organic composition of capital, the proportionate change in money-wages and the ratio of total profit to the total wage-bill (per unit period of time) in the initial situation.

tures, as a result of the opening up of the interior of America by railroads and the rapid improvement of ocean transport. But this cheapening of foodstuffs operated in a situation where labour was strong enough to resist the sweeping reductions in money-wages which earlier in the century would probably in like circumstances have occurred ; and the result was chiefly to enhance real wages, while effecting a cheapening of labour-power to employers only in minor degree.

Among the proximate causes of the crisis of 1873 events in the foreign investment-market are usually assigned a leading place ; and it has to be remembered that prior to that date foreign investment provided an important safety-valve against any tendency of the process of accumulation to outdistance the possibilities of profitable employment at home. This foreign investment was modest compared with the dimensions which it later assumed, and was by no means an unfailing device, as events were to show. But it was far from being a negligible factor. The immediate onset of the crisis was associated with an abrupt closing of this safety-valve. Between 1867 and 1873 there had been a series of loans to Egypt, to Russia, to Hungary, to Peru, to Chile, to Brazil, together with a number of special railway loans, in addition to numerous distinctly shady ventures. Of the two milliard dollars of American railway capital floated between 1867 and 1873 British capitalists subscribed a very substantial part. " The favourite business for many years before 1873 ", said Sir Robert Giffen, " had become that of foreign investment ".[1] The bankruptcy of Spain and the non-payment of interest on the Turkish debt were douches of cold water to the prevailing investment mood ; and financial difficulties in countries " more or less farmed by the capital of England and other old countries " (as Giffen put it), such as Austria and later South America (" almost a domain of England ") [2] and Russia, caused an abrupt paralysis of the market for foreign loans.

After an initial check to investment, the result was to encourage increased investment in the home market instead. This fact served to explain one of the most curious features of the depression : the extent to which production and productive capacity continued to increase at a pace only slightly moderated as compared with the decade before 1870. This expansion of

[1] *Economic Enquiries and Studies*, vol. II, 101 : " The conspicuous industry which has failed is that of the ' exploitation ' of new countries with little surplus capital."
[2] *Ibid.*, 102. The depreciation of securities in the case of the loans to Turkey, Egypt and Peru alone amounted to £150 million within a year.

productive capacity was specially marked in the capital goods industries during the middle '70's.   The number of blast-furnaces continued to grow ; and capital goods production as a whole rose from an index figure of 55·3 in 1873 to 61·6 in 1877.[1]   At the end of 1877 home investment also collapsed, as foreign investment had done some years before.   But despite this, the index of capital goods production was only eight points lower in 1879 than it had been in 1877 ; and despite an unemployment figure of over 10 per cent. the production index had only fallen between 1873 and 1879 from 62 to 60.[2]   A revival of home investment contributed to the short-lived recovery of 1880-3. But the continuing increase of productive capacity in this period, piled upon the expansion before 1873, served to exert a further downward pressure on prices and on profit-margins in the middle '80's ; and as Goschen remarked in 1885, " capitalists find it exceedingly difficult to find a good return for their capital ". Over a decade the price of iron fell by 60 per cent. or even more,[3] and the price of coal by over 40 per cent.   Steel which sold for £12 in 1874 was selling for only £4 5s. in 1884.   Much of this fall, as we have seen, was to be explained as a result of economies of cost due to technical improvement.   It has been estimated that the amount of labour in a ton of rails was only a half what it had been in the middle of the century.   The cheapening of steel was partly due to the economies of the new basic process (which British industry, however, had been slow to introduce and was inclined to neglect).   Bessemer steel in England in 1886 could be manufactured and sold at only a quarter of the price per ton that had prevailed in 1873, and only half as much coal was required to make a ton of steel rails as had been needed in 1868.[4] Economies of production in consumers' goods were on the whole much less striking, but were nevertheless appreciable : for example, real costs in the cotton industry in the decade of the '70's probably fell at an average rate of 0·5 per cent. per annum. More remarkable is the fact that nearly 400 new cotton companies were floated between 1873 and 1883.   To a small, but only minor, extent can the price-changes be attributed to a fall in money-wages, which fell by rather less than 10 per cent. between their peak in 1874 and 1880, after which they remained more or less

---

[1] W. W. Rostow, loc. cit., 154.   [2] Ibid.
[3] Scotch pig prices which stood at £5 17s. 3d. in 1873 were £2 2s. 2d. in 1884, and the price of iron rails halved between 1874 and 1880 (Lothian Bell in 2nd Report of Ryl. Comm. on Depression of Trade, p. 43).
[4] D. A. Wells, op. cit., 28.

stationary, or even rose slightly.[1]   But it seems clear that the fall in price, consequent on the increased productive capacity, must in most directions have exceeded what could be explained in terms of cost-reduction alone.   According to Sir Lothian Bell's evidence before the Royal Commission on the Depression of Trade and Industry, the production of pig-iron in the world at large had swollen by the impressive figure of 82 per cent. between 1870 and 1884, and British production alone by 31 per cent. ;   which had contributed to " a very considerable decline in price ", exceeding any compensating decline in costs, with the consequence (the witness added, no doubt with the exaggeration to which industrialists are prone on such occasions) that " workmen were getting all the profit and iron manufacturers none ".[2]   The Commission in their Final Report found that similar conditions prevailed in coal, while in textiles " profits have been much reduced " in face of production which " had been maintained or increased ".   The general conclusion they reached regarding industry and trade as a whole was expressed as follows :   " We think that . . . over-production has been one of the most prominent features of the course of trade during recent years ;   and that the depression under which we are now suffering may be partially explained by this fact. . . .   The remarkable feature of the present situation, and that which in our opinion distinguishes it from all previous periods of depression, is the length of time during which this over-production has continued. . . .   We are satisfied that in recent years, and more particularly in the years during which the depression of trade has prevailed, the production of commodities generally and the accumulation of capital in this country have been proceeding at a rate more rapid than the increase of population." [3]   A recent commentator has given this interpretation to the " over-production " aspect of the Great Depression :   " Output was expanding, the supply of men was limited, capital was not sufficiently a substitute for labour.   Although labour-saving machinery might be introduced, its results for industry as a whole were not on a scale large enough to reduce the demand for labour so sharply as to permit a reduction in money-wages ".[4]

[1] Bowley, *op. cit.*, 8, 10, 30, 34.   [2] Final Report of Ryl. Commission, p. viii.
[3] *Ibid.*, ix and xvii.
[4] Rostow, *loc. cit.*, 150.   Actually reductions of wages occurred immediately following 1873 and again in 1878–9 when unemployment had risen to over 10 per cent.   But over the whole period, these reductions were, as we have seen, relatively small : much smaller than might have been expected in view of the magnitude of the depression.

When we turn to consider the influence of the market-factor, evidence of its contribution is rather clearer, and indications are fairly plentiful that those " buoyancy-factors " which had sustained demand earlier in the century were slackening, or at least were failing to grow in influence as the immense expansion of productive capacity demanded if it was to be fully utilized. True, the stimulus of invention seemed to continue unabated ; and the rate of obsolescence of machinery (involving a greater consequential demand over the period of, say, a decade for equipment in replacement) was probably accelerated (save for a few exceptions) rather than retarded. To this the Bessemer process in steel, the turbine and improved marine engines, hydraulic machinery and machine tools (the latter largely as the result of improved precision-gauges and the spread of the custom of working to gauge), the introduction of steel rollers in flour-making, of the Siemens " tank-furnace " in glass-making, of sewing machines and the rotary press are all witnesses. Even so, there is a good deal of reason for supposing that the *proportional* effect that these innovations exerted on the market for capital goods was considerably less powerful than the influence of the inventions of the first half of the century had been on the much smaller capital goods industry of the time. Railway building, which had constituted such a powerful stimulus in the middle of the century, was tapering off, at least ; even though one cannot say, in face of the revival of railway construction in the later '80's and its spread to Africa and Asia, that it had yet reached saturation. Over the seven years prior to the crisis, the total length of railways in U.S.A. had been doubled, and during the last four years of these seven America had built some 25,000 miles.[1] After 1873 there was an abrupt freezing of construction projects ; and this sudden decline, which accompanied the financial crisis of 1873 and 1874, was a potent immediate cause of the break. Moreover, the substitution of steel rails for iron, with their greater longevity, was at the same time causing an appreciable economy in the replacement-demand for metal which a given length of existing track created.

Of particular importance for British industry was the sharp contraction of the export demand, which was only partly a consequence of the decline of foreign investment and of the cessation of railway-construction orders. In the years immediately preceding 1873 British exports had undergone a very great expansion in

[1] Clapham, *op. cit.*, vol. III, 381.

quantity and even more in value. Between 1867 and 1873 our foreign trade had risen by more than a third, and by 1873 total exports were 80 per cent. larger than they had been in 1860. The increase in export of iron and steel was even more remarkable : a growth of 66 per cent. between 1868 and 1872 alone. Then came the turn of the tide, unexpected and alarming. By 1876 exports of British produce had shrunk (in value) by 25 per cent. compared with the peak of 1872. Exports to U.S.A. alone were halved, and exports of iron and steel receded by one-third in tonnage and by more than 40 per cent. in values.[1] The collapse of the rail-iron market was specially severe. And although American railroad construction showed a cautious recovery in 1878, and there were bursts of activity again in 1882 and 1887, an increasing proportion of American railway-equipment was supplied, after the early '70's, from her own growing iron and steel industry. Never in previous depressions, as Sir Robert Giffen explained, had Britain's export trade shrunk so drastically.[2] Despite recoveries in the export figure in 1880 and again in 1890, it was not until the turn of the century that the peak-figure (in values) of 1872-3 was surpassed. Moreover, the decline of exports was accompanied by a marked increase in the surplus of visible imports over visible exports. Whereas exports in 1883 were only £240 million (in 1879 they had been only £191½ million) compared with £255 million ten years previously, imports in 1883 at declared values stood at £427 million compared with only £371 million ten years before.

If there may be some obscurity about the causation of the Great Depression, there is much less about its effects on British Capitalism. Having witnessed the drastic effect of competition in cutting prices and profit-margins, business-men showed increasing fondness for measures whereby competition could be restricted, such as the protected or privileged market and the price and output agreement. This enhanced concern with the dangers of unrestrained competition came at a time when the growing concentration of production, especially in heavy industry, was laying the foundation for greater centralization of ownership and of control of business policy. In the newer industry of Germany and the United States this centralization was to be earlier on the scene than in Britain, where the structure of business, with its foundations firmly laid in the first part of the century, had developed according to a more individualist pattern, and

[1] Giffen, *Inquiries and Studies*, vol. I, 104-6. [2] *Ibid.*, 105.

the tradition attaching to this structure was more stubborn in survival.   In the structure of economic as of human organisms ageing bones are apt to grow rigid.   In America the '70's saw the rise of the trusts, which had sufficiently grown in extent and structure to provoke the legislation against trust companies in the late '80's and the more sweeping Sherman Act of 1890 directed against " combination in restraint of trade ".   In Germany associations of producers in the iron industry and the coal industry were formed in the '70's, and over the next three decades multiplied in these and other industries, until in 1905 there were stated (by the Kartell-Commission of that year) to be something in the neighbourhood of 400 cartels : a development which, in the words of Liefmann, a well-known apologist for cartels, was " a product . . . of the entire modern development of industry, with its increasing competition, the increasing risks of capital and the falling profit ".[1]   In England stable forms of price-agreement probably did not assume considerable dimensions until the opening of the new century, and even in iron and steel the beginnings of the amalgamation movement (which was on a more modest scale than in America) date from the late '90's.[2]   But it is significant that the International Rail-makers' Agreement (for partitioning the export-market), in which British producers participated, and the start of the " fair trade " agitation, with its plea for restricting the intrusion of " dumped " foreign products into the home market, both date from the '80's. The depression of the last quarter of the century in England was relatively little marked by the extensive excess capacity which was to become so prominent a feature of the second Great Depression of the inter-war period : it was essentially a depression of cut-throat competition and cut-prices of the classic text-book type.   A leading difference between the events of the earlier and the later period, which in so many other respects provoke comparison, is that in the interval the monopolistic policy of meeting a shrinkage of demand by output-restriction and price-maintenance had come to prevail.   We have earlier quoted Professor Heckscher's characterization of the mercantilist epoch of earlier centuries as obsessed by the " fear of goods ".   The new period that was now dawning, and which already in the '80's was being spoken of as one of neo-Mercantilism, was to be

---

[1] Cit. Dawson, *Evolution of Modern Germany*, 174. Cf. also H. Levy, *Industrial Germany*, 2–18. By 1925 the number of German cartels was said to be about 3,000.
[2] Burn, *op. cit.*, 229 ; also Clapham, *op. cit.*, vol. III, 221.

increasingly obsessed with a similar fear : a fear which from one of goods was to become a fear of productive capacity.

The last two decades of the nineteenth century were also marked by another preoccupation which recalled the Mercantilism of earlier centuries : a preoccupation with privileged spheres of foreign trade. Closely joined with this went an interest in privileged spheres of foreign investment. This concern with foreign investment was a distinctive mark of the new period, having no close likeness in its prototype. The difference marked the contrast between an age of undeveloped capital accumulation and the latter days of industrial Capitalism. Of this mature Capitalism, impelled by the need to find new extensions of the investment-field, export of capital and of capital goods constituted a leading feature. In the '80's there awakened a new-found sense of the economic value of colonies : an awakening which occurred with remarkable simultaneity among the three leading industrial Powers of Europe. During that decade, as Mr. Leonard Woolf has pointed out, " five million square miles of African territory, containing a population of over 60 millions, were seized by and subjected to European States. In Asia during the same ten years Britain annexed Burma and subjected to her control the Malay peninsula and Baluchistan ; while France took the first steps towards subjecting or breaking up China by seizing Annam and Tonking. At the same time there took place a scramble for the islands of the Pacific between the three Great Powers." [1] Business interests in centres like Birmingham and Sheffield began to raise the demand that " to make good the loss of the American market we ought to have the colonial market " : and Joseph Chamberlain was to call on the Government to give protection to markets at home while taking steps to " create new markets " abroad, and to raise his glass in simultaneous toast of " Commerce and Empire, because, gentlemen, the Empire, to parody a celebrated expression, is Commerce ".[2] In similar vein, writers in Germany at the turn of the century were talking of the participation of Germany " in the

[1] Leonard Woolf, *Economic Imperialism*, 33–4.
[2] Speech to the Congress of the Chambers of Commerce of the Empire, London, June 10, 1896 ; also speech at Birmingham, June 22, 1894 ; cit. L. Woolf, *Empire and Commerce in Africa*, 18. In the latter speech he declared that he " would never lose the hold we now have over our great Indian dependency—by far the greatest and most valuable of all the customers we have ". " For the same reason [i.e. need for creating markets] I approve of the continued occupation of Egypt ; and for the same reason I have urged upon this Government . . . the necessity for using every legitimate opportunity to extend our influence and control in that great African continent which is now being opened up to civilization and commerce."

policy of expansion out of Europe, at first modestly, of late with growing decision ", as being compelled by " the enormous increase of its industrial production and its trade ", and of German activities in the Near East as " doing what we are doing in other parts of the world—seeking new markets for our exports and new spheres of investment for our capital ".[1] Mr. Rostow has summed up the effect on capitalists of their experience in the Great Depression as follows : they " began to search for an escape [from narrower profit-margins] in the insured foreign markets of positive imperialism, in tariffs, monopolies, employers' associations ".[2] The extension of the investment-field and the search for the stimuli of new markets to keep productive equipment working to capacity, the race to partition the undeveloped parts of the globe into exclusive territories and privileged markets, were quickly to become the orders of the day.   Price agreements, it is true, were no new thing—they had been common among ironmasters quite early in the century—and export of capital was no sudden novelty. But this new preoccupation represented a very different focus of interest and yielded a very different design of economic strategy from that which had held the minds of the industrial pioneers of Ricardo's day.

The Great Depression, whose course we have traced in England, by no means confined its attentions to this country. Its incidence was heavy alike in Germany, in Russia, and in U.S.A. ; although France, less deeply industrialized, felt its effects more lightly and pursued a smoother course.   In fact, in Germany the initial shock was more violent than it was here ; and between 1873 and 1877 German iron consumption fell by as much as 50 per cent.   The outcome of the depression, however, in these other countries followed somewhat different paths. In Russia the nascent factory Capitalism of the late '60's and early '70's received a sharp setback from the crisis of the middle 70's : a depression which was prolonged for ten to fifteen years. But the early 90's witnessed a quick recovery, stimulated by a renewed burst of railway building, and in the investment boom that followed the number of factory workers increased by a half and the production of factory industry doubled.[3]   In Germany there were elements of buoyancy which brought revival sooner than elsewhere and gave it more strength when it came.   For one thing, the industrial revolution had only recently begun,

[1] Cit. Dawson, *op. cit.*, 345, 348.   [2] *Loc. cit.*, 158.
[3] P. Liashchenko, *Istoria Narodnovo Khoziaistva S.S.S.R.*, vol. I, 438.

and until the unification of Germany had been restricted in scope. The events of 1866–1872 proved to be a crucial turning-point in her economic development. The last three decades of the century were to witness a rapid urbanization of Germany; and the population showed a higher annual average increase during the second half than it had in the first half of the century. The growth of the electrical industry and to a less extent of the chemical industry also played an important rôle in stimulating revival, especially in the later '90's. In U.S.A. the " expanding frontier ",[1] with its rich possibilities for both investment and markets, and a labour-reserve swelled by immigration as well as by a large natural increase of population, gave to American Capitalism in the last quarter of the nineteenth century a resilience which the older Capitalism of Great Britain could not have. The spirit of business optimism, confident that no straitness of markets or of labour-supply would rob the pioneer of his gains, continued for some decades to feed on its own achievements in the sphere of technique and industrial organization. Railway building, as we have seen, continued on the American continent to absorb both capital and the products of her growing heavy industry until the final years of the century; and her population, swollen by nearly 20 million immigrants from Europe, was almost trebled between 1860 and 1900. On the North American continent, indeed, until the first decade of the present century there was something that can be called an " internal colonialism ",[2] which goes far to explain the tardiness with which the U.S.A. turned attention to the spoils of the new Imperialism.

In England, there can be small doubt that it was the revival of capital export and the opportunities which the new Imperialism afforded which was the essential factor in that new phase of prosperity between 1896 and 1914.[3] This Indian summer caused memories of the Great Depression to fade out of mind. It rehabilitated the reputation of Free Trade, grown tarnished during the depression years. It brought renewed faith in the

[1] In a geographical sense expansion of the frontier had come to an end by the middle '70's. But in an economic sense it may be said to have continued to be a force until the end of the century.

[2] See above, p. 194.

[3] This is the period that Prof. Schumpeter describes as the upswing-phase of a new " Kondratiev " long-wave movement; 1873–96 having constituted the downward phase of the previous one. But true to his special theory of " innovations ", he appears to attribute the new prosperity-phase exclusively to technical innovation, associated with electricity (*Business Cycles*, vol. I, 397 seq.)

destiny of Capitalism to make economic progress eternal. Socialism was to be heard again as a street-gospel in the 1890's and the 1900's ; while the Labour Party was to grow to be a political force after 1906. But the belief in Capitalism as a working system was not in England seriously shaken in the decade prior to the first Great War.

Actually, foreign investment had already shown a modest recovery in the '80's under the impulse of the new colonial movement and the shift of attention in the investment market towards South America, especially Argentine, Chile and Brazil, and towards Canada and India. Land speculation in Argentine and nitrate-development in Chile were important factors both in the revived investment activity of 1887 and in the collapse of 1890, associated particularly with the name of Barings who were heavily implicated in South America.[1] In 1888 (according to C. K. Hobson's estimates) foreign investment had again reached the figure of 1872 : i.e. it had passed the £82 million mark. But in the '90's it shrank again to almost as low a level as in the middle '70's. In 1894 it was only £21 million, and in 1898 it was only £17 million.[2] In these years there was even some re-purchase by America of foreign securities previously held in Britain. In the start of the recovery in 1896 it played no noticeable part. In fact, this recovery took place at first in face of an actual decline of exports, especially to North and South America, Australia and South Africa ; and between 1897 and 1900 there occurred that dramatic rise of American export figures which provoked articles in American periodicals entitled " American Invasion of Europe ".[3] Much more important as an initial cause of recovery in that year was the introduction of the bicycle and the boom in the Birmingham bicycle industry ; also shipbuilding, a certain amount of home railway extension and to some extent electrical construction. The part that foreign investment and overseas markets played was rather that of sustaining recovery, and in particular of reviving activity after signs had appeared of a fresh relapse in the opening years of the new century. 1904 was the year when British foreign investment started its spectacular ascent. The Transvaal Loan of 1903 was followed by Japanese borrowing and Canadian and

---

[1] Cf. Wesley Mitchell, *Business Cycles*, 47–8.

[2] C. K. Hobson, *Export of Capital*, 204. Cairncross gives only 72·4 for 1888 but also lower figures for 1894 and 1898—namely, £17 m. and £14 m.

[3] Cf. Wesley Mitchell, *op. cit.*, 60, 69. Mitchell speaks of an article by Vanderlint in *Scribners* as having been the origin of this phrase.

Argentine railway issues.   The main stream of British capital
went to Canada and Argentine, also once more to U.S.A. ; to
Brazil, Chile and Mexico, and in smaller amounts to Egypt, to
West and East Africa, to India and to China.   Railways, docks,
public utilities, telegraphs and tramways, mining, plantations,
land mortgage companies, banks, insurance and trading companies were the favourite objects of this investment boom.   But,
as Mr. C. K. Hobson wrote in 1906, there had developed " during
the past few years a tendency to invest in manufactures and
industrial concerns ", such as Canadian textiles, iron and steel
and paper, in Indian jute and Russian textiles and iron ; and
" it would appear that the obstacles in the way of successful
foreign investment in manufacturing is being overcome ".[1]   In
1906 the figure of capital export stood at £104 million, over-
topping the previous peak foreign-investment years of 1872 and
1890.   In 1907 it was £141 million, or nearly 75 per cent. higher
than 1890.   From there, despite a check in 1908 and 1909, it rose
to £225 million in 1913.[2]   On the eve of the First World War
British capital abroad had grown to constitute probably about a
third or a quarter of the total holdings of the British capitalist
class and current foreign investment may even have slightly
exceeded net home investment.[3]   Of this capital held abroad
about a half was in British colonies and possessions, and of the
remainder a very high proportion was in North and South
America.[4]   During the two years 1911 and 1912 " upward of
30 per cent. more capital was exported than during the whole
decade between 1890 and 1901, and in each of the two years
vastly more than in any peak year of capital export during the
'80's and '70's ".[5]

At the same time commodity-exports climbed, even if they
were slow to move in the first years of the recovery after 1896.
From only £226 million in 1895 (and £263 million in 1890)
exports of British produce and manufactures had revived to
£282 million by 1900.   This improvement was equally shared
between exports to foreign countries and exports to British
colonies and possessions (partly because areas such as South
America, which were virtual " economic spheres of influence "

[1] C. K. Hobson, *op. cit.*, 158–60.
[2] Cf. Hobson, *op. cit.* ; Clapham, vol. III, 53.   Dr. Cairncross, who has revised
Mr. Hobson's figures, suggests slightly lower totals than these, but the difference is
inconsiderable.   He gives 99·8 m. for 1906, 135·2 m. for 1907 and 216·2 m. for
1913 (*op. cit.*, Table 14).
[3] Cairncross, *op. cit.*, 223.   C. K. Hobson gives a lower figure (*op. cit.*, 207).
[4] Cairncross, 247.   [5] Clapham, *op. cit.*, 61.

of this country at the time, were listed under the former). By 1906 the export-figure had reached £375 million, and in 1910, the year when (according to Wesley Mitchell) " England was distinctly the most prosperous among the great nations of the world ",[1] it had reached £430 million. Of that total, exports to British colonies and possessions represented about a third. In the same prosperous year exports of iron and steel were more than twice what they had been in 1895 in *values*, 70 per cent. greater in *tonnage* and more than 30 per cent. above the value-figures for 1890 and for 1900. The connection between export of capital goods and foreign investment is well shown in the fact that up to 1904 iron and steel exports registered only a modest tonnage-increase on the middle '90's, and were lower in 1903–4 than they had been between 1887 and 1890. It was after 1904 that the upward movement of tonnage, and still more of values, occurred. Export of machinery, especially textile machinery, also increased, and between 1909 and 1913 maintained an annual average that was nearly three times the level of 1881–90. In the wake of iron and steel and engineering went shipbuilding, which in 1906 attained what *The Economist* called " unprecedented activity " in launching more than a million tonnage in the year. As Professor Clapham has observed, " the 50 per cent. rise in exports between 1901–3 and 1907 was essentially an investment rise. . . . Manufacturers and all who thought like manufacturers gloried in the swollen exports. . . . Resources were turned towards foreign investment, rather than to the rebuilding of the dirty towns of Britain, simply because foreign investment seemed more remunerative." [2] But it was not only the capital goods industries that shared the fever of expanding demand. " That the roots of prosperity were overseas was fully recognized at the time. The only complaints during the three years (1905–7) came from trades mainly or entirely dependent on the home demand."[3] Although textile yarns and fabrics now formed only a third of all exports (in 1850 they had made up 60 per cent. in values), the total yardage of cotton piece-goods exported in 1909–13 was 40 per cent. larger than it had been in 1880–4.[4]

But there were elements in the situation in the first decade

[1] *Op. cit.*, 79.
[2] *Op. cit.*, 53. There was even some unemployment in the building trades at the time, by contrast with the expansion of building and of employment in the building trades in the '90's ; affording illustration of the fact (emphasized by Cairncross) that foreign and home investment were predominantly competitive.
[3] *Ibid.*, 52.   [4] *Ibid.*, 66.

of the new century that were to make the outlook for British Capitalism very different from the halcyon days of the middle nineteenth century, and different even from the sunshine years of 1867–73 before the breaking of the storm. In the first place, the population was increasing at a much slower rate than it had done four or five decades before. Between the first five years of the century and the four years preceding the First World War the population of England and Wales and Scotland grew by scarcely more than 9 per cent., as compared with a decennial increase of between 12 and 13 per cent. in the middle of the nineteenth century.[1] Capital accumulation, meantime, had been proceeding considerably faster. In the forty years prior to the First World War (i.e. between the boom years 1873 and 1913) the number of employed persons had risen by 50 per cent. ; while the total of capital invested at home had probably grown by more than 80 per cent., and the total of capital invested abroad by as much as 165 per cent.[2]

In the second place, while home as well as foreign investment was proceeding at a considerable (if compared with 1865–95 a somewhat slackened) speed, and productive equipment was consequently growing by something of the order of magnitude of 20 per cent. a decade, there were signs of a considerably slackened progress of cost-reducing improvements in industry. As Professor Clapham has written, the coal industry had been " worse than stagnant in efficiency since before 1900 " ; there was probably an actual decline in the efficiency of the building industry, as measured by labour-productivity, between 1890 and 1911 ; in cotton " most of the economies of machinery had been attained long since. There was no fundamental improvement in the blast-furnace and its accessories between 1886 and 1913. In neither industry was there any reorganization which might have made labour more productive." [3] Two recent writers on the iron and steel industry have concluded that since 1870 " the industry in Great Britain

[1] In the years prior to 1914 the birth-rate was less than 24 per 1,000, compared with almost 34 per 1,000 in the early '50's. The estimated net reproduction rate (per woman) in 1910–12 was only 1·129 against 1·525 in 1880–2 (D. Glass, *Population Policies and Movements*, 13).

[2] Cairncross, *op. cit.*, 223. The figures given here are as follows : a growth of capital at home between 1875 and 1914 from £5,000 m. to £9,200 m., and of capital held abroad from £1,100 m. to £4,000 m. Colin Clark estimates that the real capital of the United Kingdom about doubled between the decade of the '60's and the middle or later '90's and that between about 1895 and the First World War it increased again by between 40 and 50 per cent. (*Conditions of Economic Progress*, 393).

[3] Clapham, *op. cit.*, 69–70 ; G. T. Jones, *Increasing Returns*, 98 and *passim*.

has lagged behind the rest of the world both absolutely and relatively " : it was characterized by " neglect of developing technique " and " lack of flexibility ", while its entrepreneurs " were not prepared to undertake the heavy capital expenditure required for mechanization on an adequate scale ", with " a long-standing neglect of plant development and organization " as the consequence.[1]

In the third place, there are indications that the so-called " barter terms of trade " between Britain and the rest of the world—the rate at which she acquired imports in return for her exports—which had become increasingly favourable to this country in the latter part of the nineteenth century, were beginning in the decade before the First World War to turn in the opposite direction. This movement was still only slight ; and it is perhaps to be regarded as no more than a halting of the previous tendency. But since it concerned the ratio of the prices of the foodstuffs and raw materials which this country purchased and of the manufactured goods that this country sold, any movement in these terms had a crucial significance. For this price-ratio influenced the level of industrial costs, directly *via* raw material prices, and more indirectly *via* the price of workers' subsistence, relatively to the level of industrial selling-prices, and hence affected the profit-margin available. This change seems to have reflected a significant shift in the economic situation of the world at large relatively to the country which had so long enjoyed the position of industrial pioneer. In the nineteenth century we have seen that capital export had been mainly directed towards transport development and primary production. By cheapening the supply of primary products available to an advanced capitalist country like Britain foreign investment had redounded to the advantage of capital invested at home ; and every enlargement of the sphere of international trade enlarged the scope of the gains to be derived in this way. But this could be no more than a passing phase in the history of Capitalism on a world scale. As the development of other parts of the world passed from primary production to manufacturing industry and even to industries producing capital goods, the terms of inter-

---

[1] T. H. Burnham and G. O. Hoskins, *Iron and Steel in Britain, 1870–1930*, pp. 70, 80, 101, 148, 155. These writers attribute a good deal of the " inherent conservatism " of the British industry to the persistence of the family firm, with " men without any special training " at their head, to " the sense of security from inheriting wealth ", to " a marked tendency to retain aged directors " and to inadequacy or non-existence of training for works management and for foremanship (248).

change between the manufactured exports of the most advanced industrial countries and primary products no longer tended to move in favour of the former. They even tended to move in the reverse direction ; thereby depriving the most advanced industrial countries of one of the sources from which their prosperity (evaluated in terms of profit) at an earlier phase of world development had derived.

As far as influences touching the price at which industry could acquire labour-power were concerned, there was probably a more important newcomer on the horizon. The Capital-Labour Problem, the Social Question or the Class Struggle, as it had variously been termed, had caused anxiety in employing class circles on numerous occasions over the past century. It had sometimes provoked threats and repressive action to stem the rising insubordination of men towards masters. At other times it had called forth fair words and " bread and circuses " and talk of the essential harmony of interest betweeen the classes in a continued augmentation of the product of industry. By the end of the nineteenth century Labour was more highly organized than it had ever been. With the New Unionism this organization had spread to the unskilled ; and Labour's incursion into politics was about to bring a new period of State recognition of collective bargaining and the first small beginnings of a legal minimum wage. The years were approaching when the trade union movement was to undergo an expansion alike of numbers and of power such as no single decade had previously witnessed, and to reach a position of influence on the functioning of industry which was entirely without precedent and which must have scared the ghosts of Victorian ironmasters or cotton magnates with the vision of a nemesis of which in their lifetime they could have scarcely dreamed.

CHAPTER EIGHT

THE PERIOD BETWEEN THE TWO WARS
AND ITS SEQUEL

I

In many, though not in all, respects the twenty years separating the First from the Second Great War witnessed the continuation of those underlying tendencies which had shaped the economic scene in the first decade of the new century. Moreover, it was a continuation of those tendencies at a more advanced level and at an accelerated *tempo*. A common opinion in the decade of the 1920's was that the economic ills of the time had their origin in the dislocations bequeathed by the war and in post-war monetary disturbances, and that as transient maladjustments these ills would accordingly pass, once " stabilization " had been achieved.[1] For certain commentators " stabilization ", which many identified too easily with the restoration of some kind of " normal " set of price-ratios, became a magic formula, and as such a substitute for realistic thought. Close on the heels of this opinion went a kindred but more flexible interpretation. Certain structural transformations, it was said, had occurred in the body economic, in part due to the war and in part to more long-term changes in conditions of production and of markets ; and, although adaptation to these changes was being hindered by elements of friction in the situation, successful adaptation after an interval could none the less be achieved, if only freedom of enterprise and of trade were restored. The view that symptoms of economic crisis were transient was reinforced by the contrast between the troubles of Europe and the

[1] This position was substantially the one adopted in publications of the Economic Section of the League. For example, the following diagnosis which appeared as late as 1932 : " The basic causes (of the 1929 crisis) lay far back in the disorganization produced by the war and the burdens of debt and taxation which it achieved. . . . The mechanism of adjustment has worked with increasing difficulty and friction in the post-war period." For this the cure was " by extending the range and volume of international trade " and " allowing the forces of competition in world markets to rearrange territorial specialization ", to " carry and gradually liquidate the financial legacies of the war, as the similar legacies of 1793–1815 and 1870 were liquidated " (*World Economic Survey, 1931–2*, 27, 28, 30). In the previous year *The Course and Phases of the World Economic Depression* had referred to " structural changes, followed by a slow and insufficient adjustment, (which) have made for instability of the economic system " (p. 71).

prosperity which characterized some other parts of the world. Before the decade was very old, America was launched on a prosperity-phase, which was to breed a mood of optimism amounting to intoxication. A faith swept the continent of North America that their land, which was a land of expanding Capitalism and free enterprise *par excellence*, had an inspired destiny : to banish the problem of scarcity and to enrich its citizens and even to enrich the rest of the world. In the fateful year 1929 a report of the Committee on Recent Economic Changes, under the chairmanship of President Hoover, made the confident pronouncement that " economically we have a boundless field before us ; there are new wants which will make way endlessly for newer wants as fast as they are satisfied. . . . We seem only to have touched the fringe of our potentialities." When we look back on it, the temper of this period is to be numbered among the wonders of recent times. Such optimism was not destined to survive for very long. Dreams of an economic millennium were to be rudely broken by the events of 1929 to 1931 : by the onset of an economic crisis that was unmatched even by the Great Depression of the '70's and '80's as well as universal. The stark facts of these grim years, with their sudden bankruptcies, their derelict plants and their bread-lines, forced upon sobered minds the conclusion that something much more fundamental than sluggish adaptability or disordered price-ratios must be wrong with the economic system, and that capitalist society had become afflicted with what had every appearance of being a chronic malady, in danger of becoming fatal.

In its larger outline the visage of this period between wars confronts us with no difficult problem of recognition. The main features fit only too simply into a picture that we have come to associate with a monopolistic age ; and the essential character of the period is so clearly written on its face as scarcely to need analysis. The very contrasts which these decades showed to the previous Great Depression of the last century afford convincing testimony : price rigidities over a large range of major industries and the maintenance of profit-margins instead of price-collapses ; restriction of production rather than cost-reduction as the favourite remedy of industrialists and statesmen ; mounting and universal excess capacity and unemployment of unprecedented stubbornness and dimensions. Evidence of that neo-Mercantilist " fear of productive capacity ", of which we have spoken, is certainly not lacking. It was apparent alike in tariff policies, in the widespread extension of cartel-quotas and restriction schemes, in the growing vogue of large-scale advertising campaigns, concerted trade propaganda and privileged markets, and in the almost universal worship of export surpluses. It coloured the economic policies of governments. It dogged every proposal for industrial reorganization and every project of economic reconstruction. It imposed caution and conservatism, amounting at times to paralysis of the will, where once there had been enterprise and the zest for adventure and risk-taking. It even provoked the thinking of economists to defy century-old traditions and shaped economic theory to quite novel patterns.

To elucidate what we have said, let us construct an abstract model, representing the way in which we should expect a system of capitalist industry organized in the main on the basis of a high degree of monopoly [1] to function. In order to sharpen the comparison between our model and the real world, and to direct our eyes in the search for essentials, let us even exaggerate the simplicity of our model by emphasizing certain of its limbs and omitting certain features that one might expect to find in any actual system to which the abstraction was intended to be related.

In the first place, this model would be characterized by an abnormally large gap between price and cost ; from which it would follow that profit-margins (i.e. profit expressed as a ratio to current outlay) would be abnormally enhanced and that in all probability the share of industrial income going as wages would be abnormally depressed. Secondly, our model would show that reductions in demand on particular markets or in markets in general were followed by reductions of output, rather than of price (in view of the monopolist's desire and ability to maximize profits by maintaining his price in face of the fall of demand).[2] Thirdly, and consequentially, this system would tend to be characterized by extensive under-capacity working of plant and equipment and by an abnormally large reserve of unemployed

---

[1] This phrase is being used here, not only in the limited technical meaning which some economists have recently given to it, but to include a high degree of restriction of entry into an industry, approximating to full monopoly in the traditional sense.

[2] The same would apply, *mutatis mutandis*, to an increase of demand if industry was working below capacity (and prime costs per unit were consequently more or less constant in face of changes of output). But if the increase occurred in a position of full capacity working, it could not, of course, evoke (in the short period) an increase of supply, and the monopolist would presumably meet the growth of demand by raising his price.

man-power, especially at times when markets were depressed. In so far as the prevalence of restrictive practices operates in conjunction with large indivisible units of fixed equipment, such a condition of excess capacity is likely to become permanent,[1] as is also the existence of an inflated labour reserve. In other words, in such an epoch the " fear of productive capacity " will result in a portion of the existing productive power being kept out of action or under-utilized, while the industrial reserve army will be recruited by deliberate restriction of production.

Fourthly, there would tend presumably to be a decline in the rate of new investment, owing to the reluctance of the monopolies already entrenched in a certain sphere to expand productive capacity and because of the obstruction placed in the way of new firms entering these sacred preserves. In the extreme case each industry would become, if not the preserve of a single giant firm, a virtually closed corporation, from which interlopers were as jealously excluded as under the gild régime of earlier centuries. To the extent that " free " spheres remained, where entry of newcomers was unrestricted and output and investment un-controlled, this retarding of investment in the monopolized industries might be partly offset by a rush of capital into the " free " industries and an acceleration of their rate of expansion. This overcrowding of the latter would, however, have the tendency to depress the rate of profit in these industries as much as it had been raised elsewhere by monopolistic action, until a point was reached where new investment was likely here also to slow down.[2] Such a situation is likely to be marked by an outstanding contradiction. On the one hand, the concentration of wealth and of profits which monopolization brings about will tend to increase the desire to invest. On the other hand, the opportunities which exist for investment (without undermining the protected rate of profit in the monopolized sphere) will be narrowed. The outcome of this contradiction is likely to be an intensified search for outside investment outlets—an intensified drive to penetrate or to annex spheres which stand to the metro-polis of monopoly industry as " colonial " spheres.[3]

[1] This is for the reason that the indivisibility of plant (or the economies that are sacrificed if a smaller size of plant is substituted) places an obstacle in the way of reducing the size of the plant, which firms might otherwise be tempted to do in the long run as a means of saving capital-costs and raising the *rate* of profit on capital.

[2] In so far as the markets for these industries were characterized by conditions of imperfect competition, a further effect would be to accentuate the disease of excess capacity prevailing there.

[3] Cf. Paul Sweezy, *Theory of Capitalist Development*, 275–6.

Fifthly, this declining rate of investment at home (unless it were compensated by a larger export of capital for colonial development) would result in a narrowing of the market for the products of heavy industry ; while the existence of mass unemployment and the shift from wages to profit of which we have spoken would depress consumption and the market for consumption goods. One would accordingly expect an epoch of monopoly Capitalism to be characterized by an abnormal sagging of markets and a chronic deficiency of demand : a factor in the situation which would not only make for a deepening of slumps and a curtailment of periods of recovery, but would aggravate the long-term problem of chronic excess-capacity and unemployment. Moreover, of the two main groups of industry it seems probable that heavy industry would find its markets the more shrunken ; so that such an epoch is likely to be remarkable for a special crisis of heavy industry, and for the emergence of a business-strategy which lays special stress on the creation of new and privileged markets for capital goods and even on the throttling of rival industries in other countries and the annexing of their territory.

Finally, one would expect to find a tendency towards an ossification of industrial structure, both in industries dominated by the more solid forms of monopolistic organization and in those characterized by a looser cartel-form of control, which has the effect of freezing the existing pattern of each industry by the allotment of output quotas to the various firms.[1] This is not to say that monopolistic organization is altogether bereft of progressive elements. It may be in a better position to organize research and to take a broader and a longer view than the smaller firm, and be capable of concentrating production on the most efficient plants, which is unlikely to occur in a half-way state of imperfect competition. Schumpeter has even argued that a large monopolistic organization is likely to attain an unusual standard of constructive initiative, because it can marshal sufficient resources to plan business strategy on an ambitious scale, and is strong enough both to shoulder risks and to face up to uncertainties which would baffle a weaker entrepreneur : an

---

[1] Where quotas can be sold, the door is opened to change by means of the enlargement of more efficient firms (who buy the quotas of less prosperous ones) at the expense of the closing down of others. Even so, change is restricted by the introduction of an additional cost associated with change : the cost of buying additional quotas to provide the title to enlargement, at prices which may represent simply the " nuisance value " of the firms which are being bought out,

argument which seems to ignore the extent to which monopolies spend time and energy in entrenching an established position against the encroachments of rival innovations and in resisting the intrusion of enterprising newcomers on to the field—to ignore the fact that consideration of the unfavourable effect of new methods on the value of capital sunk in older methods will (during the length of life of the old plant) exercise an influence, and a retarding influence, under monopoly, which it could not do under conditions of atomistic competition.

It is, doubtless, true that the most important considerations affecting any judgement of monopoly are its effects on economic development, and not its effects on economic equilibrium with which economic analysis hitherto has been chiefly concerned. Such effects seem likely to be cumulative in character, and may alter, not merely the rate at which changes occur, but the whole path which the development of the economic system follows in a given epoch, as it so markedly did four or five centuries ago. What seems to be decisive here is that in such a régime the focus of interest is so largely shifted from considerations of production and productive costs to considerations of financial and commercial supremacy : for example, to the pyramiding of holding companies or the establishment of tying contracts or of an intimate liaison with banks, rather than to the promotion of standardization or finding the optimum location for an industry. A habit is generated of retrenchment rather than of adventure—unless it be the adventure of capturing larger tracts of exclusive territory and bludgeoning those whose activities show signs of reducing the value of a monopolist's own assets. The gains to be made by manœuvring to improve one's strategic position—to enhance the value of what Veblen called the " margin of intangible assets that represents capitalized withdrawal of efficiency "—come to be more alluring than any gains to be made by a display of initiative in the sphere of production. As a result, in the contemporary capitalist world an increasing part of the value of capital and of the profit-expectation which serves both as a criterion and as a motive of business policies represents the power to restrict and obstruct rather than to improve : a development which is expressed in the fact that (in Veblen's words again) " one of the singularities of the current situation in business and its control of industry (is) that the total face-value, or even the total market-value, of the vendible securities which cover any given block of industrial equipment and material resources and which give title to its ownership, always and greatly exceeds the total market value of the equipment and resources to which they give title of ownership ".[1]   In other words, the industrial system becomes increasingly weighed down by a mass of unproductive costs, inflated by the internecine warfare of that new " economic baronage " (as a contributor to *The Times* recently named it), battling for position and for supremacy in an age of monopolistic competition.

Resemblance to this abstract model is not difficult to trace in recent events in our own country ; and certain points of resemblance are even more striking when we compare it with the shape of things in some continental countries or in America in the decade of the '30's.   Comprehensive surveys of excess capacity are unfortunately lacking for this country.   But for America we have the much-quoted estimate of the Brookings Institute that in 1929, at the peak of that country's prosperity wave, excess capacity of plant and equipment amounted to the considerable figure of 20 per cent. : [2] a margin of wasted productive power which had grown by the year of deepest depression to 50 per cent. Such evidence as we have in this country about the condition of our basic industries, and the plenitude of modern " machine-wrecking " schemes for destroying excess capacity, like the Ship-building Securities Ltd. scheme or the Cotton Spindles Act (not to mention the agricultural schemes for limiting the area of cultivation, which are perhaps in a special position), indicate that a problem of comparable dimensions characterized the position here as well, even if a figure of 50 per cent. excess capacity might exaggerate the decline in activity in the early '30's in this country.   Unemployment in Britain during the '20's stood at an average level of 12 per cent., rose in the early '30's to a quite unprecedented figure which approached 3 million, and on the average of the years 1930–5 stood at a percentage figure of 18·5 per cent. of all insured workers, or some four times the pre-1914 average and nearly twice the peak of recorded unemployment for any year of the four decades prior to 1914. For America in the great slump of 1929–33 estimates have been

[1] *The Vested Interests*, 105.
[2] This figure takes account only of the extent to which equipment as it existed and was organized at the time was being utilized or " loaded " : i.e., it rests on a comparison between potential and actual in given conditions.   It does not rest on estimates of what an industry might be able to produce if it were appropriately re-equipped or re-equipped.

made which range up to 13 million [1] and even higher ; and for the leading industrial countries as a whole a total figure in the neighbourhood of 25 or even 30 million has been cited.   While in Britain the absorption of labour into employment continued over at least the last three-quarters of the two decades at an average rate of about $1\frac{1}{2}$ per cent. per annum, this growth over the fifteen years which separated 1923 and 1938 left the unemployed reserve army as large at the end of this period as it had been at its beginning ; and this despite the rearmament activity of the later '30's and despite a much slower natural rate of population increase than had prevailed in the century before 1914.   If we compare the employment peak after the First World War with the position in the summer of 1939, we find that total employment (in the insured trades) increased over the period by about 20 per cent., but the number of workers seeking employment grew by about 28 per cent.   In manufacturing industries alone the increase of employment over the period was much smaller, while in extractive industries employment had shrunk by nearly a third.

Of the price-rigidities occasioned by business policies of price-maintenance and restriction there have been a number of studies in the pre-war decade, most notably in America.   Of America in 1929–30, when the decline of prices was much slower than in earlier depressions, it has been written that the situation was marked by " strongly entrenched values and corresponding reluctance to reduce prices " : a circumstance which gave to the depression its " more protracted and more painful character " than previous depressions had borne.[2]   The Final Report and Recommendations of the Temporary National Economic Committee cited evidence which " for many of our basic industries showed definite curtailment of production by monopoly concerns or dominant industrial groups in order to maintain prices and insure profits " ; and one of the Monographs written for the same Committee concerning Price Behaviour pointed out that " within very broad limits there was a tendency for production to fall less where prices fell more during the 1929–33 recession : conversely where prices were maintained, production fell much more sharply ".[3]   Perhaps the most striking piece of evidence is

---

[1] Thirteen million was the contemporaneous estimate made by Kusnets, by the American Federation of Labor and by the National Industrial Conference Board for March, 1933.

[2] F. C. Mills, *Prices in Recession and Recovery*, 17.

[3] Final Report and Recommendations of T.N.E.C., 23 ; T.N.E.C. Monograph No. I, 51. Cf. also the observation of Willard L. Thorp in *Recent Economic Changes*

the comparison made by the German Institut für Konjunktur-forschung, and cited in the League of Nations Economic Surveys, between the price-fall of products subject to control by cartels or similar bodies and of products that were marketed under some degree of free price-competition. These German data show a fall between 1929 and 1933 to an index figure of 45·7 (1926 = 100) in the case of the latter and a fall to a figure of 83·5 in the case of the former. In other words, the fall in price of cartel-controlled products was only about a third as great as that to which goods on free markets were subject.[1]

A similar contrast is seen in the different price-histories of producers' goods and consumers' goods in the course of the crisis ; price-reductions being much smaller in the case of the former. This result is the more remarkable since it is the precise opposite of what used to take place prior to 1914. For example, in the 1907–8 crisis in U.S.A. the prices of producers' goods fell by twice as much, and in Germany by nearly three times as much, as the prices of consumers' goods. At first sight the contrast is surprising since *net* investment probably fell more sharply after 1929 than in previous crises; although the decline in *total* demand for producers' goods (including maintenance as well as new construction) may not have been as great as at first sight appears; and even if this decline had been a large one, there is not much reason to have expected it to exert any appreciable influence on the trend of prices.[2] Without much doubt, the difference is attributable to the greater degree of monopolistic organization in heavy industry : to " the strong resistance from the powerfully organized capital-equipment industries, many of which are cartellized and, in the process of organization, have been loaded with excessive capital obligations ".[3] Again, the fall in wholesale prices of agricultural products on world markets was greater than those of manufactured goods. In U.S.A., for example, raw materials fell by 49 per cent. and in Germany by 35 per cent. between 1929 and 1933 and

---

in the United States (1929), vol. I, 217 : " The data indicate that large corporations are subject to wider fluctuations in production and employment than the smaller concerns, but that their earnings are more stable."

[1] Economic Section of the League, *World Economic Survey, 1931–2*, 127–9 ; *World Economic Survey, 1932–3*, 62.

[2] Unless firms had previously been operating at or close to full capacity, prime costs (which are probably the relevant factor in the determination of short-period price) will be more or less constant in face of changes of output ; and the degree of monopoly and changes in it will be the principal determinant of price.

[3] *World Economic Survey, 1931–2*, 133.

manufactures by 31 and 29 per cent. respectively.[1] But in the case of agriculture certain special factors affecting production and supply were present to explain the collapse of price. This large disparity between different sets of prices—this " price-scissors " as it has come to be called, using a term that was coined to describe the divergent movements of industrial and agricultural prices in Russia in 1923—was an outstanding feature of the 1929–33 crisis, exerting a disruptive effect on the normal terms of exchange and on the volume of trade, with consequential shifts of relative income and purchasing power, and constituting a major influence in the financial disturbance of those years.

Since changes in profit will be a function jointly of changes in output and changes in price, one would expect profit-fluctuations to be particularly marked between years of boom and of depression. Moreover, since in speaking of net profit we refer to a margin between gross proceeds and gross costs which may not represent a very large fraction of either of the latter two quantities, this margin may be eliminated altogether by a proportionately small drop in price (and hence in receipts) ; and we might accordingly expect net profit to disappear and even to give way to losses in a really bad slump year. Industrial profits in the early '30's, of course, experienced some drastic shrinkages. But in contrast to what one could reasonably expect to find in conditions of unfettered price-competition, the degree to which profits in general were maintained must strike one as surprising. Estimates based on dividend-distribution do not tell the whole story ; and the real profit position cannot be fully appreciated until one knows the facts about allocation to reserves and valuation of assets. Nevertheless, the fact that (according to Lord Stamp's profit-index) dividends on preference and ordinary shares in this country maintained an average figure of more than 6 per cent. even in the bad years of 1931–3 (as against 10·5 per cent. in 1929),[2] and in no year fell much below 6 per cent., is something to be marvelled at in those grim years. Regarding the distribution of income the evidence is inconclusive. Some estimates of the share of the national income accruing to wage-earners, which have figured in recent discussion, do not suggest any marked change in this proportion either in the course

---

[1] *Ibid.*, 61.
[2] Cit. *World Economic Survey, 1934–5*, 130. Already by 1934 the index figure had been restored to 96, or nearly to the 1929 level. The *Economist* Profits Index had stood at 113 at the end of 1929 and fell to 67 in 1933. By 1938 it had risen again to 130.

of the crisis-years or as a longer-term tendency since the opening of the century. But they fail to reveal any such tendency, not because the degree of monopoly has not grown or has failed to exercise its anticipated influence, but because the effects of monopoly in reducing the share of income accruing to labour have probably been obscured by the contrary influence of largely fortuitous factors that have happened to operate at the same time.[1] If we take the share of wages in the net output of manufacturing industry (as distinct from the national income as a whole) the position is different. Here we seem able to discern a long-term tendency for this share in Britain to undergo " a slow but steady decline " : in the U.S.A. for it to decline in the course of the '20's and in the early '30's up to 1933, whereafter it rose again in the years of the New Deal ; and in Germany for it to undergo " a sharp fall " between 1929 and 1932 to a " low level maintained ever since ". Moreover, this proportion was lower in Germany and U.S.A. (where monopoly is, in general, more strongly developed) than it was in Britain, and was lowest of all in Germany since 1932.[2]

Sir William Beveridge has pointed out that in Britain the violence of fluctuation of output between boom and slump, which was tending to decrease in the decades prior to 1914, showed a very marked increase in the period between the wars and became " much more violent than it had been since the middle of the nineteenth century ".[3] His index of industrial activity shows a fluctuation which (measured in terms of the standard deviation) was more than twice as great between 1920 and 1938 than it had been between 1887 and 1913, and nearly twice as great as between 1860 and 1886 ; while for the con-structional trades alone the fluctuation in 1920–38 was nearly three times what it had been in the quarter of a century prior to 1914 and more than twice what it had been between 1860 and 1886.[4] Of the crisis of 1929–32—" a litany of woe and a commination service against increasing misfortune " as The Economist called the story of one of those years—it has been said that production " in most industrial countries was reduced to levels which could hardly have been deemed possible in the years before 1929 ".[5] In U.S.A. the production trough in the summer

[1] Cf. M. Kalečki, op. cit., 32–4.
[2] Dr. L. Rostas on " Productivity in Britain, Germany and U.S." in Econ. Journal, April, 1943, 53–4.
[3] Full Employment in a Free Society, 294.   [4] Ibid., 293, 312–13.
[5] World Economic Survey, 1932–3, 12.

of 1932 represented a fall of 55 per cent. below the 1929 peak, and the production-index of constructional goods in 1933 stood at little more than a third of 1929. In other countries the decline varied between 25 and 50 per cent., being considerably greater by 1932 in Germany, Czecho-Slovakia and Poland than it was in the United Kingdom and in Sweden. The collapse of production in heavy industry was the most spectacular. In six leading industrial countries taken together the output of pig-iron by March, 1932, had declined by 64 per cent. from the 1929 level.[1] In a number of countries the total national income (in value terms) was almost halved. Meanwhile international trade had shrunk to less than 40 per cent. of its 1929 amount in value and to 74 per cent. in physical volume.

Apart from its violence and its stubbornness, the crisis was remarkable for its ubiquity. As an American economist has written, " the severity of the second post-war depression and the difficulty of breaking it has been due in considerable part to the universality of the crisis. No nation except Soviet Russia escaped. Industrial centres and colonial areas alike felt the impact of the general decline." [2] This universality had been much less marked in the crisis of the '20's ; so much so that the latter came to be regarded as essentially troubles of war-scarred Europe. After a short depression in 1920 to 1921 America started that eight-year boom which was to carry the physical volume of production by 1929 to 34 per cent. above the level of 1922 and to about 65 per cent. above the level of 1913. So great was the rate of new construction that between 1925 and 1929 alone the demand for machine tools in the U.S. grew by nearly 90 per cent. and the demand for foundry equipment by nearly 50 per cent. Over this period it is notable that the rate of increase of capital goods production (which rose by 70 per cent. between 1922 and 1929) was almost double that of consumption goods (while the increase in durable consumption goods was also higher than that of non-durable consumption goods, partly owing to the expansion of instalment-selling as a form of monopolistic competition). Indeed, this fact that " the equipment for producing goods for ultimate consumption was being augmented at an exceptionally rapid rate " prompted economists to ask whether " too large a proportion of the country's productive energies were being devoted to the construction of capital

---

[1] *World Economic Survey, 1931–2,* 92.
[2] F. C. Mills, *Prices in Recession and Recovery,* 37.

equipment ".[1] But, in addition to a large volume of home investment, it was during this prosperity phase that the enormous expansion of American export of capital also occurred ; and " although the transition of the country from debtor to creditor status was not so abrupt as is sometimes supposed, the rapidity with which it acquired foreign investments is unparalleled in the experience of any major creditor country in modern times ".[2] Much of this took the form of direct investment through, or under the control of, American corporations (e.g. through subsidiaries of Standard Oil or General Motors, through specially formed subsidiary companies or companies in which American capitalists held the major control) ; and something like $3 milliard was invested throughout the decade in this form.[3] An expansion of considerable magnitude characterized also other non-European countries during the '20's. Already by 1925 the general production index for North America showed an increase of 26 per cent. on 1913, and for all other countries outside Europe an increase of 24 per cent. (as against an increase of only 2 per cent. for capitalist Europe as a whole).[4] Much of this growth was in primary production. But it also included substantial rates of increase for certain types of industry in countries of South America and in Japan.

Thus the fact that during the 1920's the continents stood in such marked contrast made the universality of the crisis in 1929 the more surprising. Indeed, when the crash came upon American industry in 1929, the collapse of production was correspondingly more severe than the average of the world as a whole, and markedly greater than in Britain, Sweden or France. Mr. Solomon Fabricant has estimated that over the period 1899 to 1937 the aggregate manufacturing output of U.S.A. increased by two and three-quarter times, or at an annual rate of 3·5 per cent. ; and that over this stretch of four decades there were nine occasions on which manufacturing output suffered an absolute decline, most of them covering only one year. By contrast with the previous thirty years, the contraction of 1929–32 was the

---

[1] F. C. Mills, *Economic Tendencies in the U.S.*, 280–1. This tendency had also characterized development between 1900 and 1913. Over the whole period between 1899 and 1927 the value of industrial buildings increased some three and a half times. Over the two decades, 1899–1919, the primary power per wage-earner in industry increased 47 per cent., and in the six years between 1919 and 1925 it grew by the remarkable figure of 30·9 per cent. (*Recent Economic Changes in the United States* (1929), Vol. I, 104, 136–7).
[2] U.S. Dept. of Commerce, *The United States in World Economy*, 91.
[3] *Ibid.*, 100–1.   [4] *World Economic Survey, 1931–2*, 23.

" most severe as well as the longest in duration " ; by 1932 output had dropped back to the level of 1913 ; and even by 1937, after several years of recovery, manufacturing output had not managed to do more than just top the 1929 peak.[1] From the 1937 level there was in the following year a further relapse ; the Federal Reserve Board Index of Industrial Production showing a decline from 113 in 1937 (1929 = 110) to no more than 88 in 1938 : a fall that was nearly as great as that of the majority of European countries after 1929.

In the capitalist world as a whole the recovery after 1932, when it came, was tentative and uneven. The system evidently lacked the resilience it had once had. In the middle 1930's the League's *Economic Survey* could only describe recovery to-date as " superficial rather than fundamental " and as " proceeding slowly and unevenly ", and (speaking of 1935, six years after the 1929 collapse) had to confess that the economic outlook was " confused and unpromising ", and that it would be " idle to pretend that the evidence of increasing economic activity over a wide area is sufficient to indicate the final passing of the depression ".[2] In the previous year the author of the *Survey* had written : " In past depressions, after a fairly long and painful period of reconstruction and stabilization, business enterprise could count upon renewed opportunities of profit under much the same conditions as existed before the depression began. At the present time, business enterprise emerges from its readjustments to find a very different situation confronting it." [3] This altered situation was largely conditioned by the enhanced restrictionist measures, the drift to autarkie, and the currency disorganization which had been the expedients—and so predominantly beggar-my-neighbour expedients—that business and the governments reflecting business-interests had adopted in response to the crisis. Moreover, the situation was different in another and highly significant respect, even in 1936 and 1937 when signs of recovery had become more general and less tentative. The recovery-phase of 1933 to 1937 stood in contrast to previous periods of this kind in the extent to which the expansion of production depended on government policy : [4] at first on currency- or tariff-policies favourable to industry, as for example the depreciation of the pound sterling in 1932, with the

[1] Solomon Fabricant, *Output of Manufacturing Industries, 1899–1937*, 6–7, 44.
[2] *World Economic Survey, 1934–5*, 6–7, 275.
[3] *Ibid., 1933–4*, 14.   [4] Cf. *Ibid.*, 10–12.

temporary fillip that it gave to British export industries ; on government policies designed to lower interest-rates and hence stimulate building activity ; and finally on armament expenditure, earliest and most powerfully in Germany, more tardily and weakly in Britain.   In other words, the expansion of demand, whether from investment in capital goods or from consumption, which prompted the halting recovery of the '30's, no longer came, to any considerable extent, from within the system and from its native powers of resilience, even in the case of America. It depended on stimuli which came, as it were, from outside the system and had a political source ; taking the form of government expenditure and of government measures to stimulate investment and to fence off markets as preserves for particular enterprises. As *The Economist* remarked in an article entitled " The Cartelization of England " : " since 1932 the State has no longer appeared to industry solely in the guise of monitor or policeman ; it has had favours to dispense " ; " the attitude of industry to the State " has been revolutionized and " the policeman has turned Father Christmas ".[1]

II

Yet when we approach the detail of this period there are a number of special features, both in this country and elsewhere, which do not fit into the simplified model that we have sketched above, and which even appear in certain respects to stand in contradiction to it.   First of these is the extent to which, despite the abnormal dimensions of the labour reserve army in all countries, real wages of those who kept their employment were maintained or even rose in the crisis-years of the early 1930's. This feature of the depression was more pronounced in Britain than elsewhere ; and it afforded in this respect a parallel to the position in the 1870's.   In fact, money-wages in Britain, taking industry as a whole, fell by considerably less than they had done after 1873.   In other countries the fall was much greater. Labour costs were estimated to have fallen by 20 per cent. between 1929 and 1933 in Germany and in U.S.A. by as much as between 30 and 40 per cent.[2]   This phenomenon is not difficult of explanation.   It evidently was the expression of the

---

[1] *Economist,* March 18, 1939.
[2] *World Economic Survey, 1933–4,* 51–2.   The fall in labour costs was not, of course, the same thing as the fall in money wages, since it reflected also the results of any change in productivity.

unprecedented strength of organized labour which, despite its setback after the collapse of the British General Strike of 1926 and despite the decline of Trade Union membership since 1920, was capable of maintaining wages in most of the highly organized trades, while the existence of the Trade Board machinery did much to cushion the downward pressure which ruthless competition for jobs would otherwise have exerted (and in many countries successfully exerted [1]) on wages in the unorganized trades. In other words, this fact stands as witness that the mechanism of the industrial reserve army, on which Capitalism had traditionally relied to maintain both discipline and cheapness in its labour force, had virtually ceased (at any rate in Britain) to perform its age-long function—at least a crucial part of that function ; and, except in Germany where Fascism introduced the Labour Trustee and the Wage-Stop, to supplement its liquidation of trade unions, Capitalism lacked any mechanism that could function in its place.

But to an explanation of the actual increase (even though a small increase) of real wages in this period more is needed than the mere strength of organized labour and its ability to win defensive successes. As in the '70's and '80's, the result was primarily due to a cheapening of imported foodstuffs, which was a direct result of the " scissors " movement of agricultural and industrial prices on world markets, to which we have referred above. In fact, it had been the case in the decade of the '20's as a whole that, compared with the pre–1914 situation, the prices of British imports had fallen relatively to the average price of British exports. But now the ratio between the two was to undergo a further movement in our favour. Since Britain had maintained her traditional policy of free food imports, this sharp turn in the terms of exchange between agriculture and industry was reflected in a fall in the cost of living, and hence in a rise in real wages : a rise in real wages which, since it arose from the external relations of the country, did not involve any rise in the wage-cost of output to British industry. A striking example of this is that within the space of two years the wheat imported into this country lost nearly two-thirds of its value on the world market. Had it not been for this eventuality, the plight of the British working-class in these years of

---

[1] A good example of this is Poland, where a large disparity developed between wages in the strongly unionized main industries (which happened also as a rule to be the cartellized industries) and in the unorganized sweated trades.

hunger-marches and insecurity would have been very much worse than it was. Without it we probably should not have witnessed that growing division in the ranks of Labour (which, again, had its parallel in the 1880's) between the temper of those who felt on their persons the main brunt of the crisis and of that more fortunate 40 per cent. of the wage-earning class who were immune from unemployment throughout the depression years. In fact, we witnessed the strange spectacle of this island remaining surprisingly aloof from the social and political currents that were convulsing large areas of the Continent, and the contradictory phenomena, so baffling to many observers, of moods of protest and revolt among the mass of those whose livelihood was threatened coexisting with a conservative, rather than a radical, turn of policy in both the industrial and the political wings of the official Labour movement.

Secondly, there is a feature of these years which, at first glance, seems less susceptible to explanation. This is the fact that the productivity of labour showed a quite unusual rate of increase, not only in America but also in this country. What is even more remarkable, this increase of productivity continued (as it had done in the '70's and '80's) throughout the depression years. One estimate places the growth in output per worker in British industry between 1924 and 1930 at a figure of 12 per cent. and in the depression years of 1930–4 at a further 10 to 11 per cent.[1] As an illustration of the type of change to which this was attributable, we may note that " the capacity of electric motors installed in all trades except electricity supply undertakings increased 37·2 per cent." between 1922 and 1930.[2] This increase was a modest one compared to what was happening in the United States. The growth in output per wage-earner in manufacture in U.S.A. has been estimated at as much as 43 per cent. over the ten years between 1919 and 1929,[3] and a further 24 per cent between 1929 and 1933.[4] The same phenomenon can be observed in other capitalist countries of this period. In Sweden output per worker between 1920 and 1929 rose by

---

[1] Witt Bowden in *Journal of Pol. Economy*, June, 1937, 347 seq. The comparison between 1924 and 1930 relates to industries included in the census of production for G.B. and N.I., and that between 1930 and 1934 to industries included in the Production Index of the Board of Trade. Between 1928 and 1934 in industries covered by the latter, average output per employee rose by 16·5 per cent., including 14 per cent. in mines and quarries, 16 per cent. in iron and steel and 26 per cent. in non-ferrous metals.
[2] *Ibid.*, 368.   [3] F. C. Mills, *Economic Tendencies in the United States*, 192, 290.
[4] *World Economic Survey, 1933–4*, 10.

something in the neighbourhood of 40 per cent. ; while " in Germany the number of employed workers seems to have been not quite 5 per cent. higher in 1929 than in 1925, while the volume of production index was 27·5 per cent. higher ", indicating accordingly " an annual increase of output per man of about 5 per cent.".[1]

Such a surprising growth in productivity affords *prima facie* evidence of considerable advances in technique ; and in the case of Britain of some resumption (under the banner of " rationalization ") of improvement in industrial organization and equipment, which we have seen was virtually lacking in the decades immediately preceding the First Great War. In Britain the " rationalization " movement of the '20's may have been no more than making up some of the leeway that had been lost. But since the improvement was not confined to Great Britain, it must have had other significance than a tardy adoption of changes which properly belonged to an earlier decade. Speaking of America, Mr. F. C. Mills has pointed out that prior to 1923 " the chief factor in expanding production was an enlarged body of wage-earners ", whereas since that date " better technical equipment, improved organization and enhanced skill on the part of the working force seem definitely to have supplanted numbers as instruments of expanding production ".[2] Whether this turn of investment towards a " deepening " of capital represented an answer to the growing strength of organized labour ; whether it was the sign that, as Dr. Paul Sweezy has expressed it, monopoly implies that " labour-saving becomes more than ever the goal of capitalist technology and that the rate of introduction of new methods will be so arranged as to minimize the disturbance to existing capital values " ;[3] or whether it was evidence of a new harvest season of scientific achievement, powerful enough to force a measure of industrial progress despite the fetters of straitened markets and of a monopolistic age ; this technical revolution was of outstanding consequence, and some have even gone so far as to compare it with events at the end of the eighteenth century.

Certain of its consequences, however, were not those which would formerly have been expected. Operating in an environment from which the earlier buoyancy of demand had so largely departed, it served to augment the problem of unemployment,

[1] *Course and Phases of the World Economic Depression*, 66–7.
[2] F. C. Mills, *op. cit.*, 291.   [3] P. Sweezy, *op. cit.*, 276.

since its effect was to diminish the amount of human labour required to yield a given result, without effecting a compensating expansion of total output in sufficient degree.   Indeed, in U.S.A. the fact that between 1923 and 1929 the number of wage-earners in manufacturing industry fell by some 7 or 8 per cent., while the physical volume of production rose by 13 per cent.,[1] occasioned a whole literature about " technological unemployment " as a leading peculiarity of the modern age.   Because the incidence of improvement was very unevenly distributed between different industries and different countries and even between different sections of an industry within the same country, it was a potent influence behind the disturbance of price-ratios and terms of trade which was a feature of the crisis of the early '30's, and the sharp conflicts of interest which these evoked.   Since these cost-reducing innovations were introduced into an industrial environment where competition was so blunted and hemmed in, their appearance often served merely to inaugurate a period of chronic under-capacity working and diminished profitability all round.   The normal mechanism by which the low-cost method in the course of time replaced the high-cost method no longer operated ; and instead of being driven into liquidation the latter were frequently prompted to impose on the industry schemes of price-minima or output-quotas to muzzle the former and preclude it from bringing its potential capacity into play.   This was specially in evidence among a number of primary products, of which rubber, sugar, coffee and tin are familiar examples.   But examples from manufacturing industry are by no means lacking. In such cases the expansion of capacity in the form of new and cheaper methods had as its principal effect to precipitate a crisis of the industry, from which there emerged, not reconstruction on a new basis, but an epidemic of restriction-schemes and internecine warfare between low-cost and high-cost producers over the allotment of quotas and the price-target at which restriction should be aimed.

But it would be a mistake to conclude that even in the '30's such changes lacked altogether the accompaniment of expanding output, or that between the two wars investment exclusively took the form of " deepening " and not of " widening ".   It is true to say that in Britain the growth of industrial output proceeded much more slowly over these two decades than it had proceeded before ; while in the U.S.A. industrial output in

[1] F. C. Mills, *op. cit.*, 290.

1939 was still below the level that it had attained ten years before. It is also true that in Britain's basic industries an increase in productivity was accompanied by a shrinkage of total output over most of the period. At the same time there were expanding industries, where not only output but also employment grew at a quite surprising rate. That this was so has often been cited as an indication that there was still buoyancy in the market situation, and that recovery was merely a question of structural adaptation to the changing pattern of demand. That every element of buoyancy had not gone out of the market is, of course, true ; and it would be absurd to contend that either the demand for investment goods or consumption were incapable, after 1929, of again showing any marked expansion. But when we examine the reasons which accounted for the expansion of output occurring in Britain in the '20's and in the first half of the '30's (i.e. before the special stimulant of rearmament came upon the scene), we shall find that this expansion was mainly the product of rather special causes, which showed no signs of exercising an influence that could compare with the nineteenth century either in potency (relative to contemporary productive capacity) or in persistence.

The chief advancing industries of the period were electrical engineering, road transport, motors and aircraft, artificial silk, and the catering trades. The number of workers employed in the electrical industry doubled between 1924 and 1937, and the output of electricity doubled between 1931 and 1937.[1] The output of motor vehicles, which was hardly affected at all by the slump of 1929–30, was similarly doubled between 1929 and 1937.[2] In the course of the '30's there occurred a remarkable expansion of building, especially of houses for sale by private builders ; and there was also some expansion in non-ferrous metals, owing to their connection with motors, aircraft and the electrical trades.

Contributing to this expansion were three main factors. First, the effect of cheaper foodstuffs, of which we have spoken, was to increase appreciably the residual income in the hands of the more well-to-do section of the working class, such as the employed workers in the more prosperous south, where unemployment was relatively small, and also among the lower middle

---

[1] *Britain in Recovery* (a Report of the Econ. Section of the British Association), 256, 259.
[2] *Ibid.*, 62.

class, which could create a demand for such things as clothes, radio-sets, furniture and even new houses.   Secondly, in certain directions State activity, though it was of modest dimensions in the 20's and early 30's, was already beginning to exert an influence such as it had not done in the nineteenth century.   Most of the £27 million spent by the Electricity Grid was expended during the slump years of the early '30's, and was an important factor in the market for the electrical trades.   Newly imposed tariffs affected motor-cars and iron and steel ; and the " cheap money " policy pursued by the Treasury after 1932, combined with the guarantee to building society loans, prompted the building boom of that decade.   Thirdly, this expansion was partly occasioned by technical innovation, and was to this extent reminiscent of the expansion of former decades.   The two inventions which have hitherto had special economic significance in the present century are the internal combustion engine and electrification.   The former was the creator of the new industries of motors and aircraft, as it was also of road transport ; and it had also an important application to agriculture such as steam-power had never had.[1]   Electricity, in the development of which Britain had previously been exceptionally backward, now spawned a family of related spheres of investment, such as rural electrification, electrical heating, electrification of industrial processes and of traction, and the radio industry.   To some extent it may also have been true that part of the investment at the time represented a crowding of capital and enterprise into spheres where the entry of newcomers was still relatively unrestricted, which led to a forcing of the pace of expansion in the interstices of a monopolistic régime or in uncharted territory where the combine and the cartel had not yet ventured.   As for the expansion of the distributive trades, about which there has been a fair amount of debate : this was evidently in large part a symptom of the multiplication of the unproductive costs incidental to an era of monopolistic competition, in which rivalry takes the form, not of price-cutting, but of selling-campaigns to influence demand and annex a private market.

But by the end of the decade of the '30's there were signs, in Britain as in America, that these expansionist influences were

---

[1] The number of combine-harvesters manufactured in U.S.A. on the eve of the First World War was only a few hundred ; by 1929 this figure had grown to between 30,000 and 40,000.   The number of tractors in use in 1916 was about 30,000 : a figure which had grown by the end of the 1920's to between three-quarters of a million and a million.

beginning to be spent. By the end of 1937 both motors and electrification gave indications that they had already passed their peak ; and a decline in output both of motors and of furniture started a recession which was only arrested by a stepping-up of armament expenditure in the course of the Munich year. There were signs even of a forthcoming decline in building, to judge from the fall in building plans passed in 1938 ; although the decline of activity was here postponed (as it was also in shipbuilding) by the considerable time-lag existing between the placing of contracts and their fulfilment ; [1] and there seems to be " some evidence . . . that consumption reached its peak in the spring or summer of 1937 ".[2] In the summer of 1939 *The Economist* was speaking in grave tones of " a permanent bias in the American economy towards deflation, which heavy Government expenditures can only temporarily and precariously reverse ", of " recovery in America turning into stalemate ", and of a " definite setback " in the spring of the year. Even of the recovery in Britain, prompted by growing armament expenditures, we were advised to have " caution in prophesying its continuance ".[3] As Sir William Beveridge has said, " a repetition of 1929–32, even more severe, was setting in ". But although the approach of war forestalled the onset of a fresh crisis, rearmament activity no doubt tended in certain directions to store up trouble for the future in the shape of excess productive capacity which might prove a heavy millstone around the neck of industry if reliance had to be placed once again on private demand as determinant of activity and employment. It was suggested, for example, just before the war that " the recent great increase in steel-making capacity may prove financially embarrassing once the rearmament programme has been completed and recession from the peak production of 1937 begins. . . . The restoration of the volume of export trade is imperative if output is to be kept close to productive capacity ".[4]

The third feature of the inter-war situation which confronts us with an apparent contradiction is that, alongside the tendency towards concentration of production and control and the extension of monopolistic or quasi-monopolistic forms of organization, there has been a most marked persistence of the small firm. This survival of economic forms typical of an earlier epoch into the modern world should not necessarily surprise us. It

[1] *Britain in Recovery*, 64.   [2] *Ibid.*, 65.
[3] *The Economist* on " A Distorted Boom ", June 3, 1939.
[4] *Britain in Recovery*, 372.

has been a pronounced feature of each stage of economic history, and without an appreciation of the extent to which every economic system is in some degree a " mixed system " any full understanding of economic movement and development, so largely influenced by interaction of these conflicting elements, is impossible. As we have seen, town markets and elements of money economy and even hired labour coexisted with the natural economy of feudalism ; the independent artisan and the local craft gild continued into the period that was predominantly characterized by the capitalist manufactory and the putting-out system ; while elements of the putting-out system and the small handicraft workshop continued into the late nineteenth century and even up to the present day. What might seem, however, to be particularly surprising about the persistence of the small firm to-day is the extent and the stubbornness of its survival in view of the fact that the quintessence of monopoly is its all-embracing character—that it succeeds in its aims in the degree that it can dominate the whole of its field. Our surprise may be qualified by two considerations. First, what is important here is not mere numbers of business units, but economic " weight " : that concentration of production (in the sense of control over output) will tend always to be much greater than a survey of the mere number of economic units suggests and that it is control over " key " spheres of industry and " key " lines of production that are of principal significance. Secondly, there are various ways in which a large concern, even if it does not control a major part of the output of an industry, may in fact exercise industrial leadership or dominance over the numerous small-scale independents that survive in apparent competition with it, by means of some industrial treaty or the influence of the large concern over some trade association or cartel, or by *liaisons* which the large concern has established with the banks, or simply from the fact that the threat of being driven to the wall, should they throw down a challenge to their stronger neighbour, may suffice to cause the smaller firms to accept the *de facto* leadership of the former. But even when these qualifications have been made, an element of surprise remains.

The facts of industrial concentration in the modern world are almost too familiar to need much emphasis here. In Britain, as is well known, this tendency was already a marked one prior to the First Great War, even if it operated less strongly than in Germany or America ; and as the Final Report of the Committee on Industry and Trade observed in the 1920's, " the information available shows a strong tendency, both in this and other industrial countries, for enterprises engaged in production to increase in average size, a tendency which shows no sign of reaching its limit ".[1] A well-known inquiry made by Sir Sydney Chapman and Professor Ashton in 1914 showed that in the cotton industry " the ' typical ' size of a spinning firm more than doubled between 1884 and 1911 ".[2] In 1884 very few spinning firms had more than 80,000 spindles, while in 1911 over one-third were of this size ; while at the lower end of the scale the proportion of firms owning 30,000 spindles or less had fallen between 1884 and 1911 from one-half to under one-third. In the manufacture of pig-iron " the average output capacity per undertaking, taking into account both the size of blast-furnaces and the number owned by each business ", more than doubled between 1882 and 1913, and nearly trebled between 1882 and 1924.[3] In 1926 twelve large groups (since reduced in number) were between them responsible for nearly half the pig-iron output and nearly two-thirds of the steel ; and in 1939 39 per cent. of iron and steel was produced by the three largest firms.[4] In British industry at large in 1935 about half the output and nearly half the employment was provided by large business units employing more than 1,000 persons each.[5] In Germany the proportion of collieries producing less than 500,000 tons a year fell from 72·7 per cent. in 1900 to 23·7 per cent. in 1928, while the proportion of collieries producing between half a million and a million tons rose correspondingly from 27·2 per cent. to 60·2 per cent.[6] Between 1913 and 1927 the output of German pig-iron furnaces in blast rose by approximately 70 per cent. per furnace[7] ; and by the latter date nearly three-quarters of the iron and steel output was accounted for by five leading producers.[8] In certain branches of the chemical industry there

[1] P. 176.
[2] *Journal of Royal Statistical Society*, April, 1914. In weaving, however, " the ' typical ' number of looms in a firm rose by less than 50 per cent." over the period.
[3] Committee on Industry and Trade, *Factors in Industrial and Commercial Efficiency*, 4.
[4] Comm. on Industry and Trade, *Survey of Metal Industries*, 33 ; H. Leak and A. Maizels paper to Ryl. Statistical Society, Feb. 20, 1945, reprinted in *Journal of the Royal Statistical Society*, vol. CVIII, Pt. II, 1945.
[5] *Ibid.* The number of such firms was 938. This figure probably *under*-estimates the degree of concentration of *control*, since many of the businesses which appear as independent units in these figures may come under the *de facto* control of other firms. The proportions relate to all firms employing more than ten workers.
[6] H. Levy, *Industrial Germany*, 26. [7] *Ibid.*, 57.
[8] Comm. on Industry and Trade, *Survey of Metal Industries*, 33.

was in several countries an unusually high degree of concentration approaching complete monopoly. " According to a quotation of the Dresdner Bank, in the German synthetic dyestuff industry in 1927–8 about 100 per cent. of the actual national production was controlled by the I.G. Farben, Imperial Chemical Industries Ltd. controlled about 40 per cent., in France the Établissement Kuhlmann about 80 per cent. of the national output.   Of the production of syr.thetic nitrogen the German trust was responsible for about 85 per cent. of the national output, while Imperial Chemical Industries controlled about 100 per cent., Établissement Kuhlmann about 30 per cent., the Montecatini trust in Italy about 60 per cent., and the E. J. Du Pont de Nemours concern in the U.S.A. a certainly dominant percentage of national production." [1]

In U.S.A. a more marked tendency towards concentration than in Britain was visible both before and after 1914.   Between 1899 and 1914 the index of output per establishment, according to a study of production in some sixty industries made by Mr. F. C. Mills, " reveals a clear tendency towards large-scale production, with a declining number of establishments, except between 1904 and 1909 ".   Again in the boom period between 1923 and 1929 there was " a drop of 6·2 per cent. in the number of establishments, with a gain of 20·5 per cent. in production per establishment ".   Over the whole thirty-year period between 1899 and 1929, while the number of establishments in the industries studied was " slightly higher " at the later date, the output per establishment was 198 per cent. greater ; while over the last decade of the three the number of establishments fell by nearly a fifth and output per establishment rose by more than two-thirds.   This author concludes that " integration and the concentration of production in establishments turning out constantly larger quantities of goods has proceeded more rapidly during the last decade [i.e. the '20's] than in any similar period we have covered ".[2]   This " definite tendency during the past three decades for the average size of manufacturing establishments to increase " (in the words of the Final Report of the Executive Secretary of the Temporary National Economic Committee) showed an " unusual increase " in the '30's ;[3] and over the whole period between 1914 and 1937 the average number of wage-earners per establishment rose by 35 to 38 per

[1] Levy, *op. cit.*, 66.   [2] F. C. Mills, *op. cit.*, 45, 300–1.
[3] Final Report of Exec. Secretary, T.N.E.C., 32.

cent., and the real volume of production per establishment by 80 to 85 per cent.[1]

Of the degree of integration of financial control in American business the most striking evidence is the much-quoted conclusion of the exhaustive study of American corporate wealth made by Messrs. Berle and Means. This showed that approximately a half of all non-banking corporate wealth in U.S.A. in the late '20's was controlled by no more than 200 companies; that these giant corporations had been growing between twice and three times as fast as all other non-financial corporations; and that, if the rate of growth of large corporations between 1909 and 1929 were maintained, it would take only forty years (and thirty years at the rate of growth of the years 1924–9) for all corporate activity, and practically all industrial activity, to be absorbed by these 200 giants.[2] More recently the Temporary National Economic Committee (a section of the Securities and Exchange Commission) have studied the same ground again, and have revealed that in these 200 companies one-half of all the dividends went to less than 1 per cent. of the shareholders.[3] In manufacturing industry some 28 per cent. of the total value of production (and 20 per cent. of the *net* value of output) was supplied by 50 companies, covering one-sixth of all wage-earners; while the largest 200 companies controlled 41 per cent. of total value produced (and 32 per cent. of the net value) and employed 26 per cent. of the wage-earners.[4] As Messrs. Berle and Means observe in summarizing their conclusions: " The rise of the modern corporation has brought a concentration of economic power which can compete on equal terms with the modern State . . . (and which) the future may see possibly even supersede it as the dominant form of social organization."

Yet at the same time there remained in Britain nearly 1,000 separate concerns in the coal-mining industry (even though some four-fifths of the output came from some 300 firms, each employing more than 1,000 persons). Both the cotton industry (especially its weaving section) and the woollen industry continued to be the preserve of the small firm. In cotton in the '20's there were between 800 and 900 spinning firms (no more than 230 of them vertically integrated so as to embrace weaving as well), and in weaving over 900 firms. Even in U.S.A. the

---

[1] T.N.E.C., Monograph No. 27, 4.
[2] *The Modern Corporation and Private Property, passim.*
[3] T.N.E.C., *Investigation of Concentration of Economic Power*, Monograph No. 29, 13.
[4] Final Report of Executive Secretary of T.N.E.C., 45–6.

average number of employees per establishment in the woollen industry was only 206 ; although this represented a doubling of the figure since 1899, accompanied by a decrease in the number of establishments.[1] In the British boot ánd shoe industry there are some 800 individual firms, employing on the average no more than 150 workers. In many types of engineering and woodworking the small unit predominates ; and despite the recent rise of some considerable joint-stock companies in the building industry, this trade remains chiefly the preserve of the small one-man business or partnership, in the shape of the local contracting or speculative builder.[2] In industry at large in Britain we meet the surprising fact that in " factory trades " the average number of employees per firm among those covered by the Census of Production of 1935 was only about 125 (and in " non-factory trades " about 172) ; that in the middle 1930's there were over 30,000 firms having between ten and a hundred workers each, covering between them about a fifth of all factory workers ; and that, in addition, there were probably another 130,000-odd firms in the " factory trades " (and a further 71,000-odd in " non-factory trades ") who employed no more than ten workers each, these dwarf enterprises in all giving employment to about half a million persons.[3] In this respect there is a contrast between Britain, on the one hand, and Germany and U.S.A., on the other, at least so far as the main industries are concerned. Compared with over 2,000 mines owned by more than 1,000 separate undertakings which existed in the British coal industry at the end of the '20's, there were in Germany 175 collieries owned by some seventy companies. The average annual output-capacity of British blast-furnaces in 1929 was only 48,000 tons, compared with 97,000 in Germany and 138,000 in U.S.A. Nevertheless, even in U.S.A. small firms with less than twenty workers compose more than nine-tenths of the total number of firms of all kinds and cover about a quarter of all employed workers.[4]

[1] Comm. on Industry and Trade, *Survey of Textile Industries*, 24–5, 257.
[2] The three largest firms in the building and contracting industry in 1939 included only 4 per cent. of all workers employed in the industry, in clothing industry only 13 per cent., in mining and quarries only 10 per cent. (H. Leak and A. Maizels, *op. cit.*).
[3] Fifth Census of Production, 1935, Final Summary Tables. The average number of workers per *establishment* was about 105. Of large firms in factory trades employing more than 1,000 workers each there were 649, covering some 1·6 million workers, or nearly a third of all factory workers. Of *establishments* with more than 1,000 there were 533, covering between a fourth and a fifth of all workers.
[4] Final Report of Executive Secretary of T.N.E.C. on *Concentration of Economic Power*, 298.

What seems to have emerged, therefore, over large sections of industry is a development of forms of monopolistic or quasi-monopolistic control over output and prices which permits the small concern to survive subject to surveillance and restriction in various ways. To organize small-scale units and co-ordinate their marketing policy has been the essential function of the Trade Association and the Cartel. In some cases this has occurred in industries where technical conditions have not been favourable to the large-scale unit, either because of technical backwardness (as in some British industries) or because of peculiarities in the application of technique to the manufacture of the type of commodity that is their concern. In other cases it has been a sort of compromise, possibly no more than temporary, between the giant firm and its smaller rivals, under which the dominance of the former over the marketing policy of the whole industry has been maintained. So far as this is the case, we may have the curious situation that the half-way house combines in itself the defects of the two extremes, while forfeiting their advantages, and at the same time actually encourages the preservation of the small concern. In so far as the obsolete type of industrial organization and technique is enabled to survive because the existing structure of industry is frozen by the blunting of competition and the clamping down on the industry of a system of output-quotas, progress is retarded, the difference between the highest cost and the lowest cost production-unit tends to be enhanced, and the advantage of concentrating production on the most efficient unit, which a completer type of monopoly might effect, is sacrificed.

Yet again, small firms may continue to thrive (and even be multiplied in number) in order to supply the needs of larger firms for special components or special lines, or to help out certain stages of production at periods of peak demand ; these small firms filling the rôle of sub-contractors to the large firms on a kind of modern putting-out system practised between large capitalists and small, as war experience has shown to be such an extensive feature of armament production. To the extent that these varying types of industrial relationship are found, the unevenness of development and of circumstances, and the divergence of interests within the ranks of capitalist business itself, are evidently much accentuated in the present age. Yet when all these variants have been listed, it remains true that there persist to this day important elements of competition of the nineteenth-century type—even if even here such competition is increasingly "imperfect" and at a good distance from the text-book type—both on the fringes and in the interstices of giant industry and also over some "autonomous" tracts of economic country that are by no means negligible in extent.

III

Among the novel features of Capitalism in its latest phase some commentators have stressed the rise of a new middle class ; and Mr. Durbin has even spoken of the "embourgeoisement" of the proletariat, with its Council houses and gardens and radio-sets and hire-purchase furniture, as a twentieth-century development which Marx and his school never foresaw.[1]   This emphasis is intended, presumably, to imply that latter-day Capitalism finds the class struggle mollified and acquires accordingly greater stability than it formerly had.[2]   It is certainly true that the requirements of modern industry have caused a growth of office staffs and of technical grades both absolutely and relatively, and have given these grades an importance in the productive process that had no counterpart in the days of more primitive technique.   Alongside a decline of the old type of skilled crafts-man in favour of the semi-skilled machine operator has gone the rise of a salariat and a new type of superior technician. Salary-earners in Great Britain have been estimated as numbering rather more than 4 million, or about one-fifth of the occupied population, in the early '30's and as receiving about a quarter of the national income ; this figure of rather more than 4 million showing an increase of about a third since 1911 (when they made up approximately one-sixth of the occupied population), most of this increase taking place between 1921 and 1928.[3]   It is also true, as we have seen, that the section of wage-earners who were fortunate enough to retain their employment through the crisis years improved their position, even while those in the depressed areas and the stricken trades suffered a grave worsen-ing.   But it does not follow that facts such as these have the significance that some writers have placed upon them.   The new stratum of technicians and office workers is in no way a

---

[1] *Politics of Democratic Socialism*, 107 seq.
[2] Mr. Durbin writes : "A society that is increasingly proletarian is a thing of the past. The society in which we live is increasingly bourgeois" (*ibid.*, 112).
[3] Colin Clark, *National Income and Outlay*, 38, 100–1 ; Durbin, *op. cit.*, 370–1.

middle class in the same sense as were the old master craftsmen of the manufacturing period of Capitalism—the sense in which Marx spoke of the middle class as dying out. The latter were men of some, if meagre, economic independence by virtue of being small owners and entrepreneurs. They constituted in-dividual economic units, in direct touch with the market, at times themselves employing the labour of others, and their pro-ductive activity was joined to means of production which they themselves possessed and controlled. Hence they occupied a special rôle in society as representatives of the petty mode of production. This type of " worker on own account " (to use our Census classification) represents to-day only some 6 per cent. of the occupied population ; and Mr. Colin Clark has estimated that the total of employers and independent workers combined showed a fall of 14 per cent. in the very period in the '20's when the number of salaried workers was increasing with particular rapidity. From this and from the fact that " the major part of the increase in the salaried population is in the higher category " of persons with more than £250 a year, Mr. Clark concludes that this increase may largely have represented a substitution of salaried employees for independent employers (presumably owing to the growth of joint-stock companies and the large firm, and a corresponding decline of the small business).[1] When we bear in mind that three-quarters of all salary earners before the war earned less than £250 a year, and hence were on the same income-level as better paid manual workers ; that between the wars these strata were afflicted by unemployment only a little less than skilled manual workers, and like manual workers increasingly became organized in trade unions ; and that approaching 90 per cent. of the occupied population are persons employed on a contract of service (from which they derive all but a small fraction of their income), there seems little ground for questioning the overwhelmingly proletarian character of present-day society in Britain—unless it be questioned by those who identify " proletariat " with " lumpen-proletariat ", and by those who assume a wage-earner's class status to be forthwith transformed if his clothes are not threadbare, if he chances to draw a pound or two a year as interest on savings bonds or if he digs potatoes on an allotment.

A further development in modern Capitalism to which a good deal of attention has been paid in recent discussion is the

[1] *Op. cit.*, 38-40, 100-1.

rise of what has variously been termed " absentee Capitalism " and " the divorce of ownership from control ". It often used to be maintained that the spread of the joint-stock company had exercised a democratizing influence on the ownership and control of business, giving the small saver a stake in the business and putting the entrepreneur of small capital on a more equal footing with the wealthy entrepreneur. But of any such influence there is very little sign. On the contrary, not only does the growth of the company system seem to have strongly favoured the concentration of ownership rather than retarded it,[1] but the company system has served to encourage a high degree of concentration of *de facto* control. Modern forms of company organization have provided an opportunity for the multiplication of a *rentier* element, drawing their share in profits and possessing legal titles of ownership to portions of the equipment of industry but in fact quite removed from (and often quite innocent of) industry. As holders of mere titles, negotiable titles, to ownership, their economic rôle is a purely passive one, and being separated from the active process of production they are generally impotent to exercise any control over it even if they so desire. Certain features of joint-stock company procedure, such as proxy-voting, make it unlikely that the general run of smaller shareholders could exercise any influence on policy ; and sometimes they are deliberately excluded by the division of shares into classes, some voting and others non-voting, and by the concentration of the majority (or a decisive fraction) of the former in the hands of a minority-interest which dominates policy. When such features are combined with financial devices like the voting trust or the pyramiding of holding companies, the effective control exercised by the overwhelming majority of shareholders is still further reduced. The result is to concentrate *de facto* control over policy much more closely than would appear from inspection of legal titles to ownership ; to set up from time to time a conflict of interest between *rentier* and managing group ; to reinforce the tendency for primarily financial motives (e.g. concerning short-term changes in capital values) to dominate business policy ; and moreover so to transform the content, by contrast with the legal form, of property-

---

[1] Cf. J. Steindl in " Capital, Enterprise and Risk " in *Oxford Economic Papers*, No. 7, March, 1945, 40–3. Mr. Steindl's conclusion is : " The outstanding effect of the introduction of the joint-stock system is the strengthening of the superiority of the big entrepreneur. Far from favouring a more even distribution of controlling ownership of enterprises, it accelerated the process of concentration of this ownership."

rights as to deal the *coup de grâce* to the ideology of private property which has traditionally held a leading place in the *apologia* of Capitalism.[1] Considerations of power become intermingled with considerations of profit in this new epoch of " economic empires ".

Such *penumbra* of twentieth-century Capitalism have no mean importance for the history of our time. Yet here again certain interpretations have been placed upon them which are very ill-supported by the facts. Some have rushed to conclude that the divorce is so complete that control of policy is no longer vested in capital at all, and that Capitalism has thereby ceased to be Capitalism, properly so-called. One writer has even discovered a " managerial revolution " as a world-wide phenomenon of our epoch. This kind of interpretation, where it is not facile speculation, seems to rest on a misreading of some of the data disclosed by the study of Messrs. Berle and Means. The Temporary National Economic Committee has pointed out that the cases of pure " management control " (as Messrs. Berle and Means termed it) where control was vested in persons who owned no capital (or a negligible amount of it) were a distinct minority of the whole ; and that, while control by a few individuals, and by a small fraction of the share-capital, was very frequent, the persons who exercised this control were in most cases substantial shareholders. " In about 140 of the 200 corporations the blocks of stock in the hands of one interest group were large enough to justify the classification of these companies as more or less definitely under ownership control " ; and the 2,500-odd officers and directors of these 200 largest corporations owned between them over 2 milliard dollars of capital in their respective companies, this sum being largely concentrated in the hands of the 250 men who occupied the decisive executive positions.[2] The divorce between ownership and control, in other words, while it is of outstanding importance, is no more than partial,

---

[1] Cf. " Physical control over the instruments of production has been surrendered in ever-growing degree to centralized groups who manage property in bulk, supposedly but by no means necessarily for the benefit of the security holders. . . . There has resulted the dissolution of the old atom of ownership into its component parts, control and beneficial ownership. This dissolution of the atom of property destroys the very foundation on which the economic order of the past three centuries has rested. . . . The explosion of the atom of property destroys the basis of the old assumption that the quest for profits will spur the owner of industrial property to its effective use " (Berle and Means, *op. cit.*, 7–9).

[2] T.N.E.C. Monograph No. 29, *Distribution of Ownership in the 200 Largest Non-Financial Corporations*, 56–7, 104 seq. Also cf. P. Sweezy on " The Illusion of the Managerial Revolution " in *Science and Society* (N.Y.), vol. VI, No. 1.

and it follows the lines of a division between numerous small owners and a small number of large.

An aspect of the modern concentration of economic power to which this type of recent discussion has given prominence is the inevitable distortion that is given thereby to the operation of political democracy. This " new baronage " of an era of " economic empires "—" usurping the sovereignty of the people " in Mr. Henry Wallace's words [1]—is no mere rhetorical phrase. That capital, through its influence on the Press and other organs of opinion and on party funds, can purchase political influence and frequently convert both local and national governments into its mouthpieces has for long been a commonplace, even if its full implications for political theory have too seldom been appreciated. Regarding tariff and colonial policies and even diplomatic policy abroad, examples of such influence have been so numerous as to leave little doubt as to where the real power over such matters ultimately resides. Of the decades immediately preceding the war of 1914 Professor H. Feis has written that " the habits and structure of British society contributed to foster a national harmony of action [between finance and politics]. In the small circles of power, financial power was united with political power, and held mainly the same ideas. Partners of the important issue houses sat in the House of Commons or among the Lords, where they were in easy touch with the Ministry. . . . As highly organized industry and commerce attained a steadily growing part in deciding Great Britain's political course, the demand increased that the government use the power of the State to aid British industry to secure openings and contracts abroad, and in response to the demand, the government yielded." [2]   Thus in the case of China the British Government used threats of force to secure concessions for British companies ; in the case of Greece it " undertook the direct support of an organized British group, controlling a vast investment, against a small republic " ; while with regard to Africa " the Colonial Office was geared to forces stronger than itself " and " government and private enterprise became often part of one mechanism ".[3]   Needless to say, such conditions were not peculiar to Great Britain in the decades of Imperialism. Of Germany the same author remarks on the " close partnership of effort between the government and the banks " and of the

---

[1] Speech at Chicago, Sept. 11, 1943,
[2] *Europe the World's Banker, 1870–1914*, 87, 96.   [3] *Ibid.*, 98–9, 102, 111.

government as " the driving power in much of German foreign investment " ; while in the case of France, " for railway and banking opportunities in the Balkan States entrusted to French capital French diplomacy worked in a half-dozen capitals ".[1]

But it is in its dealings with labour that this monstrous regiment of concentrated economic power is most in evidence, and often shows itself as a dominion that operates, not through, but independently of the machinery of government. In non-proletarian walks of life the influence of capital over political life may appear as no more than occasionally obtrusive. We now know something of the tyrannies that were exercised over the lives of workpeople in this country in the early days of trade unionism, even if at the time such things were accepted as so much part of a traditional and hallowed order of things as to arouse little comment. We now know of the tyrannies of the tommy-shop and of truck, of the employer-owned house and the eviction of employees who took action displeasing to their masters, of a master's power to victimize a workman for his opinions or his activities by depriving him of his employment and black-listing him among fellow employers ; of the bias both of the law and of its interpretation by the local magistrates' bench, which for long virtually deprived the working class of the right of association and the right of independent political assembly. With the victories of trade unionism in more recent times in the fight for *de facto* recognition and for legal sanction for collective bargaining, these cruder forms of tyranny of Capital over Labour have largely, though not completely, in England receded into the past ; and attempts at retaliation against the newly-won rights of trade unionism by the fostering of company unions have provided on the whole a record of failure, even in the mining industry after the defeat of the miners in the stubborn struggle of 1926.

Outside the countries of Fascism, it is in America that fullest evidence is to be found in recent times of the powers exerted by large business corporations to deprive workpeople of their rights of association and assembly and opinion, and, after the passing of the National Labour Relations Act of 1935, to frustrate the aims of the Federal legislature. The story of this has been told in voluminous records of a Senate committee of investigation : the La Follette Committee. In parts the story has quite a mediæval flavour with its private bands of

[1] *Ibid.*, 144, 187.

condottieri, kept by big corporations for use against their own employees ; with the interpenetration of business personnel and the local administration ; with its *maffia*-like methods and the employment of private espionage, bribery and thuggery on an ambitious scale. The National Association of Manufacturers, a powerful federation of 200 employers' associations in various parts of U.S.A. and in various branches of industry, organized a nation-wide campaign to defeat the purposes of the National Labour Relations Act, which had established the legal right of trade unions, if sufficiently representative of their trade, to negotiate on behalf of their members. In the Los Angeles district the local Association organized firms to refuse to entertain any dealings with unions, bringing pressure to bear (e.g. through their bankers) upon employers unwilling to come into line, ran a special bureau for the supply of strike-breakers and established liaison with the police for purpose of espionage among their employees. " The most influential business and financial interests in Los Angeles ", says the Report, " have deliberately attempted to sabotage the national labour policy of collective bargaining as expressed in the National Labour Relations Act. . . . They engaged in a series of organized conspiracies to destroy labor's civil liberties. . . . They concluded alliances with the local press, local police, local law-enforcement officials. Behind their illegal and anti-social policy they concentrated economic and political power that defied any local application of the law and custom of the nation. . . . Organized conspiratorial interference with collective bargaining included the mass application of the common anti-union devices such as labor espionage, the use of professional strike-breakers, the use of industrial munitions, the blacklist, discriminatory discharge and a host of similar weapons. . . . Behind this vast and powerful movement stood the leaders of business and industry, titular and real, the banking and financial groups, leaders of the local press and until recently many of the public officials." In all this California by no means stood alone : it was " but a symbol of many other areas in various parts of the Nation ".[1]   At the same time in the country districts of California

[1] Report on *Violations of Free Speech and Rights of Labor : Employers' Associations and Collective Bargaining in California* (1943), Pt. VI, 792–3, 1019–1021. A somewhat similar story is told in another part of the Report of the Cleveland Industries, where, in defiance of Federal law, " the labor relations policy of the Associated Industry is demonstrated to be productive of strife, bitterness, strikes and industrial warfare of the most ruthless and relentless sort " (Report, *Labor Policies of Employers' Associations*, Pt. 2, 185).   The Bethlehem Steel Corporation is accused of " prefer(ring)

" groups similar to the Associated Farmers [which were financed by big business interests] . . . have proceeded with impunity to perpetuate a system of tyranny which should be a cause of national shame and concern " in the attempt to smash incipient trade unionism among farm workers, to the accompaniment of organized " red scares " and the use of gunmen, espionage and violence.[1]

Leading American firms, such as the Republic Steel Corporation, the U.S. Steel Corporation, Carnegie's, Bethlehem Steel and the Goodyear Tyre Company spent large sums on the purchase of munitions and made a practice of employing a corps of armed guards for use against strikers and trade union organizers. These " industrial munitions " consisted, not only of revolvers, army rifles, sawed-off and repeating shot-guns, but also of army-type machine-guns and " prodigious quantities of gas and gas equipment ", including gas-guns and gas-grenades " entirely unsuited for use except in carrying out offensive action of a military character against large crowds of people ". Industrial corporations, indeed, were purchasers of tear-gas " in quantities many times greater than those required by the police departments of some of our largest cities ". The plea that such munitions were intended for purely defensive use is rebutted by the fact that they were generally used against picket-lines outside the works boundaries, and not against crowds invading the plant ; and in specific cases of their use, which were investigated by the Commission, " there was no threat of damage to the plant at any time ".[2] Mr. La Follette himself in two summary interim reports speaks of the " usurpation of police powers by privately paid ' guards ' and ' deputies ', often hired from detec-

to settle industrial disputes, not in a peaceful fashion through negotiation, but by means of fostering municipal corruption and vigilante movements in the city of Johnstown " (*ibid.*, Pt. 3, 144).
[1] Report on *Employers' Associations in California*, Pt. VIII (1944), esp. pp. 1375–80, 1617.
[2] Report on *Violations of Free Speech, etc. : Industrial Munitions*, 185–7, 123. The Report concludes that the cases investigated " clearly demonstrate the invalidity of any claim that employers need arms as protection against the arms of their employees ". In a notorious case of the Little Steel Strike of 1937, " the whole course of the strike does not exhibit a single instance of the use of industrial munitions to protect plant property from invasion or attack " (*ibid.*, 124). Cases are also cited where " police officials are armed by one side of an industrial dispute for the purpose of having them use the arms against the other ". " Approximately one-half of the sales of gas weapons in the country goes to industrial employers " and " there are no recorded sales to labor unions " (*ibid.*, 188, 185). Two-thirds of the gas-shells purchased by one company were long-range shells, not short-range. In the 1934 longshoremen's strike at San Francisco the gas used by the local police to break the strike was paid for out of the employers' funds (*ibid.*, 72, 104).

tive agencies, many with criminal records ", as being " a general practice in many parts of the country " ; of " areas where no union officer can go without risk of personal violence " ; and of the " menace to democratic government " inherent in the " willingness of great business men's organizations . . . to foment the means whereby pecuniarily interested parties can become a law unto themselves ".[1]

The use to which these " industrial munitions " were put is fully illustrated in the record of these private armies. " Rough shadowing " (or the shadowing of an individual at all times and all places so as to amount to intimidation) [2] and the planting of spies in every labour union, with the intent not merely of espionage, but of disrupting the organization and even acting as *agents provocateurs*,[3] were among the less menacing of their activities. They engaged in assaults upon individuals, the beating-up and shooting of union organizers, the breaking up of meetings and demonstrations, and the wrecking of trade union offices.[4] The use of private police systems is announced by one of the Reports to have led to " private usurpation of public authority, corruption of public officials ; oppression of large groups of citizens under the authority of the State ; and perversion of representative government ".[5] Those employed as company police were often " men with criminal records ",[6] and the professional strike-breaking gangs were " for the most part a specialized kind of ruffian . . . well-versed in violence and sometimes a gangster ".[7] In a town dominated by Republic Steel " civil liberties and the rights of labour were suppressed by company police. Union organizers were driven out of town ".[8] In certain coal company towns in Harlan County, not only were stores and houses company-owned but there were company-gaols ; while company guards, who " persecuted residents of the town and visiting labour organizers ", constituted " the only law-enforcement officers ".[9] Throughout the county " private gangs terrorized

---

[1] Report dated May 12, 1936, and Interim Report dated Jan. 5, 1938.
[2] Report on *Private Police Systems : Harlan County* (1939), 53.
[3] Report on *Industrial Espionage* (1937), 63.
[4] Report on *Industrial Munitions*, 80–4, 86–7, 104, 109–10 ; Report on *Private Police Systems : Harlan County, passim.* One case of wrecking of union offices was by employees of the Goodyear Company ; in 1935 at a plant owned by Republic Steel armoured cars were used to break up the picket-line and union organizers were assaulted and severely injured by private police of Republic Steel.
[5] *Ibid.*, 214.   [6] *Ibid.*, 211.
[7] Report on *Strike-breaking Services* (1939), 136.
[8] Report on *Private Police Systems : Harlan County*, 211.
[9] *Ibid.*, 208, also 48–52.

union members, . . . acting as auxiliaries to the force of privately paid deputy sheriffs ", and operated " a reign of terror directed against miners and union organizers ". Deputy-sheriffs and " thug gangs " kept by the coal companies " repeatedly fired on union organizers, from ambush on public highways, in open country and in their own homes. They kid-napped and assaulted union officers and dynamited the homes of union organizers ", while at the same time they " subverted and corrupted the office of high sheriff . . . through many extraordinary financial favours ", as they did also the Common-wealth Attorney and a County Judge.[1] Yet this reign of terror was directed against workers who were simply " exercising the rights guaranteed by Section 7(a) of the National Industrial Recovery Act ". Between the methods of Fascism and the " normal " labour policies of powerful capitalist concerns a line is apparently hard to draw. The use of such methods, even were they exceptional (which the American evidence suggests that they were far from being), is a witness to the immense and irresponsible power residing in modern business units and to the constant menace of " a concentration of economic power which can compete on equal terms with the modern State . . . and may even supersede it ". When business policy takes the step of financing and arming a mass political movement to capture the machinery of government, to outlaw opposing forms of organization and suppress hostile opinion, we have merely a further and logical stage beyond the measures we have been describing.

IV

We have several times had occasion to observe the growing obsession of capitalist industry in its latest phase with the limita-tion of markets : an obsession which had little parallel in the nineteenth century, except in the years of hesitancy during the Great Depression. This is manifestly connected with the fact that the expansion of consumption and of opportunities for profitable investment have come to lag chronically behind the growth of the productive forces. But for this obsession there seems also to have been a deeper reason connected with the nature of modern technique. That certain of the technical changes in the productive forces which have characterized the

[1] Report on *Private Police Systems : Harlan County*, 209-11 ; also 88-111.

twentieth century, and especially the period between wars, have had a significance much greater than was noticed at the time is now coming to be widely recognized. The possibility that they may have effected certain radical alterations in the whole setting of the economic problem, and in the reactions of capitalist entrepreneurs to it, has more rarely received attention.

These technical changes of recent years have had a number of features in common, which have come to be popularly referred to under the vague designation of " mass production ".[1] A characteristic of many of them has been the introduction (aided to some extent by electricity as a tractive power) of continuous-flow methods, by which the movement of the product through its successive stages is governed by a single machine-process. " A basic feature of much of our modern mass production is the serialization of machines and processes in such a way as to reduce handling to a minimum and arrange the assembly and other processing operations along a continuously or intermittently moving conveyor, with the processes highly subdivided and standardized ".[2] In this way successive stages, which previously were separate acts of production loosely co-ordinated, are firmly integrated. Production becomes continuous instead of intermittent.

Not only does this transform and extend the division of labour by requiring a more intricate subdivision of operations between the various stages of the production-flow, but it also carries the subordination of work-operations to the machine process an important stage further, so that little trace remains of the initiative of the old-style artisan or craftsman as an independent productive agent (governing the *tempo* of production by his own work-movements), and in the extreme case the worker becomes simply a machine-minder. But while from one aspect the worker appears as more completely a " slave to the machine "—an aspect which certain critics of industrialism have stressed, indicting " the Machine Age " rather than Capitalism as cause of the degradation of human beings—from

[1] " Mass production " methods, as the term is usually employed, started in America in the first decade of the present century ; but in British engineering they were not adopted at all extensively until after 1918. One writer has said that it " started, as so many great movements have done, almost by accident. It was not started originally as a means of reducing production costs. It was tried as a means of greatly increasing output-rate " (L. E. Ord, *Secrets of Industry*, 15). (When he speaks here of production costs, this author is presumably referring to prime costs. An increased output-rate generally, of course, has a reduction in total unit-cost as its consequence.)

[2] H. Jerome, *Mechanization in Industry*, 395.

another aspect the worker under modern technique acquires a new kind of independence, at least potentially. From being " an extension of the workers' own fingers " the machine has become a robot productive agent which all but supplants human limbs and fingers, and human labour has become (or is in the process of becoming) its overseer. Thereby the workers collectively tend to acquire a new sense of power as governors of the limbs of a machine-process which is subordinate to their own limbs and purposes. The subjective, or active and conscious, rôle of labour in production receives a new emphasis ; only now, not in association with individual possession or pride of a distinctive craft, but in a novel collective setting, where man sees himself as brain and nervous system to machinery as part of a co-ordinated human team. The potentialities, at least, are discernible for a new status and dignity of man as a producer, different in kind, but no meaner than that of the old-time individual craftsman : potentialities which, the more they contrast with present actualities of social status, must profoundly influence the psychology of labour and quicken its aspirations. Man as technician in the production process increasingly stands in opposition to labour-power as a commodity, which is the bases on which Capitalism rests.

In many ways more important than these new forms of the division of labour and of the workers' relation to the mechanical productive forces is the closer unity given to the productive process, of which each constituent part has to be closely geared to the rest with a discipline that is something akin to that which co-ordinates the separate instruments of an orchestra. Production has to be a vertically balanced process and to observe a common rhythm, a disturbance of which at any point quickly disrupts the whole. The demands of this balanced process often extend beyond the boundaries of what was previously a separate enterprise, and involve the vertical integration under one control of what were once autonomous units and even the geographical association in one place of previously dispersed stages of production. Of this newer type of integrated continuous production-flow there are varying examples, each with peculiarities which distinguish its character from that of analogous cases. In many branches of heavy chemicals we find a most complete form of mechanical co-ordination of successive processes as a virtually single and autonomous technical whole. In the metal industries we find the continuous strip-mill or billet-mill or universal beam-mill and the modern association in a complex integrated unit of blast-furnaces, coking-plant, steel-furnaces and rolling-mills. In engineering we have the continuous assembly-belt in the manufacture of motor-vehicles and aircraft, and analogous to it (if with more weakly marked characteristics) the conveyor-belt system to be found in other finishing industries such as the clothing industry. " A modern factory ", it has been said, " producing automobiles, sewing machines, clocks or shoes, is like a river, the various elements *flowing* like tributaries from the several departments and merging smoothly into the stream of finished production which comes from the assembly floor." [1] In such forms we witness the highest development of production as a unitary mechanical team-process—of what Engels termed " social production "—by contrast with the atomized individual production of the " manufactory " with which Capitalism began. Even after the industrial revolution, factory-industry retained much of the character of this earlier phase out of which it had come, and continued to do so throughout a major part, at least, of the nineteenth century. For example, in lathe-work in engineering or mule-spinning in textiles, each operative at his lathe or each minder with his team of mules is largely a unit-process, the speed of which is governed by the individual operative and which can be closed down or started up independently of others. An important result of this was that the output of the factory as a whole could be varied within very wide limits both by changes in the number of such individual units that were working and by changes in the independent *tempo* of each unit. But in the degree that these relics of the older individual forms of production give place to the most recent technique, this possibility begins to disappear. Output can no longer be varied in this simple and continuous manner. Output is dictated by the capacity of the unified machine-process. It can be zero if the machinery is stopped, or it can be equal to the normal capacity of the process to yield its flow ; but it cannot (or cannot without difficulties which had no parallel in an earlier age) be intermediate between the two.

In the picture which economists have traditionally constructed of the working of economic processes discontinuities of supply and of cost-conditions have been regarded as exceptions, or as covering too small an area to be important relatively to the scale on which things were being viewed. Discontinuities, whether due to large and indivisible [1] units of plant or to elements of " joint supply ", have been regarded as exceptions ; so that theorems have been constructed on the assumption that the economic world is characterized by continuous variation. The significance of the kind of technical innovations that we have been describing is that technical indivisibilities and elements of " joint demand " and " joint supply ", imparting rigidity into the system of economic relationships (reducing, for example, the possibilities of substitution), are considerably enlarged in importance, whether they apply to components or to productive-agents or to final products. Moreover, rigidities imposed by technical conditions apply, not only to successive stages in the production-process, or to such things as by-products, but also to the output-flow of the plant, or congeries of plants taken as a whole. It is, no doubt, rare to find this rigidity absolute : to find that it is physically impossible to vary the size of the plant itself or the rate of output of the plant once in operation. But to the extent that the production-process becomes a unified whole, rather than a collection of atomic units, there is imposed at least a minimum size below which a plant cannot fall ; and to the extent that fixed or overhead costs are increased while direct or prime (or variable) costs are simultaneously decreased, the practicability of varying output from a given plant (e.g. by staffing the plant with a smaller labour-force) is at the same time reduced. Technical change in the past has generally had the tendency to raise the ratio of fixed to prime costs ; but a mere change in this ratio does not necessarily alter the manner in which output is determined in face of a given state of demand. What seems to be novel about the kind of technical developments of which we have been speaking is that they actually reduce (both absolutely and relatively) the types of expense that can properly be classed as direct costs by including labour as an integral part of the unitary machine process, thereby converting wages into a kind of overhead (in the sense of a cost that will not be reduced by a reduction of output).[2] If direct

[1] In the sense that the plant (or some part of it) is, for all practical purposes, a minimum unit, which cannot be reduced in size.

[2] This is true if the workers are paid on time-rates (as tends to be common on production methods of this type, since the rate of output is controlled by the machine and not by the individual operative, and the employer has accordingly no motive to put his workers on piece-rates). Where, however, the workers are paid on a piece-rate basis, the earnings of the workers will fall, if output is reduced, down to the level of the basic minimum time-rate which actually or virtually accompanies most payment-by-results systems.

It will, of course, generally be possible to reduce output by reducing the " feed "

(prime) costs are reduced sufficiently, they may well become a negligible influence on the output-decisions of a firm. Moreover, the very change in the technical situation which converts wages into a kind of overhead at the same time enlarges the size of that category of costs which can be avoided by a complete closing down of the plant (or of the particular unit-process), but which cannot be substantially altered by any reduction of output falling short of this. In other words, these latter are costs which disappear when output is zero, but will exist as a fixed sum for any positive level of output. This type of cost corresponds, I believe, to what Mr. R. F. Kahn has christened " running overhead costs ". In the situation of which we are speaking, the only way in which the employer can secure any appreciable reduction of his wage-bill is by stopping the machine-process altogether ; so that the whole (or virtually the whole) of his wage-bill may become in this sense a " running overhead cost ". The existence of " running overheads " that are large relatively to direct costs and to total costs will mean that, even if it is *physically* possible to vary the rate of the production-flow, such variation may nevertheless be *economically* impracticable ; since any reduction of output (in face, for example, of a fall of demand) as soon as it reduced net receipts (i.e. gross receipts less direct costs) below " running overheads " will make a complete closing down of production the preferable alternative. In the extreme case [1] there will be no intermediate

of raw material into the machine-process, or by slowing the rate at which the machine-process moves. Thereby there will be saving on expenditure on materials. But the extent to which the number of distinct operations to be performed, and hence the number of operatives, can be reduced will tend to be very limited, short of complete reorganization of the whole process. Changes in the number of operatives will probably be limited to the possibility (if the rate at which the machine-process moves is slowed down substantially) of one operative taking over what were previously two distinct operations (e.g. on an assembly-line) : a possibility which is not likely to be very extensive since a fundamental principle of continuous-flow production is that the time taken by each unit-operation should be equal, to avoid interruption of the flow. Even if the possibility is extensive, the number of intermediate positions between zero output and full-capacity output will be very small. Moreover, unless the change of output is expected to continue for a time, an employer will be unwilling to resort to such " doubling " of operations, since, once he has discharged operatives who have specialized on one of the pair of operations that are now " doubled ", the difficulty of obtaining them again may be a barrier against subsequent expansion of the rate of output.

It has been maintained that one result of mass-production methods has been to reduce the ratio of " unproductive " to " productive " workers, thereby effecting an economy of overhead costs. The reason suggested is the reduction of " paper work " (L.C. Ord, *op. cit.*, 34, 117–18). But this does not invalidate the statement made above that the wages of " productive " workers cease to be a direct cost variable with output.

[1] The extreme case will be where " running overheads " are equal to net receipts at full capacity working (the price being taken as given by the degree of monopoly

level of output that is practicable between full-capacity output and zero output.

It would be absurd, of course, to suppose that this situation is at all frequently found in its extreme form. Nor can it be said that the tendency towards it is common to all industry. But over important spheres of industry, and especially in some industries such as the chemical industry which show promise of being among the leading industries of the future, something approaching this situation seems to have been the outcome of the technical development of recent decades : developments which are themselves so largely children of electrical power and of modern industrial chemistry.

In the case of iron and steel, particularly in the modern type of integrated plant, we can find striking examples of this in some, though not in all, branches. In the case of the blast-furnace we have the indivisibility of the furnace as a unit : a unit which (for efficient operation) is nowadays of a considerable size. Either it is worth keeping in blast or it is not ; and although a furnace may be worked more or less slowly by varying the amount of air that is blown into the stack, this possibility of varying the pace is no more than a limited one, and the labour required to tend the furnace is not appreciably altered thereby. True, a plant usually consists of several furnaces ; and it might seem as though output could be fairly easily varied, with a proportionate variation of cost, by altering the number of furnaces in blast. In practice, however, this is seldom practicable except in cases where furnaces are of small capacity and the whole plant is large enough to include a considerable number of such furnaces, operating side by side. In particular, the existence of large stopping-and-starting costs militates against the use of this method of varying output and makes for rigidity in face of anything but changes in demand which are very large or are expected to be of long duration. In blast-furnaces " stopping or starting may be costly and stopping may occasion serious deterioration of part of the unit ". Moreover, it is often considered " desirable to have several furnaces supply iron to the mixer in a steelworks to ensure uniformity ".[1] In the case of coke-ovens these factors

in relation to direct costs). This is unlikely to be the case unless *all* overheads are " running overheads " and hence is extremely unlikely to be found as a normal case in practice. But there may be approximations to it.

[1] D. L. Burn, *Economic History of Steelmaking*, 521, 522. Mr. Burn adds : " Blast-furnace linings are not necessarily hurt by stopping, but they may be, and the process of stopping is prolonged and costly."

which make for output-rigidity are even more in evidence. " Silica linings are ruined by cooling, hence continuity of work is essential " ; and although to a limited extent it is possible to reduce output by reducing the pace, " the labour force remains almost unchanged " and total labour-costs are nearly the same for the smaller output as for the larger.[1] By contrast, in open-hearth steel furnaces, since stopping-and-starting costs are not appreciable and furnaces are customarily stopped at week-ends in any case, output can be fairly easily adjusted at any time by taking off a furnace ; and in rolling-mills the usual method of meeting changes in demand is by changing the number of working shifts.

An additional influence which makes for rigidity in the output of a modern integrated iron and steel plant is the existence of joint products, and moreover the use of the joint product of one process as an essential constituent of another process ; as, for example, the use of blast-furnace gas for heating the steel-furnaces or the basing of an electric power plant, serving the steel plant and associated works, on blast-furnace gas as fuel. Hence the scale of output at one point in a complex integrated plant cannot be changed without affecting the output at other points ; the output-flow not merely of different stages but of different products in the complex plant will be geared together. Similar considerations again apply to the chemical industry, which has been called by one writer " the industry *par excellence* of by-products and joint production ".[2] As the same writer has said : " In case the entire by-product is disposed of within the combine itself (for instance, when the mines, steelworks and rolling mills of the integrated works are supplied with energy from the furnaces), it is impossible to curtail the production of the principal commodity if it is coupled with the generation of energy. Thus in this case the production of pig-iron cannot be reduced without cutting off the by-product ' energy ' so indispensable for the operation of the whole complex of works." [3] The possibility of variation is somewhat greater than this writer

[1] D. L. Burn, *Economic History of Steelmaking*, 522. Mr. Burn quotes figures to show that labour cost per ton would be almost double if the output of " a modern battery of ovens fell by one half ".

[2] Von Beckerath, *Modern Industrial Organization*, 80.

[3] *Ibid.*, 80–1. Cf. also : " If we consider a steel firm, the rolling mill, the soaking pits or reheating furnaces, the coking plant, the blast-furnaces, have been designed in such a way that their output balances when working at full capacity. At that capacity the plant will be highly efficient. But if for some reason it becomes necessary to produce at 30 per cent. less than full capacity, the whole plant will be at sixes and sevens " (E. A. G. Robinson, *Structure of Competitive Industry*, 95).

implies, owing to the possibility of varying the ratio of pig-iron to scrap in the steel-furnace. But this variation is usually practicable only over a comparatively restricted range, and there remains substantial truth in the statement that the output-policy of a complex production unit of the present day, whether metallurgical or chemical, tends to be determined within fairly narrow limits, once the scale and lay-out of the plant have been established and the original investment has been made. At any rate, the changes attendant upon modern technique have robbed those industries of much of the output-flexibility of the economic text-books, and have caused technique increasingly to dictate to the makers of economic decisions.

So far as the output of a whole industry is concerned (as distinct from the output of an individual plant), this tendency to reduce the range of output-variation is reinforced by the growing prevalence, as specialization develops, of what may be termed " one-firm industries ", or rather " one-plant industries ". The meaning of an industry is something to which economists have been unsuccessful in attaching any consistent definition ; and it would seem that any clear-cut definition is from the nature of the case impossible. In popular speech the word industry is usually taken to mean a broad class of similar products, embracing numerous plants and firms. Thus iron and steel is customarily spoken of as an industry ; and sometimes one even meets a reference to a conglomerate entity entitled " the metal industry ". But for many of the economist's purposes a much narrower definition than this is necessary, and logical consistency requires him to draw its boundaries round the production of a separate commodity which has a separate market, in the sense that other similar products are not in practice regarded as perfect substitutes for it. The more one approaches to this latter, and narrower, definition of an industry, the more is it likely (if production is efficiently organized) that this particular " commodity " or " line " will be the product, not of several firms, but of one specialized plant (or section of a complex plant). To the extent that this is so, monopoly in the supply of distinguishable commodities will be more common, and competition between numerous firms serving the same market less common, than would appear at first sight when industry is more widely defined and when the homogeneity of a wide and varied range of products is stressed rather than their heterogeneity.

In considering the mechanism of adjustment of output and

price to demand, economists have generally focused their attention on three main variables : firstly, the *number* of firms (or
plants) in an " industry " ; secondly, the *size* of each plant ;
thirdly, the amount of " prime factors " (labour and materials)
that are combined with the " fixed factors " in each plant at any
time—or the " output load " of an individual plant. To the
extent that a particular type of product is the monopoly of a
single plant, the first method of variation of the output of an
industry will be excluded.[1]   The second type of variation is only
possible over a period long enough for the reconstruction of the
plant to be undertaken ; and its possibility even in the long run
will be reduced in so far as technique imposes a limit (owing
to indivisibilities) upon the number of sizes of plant that it is
practicable to choose. The third type of variation, as we have
seen, tends also to be much more restricted to-day than formerly
by certain features of modern technical methods. With such
important elements of discontinuity at each of these levels, it
might seem as though the nice adjustments of revenues to costs
at a margin, in terms of which economic theory has come to
state the economic problem—moreover to state it with sufficient
generality to apply to any type of economic system—have a
diminishing degree of relevance ; and the economic situation,
and the crucial forces moulding it, have a different shape from
what has been traditionally assumed.

The consequences of these new developments in the technical
situation are various, and certain of them seem to be more far-
reaching than might initially be supposed. Firstly, they would
appear to increase the extent to which any important changes
in technique and in industrial structure have to take place by
revolutionary leaps rather than by a gradual succession of small

[1] It may be objected that the smaller degree of variability in this case is purely
formal, being due simply to a narrowing of the definition of an industry. But it
contains an implication for economic theory of crucial importance. This is that
variability is relegated to a sphere which falls *outside* the territory of *particular demand
curves*, and is concerned with the question of *how many commodities* (or how many varieties within a commodity-group) shall be produced. The latter is, in a sense, an
arbitrary element in any system of economic analysis (whether of particular or
general equilibrium). Like the question of " new commodities ", to satisfy " new
wants ", it is generally governed by the initiative of producers and not by consumers'
choice (since consumers in practice seldom have simultaneously before them, to choose
between, the larger assortment of commodities, at the prices appropriate to the
more varied production, and the smaller assortment, at prices appropriate to more
standardized production—even if under pure competition this alternative *may* be
presented if one competitor takes the risk of specializing and offering a standardized
commodity at a cheapened price in rivalry with higher-priced variety).   It is not a
matter, therefore, that can be simply treated as part of the mechanism by which
supply is regarded as adapting itself to a *given* pattern of demand.

adaptations, thereby increasing at the same time the danger of the ossification of an existing structure owing to the reluctance or inability of entrepreneurs to face the cost and the risks attendant upon such large-scale change. The study of economic processes is increasingly being influenced by the recognition that what may be called the " time-horizon " of business men plays a major part in determining the expectations and hence the actions of entrepreneurs, and is frequently decisive in that choice between the short-term and the long-term view upon which so much in the development of industry turns. In a world of uncertainty as to the plans and intentions of other firms and other industries there is always a bias in favour of the shorter rather than the longer view with its multitude of imponderables ; and every increase in the costs attendant on innovation—costs which are close to the eye and calculable, whereas the fruits of innovation are distant and uncertain—augments this bias towards the short-term view and towards adherence to the familiar *status quo*. With examples of such a bias the recent history, particularly of British industry, teems ; and there are signs that the tendency of modern developments is to increase it. Von Beckerath has pointed out that in modern industry the growing inter-relationship of the several parts of a productive organization, not only " diminishes the adaptability of a complex plant to fluctuations in the demand for the products of its different sections ", but also increases the difficulties attendant on technical transformation and innovation. " A mechanical combination of labour cannot easily be changed, and the transformation of the machinery in a factory usually causes very expensive changes of the whole system. The more thorough the mechanization, the greater the expense." [1] Similarly Mr. E. A. G. Robinson has pointed out that " the more elaborate a firm is, the more highly specialized in equipment, the better adapted in lay-out to the existing rhythm of production, the more expensive and difficult will be its re-equipment, the more complicated the task of moving and adjusting to their new functions heavy and capricious pieces of machinery ".[2] In so far as this is the case, it may well happen that larger sums are needed to finance reorganization than can at one and the same time be provided out of the reserves even of a large concern (unless, at least, such reserves have been far-sightedly accumulated over the period of a decade or decades of unusually profitable trade

---

[1] *Op. cit.*, 86–7.   [2] *Op. cit.*, 85–6.

conditions) or be raised by an ordinary issue of new capital.[1] The result is apparent in the increasing reliance of industry, in financing technical innovations, on the aid of banks, or of financial institutions that are filial to the banks, and even on the State ; thereby strengthening the tendency towards what has been termed " finance capital ", and even towards a measure of " State Capitalism ".

Secondly, the special risks attendant on the operation of a plant of modern type in an unplanned economy (where fluctuations of demand are so largely incalculable) may preclude its adoption and establish a preference for a technical form of an older and less efficient type. The fact that the plant can only be operated profitably at or near to full capacity, and that if demand is smaller than this substantial losses may be made owing to the inflexibility of costs, may confront the entrepreneur with a conflict between the financial *optimum* of type and size and the technical *optimum*, in which he is likely to choose the former.[2] For example, the greater size of American iron and steel furnaces, compared with British, and the much greater frequency of large integrated plants in the former country, has often been attributed to the greater chance which American plants have of maintaining full capacity working in view of their larger and more secure home market. In the U.S.S.R., with its planned investment-programme extending over a period of half a decade, and the greater possibility which this gives for gearing productive capacity in heavy industry to the demand for the products of heavy industry, the size of the more modern steel plants tends to exceed even that of American plants, and standardization is generally carried much further than in America.[3] With this conflict between financial and technical *optima* is connected the well-known tendency of " monopolistic competition " to take the form

[1] An example is the finance of British iron and steel rationalization as it was discussed in the late '20's or of the re-equipment of the British coal industry after the war.

[2] I.e. of two methods, one of which is the more efficient *when* operated at or near to full capacity and the other much less efficient but involving a larger proportion of variable costs, which are reducible when output falls, he will tend to choose the latter as involving less risk of loss if and when demand is insufficient to make full capacity working possible.

[3] An example of standardization in capital-goods is that, under the Second Five Year Plan, Soviet industry concentrated on producing four types of tractor for agriculture, each in a specialized plant : a 15-h.p. light tractor at Kharkov, a 48-h.p. caterpillar tractor at Cheliabinsk, a special type for row-crops at the Putilov works in Leningrad, and a fourth type at Stalingrad. This compared with about eighty different types produced in U.S.A., although the U.S.S.R. led the world in tractor-production (Gosplan, *The Second Five Year Plan*, 138-9.).

of multiplying varieties, and of maintaining or creating for each its distinctive private market or clientèle of customers attached to each firm, instead of striving after methods of cheapening prices. This tendency militates against standardization, whether of consumer goods or capital goods, and results in a large number of commodities and plants, each with its limited market, in preference to a smaller number, each serving a larger and less variable [1] market in which the full potentialities of modern technical methods could be exploited. Mass production has been called " the art of manufacturing the maximum quantity in the minimum of variety ".[2] In some cases the difference in efficiency between the production of numerous varieties, each on a relatively small scale, and of more standardized production on a larger scale is quite staggering. Mr. N. Kaldor recently stated that " for a wide range of durable consumers' goods—like furniture, heating or cooking appliances, vacuum cleaners, radio sets, refrigerators or even motor-cars—the pre-war prices were in many cases three or four times as high as they need have been if full advantage had been taken of the potentialities of standardized mass-production, and if they had been marketed in a reasonably efficient manner " ; citing the fact that " the man-hour productivity of the American motor industry was three to four times as high as that of Britain's " as evidence of the potentialities of standardized mass-production in a country where the market was large relatively to the number of varieties produced.[3]

Thirdly, a situation is created where a quite unusual premium is placed on measures to enlarge the market or to capture demand. We have already spoken of the tendency of monopoly to curtail output in the interest of price-maintenance. To the extent that technical conditions make for output-rigidity this business instinct will be thwarted ; and if this instinct is thwarted, it might seem to follow that fluctuations in output and employment will be moderated and business policy have less anti-social effects than the theory of monopoly generally implies. Either a choice must

---

[1] Less variable as well as larger, since the more that commodities and " lines " which are fairly close substitutes for one another are multiplied, the more sensitive will the market for each be to changes in supply and price in other markets.

[2] L. C. Ord, *op. cit.*, 35.

[3] *The Times*, Jan. 10, 1945; Feb. 1, 1945 ; Cf. also the figures for output per head in certain manufacturing industries in the United Kingdom and the United States given by Dr. L. Rostas in " Industrial Production, Productivity and Distribution in Britain, Germany and U.S., 1935-7 ", *Economic Journal*, April, 1943, 46. These show that physical output per operative in motor-cars in U.S. was four times that of G.B., in radio nearly five times, and in industry at large rather more than double.

be made initially in favour of a less efficient production-unit with a smaller output-capacity, or where this is impracticable or for some other reason this alternative has not been chosen, the cost-situation will encourage the maintenance of output near to the full-capacity level, even in face of a contraction of demand. The latter may well be the likely consequence in face of short-period fluctuations of price ; especially where output can be made for stock (or, as sometimes happens in a large metallurgical combine, used for repair and maintenance purposes within the combine), so that output can be maintained without any great price-sacrifice as a consequence.   But where the holding of stocks is difficult or risky, fluctuations of demand that are expected to be other than temporary will more probably encourage violent alternations between full working and the complete closing down of plants, or unit-sections of a plant ; with the consequence of discontinuous and exaggerated fluctuations of output, and a desperate resort, when demand is inadequate, to those concerted measures to destroy productive-capacity that were such a notorious feature of certain industries between the wars.   Under-capacity working, in other words, may take the form of derelict plants and subsidies to the machine-breaker rather than of slackened pace of working and partial reductions of staff all round.

But whatever the precise effect on output-policy may be, it is evident that in any situation where output-reduction and price-maintenance is rendered difficult, monopolistic industry will be impelled towards the alternative of taking measures to sustain demand.   In a situation where there was some physical necessity for choosing between full-capacity working and no output at all, one could say that business-policy, intent on maximizing profit, would have no alternative than to exert its efforts towards enlarging the market, even if these efforts involved considerable expenditure.   But even where there is no such physical necessity, the combination of relatively low direct or variable costs with large fixed costs, and particularly with large non-variable operating costs or " running overheads ", may make such measures the only alternative to substantial losses.   One can put the matter in another way by saying that under such conditions the gross profit-margin on each *extra* unit of output will be so great as to place a very obvious and unusual premium on any measures that can expand demand ; and if such measures are sufficiently successful, they will not only make sales sufficient to absorb the full capacity of the plant, but may enable the selling-price to be raised as well. Whereas price-maintenance by restriction is the first chapter of monopoly-policy ; the second chapter consists of high-pressure campaigns to sustain demand.

Such policy may take a variety of forms, each of which has had its familiar place in the economic history of recent years. It may take the form of concerted sales-drives, organized boycott of rival sources of supply, the capture and fortification of protected markets, forward integration to control or influence the use of the product, or the exertion of political pressure to secure the assistance of the State or of public bodies as consumer and contractor. But while such measures may be successful in improving the fortunes of one firm, and even of a whole industry, by diverting demand from rivals, as a general policy they soon meet serious limitations. In the case of consumption-goods industries there is the limit imposed by the level of incomes of the majority of consumers, which can only be substantially enlarged at the expense of reductions in the inequality of incomes and hence of the income of the propertied class. In the case of investment-goods industries, expansion of the market depends on a rise in the rate of investment, which is limited by the prevailing " fear of productive capacity " and the reluctance of capitalists to increase it.

Of measures adequate in a substantial degree to affect the sales of any extensive section of capitalist industry two stand out above all others. Firstly, there is political control of foreign territories, designed to open these as new development areas and as protected and preferential markets ; which has been a leading feature of capitalist expansion since the closing decades of the last century. Secondly, and more recently, there is armament expenditure by the State, in furtherance of the requirements of twentieth-century mechanized warfare, with its dominating effect on a whole chain of industries and in particular on heavy industry : a mode of expenditure which has the unique advantage for capitalist society of bringing into existence instruments of destruction instead of additional instruments of production and of being rooted in a demand that is apparently insatiable. In view of the leading importance of these two expedients it is not surprising that business strategy should have come so largely to assume a political character, to an extent which probably only finds a parallel in the very early history of the bourgeoisie.

In Fascist economy, and most markedly in the case of Nazi

Germany, both these policies were combined : systematic territorial expansion by the State and organization of the normal economy of peace-time on the lines of a war-economy, with State armament orders as its fulcrum.   In this fusion of two policies each was reinforcement to the other.   With them, as logical accompaniments, were combined two others : extensive measures of State control over the economy, including control of investment and of prices, and the liquidation of trade unions as prelude to measures of authoritarian wage-control.   These measures were reminiscent of that régime of economic regulation which we find in certain stages of the infancy of Capitalism ; and wage-control in particular performed the function, like its prototype, of stabilizing the labour market in a situation where jobs were in danger of becoming as plentiful as men, and of braking any upward movement of wages which might arise from the upward pressure of demand.   As a result, between 1933 and 1938, in face of a large increase in employment " there was a marked fall in real wage-rates and probably also a decline in the purchasing power of hourly wage-earnings ", while " profit-margins were extraordinarily high compared with conditions in other countries or with conditions prevailing in Germany in the '20's ".[1]   At the same time, control over investment enabled a limit to be placed on expansion of productive capacity ; the installation of new equipment in a whole range of industries being prohibited except with official approval.   These measures were among the first efforts of the the Nazi government at control.[2]

In its policy of territorial expansion, Fascist economy introduced two significant improvements upon the older imperialism.   Imperialism of the pre-1914 type had turned its eyes towards undeveloped agricultural areas of the world, with export of capital as its guiding preoccupation.   The objects of investment had chiefly been the development of primary production such as mining and plantation economy, railways, telegraph and harbour building—all capital-absorbing objects in high degree—and to some extent of industries engaged in processing local raw materials.   But the development of industry in these colonial areas was limited by the fact that, if any

[1] K. Mandelbaum in *The Economics of Full Employment* (Oxford Institute of Statistics), 194–5.

[2] Cf. Otto Nathan, *The Nazi Economic System*, 154–62.   " Between 1933 and the outbreak of war in 1939, seventy-two decrees regulating capacity were promulgated under the authority of the Compulsory Cartel Law.   Generally issued for periods between three months and two years, most of them were renewed again and again and were still in force by December 31, 1939 " (*ibid.*, 156).

extensive industrialization had occurred, this would inevitably have resulted in harmful repercussions upon the value of capital invested in similar industries in the home country. Carried to completion, of course, such a process of industrialization would have resulted in the economic decolonization of the colony. It was to be expected that interest-groups which were finding an outlet for part of their capital in colonial development should seek to make this development complementary and not rival to their investments at home ; and to ensure that in what they had designed as preferential markets for themselves competitors should not be reared. The greater the extent to which the interest-groups concerned in the colonies were the same as, or affiliated to, the interest groups concerned in the main industries at home, the more was this likely to be so. But even if these groups had been altogether separate, it was to be expected that the imperial State, as custodian of the interests of capital as a whole, would have shaped its colonial economic policy with an eye upon the probable effect on capital-values in the home country. Hence the advantage of these colonies as fields of investment always tended to be overshadowed by the concern to retard their industrial development, at any rate along autonomous lines, in order to maintain colonial economy as reciprocal to the economy of the metropolis, just as in earlier centuries Mercantilism had also been concerned to do. Thus, as time went on, the two dominating economic motives of Imperialism—the desire to extend the investment-field and the desire to extend the market for the industrial products of the imperial metropolis—came to stand in contradiction with one another.

The decades of the First World War and of the 1920's witnessed the appearance of colonial nationalism, although a newcomer, as a leading figure on the historical stage. Born as a reaction against the exploitation of colonial territories for the benefit of the leading capitalist Powers, it nursed the ambition to convert the colonial areas into autonomous units, in an economic as well as a political sense, pursuing policies of industrialization, independently of foreign capital, and aided by autonomous tariff and financial policies shaped to this end. Such aspirations were beginning to win some substantial, if as yet limited, successes in the period between wars ; and in the degree that they were doing so, they were setting barriers against any extension of the privileges of foreign capital in these spheres.

As a factor of buoyancy for the capitalist economy of the Old World, colonial markets and investment-fields seemed to have had their day. At least, the opportunities of further expansion in these fields along traditional lines were growing markedly narrower. Tariff barriers giving preference to native industries, a boycott of foreign products and foreign fashions, a movement towards autonomous banking policy and the withdrawal of special political and economic privileges for foreigners, such as rights of extra-territoriality in China, were all important pointers to the prevailing wind ; and popular movements that had so recently gathered momentum in India and China, in the Near East and in Latin America, might very well spread to the African continent to-morrow. If Imperialism was to continue to represent an expansive force for Capitalism in the older countries, it had to find either new territory or a new technique.

This, to a very large extent, Fascist imperialism endeavoured to do. Of necessity, perhaps, rather than of design, German Fascism turned its attention to contiguous countries on the continent of Europe : countries that were already industrialized or partly industrialized. These afforded no *tabula rasa* for capital investment as Africa or China had done for British or French or German capital in the second half of the nineteenth century. Here the export of capital could not be the kernel of policy. Instead, it had rather to be a matter of gearing their economies to that of Germany as economically dependent satellite economies. Such a design inevitably involved measures of de-industrialization (at least partially) of these new colonial areas : measures which were to become the unconcealed objective of Hitler's New Order in Europe ; as proclaimed, for example, in the famous speech of Dr. Funk in July, 1940, and proclaimed as an objective of long-term policy and not simply as a war-time expedient.[1] In these satellite territories German industries would find new and preferential markets, where they could enjoy a monopoly, or quasi-monopoly. So far as heavy industry was concerned, the rôle of capital-export in establishing an outlet for their products had already been taken over (for the time being, at least) by State orders for armament needs. The analogy with Mercantilism was carried a stage further, while at the same time being fitted to the conditions of a modern type of economy where heavy industry bulked so large. The initial subordination of these

[1] Cf. C. W. Guillebaud in *Econ. Journal*, Dec., 1940.

neighbouring States was made the easier by the fact that, since they were already capitalist States, their ruling class was afflicted by an up-to-date fear of social revolution : a fear that predisposed them to be allies of a movement which claimed to have stamped out the class struggle at home and was raising the banner of an Anti-Comintern Pact abroad. This new Fascist technique of political penetration, on the contrary to being an expression of stubborn survival of nationalism, is a witness to the overshadowing significance during the inter-war period of class antagonism within each national area ; and as such it was squarely rooted in the actual class relations of mature capitalist societies in the contemporary world.

Once an initial political control over these areas had been achieved, the methods by which the subordination of their economic systems as satellites to the Reich was subsequently achieved were also in some degree novel. These methods in-cluded the acquisition of industrial assets in these countries through the medium of German banks, or local filials of German banks [1] (acquisition which often seems to have been financed out of credits in favour of Germany in the local clearing-accounts, or simply by credit-creation, and accordingly did not involve the transfer of any *quid pro quo* to the country in question in fulfilment of the purchase) ; by regimenting their industries under schemes of State-organized monopoly, which had already been tested in Germany ; and by an extension of the régime of compulsory cartellization, inaugurated in Germany by the well-known Act of 1933, to the whole imperial area, and by the allocation of raw material supplies through centralized raw material controls.   An early example of the operation of this policy was the German-Roumanian agreement of March 1939. By this a programme of development was agreed upon under which Roumania was to become primarily a producer of raw materials and food-stuffs, the bulk of her oil and other raw products being exported to Germany, while German capital was given extensive privileges for the development of raw material production. For the agricultural regions of the Slavonic world further east, which it was an aim of the war to subjugate, something like a return to serfdom of the native producers, under German overlords and *ministeriales*, was apparently envisaged : a development irresistibly reminiscent of German expansion east of the Elbe in the twelfth

---

[1] In Austria, for example, control over industry was achieved by annexing the big banks to the large German banks.

and thirteenth centuries. At any rate, it was designed to be an Imperialism of a much improved and more predatory type : more ruthless and uncompromising, more organized and systematically planned, and to a large extent following the lines of plantation economy, equipped with modern technical methods but resting on the labour of a population depressed to a bare subsistence level of consumption. A glimpse of this design was seen in the German economic plan for Poland. The western and more industrialized part was incorporated in Germany, and was to be peopled with a German population, and the Polish population expelled, except for some imported labour forming a depressed class employed at a low wage on unskilled jobs. The eastern half of what was pre-1939 Poland (and is now the Ukraine or White Russia) was to be divided off as a primarily agricultural region, except for a few raw material- and food-processing plants, to be taken under German management, and based on cheap local labour. Import into this area was restricted, especially in the case of foodstuffs and raw materials, of which the import was virtually prohibited ; while an export surplus of raw produce to Germany was secured by a system of obligatory delivery-quotas imposed on all farmers.[1] It is clear that in this novel and grandiose imperial system, the apotheosis of State-organized monopoly over the area of a whole continent, the fruits of exploitation were enjoyed, not only by the German capitalist class and the new bureaucratic strata, but in some measure even by the humblest among the *herrenvolk*.

One feature, however, German Fascism had in contrast with Mercantilism, at least superficially. Instead of worshipping export-surpluses, as had been the traditional obsession alike of modern Imperialism and of Mercantilism, German economy in the late '30's adopted a policy of import-surpluses. Partly this was an accidental result of shortage of raw materials to feed the armament programme and shortage of foreign valuta with which to buy them in the world market : a circumstance which placed a premium on the acquisition of an import-surplus from any country over which Germany could exercise political or economic pressure. This was done through the mechanism of bilateral exchange-clearing agreements with countries of south-eastern Europe in ways that are now familiar. The import surplus was offset by a growing credit in favour of Germany in

---

[1] Cf. *Polish Fortnightly Review*, pubd. by Polish Ministry of Information, Jan. 15, 1943.

the clearing-account, which meant that it had in fact to be financed (so long as the import surplus continued) by the central banks of the satellite countries themselves. It represented essentially a commodity loan by these countries to Germany, which Germany showed no haste to repay, and which she was free to repay, when she did, largely in commodities of her own choosing. The system probably had the further result of raising the level of agricultural prices in the satellite countries (since it was products of agriculture and the extractive industries that Germany was mainly importing) relatively to industrial prices, thereby tending to discourage local industries [1] and identifying the interests of exporters in these countries with German policy.

Seen in a larger setting, however, this striving after import-surpluses was an incident in a policy of turning the terms of trade with the satellite economies in favour of Germany : an object which we have seen in an earlier chapter that Mercantilism also pursued. This " exploitation through trade " was an essential object of the Schacht Plan with its elaborate mechanism of exchange-control. It was furthered by a series of agreements by which the rates of exchange with these new-type " colonial countries " were established at a figure which represented a substantial over-valuation of the mark (thereby cheapening the colonial products in terms of marks and raising the price of German exports in terms of the " colonial " currencies). Notable among these was the agreement with Roumania in 1939 providing for a change in the parity of the lei-mark exchange from 41 lei to 50. Later the rates of exchange with German-occupied countries were changed in a similar way : for example, the devaluations of the Dutch guilder and the French and Belgian franc. The essence of the policy was this. Armament orders had replaced the need for export markets as a means of maintaining German industry at full capacity ; and State and cartel control over any extension of existing equipment was a brake upon the creation of excess capacity. It now became the preoccupation of industrialists, not merely to obtain a greater quantity of raw materials, but to lower the price at which these could be acquired by industry and to cheapen the goods on which

[1] Against this, on the other hand, was the expansionist effect of the policy in enlarging the home market, which may in some cases have resulted, on balance, in benefit even to producers for the home market. It also tended to maintain a higher level of employment, both directly through the export demand and indirectly through the expansionist influence of this on the home market.

workers spent their wages, in order thereby to widen the profit-margin.

The obsession with demand which the modern economic situation in the capitalist world occasions is apparent also in democratic countries like Britain and U.S.A., even if here it has taken other forms. A witness to this is the willingness of industrialists, at least of certain sections of them, to contemplate a new function for the State after the war to replace armament orders : the function of financing an expansionist programme of expenditute to sustain the market. In face of the immense problem presented by cessation of war-time expenditure by the State, and the memories of 1929-33 which this prospect arouses, a substantial section of the American business world seems willing to tolerate, even to advocate, large-scale State expenditure as a normal peace-time policy after the war. At the same time the British Government in 1944 accepted the quite new principle of admitting " as one of their primary aims and responsibilities the maintenance of a high and stable level of employment after the war ", and advanced proposals for government expenditure designed with the sole purpose of maintaining demand.[1] True, those proposals kept cautiously within the limits of a traditional " public works " policy, supplementing attempts to stabilize investment by capitalist industry ; with government expenditure to be switched on and off according to the general state of the market for investment goods and consumption goods. As such it did not propose substantially to enlarge the sphere of public expenditure ; and has been criticized on the ground that " it is concerned almost wholly with the timing of demand, and proposes nothing for its expansion ".[2] Other proposals, however, such as those of Sir William Beveridge, which involve no substantial inroads upon the structure of capitalist society, would assign to State expenditure both a larger and more continuous rôle in peace-time economy ; and the signs are that it is in this direction that the logic of events will compel future governments to travel.

But the adoption of such expedients as a normal policy in peace-time would seem to be confronted with certain crucial difficulties : difficulties which have nothing to do with the productive situation per se, but arise from the peculiar social relations which constitute the capitalist mode of production.

[1] White Paper on Employment Policy, Cmd. 6527.
[2] W. Beveridge, Full Employment in a Free Society, 269.

In the first place, measures which attempt to remedy excess capacity within the framework of Capitalism must evidently pay court to that " fear of productive capacity ",[1] of the prevalence of which economic experience between the wars has afforded accumulating evidence. It may be that, so long as State expenditure can sustain demand, this fear may become less dominant an obsession than it was in the 1930's. But so long as the maximizing of profit remains the ruling motive of business, it is unlikely to pass altogether out of mind. Hence, if they are to be tolerated by business interests, particularly in the industries where monopolistic organization affords the means as well as the desire to restrict productive capacity, the measures designed to sustain demand and to give industry the opportunity of working to full capacity must not be such as will increase the capital equipment of industry. Any suggestion that State expenditure is to involve investment in lines which compete with existing capital in private hands is likely to evoke strenuous opposition, on the ground that it endangers existing capital values. Of this the opposition of interested parties to the American Tennessee Valley scheme, which threatened competition with private capital in the field of public utilities, is a notable example. Armament expenditure has the inestimable benefit for Capitalism that it involves no such contradiction. It conjures a new destination for the products of heavy industry outside industry itself; thereby performing something of the rôle of railway building in the nineteenth century. But in peace-time, apart from house-building, road development and electrification, there is little, as a permanent object of State investment, which seems capable of stepping into its shoes.

If capitalist industry should decide to grasp this nettle firmly, and to accept the necessity for State-aided investment in the consumption-goods industries as the only means of providing an adequate market for the products of heavy industry, then it will have laid one spectre only to raise another. The problem of excess capacity in the consumption-goods industries cannot in such a case be prevented for long from emerging once again, unless in the meantime the consuming power of the mass of the population has been increased : an increase which can hardly occur on any substantial scale unless the inequality of income,

---

[1] Cf. the remark of V. Gaiev in an article on " Plans for the ' Full Employment ' of Labour Power after the War " in *Voina i Rabotchi Klass* (*War and the Working Class*) No. 11, 1944 : " A characteristic feature of all these projects is the fear of a growth of productive power " (p. 20).

characteristic of capitalist society, is reduced by making heavy inroads on the share of property-income. It is, again, possible that an outlet for the products of industry might be sought in large-scale financing of the industrialization of colonial countries, thereby enlarging the market for capital goods in providing the equipment of colonial industry and also the market for consumption goods in the increased purchasing power which greater employment in colonial industry and on construction work would bring. There are even signs that this is the solution which certain capitalist circles in America favour as alone consistent with post-war prosperity.[1] For a decade or two this might well provide a temporary solution. In the long run it would involve the economic decolonization of what formerly had been economically dependent territories, and hence the jettisoning of those monopoly-advantages which capital in the imperialist countries had previously enjoyed, and which, as we have seen, it was the object of Fascist Imperialism to extend. Yet the problem of excess capacity has to-day assumed such dimensions,[2] particularly in American industry, that it is not impossible that the short-term expedient may be seized upon by an important section of business interests, even though this be at the expense of certain long-term advantages, whose survival for long may anyhow be open to doubt. Where doubt and uncertainty prevail, short-term expedients that offer some quick advantage tend to have more attraction than long-term strategies which, should they succeed, hold the promise of a larger and more enduring gain. So far has the unbounded optimism of the American prosperity wave of the '20's receded ; so much has the alternative for many industries become one between maintaining a state of full-capacity working or facing a collapse in which profits are unlikely to be earned at all. To so great an extent have the " productive forces created by the modern capitalist mode of production come into burning contradiction with that mode of production itself." [3] It has been estimated that in America productive power has so grown, as well as the labour force, over the quinquennium 1940–5 as to require an increased market (compared with 1940) equivalent to the output of

---

[1] Another example of this tendency (if only a cautious tendency so far) is the Government of India Plan for industrial development.

[2] We have seen above that the recovery of the '30's was very hesitant, and was largely built on State intervention, and already showed signs on the eve of the war of giving way to a fresh collapse.

[3] F. Engels, *Anti-Dühring*, 179.

between 10 and 20 million workers, if a condition of full-capacity working is to be maintained. There is no present evidence that American Capitalism is capable of expanding either its export of capital or mass consumption at home by anything approaching this order of magnitude.

But in all such policies for a capitalist society there is a further difficulty which is even more fundamental. Each section of capitalist industry will profit from any expansion of its market, provided that this is not at the expense of rearing new competitors within its own sphere. But as soon as such an expansion of the market has become general, and resulted not only in the full working of plant but also in the full employment of the labour force, the whole balance of the labour market will have been transformed. In Sir William Beveridge's words, the labour market will have become " a seller's market rather than a buyer's market ".[1] The labour reserve will have disappeared, and governmental policy will have assumed the obligation of preventing its reappearance. The weapon of industrial discipline on which capitalist society has always depended, and to the blunting of which we have seen that it has always been so abnormally sensitive, will have been struck from the capitalists' hands.[2] This does not mean that workers, lacking the goad of starvation, will prefer idleness to labour and will no longer work, as some have claimed with groundless exaggeration. But it means that the proletariat will be in a much stronger position than at any previous stage in its history to influence the terms upon which work shall be done. A sharp upward movement of wages, and a growing share of the national income, will for the first time lie within the easy reach of organized labour to command ; and against this threat the propertied class will no longer have an economic protection, save in a general and continuing inflation of prices (due, for example, to the inelasticity of the consumption of the rich, who have reserves of money out of which to maintain their consumption in face of any rise of prices) or in the re-creation of unemployment. Not only would a rising general wage-level be the likely outcome, but also a radical alteration of the structure

---

[1] *Full Employment in a Free Society*, 19.

[2] Cf. : " Under a régime of permanent full employment, ' the sack ' would cease to play its rôle as a disciplinary measure. The social position of the boss would be undermined and class consciousness of the working class would grow. . . . Their (employers') class interest tells them that lasting full employment is unsound from their point of view and that unemployment is an integral part of the ' normal ' capitalist system " (M. Kalečki in *Political Quarterly*, Oct.–Dec., 1943, 326). Also cf. Oxford Institute of Statistics, *Economics of Full Employment*, 207.

of relative wages so as to increase the relative attractiveness of the most dangerous and arduous and unpleasant occupations which in the traditional state of the labour market have generally been among the lowest paid. It is fairly plain that in such a situation the stability of a class society would be seriously threatened ; and that, if income derived by virtue, not of a contribution to productive activity, but of property-rights should continue to exist, this would be by reason of a self-denying ordinance on the part of Labour, and no longer because Labour lacked the power of terminating its subjection to those who own the instruments of production and of refusing the tribute that for centuries it has had to pay. While a class society exists, with its two contrasted categories of income, one of them obtained by economic privilege and not by productive activity, it may well be asked whether Labour is likely to observe any such self-denial for long.

It is not difficult to see that alarm at the prospect of such a situation lies behind much of the reluctance shown in certain quarters to sponsor unreservedly a policy of full employment. This fear seems even to underlie a good deal of contemporary monetary controversy concerning the advantages of a currency system which operates " automatically ", compared with various types of " managed currency systems " capable of serving the ends of particular governmental policies. It is clear that the decisive advantage which some have seen in the former is, not only its automatism, but that it operates as an automatic check on any upward movement of the wage-level by tending to re-create unemployment : unemployment which is lifted out of the sphere of human policy and made to appear as product of the natural order of things. For example, in answer to a recent statement by Lord Keynes that " the error of the gold standard lay in submitting national wage-policies to outside dictation ",[1] Professor F. D. Graham, of Princeton, has asserted that " the original gold standard did not submit wage-policies to *dictation*, by governing authority anywhere, but made them the resultant of impersonal forces ", and has advanced as a crucial objection to any " perfectly free monetary system " that it would fail to " confine such tendency as (money) wages may have to rise beyond the limits within which it is possible to preserve a stable price level ", and that " if we refuse even to accept the threat of

---

[1] *Econ. Journal*, June–Sept., 1943, 187. Lord Keynes here quotes the opinion that " a capitalist country is doomed to failure because it will be found impossible in conditions of full employment to prevent a progressive increase of wages ", and adds : " Whether this is so remains to be seen."

unemployment under any conditions whatever, we shall, under any ' natural ' tendency of wages to rise faster than efficiency, be forced to pay whatever money-wages labourers may be pleased to demand ".[1]

In view of this situation, some have concluded that Capitalism, if it continues, must everywhere pass into some kind of Fascist phase, at least to the extent of reverting to measures of compulsion by the State over labour, in particular over wages.   Each new development in the direction of State Capitalism they accordingly view with apprehension as a step in this direction, since, whatever the initial intention of State control may be, the pressure of monopoly groups will inevitably turn it to the service of their interests.   These interests will demand the dissolution of independent trade unionism and the fettering of labour, the reinforcement of monopoly with the arm of legal sanctions, and the use of the power of the State externally to promote the control of satellite territories and the regimenting of their economic life in the way that Hitler's New Order in Europe designed to do.   A movement from contract back to status, the clamping of industry into the straitjacket of a new kind of State-chartered gild régime would usher in the return of the Servile State. Attendant on it would come a new age of chivalry where armed might was worshipped, both as the prerequisite of all profitable economic dealings and as the source of those State orders on which modern industry relied for its perpetual re-invigoration.

It is true that evidence is not lacking of tendencies in this direction even among the democratic capitalist countries in the decade before the Second Great War.   State intervention in industry more often took the form of reinforcing monopoly than of curbing it (e.g. the British Coal Mines Act of 1930, and British Government policy towards the steel industry), of serving the ends of restriction and the dismantling of productive capacity (e.g. the British Cotton Spindles Act of 1936 and the record of governments in relation to international commodity restriction-schemes) than of expansion, and of offering stimulants to bankrupt industries, to stave off the collapse of capital values, and not of planning large-scale economic reconstruction in the social interest.   It was a policy so aptly summarized by Mrs. Barbara Wootton as " a community more planned against than planning ", and actuated by the principle of " making one blade of grass grow where two grew before ".   The doctrine was not only preached

[1] *Econ. Journal*, Dec., 1944, 422–9.

in Germany that the State should retard the march of technical innovation for fear of the economic damage caused to those who had invested in older methods. State Capitalism which means State-reinforced monopoly—monopolistic restriction and monopolistic aggrandizement with the sanction and by the arm of the law—has a sufficiently established record to stand as a warning of one road along which State Capitalism may travel. There can be no doubt that among the propertied class there will be many who in their hearts will wish to travel along this road.

What is customarily described under the generic title of State Capitalism includes, however, a number of species, very different in their social content and significance. The difference depends on the form of the State, the condition of prevailing class relations, and the class interests which State policy serves. The common element in these various species is the coexistence of capitalist ownership and operation of production with a system of generalized controls over economic operations exercised by the State, which pursues ends that are not identical with those of an individual firm. This system may or may not include a limited amount of nationalized and State-operated production. Lenin used the term to mean " unification of small-scale production " under the ægis of the State ; and applied it in 1918 and in the early 1920's in Russia to the situation in which the Soviet State exercised control over a mixed type of economic system, including large areas of private enterprise, some of it non-capitalist (small and middling peasant economy) and some of it capitalist in type (e.g. concession-enterprises in the 1920's and non-nationalized private firms in 1918). At the same time he used the term with reference to the war economy of Germany in the First World War.[1] By extension of this meaning, it can presumably be applied to the kind of State-organized system of monopoly of which we have been speaking, and of which Fascist economy is the most developed type.

In the nightmare years of the Second World War much was changed both in politics and in economics ; and the situation at the end of the war gave no ground for supposing that the shape of events in the post-1918 years would necessarily be repeated or

---

[1] *Selected Works*, vol. IX, 169. He also used the term " state monopoly capitalism " and speaks of it as representing " in a truly revolutionary-democratic state " [which he distinguishes from a Soviet State or a Socialist State] " progress towards Socialism " (*ibid.*, 171).

that tendencies which operated in the 1930's would be resumed. Rather was there reason for the contrary conclusion in a world where Fascism as a political form and an economic doctrine had been vanquished and as an ideology discredited. Much was changed after the war years, both in the balance of power between nations and in the balance of power between classes. Much that was formerly regarded, at least until the late 1920's, as an integral part of the economic structure of society now lay in ruins. It was plain to all that expedients tried in earlier decades would no longer suffice to achieve results in the contemporary situation ; and that, even where these were capable of working, the interests that would profit from their operation often lacked the power to carry them into effect.

Outstanding among the changes resulting from the Second World War has been the extension of influence of the U.S.S.R. both in Europe and in Asia ; and with this has gone an extension of that sector of the world where Capitalism has been dethroned and the foundations laid for a new form of economy—a socialist economy. The emergence of the so-called " new democracies " of eastern and south-eastern Europe and of a Communist-led China has radically transformed the balance both of Europe and of Asia. At the same time the U.S.A. emerged from the war with a greatly expanded productive power and holding a position of hegemony in the capitalist world which was without equal in the history of Capitalism to date. Despite the hopes aroused by the war-time coalition between the Western capitalist Powers and the U.S.S.R. and by the post-war Potsdam agreement, tension between the two worlds of Socialism and Capitalism has rapidly grown more acute. And while tension between the two worlds has developed into the " cold war " on the international field, within each country conflict has sharpened between the adherents of the new world and the adherents of the old. This, indeed, is no more than one would expect in an epoch of revolutionary change. The day of " mixed economies ", in which many placed their faith as a stable resting-place, has come and gone. In common with broad coalition governments, uniting bourgeois and proletarian class-interests on a basis of national unity for post-war reconstruction, such transitional forms have proved unstable and have rapidly divided either to the right or to the left. It is the nature of transitional economic and social forms to contain a mixture of elements from different systems and to rest on a precarious balance of conflicting class forces ; from which it follows that they are apt to have problems peculiar to themselves, and being inherently unstable they can offer no more than an illusory middle way.

We have seen how the close of the Middle Ages, faced with loss of the labour services on which the feudal order relied, attempted a Feudal Reaction, to fetter the producer more securely to his traditional obligations. But only in certain parts of Europe did this meet with success. Conditions were such that elsewhere it could scarcely even be attempted. The will was doubtless there ; but those who will may often lack the means. That the tendencies towards State Capitalism in the post-war world can be made the servant of a similar capitalist reaction, bringing legal regimentation of labour and a new servitude for the producer, is a possibility which cannot be denied. With the storm-clouds of a new economic crisis upon the horizon, the probability of such a period of reaction in the west is, indeed, much greater than it seemed on the morrow of the war. That it can succeed as a stable solution for any length of time is much more doubtful than that it will be attempted. The traditional order, in Europe at least, has emerged from the war as a shattered structure, no longer capable of inspiring unquestioning faith and obedience. Certainly the mass of ordinary men and women are unlikely for long to tolerate those who preach the economics of restrictions and of unemployment in a Europe where—

> All her husbandry doth lie on heaps
> Corrupting in its own fertility
> . . . Vineyards, fallows, meads and hedges
> Defective in their natures, grow to wildness.

In the contemporary world property-rights divorced from social activity are universally despised and are on the defensive ; whereas the working class has everywhere emerged stronger, more conscious of its strength and more purposeful than was ever the case before. The vision of a future rich in promise, once productive power has been harnessed by the community to the service of man, has begun to fire minds with a new faith and new hopes. Even though some will doubtless try to do so, the clock is not easily turned back, either to the Capitalism of the nineteenth century or to the Capitalism of the 1930's.

POSTSCRIPT:

AFTER THE SECOND WORLD WAR

If we look back over the decade and a half since the end of the Second World War, there are two major features of the capitalist world that immediately stand out and call for remark. Firstly there is the marked extension in America and in Western Europe of the economic activities of the State : i.e. developments, to a large extent novel both in degree and in kind, of what has been variously called State Capitalism or State Monopoly Capitalism.[1] Secondly, on a world scale there is the radical change in the position of large areas of the former colonial and semi-colonial sector, especially in Asia and Africa, and consequently in the relations, both political and economic, between these areas and the imperialist countries to which they were formerly subordinated.

State Capitalist tendencies were, of course, nothing new at the time of the Second World War. There had been some similar tendencies even during the First World War, and in a number of European countries, including Britain and Italy, between the wars, and especially in the 1930's. One consequence of the economic crisis of 1929–31 was the emergence in the U.S.A. of the Roosevelt 'New Deal', with its measures of intervention in what was predominantly a "free market economy".

But the Second World War and its aftermath witnessed a sufficiently large extension of the economic functions of the State as to make it a qualitative dividing-line in this respect. The form which this extension took was less any direct control over, or participation in, industrial production than a large extension of State *expenditures*, and hence of the influence of such expenditures over the market, especially for means of production or capital goods. Under the Labour government of the immediate post-war years, some measures of nationalization were taken : railways, coal-mining, iron and steel, road transport and the Bank of England. Certain war-time controls over the economy

[1] The latter, as we have noticed, was the term used by Lenin for developments during the First World War, e.g., when in 1921 he called for a study especially of "the State capitalism of the Germans" (Article on The Food Tax, April 21, 1921).

were also continued into peace time. But at most this State sector of the economy extended to no more than some 20 per cent. (measured in terms of employment) ; and after the change of government in 1951 the new Conservative government proceeded to denationalise steel and road transport. In France, Austria and Italy there were some State companies established (Renault in France and the famous E.N.I. in Italy), including in the latter mixed companies and State finance companies like the Italian I.R.I. which acted as holding companies over sections of industry or fuel and power-supply.

In Britain, however, the importance of the State sector was much greater as regards its share of gross investment expenditure (which in certain years approached a half of all investment expenditures) than as regards the amount of production which it directly controlled. In U.S.A., where the State sector was virtually non-existent, government expenditures (Federal, State and local) have amounted to as much as one-fifth, and even in recent years to one-fourth, of the gross national product. About a half of this represents military expenditures ; and to this extent the increasing influence of State expenditures upon the economy is connected with the growing militarization of the economy in the epoch of cold war and struggle between two world systems.

With the high degree of economic concentration that is characteristic of this monopoly-age, it is inconceivable that such State-capitalist tendencies *per se* should introduce any radical change either in the character of the State or in the prevailing system of social relations (as some have supposed). To countenance such a possibility is to take a purely superficial view of capitalism as an economic system and to ignore those basic historically-determined characteristics of the system which these present *Studies* have sought to reveal.

But this is not to say that such State capitalist developments are incapable of modifying, in this or that respect, the functioning of the economic system. In certain respects they evidently have done so. Both the extent and the direction of any such modification will, however, depend essentially upon the balance of social forces within the economy, and especially upon the political and economic strength of the labour movement. Again, these changes have been exaggerated by some writers, especially by those who like to depict the capitalist system as already transformed or in process of " socializing itself ". At first sight it might seem that this is a sufficient explanation of the changed character of the ' trade cycle ' in the course of the past decade and a half. But further investigation reveals that the situation is less simple than such a statement implies.

The main facts about the post-war cycle can be summarized in this way. There have been economic crises or ' recessions ' on four occasions since 1945: namely in 1948–9, in 1953–4, in 1957–8 and again in 1960–1 in U.S.A. (although not at the latter date in some countries of Western Europe such as West Germany, France and Italy, which continued the upward movement of the previous two years). At the time of writing this Postscript there is again talk of the prospect of a new American ' recession ' in 1963. Thus downturns in economic activity have been more frequent than formerly, and development has certainly not been crisis-free. At the same time, these downturns or depressions have been both shallower and more short-lived than those of the nineteenth century and of the pre-1939 decades of the present century; and nothing approaching the 1929 crisis in severity and duration has appeared (as many persons continued to expect for some years after the war). The extent of the fall in industrial production on successive occasions in U.S.A. has been as follows : in 1948–9, 10·5 per cent. ; 1953–4, 10·2 per cent. ; 1957–8, 11·6 per cent. ; 1960–1, 7 per cent. (By contrast production fell in the first twelve months of the U.S.A. crisis in 1929–30 by 25 per cent., and between 1929 and the low point of 1931 by 40 per cent.) A general feature of all of them has been a surprising stability of consumption : in each case it has been a decline of investment that has been the leading influence in the downturn of production. But as the downturns have been relatively short-lived, so also have the periods of recovery and boom, which in recent years seem to have become shorter. On this the U.N. *World Economic Survey 1960* recently remarked that the period of rising industrial production in 1958–60 in U.S.A. had lasted for scarcely two-thirds of that of 1954–7 and for scarcely more than a half that of the recovery period of 1949–53 (when the Korean War was a factor in giving impetus to the boom).[1]

Two further features of the past decade in U.S.A. have been a stagnating growth-rate and an increasing margin of unemployment. On this a writer in the *Westminster Bank Review* [2] has

---

[1] The expansion phase in 1949–53 lasted some 45 months, that of 1954–7 about 35 months and that of 1958–60 only 25 months.

[2] November 1961, pp. 6–8.

commented : " The American economy is growing more slowly than most other advanced economies and its rate of growth has slowed down in recent years . . . Starting at 1947 and taking 1953 and 1960 as roughly comparable years, since in both of them a peak was reached and a downturn began, we get average annual rates of growth of real national product per head of 3 per cent. for 1947–1953 and 1 per cent. for 1953–60." Meanwhile "improvement in unemployment typically lags behind improvement in activity ", the unemployment percentage being close to 7 per cent. in 1961 (in absolute figures, nearly 5 million). By contrast, the British economy, although also showing a low and stagnating growth-rate, has been close to a full employment level for a decade, the unemployment percentage being for most of the time around 1 per cent.[1]   Meanwhile countries of Western Europe, such as West Germany for some years and more recently France and Italy, have been showing considerably higher rates of growth.   In this respect, West Germany, Italy and Japan have stood out in the capitalist world in showing what (for capitalist economics) are remarkably high growth-rates for a number of years ; but these seem to have been for special reasons and to be showing signs (in Germany and Japan at least) of coming to an end.[2]

During this period inflationary pressures and associated conflicts and crises (e.g. balance-of-payments crises) seem to have taken the place, temporarily at least, of deflationary pressures. For this the high level of governmental expenditures has been largely though not wholly responsible.   There have been other factors in the situation as well.   While military and stockpiling expenditure during the Korean War intensified the boom in 1950 and 1951, recovery had already started in 1949 before the onset of War.   Again, the recovery and investment boom of 1954–6 in U.S.A. occurred in face of a fall in American defence expenditure, and for the first year (up to 1955) a fall in total expenditure of the Federal Government.   To a predominant extent it was a boom of *private* investment.[3]

---

[1] At the time of writing it has recently gone above 2 per cent.—for the first time for some years.

[2] Cf. articles on W. Germany and Japan respectively by M. Kalecki and S. Tsuru in *Economic Weekly* (Bombay), May 12th and June 9th, 1962. (Professor Kalecki's article appeared originally in Polish in *Ekonomista*, 1961, No. 6.)

[3] Between 1954 and 1955 total private investment increased by $12 milliard, or 25 per cent., while Federal Government expenditure continued to fall (Federal, State and local government expenditures combined rose slightly by 2 milliard). Between 1955 and 1956 private investment rose a further 5½ milliard and Federal State and local government expenditures by the same amount.

Two additional elements in the post-Second World War situation have undoubtedly played a significant rôle, at least a supplementary rôle : namely the enhanced level of total working class earnings as a result of the high level of employment and a ' cluster ' of technological innovations which have served to maintain gross investment (and hence demand for products of what Marx called Department I) at a higher level.   The fact that the size of the industrial reserve army has in Western Europe been much smaller than in the inter-war period has itself strengthened the bargaining power of trade unions and improved the position of labour within the prevailing system of social relations. Thus wage-rates have been maintained as well as total earnings through higher employment.   But again one must avoid the exaggeration of these developments that has been rife in Britain and America.   While there has been a rise both of money and of real wages, profits have also risen and there has been no appreciable change in the *proportionate share* of national income accruing to wage-earners.   Nor has there been any radical change in the pattern of personal income-distribution, despite alteration in the top income-brackets, mainly in their share of *post-tax* income as a result of more steeply graduated tax-rates—an alteration partly counterbalanced, however, by expenditure out of capital gains and from business expense-accounts.   In U.S.A. the share in total income of the lowest three-tenths of income-receivers actually declined as compared with pre-war.

Technological change, prompting extensive re-equipment of industry (largely out of accumulated company reserves), has taken the form of extended automation of industrial processes— a continuation of those trends towards continuous industrial processes which have been mentioned above as a significant influence between the wars.   This new phase in the revolution of technique has been associated particularly with the use of electronic controls and feed-back mechanisms, and hence with scientific developments that received a special impetus from the demands of a war economy.   Automation as a general process in industry at large is clearly still at no more than a preliminary stage, and its extension beyond a few industries remains limited. The technological revolution which it represents is retarded by reluctance of business firms to undertake the extensive investments involved in face of existing excess capacity in the relevant industries—an excess capacity which has been increasingly in evidence in the past few years.   One development in company finance, however, considerably helped the extension of re-equipment in the early and middle 1950's.   This was the large increase in company reserves (undistributed profits) in the post-war years, which laid the basis for so-called 'internal financing' out of this internal accumulation by companies.   As a result, a remarkably high proportion of gross investment during the 1950's, both in Western Europe and America, was financed in this way ; industrial re-equipment and extension of productive capacity being to this extent independent of the capital market and of the banks (and hence of restraints through monetary policy).

Of capitalism as a whole one can confidently say that those tendencies to economic concentration of which we have spoken earlier, and with it the degree of monopoly in its variety of forms, have continued to operate.   In certain respects, indeed, the very growth of State capitalism has served to reinforce these concentration- and monopoly-tendencies, especially during the war. Already in 1947 a survey of the U.S. Federal Trade Commission indicated that 135 manufacturing corporations in U.S.A., or in number less than one per cent. of all such corporations, embraced within their control as much as 45 per cent. of the net capital assets of manufacturing corporations.[1]   This has been accompanied politically by a pronounced drift to the Right since the immediate post-war years.   Partly a product of growing American influence (exercised economically through financial loans and aid as well as militarily through her influence in NATO and SEATO as dominant nuclear-weapon partner) and of cold war policies and ideology, this has been exemplified not only in McCarthyism and the Eisenhower régime in U.S.A., in Rightward governmental shifts in Britain and France (Italy may prove to be in some respects an exception), but more recently in the formation of the new Adenauer- de Gaulle axis and the restoration of (Western) Germany, to something approaching its previous position of hegemony on the continent of Europe.

As regards the world at large, beyond the bounds of Western Europe and North America, the two leading developments have been the emergence of the socialist sector of the world to be a major factor in the world situation, both economically and in its geographical extent, and the simultaneous emergence in the post-war years of an increasing number of former colonial countries into more or less independent countries : countries which (despite the so-called 'neo-colonialism') occupy a special place,

[1] *Review of Economics and Statistics*, November 1951.

both economically and politically, in most cases distinct from, and uncommitted to, either of the two main camps into which the post-war world has divided. The former of these two developments has doubtless had, not only an effect in sharpening the conflict between the two world systems, but also an appreciable impact upon the internal functioning of capitalist countries themselves. In the future it may well exert a growing influence upon the economic and social development of the third group of semi-colonial or ex-colonial countries, which are already turning, in varying degrees, towards measures of economic planning and of State capitalism to overcome their heritage of economic backwardness. It is, indeed, a characteristic of these countries that they have been precluded by their heritage of dependence and of backwardness from following the traditional path of capitalist development as trodden by the older industrial countries of Europe in the nineteenth century during the epoch of the classic industrial revolution.

A Postscript is scarcely the place to enlarge on the probable future course either of the socialist sector of the world or of the underdeveloped countries of three continents. It seems likely, however, that future historians will in retrospect see these two developments as the outstanding landmarks of the mid-twentieth-century watershed between historical epochs.

INDEX OF AUTHORITIES

INDEX OF SUBJECTS